WOMEN AT THE GATES

In the annals of industrialization, the Soviet experience is unique in its whirlwind rapidity. The vast transformations that shook western Europe over the centuries – proletarianization, industrialization, urbanization – were in the Soviet Union telescoped into a mere decade. The working class grew at an unprecedented rate, changing in size and social composition. Even more striking was the critical role of women: in no country of the world did they come to constitute such a significant part of the working class in so short a time. As women flooded industries traditionally dominated by men, they undercut strict hierarchies within the factories and forced male workers to reexamine their ideas about skill, "masculine" and "feminine" work, and the role of women in the workplace. The state's use of female labor was closely intertwined with the great upheavals of early Soviet history: accumulation of capital for the industrialization drive, the urban food crisis, collectivization, and peasant migration to the cities. Based on new Russian archival materials, *Women at the Gates* is the first social history of Soviet women workers in the 1930s. It is the story of a world remade, from above and from below, as planners "regendered" the entire economy and women entered the ranks of waged labor in unprecedented numbers.

Wendy Z. Goldman is Professor of History at Carnegie Mellon University. She is author of *Women, the State and Revolution: Soviet Family Policy and Social Life, 1917–1936* (Cambridge University Press, 1993), which won the Berkshire Prize for the best book in history written by a woman. She travels frequently to Russia and is the author of many articles on Soviet social history.

T0381829

WOMEN AT THE GATES

GENDER AND INDUSTRY IN STALIN'S RUSSIA

WENDY Z. GOLDMAN

Carnegie Mellon University

CAMBRIDGE
UNIVERSITY PRESS

CAMBRIDGE UNIVERSITY PRESS
Cambridge, New York, Melbourne, Madrid, Cape Town,
Singapore, São Paulo, Delhi, Tokyo, Mexico City

Cambridge University Press
32 Avenue of the Americas, New York, NY 10013-2473, USA

www.cambridge.org
Information on this title: www.cambridge.org/9780521785532

© Wendy Z. Goldman 2002

This publication is in copyright. Subject to statutory exception
and to the provisions of relevant collective licensing agreements,
no reproduction of any part may take place without the written
permission of Cambridge University Press.

First published 2002
Reprinted 2011

A catalog record for this publication is available from the British Library.

Library of Congress Cataloging in Publication Data

Goldman, Wendy Z.
Women at the gates : gender and industry in Stalin's Russia /
Wendy Z. Goldman.
  p. cm.
Includes bibliographical references.
ISBN 0-521-78064-0 – ISBN 0-521-78553-7 (pbk.)
  1. Women – Employment – Soviet Union – History. 2. Industrialization – Soviet
Union – History. 3. Soviet Union – Economic policy – 1917–1928. 4. Soviet Union –
Economic policy – 1928–1932. 5. Women – Soviet Union – Social conditions. I. Title.
HD6166 .G65 2001
331.4´0947 – dc21   2001035060

ISBN 978-0-521-78064-0 Hardback
ISBN 978-0-521-78553-2 Paperback

Cambridge University Press has no responsibility for the persistence or accuracy of URLs
for external or third-party Internet Web sites referred to in this publication and does not
guarantee that any content on such Web sites is, or will remain, accurate or appropriate.

*This book is dedicated
to Marcus Rediker
and
to the memory of our beloved friend
Steven Sapolsky*

Contents

Acknowledgments

I am grateful for the help of many people and institutions. Grants from the John Simon Guggenheim Memorial Foundation and the National Council for Soviet and East European Research gave me the opportunity and the time to research and write. The History Department of Carnegie Mellon University generously provided travel funds for research in Russia. The exchange between Carnegie Mellon University and Russian State University for the Humanities made possible regular research visits to Russian libraries and archives. I am grateful to Yuri Afanas'ev, Natalia Basovskaya, Irina Karapetiants, Peter Stearns, and Steven Schlossman for their administrative support of the exchange. I would also like to thank the staffs of Hunt Library (Carnegie Mellon University), Hillman Library (University of Pittsburgh), the Library of Congress, the Institute for Scientific Information for the Social Sciences (Moscow), the Russian State Archive of Social and Political History, the State Archive of the Russian Federation, and the Russian State Archive of the Economy for their help in locating materials. I would like to thank the staff of the State Central Museum of the Contemporary History of Russia for permission to reprint selections from their archive of historical photographs. Nathaniel Rattner, a New York philatelist, searched his extensive collection for stamps of Soviet women workers, shared their history with me, and permitted me to include them in the book. Thanks to the editors of *Slavic Review*, where an earlier version of Chapter 2 first appeared as "Industrial Politics, Peasant Rebellion, and the Death of the Proletarian Women's Movement in the USSR" (Spring 1996).

I am indebted to my Russian friends and colleagues Natalia Basovskaya, Sergei Karpenko, Aleksei Kilichenkov, and Vladimir Strelkov for all of their help. Their friendship, generosity, and hospitality have deepened my feelings for the people and the history of their country. Elena Parfenova and Elena Bakhtina both proved able and assiduous research assistants, helping me to locate much useful material.

I would also like to thank Mary Buckley, William Chase, Barbara Clements, Robert W. Davies, Donna Harsch, Naum Kats, Katherine Lynch, Melanie Ilic, Arfon Rees, Steven Schlossman, Lewis Siegelbaum, Carmine Storella, Kenneth Straus, and the members of the University of Pittsburgh's Working Class History Seminar (Center for Social History). All offered useful suggestions and comments on various sections of the manuscript. I am particularly indebted to Arfon Rees, Robert W. Davies, and Zoya Kotkina for their help with Soviet labor statistics. Susan Pennybacker, a great fellow traveler, shared many a Moscow adventure with me. My parents, Judith and Lawrence Goldman, still maintain an abiding interest in the fate of Russia's working people and of socialism. Their interest buoys my own, even amid the rising tide of globalization.

Finally, I would like to thank my husband, Marcus Rediker, whose interest in people's resistance to capitalist development has shaped my reading of "primitive accumulation" in a different context. In reading and discussing countless drafts of this work, his warm encouragement and incisive comments have been invaluable.

Illustrations

Tables

xiii

Acronyms and Abbreviations

Agitmass	Department for Agitation and Mass Campaigns
CEC	Central Executive Committee of the Congress of Soviets
CC	Central Committee of the Communist Party
delo (d.)	file or folder
fond (f.)	collection
GARF	State Archive of the Russian Federation
Gosbank	State Bank
Gosplan	State Planning Commission
kolkhoz	collective farm
Kolkhoztsentr	Union of Agricultural Collectives
KUTB	Committee to Improve the Labor and Life of Women
Narpit	Union of Public Dining and Dormitory Workers
NEP	New Economic Policy
NKT	Commissariat of Labor
obratno (ob.)	back of numbered page in archival folder
opis' (o.)	inventory
Rabkrin	Workers' and Peasants' Inspectorate
RGAE	Russian State Archive of the Economy
RTsKhIDNI (RGASPI)	Russian Center for the Preservation and Study of Documents of Contemporary History, formerly the archive of the Communist Party, now Russian State Archive of Social and Political History
SNK	Council of People's Commissars
sovkhoz	state farm
STO	Council of Labor and Defence
Tsentrosoiuz	All-Union Central Union of Consumers' Societies

Tsentrozhilsoiuz	Central Housing Union
VSNKh	Supreme Council of the National Economy
VTsSPS	All-Union Central Council of Trade Unions
ZhAKT	Association of Housing Cooperatives
Zhenotdel	women's department of the Central Committee of the Communist Party
ZRK	closed system of workers' cooperatives

This postage stamp and the one on page 286 depict women workers. The stamps were issued from 1929 to 1931 as part of a set featuring two women workers and two collective farmers. They were issued as regular or definitive, not commemorative, stamps, and were reissued from 1937 to 1952. The stamps reflect the importance the state attached to the role of women workers during the 1930s.

WOMEN AT THE GATES

Introduction

In the annals of industrialization, the Soviet experience is unique in its whirlwind rapidity. The vast transformations that shook Western Europe over centuries – proletarianization, industrialization, urbanization – were in the Soviet Union telescoped into a mere decade. The working class grew at an unprecedented rate, changing in size and social composition. Even more striking was the critical role of women: in no country of the world did they come to constitute such a significant part of the working class in so short a time. In 1930 alone, 473,000 women entered industry, more than four times the number of new women workers in 1929, to be followed by 587,000 more in 1931. Between 1929 and 1935, almost 4 million women began to work for wages, 1.7 million of them in industry. More women took jobs in industry than in any other sector of the economy. By 1935, 42 percent of all industrial workers would be women. In 1932 and 1933, women were the only new source of labor for the developing economy.[1]

Not only did women pour into the labor force in record numbers, they also flooded industries that had traditionally been dominated by men. They crossed the older lines of sex segregation that had persisted in Soviet industry through the 1920s, entering new industries such as machine building and electrostations as well as expanding branches of older industries such as mining, metallurgy, and chemical manufacture. They filled newly created jobs and older jobs previously held exclusively by men, working mainly as unskilled and semiskilled labor. As women undercut the strict hierarchies of skill and gender within the factories, they forced male workers to reexamine their ideas about skill, "masculine" and "feminine" work, and the role of women in the workplace.

---

[1] *Trud v SSSR. Statisticheskii spravochnik* (Moscow: TsUNKhU Gosplana, 1936), 10–11, 25. These figures include all women in industry: workers, apprentices, and others.

Many historians have written about workers in Soviet industrialization, but few have specifically considered women.[2] Western historians of labor in the 1930s have concentrated instead on the relationship between workers and the state, on mapping policy, on labor legislation, on the clash of interests among workers, managers, and Party officials in the factories, and on the great shock work and Stakhanovite campaigns for production.[3] More recently, historians have shown a growing interest in workers' social identities as older "*kadrovye*" workers, new peasant migrants, and youth, and in their relationships to the uniquely "Soviet" beliefs, lexicon, and worldview that shaped their lives.[4] Russian historians have produced numerous carefully researched accounts of working-class growth and accomplishment during industrialization. The Party's ideological insistence on the centrality of the working class impelled historians to focus on labor, but it also constrained their questions and conclusions.[5] As a result, Russian historians today show a strong allergic reaction to those privileged categories, such as labor, that once dominated Soviet historiography. Despite their differences, however, Western and Russian labor historians have almost unanimously agreed that women merit but a few

[2] Among the few books on women workers in the 1930s are Melanie Ilic, *Women Workers in the Soviet Interwar Economy: From "Protection" to "Equality"* (London: Macmillan, 1999); Alistair McAuley, *Women's Work and Wages in the Soviet Union* (London: Allen and Unwin, 1981); Michael Paul Sacks, *Women's Work in Soviet Russia: Continuity in the Midst of Change* (New York: Praeger, 1976); G. A. Prutsenskii, A. P. Stepanov, and B. I. Eidel'man, *Voprosy truda v SSSR* (Moscow: Gosizdat Politicheskoi Literatury, 1958); *Sovetskie zhenshchiny i profsoiuzy* (Moscow: Profizdat, 1984).

[3] See for example, R. W. Davies, *The Soviet Economy in Turmoil, 1929–1930* (Cambridge, Mass.: Harvard University Press, 1989); Donald Filtzer, *Soviet Workers and Stalinist Industrialization: The Formation of Modern Soviet Production Relations* (Armonk, N.Y.: M. E. Sharpe, 1986); Hiroaki Kuromiya, *Stalin's Industrial Revolution: Politics and Workers, 1928–1932* (New York: Cambridge University Press, 1988); Solomon Shwarz, *Labor in the Soviet Union* (New York: Praeger, 1951); Lewis Siegelbaum, *Stakhanovism and the Politics of Productivity in the USSR, 1935–1941* (New York: Cambridge University Press, 1988); Kenneth Straus, *Factory and Community in Stalin's Russia: The Making of an Industrial Working Class* (Pittsburgh: University of Pittsburgh Press, 1997).

[4] On working-class identity, see David Hoffman, *Peasant Metropolis: Social Identities in Moscow, 1929–1941* (Ithaca, N.Y.: Cornell University Press, 1994); Stephen Kotkin, *Magnetic Mountain: Stalinism as Civilization* (Berkeley, Calif.: University of California Press, 1995); Lewis Siegelbaum and William Rosenberg, eds., *Social Dimensions of Soviet Industrialization* (Bloomington, Ind.: Indiana University Press, 1993); Lewis Siegelbaum and Ronald Suny, eds., *Making Workers Soviet: Power, Class, Identity* (Ithaca, N.Y.: Cornell University Press, 1994).

[5] *Rabochii klass – vedushchaia sila v stroitel'stve sotsialisticheskogo obshchestva, 1927–1937*, tom 3 (Moscow: Izdatel'stvo "Nauka," 1984); A. M. Panfilova, *Formirovanie rabochego klassa SSSR v gody pervoi piatletki, 1928–1932* (Moscow: Izdatel'stvo Moskovskogo Universiteta, 1964); O. I. Shkaratan, *Problemy sotsial'noi struktury rabochego klassa SSSR* (Moscow: Izdatel'stvo "Mysl'," 1970); A. I. Vdovin and V. Z. Drobizhev, *Rost rabochego klassa SSSR, 1917–1940* (Moscow: Izdatel'stvo "Mysl'," 1976).

pages of text, a brief index entry, and perhaps a short paragraph of statistics. In no sense, moreover, did such limited efforts at inclusion change the larger narrative of the creation of the Soviet working class.

This book makes women's experiences central to the great industrialization drive in the Soviet Union in the 1930s. It reconceives the formation of the Soviet working class by recovering the role of women and analyzing its larger implications for capital accumulation, wages, workers' mobility, and the proletarianization of the peasantry. It uses gender not simply to fill a descriptive gap or to add a missing piece to a largely completed puzzle but rather to rearrange the puzzle itself. The text covers the period from the October 1917 revolution through the second five-year plan (1933–1937), focusing primarily on the first five-year plan (1929–1932), a time of wrenching transformation. It examines the sex segregation of Soviet industry, the urban and rural upheavals that propelled women into waged labor, the mass Party campaigns to recruit women to work, the state's plans to "regender" the economy, conflicting interests within the planning process, and social relations between male and female workers.

The grand deployment of women and the rapid pace were not the only features that distinguished Soviet industrialization from its Western equivalents. The Soviet state committed itself to gender equality, to the abolition of the "free" market as a determinant of wages, prices, and the allocation of labor, and to the substitution of planning for profit as the driving force of industrial transformation. Yet despite these differences, women's experiences with industrialization under capitalism and under socialism share some striking similarities.[6] Although this book explores the Soviet experience, its perspective is informed by a wider study of women in the development of capitalism in Europe and America. The comparison

6   On gender and industrial capitalism, see, e.g., Ava Baron, ed., *Work Engendered: Toward a New History of American Labor* (Ithaca, N.Y.: Cornell University Press, 1991); Mary Blewett, *Men, Women, and Work: Class, Gender, and Protest in the New England Shoe Industry, 1780–1910* (Chicago and Urbana, Ill.: University of Illinois Press, 1990); Kathleen Canning, *Languages of Labor and Gender: Female Factory Work in Germany, 1850–1914* (Ithaca, N.Y.: Cornell University Press, 1996); Dorothy Sue Cobble, ed., *Women and Unions* (Ithaca, N.Y.: ILR Press, 1993); Judith Coffin, *The Politics of Women's Work: The Paris Garment Trades, 1750–1915* (Princeton, N.J.: Princeton University Press, 1996); Thomas Dublin, *Transforming Women's Work: New England Lives in the Industrial Revolution* (Ithaca, N.Y.: Cornell University Press, 1994); Laura Frader and Sonya Rose, eds., *Gender and Class in Modern Europe* (Ithaca, N.Y.: Cornell University Press, 1996); Alice Kessler-Harris, *Out to Work: A History of Wage-Earning Women in the United States* (Oxford: Oxford University Press, 1982); Sonya Rose, *Limited Livelihoods: Gender and Class in Nineteenth-Century England* (Berkeley, Calif.: University of California Press, 1992); Leslie Tentler, *Wage-Earning Women: Industrial Work and Family Life in the United States, 1900–1930* (Oxford: Oxford University Press, 1979); Deborah Valenze, *The First Industrial Woman* (Oxford: Oxford University Press, 1995).

between the Soviet Union and the West raises important questions about the causes, structures, and cultural tenacity of women's subordination across economic systems. For example, in what ways were women's opportunities expanded under a system that self-consciously professed gender equality? Was the planned, socialist development of industry free of the labor market segmentation and occupational segregation that were so marked under capitalism? Did male workers under capitalism and socialism react differently to the introduction of female labor? To what extent is women's traditionally subordinate economic position linked to profit, the free market, and capitalist forms of organization? These questions are of interest to all students of proletarianization and industrialization, those complex processes that first rent England in the eighteenth century and that continue to transform entire continents today.

1

Guarding the Gates to the Working Class: Women in Industry, 1917–1929

In the 1920s, the male labor force poured in from the countryside and began to replace women in production. This frequently occurred under the banner of "rationalization," but in fact, one group was laid off and another hired.   S. Gimmel'farb, planner and labor expert[1]

Women fared badly in the mass layoffs on the railroads. When men and women held the same job, women were the ones to be laid off. There was a definite tendency to lay off women whose husbands were working.
1929 report on union work among women employed on the railroads[2]

At the end of the 1920s, a poor peasant woman named Zaminskaia was abandoned by her husband. Left to fend for herself and her two children, she went to the city in search of work. She tried to register at the labor exchange, which dispensed both jobs and unemployment benefits, but was told she was eligible for neither. "You must first work six months for wages," an official explained. Feeling increasingly hopeless, she ran from one state agency to another, from the Department of Labor to the local soviet to the Workers' and Peasants' Inspectorate. She heard the same story from every official. Without previous work experience, she could not register to work. Finally she wrote a despairing letter to *Rabotnitsa*, a journal for women workers. "I am sick and I am starving," she noted. "I have appealed everywhere."[3] Zaminskaia was typical of thousands of women (and men) who sought to enter the waged labor force throughout the 1920s. She found that jobs were few, unemployment was high, and the Communist Party and unions favored and protected

[1] S. Gimmel'farb, "Likvidatsiia Bezrabotnitsy v SSSR i Problema Kadrov," *Problemy ekonomiki*, 1931, nos. 4–5: 30.
[2] GARF, f. 5474, o. 10, d. 342, "Sostoianie Profraboty Sredi Zhenshchin na Zakavkazskom Zheleznodorozhnom Transporte," 30.
[3] Letter cited by M. Gal'perin, "Uskorit' Utverzhdenie Zakona o Priniiatii na Uchet Birzh Truda Odinokikh Zhenshchin," *Rabotnitsa*, 1930, no. 21: 19.

those unemployed workers who had previously worked for wages. Was Zaminskaia a worker? She fiercely wanted to be. Should she have been entitled to the same privileges as an unemployed union member? Her experience raised a profound political question: Who defined the working class? Who held the keys to the gate that separated the dispossessed from the proletariat?

Throughout the 1920s, the definition of "proletarian" was strongly contested by a variety of social groups. In a state that proudly and self-consciously defined itself as a "dictatorship of the proletariat," the definition of a worker was linked, ideologically and materially, to numerous privileges. It determined who would receive unemployment compensation, preference in hiring, and union membership, all important and eagerly sought material advantages. The question of who qualified as a "worker" was thus critical to peasants, housewives, employed union members, unemployed union members, and those who needed a job but had never worked for wages. The Communist Party, too, had a real interest in defining and understanding the category of "worker," for in its view, it was axiomatic that a person's class position ultimately determined his or her consciousness, behavior, and interests. The Bolsheviks' victory in 1917, as well as their ability to retain state power, depended on the support of a staunch cadre of experienced, class-conscious workers. The questions of who had made the revolution, who would benefit directly from socialism, and who could be trusted to be a reliable mainstay of the regime's policies were not idle theoretical musings. Such questions took on an added urgency in a country that was overwhelmingly peasant. The answers would determine the strength of support for the new socialist state and, ultimately, whether it would survive.

The composition of the working class was in large part a consequence of how the Bolsheviks chose to define it and the policies they promoted. Until 1930, when a sharp labor shortage forced the Party to broaden its understanding of the working class, its definition of "worker" was quite narrow. The Party's understanding of the "working class," in an ideological, administrative, and symbolic political sense, was never synonymous with the poor, the dispossessed, the oppressed, or the disenfranchised. Although impoverished and miserable, the "working class" was not "the wretched of the earth." The worker was not a peasant, a simple toiler, or a member of the laboring mass; according to Marxist theory, the peasantry had little inherent interest in socialization of the means of production or industrialization. The worker was not female, though the Party recognized both practically and politically that thousands of women labored as domestic servants, laundresses, or landless laborers and in textile mills, chemical and tobacco plants, and other branches of industry. The Party held specific criteria for a worker: he was removed from the customs, beliefs, and worldview of his peasant forebears; he had severed his ties to the land; and he depended solely on a money wage. He was a "hereditary" worker whose parents had also been workers. He held prerevolutionary *stazh* (seniority) and industrial skills. The worker could be expected to support and benefit from socialism, not simply because he was poor but because of his particular relationship to the means of production. O. I. Shkaratan, the well-known Soviet labor historian, called this worker, the "*kadrovyi, promyshlennyi rabochii*" or the "*chistyi proletarii*," the rank and file industrial worker or the "pure proletarian."[4] The "*kadrovyi* worker" represented not only thousands of real workers but also an idealized projection of the Bolshevik political imagination. From the Bolshevik perspective, this "pure proletarian" made the revolution and stood to benefit immediately and directly from the socialization of the means of production in a way that the peasantry, the intelligentsia, and the petty bourgeoisie did not. Thus the "pure" or "*kadrovye*" proletariat provided the only real, reliable social base of the new revolutionary order.

By 1921, however, the actually existing working class was hardly the idealized projection of the Bolshevik imagination.[5] Making up only a small minority within a largely peasant country at the beginning of World War I, the working class was even smaller by the end of the civil war. With the collapse of industry, the destruction of the railroads, and the disintegration of trade, the working class contracted sharply.[6] Between 1917 and 1920, industry lost 30 percent of its workforce and 40 percent of its men.[7] Thousands of the Party's strongest supporters were killed in the civil war. As Shkaratan has demonstrated in his careful study of the composition of the working class, by 1920 the ranks of the working class were filled with women, urban traders, small shopkeepers, former tsarist

---

[4] O. I. Shkaratan, *Problemy sotsial'noi struktury rabochego klassa SSSR* (Moscow: Izadatel'stvo "Mysl'," 1970), 246, 261. For an excellent discussion of the meanings of class, see Lewis Siegelbaum and Ronald Suny, "Class Backwards? In Search of the Soviet Working Class," in their collection *Making Workers Soviet: Power, Class and Identity* (Ithaca, N.Y.: Cornell University Press, 1994).

[5] Numerous historians have noted this problem. See, e.g., Isaac Deutscher, *The Prophet Unarmed: Trotsky, 1921–1929* (London: Oxford University Press, 1959), 7; Sheila Fitzpatrick, "The Bolsheviks' Dilemma: The Class Issue in Party Politics and Culture," in *The Cultural Front: Power and Culture in Revolutionary Russia* (Ithaca, N.Y.: Cornell University Press, 1992), 17–19, and "The Problem of Class Identity in NEP Society," in Fitzpatrick, Alexander Rabinowitch, and Richard Stites, eds., *Russia in the Era of NEP: Explorations in Soviet Society and Culture* (Bloomington, Ind.: Indiana University Press, 1991), 12–18; Moshe Lewin, "The Social Background of Stalinism," in *The Making of the Soviet System: Essays in the Social History of Interwar Russia* (New York: Pantheon Books, 1985), 258–60; Elizabeth Wood, *The Baba and the Comrade: Gender and Politics in Revolutionary Russia* (Bloomington, Ind.: Indiana University Press, 1997), 44–45.

[6] *Rabochii klass – vedushchaia sila v stroitel'stve sotsialisticheskogo obshchestva, 1921–1927*, tom 2 (Moscow: Izdatel'stvo "Nauka," 1984), 28.

[7] Shkaratan, 203.

bureaucrats, and ex-peasants – all "class aliens" in Bolshevik phraseology. According to A. Anikst, the head of the labor market department, "an entire layer of half workers" filtered into the factories during the civil war.[8] No one was more morbidly attuned to this problem than the Bolsheviks, for if class determined consciousness, what possible support could the newly victorious regime expect from a working class composed not of *kadrovye* workers but rather of a motley, declassed collection of desperate individuals dreaming of former privilege and small business?

The Party was anxious to preserve the *kadrovye* workers, to expand their numbers, and to protect them against an influx of peasants, women, and declassed individuals in search of work. Shkaratan, reflecting the Party's early perspective, notes with marked relief that "thanks to the regulating activities of the state, streams of peasants from the country-side did not adversely affect the composition of the working class" after the civil war.[9] The "regulating activities of the state" also ensured that men would replace women. Thousands of women workers were sum-marily dismissed from industry and transport after the civil war. Others, widowed by war, "freed" by the new revolutionary divorce laws, or aban-doned, like Zaminskaia, by their husbands, desperately sought to enter the waged labor force for the first time in order to support their families. They crowded the courts and labor exchanges, petitioned the Central Control Commission, the Workers' and Peasants' Inspectorate, and local soviets in search of alimony, wages, and support for their children. Ad-vocates for women spoke about their plight in the labor press, women's journals, and Party newspapers throughout the 1920s and early 1930s.[10] Working-class and peasant women, assisted by the Zhenotdel (the wom-en's department of the Party) and by women's activists within the unions, sought to broaden the Party's definition of the worker and to open the working class to the needy and the poor. The struggle over the "right to work" was waged throughout the 1920s among the unions, male workers, peasants, women, and the Party. Each of these groups doggedly pursued its own interests. The unions sought to protect their members, male work-ers maneuvered to maintain their monopoly on skilled positions, peasants and women aimed to break into the labor force, and the Party tried to mediate among these interests while maintaining its primary commitment to workers – male, skilled, *kadrovye* – as its main bulwark of support.[11]

---

[8] Ibid., 200.   [9]   Ibid., 257, 259.
[10] See Wendy Goldman, *Women, the State and Revolution: Soviet Family Policy and Social Life, 1917–1936* (New York: Cambridge University Press, 1993), 101–44, 214–54, 296–337.
[11] On the struggle over employment, see Wood, 151–61; Douglas Weiner, "'*Razmychka?*' Urban Unemployment and Peasant In-Migration as Sources of Social Conflict," in Fitzpatrick et al., 144–55.

This chapter explores this contested arena. Focusing on the experience of women, it provides a structural overview of women's industrial-labor-force participation in the period from World War I to the beginning of the first five-year plan, paying particular attention to the gendered nature of Russian/Soviet industry both horizontally (by skill and wage) and vertically (by industrial branch and occupational sector). Concentrating on the impact of World War I, the civil war, and the New Economic Policy (NEP), it examines how each of these upheavals affected gender segregation and the role of women within industry. It analyzes the impact of Party policy on women's prospects for employment and promotion and considers how union and Party officials understood the concept of skill. Finally, it traces the development of state policy toward the labor market in the context of the Party's fears about the "purity" and "contamination" of the working class.

Women's Employment: 1914–1928

Russian industry began to grow rapidly between 1885 and the beginning of World War I, producing a small but stable working class permanently based in the towns. By 1914, almost 25 million out of a population of 139.3 million (or 17 percent of all Russians) lived in towns and cities. By 1917, approximately 18.5 million Russians had some relationship to waged labor. About 3.6 million worked in large-scale industry, 1.7 million in transport, 1.25 million in construction, another 1.25 million in small industry, and 4.5 million in agriculture. The mining and oil industry was the largest single employer, with 872,900 workers, followed by textile, with 724,000, and metal and machine production, with 544,100. Metal and machine production and the state-owned defense and railroad industries had all grown rapidly during the war, employing a total of 1,184,200 workers mostly in large plants and factories by 1917.[12]

Women were a significant part of Russian industry almost from its inception. By 1885, they comprised 22 percent of the factory workforce. They held even larger shares of the textile (37 percent), paper (36 percent), and tobacco industries (47 percent). The majority (80 percent) of women who worked for wages, however, were either servants or landless agricultural laborers based in the villages. Only 13 percent of waged women worked in industry or construction. Yet over time, both the number of women workers and their percentage of the industrial labor force

---

[12] V. P. Danilov, *Rural Russia under the New Regime* (London: Hutchinson, 1988), 38; A. I. Vdovin and V. Z. Drobizhev, *Rost rabochego klassa SSSR, 1917–1940* (Moscow: Izdatel'stvo "Mysl'," 1976), 68–70.

grew steadily. Rose Glickman writes, "From 1885 to 1914 the salient feature of the history of women workers was the slow but steady increase
not only of their absolute numbers in the labor force but of the percentage of their representation in the total as well.... Whether the total labor
force increased or diminished, whether industry flourished or declined,
the proportion of women in factories rose relentlessly."[13]

The expanding deployment of women was motivated largely by the
search for profits. One factory inspector's report noted that throughout
the country, factory owners were endeavoring to reduce their wage costs
by "replacing men with women." Factory managers turned to women as
a cheap source of labor, and following the adoption of child labor laws
in 1882, they used women to replace children as well. Women were the
fastest-growing group in the labor force: by 1914, more than half a million
women constituted almost one third of the total number of factory workers. Slowly having gained a predominant position in the textile industry,
they represented by that year more than half of Russia's textile workers.
And after 1900, especially in regions where there were few textile mills,
women had also begun filtering into industries previously reserved for men.

Women workers, like men, became ever more firmly established in cities,
retaining fewer ties to the villages and peasant life. Casual and episodic
labor gave way to steadier work. More women remained in the factories even after they married and had children. In her pioneering study
of Russian factory women, Glickman notes that by the early twentieth
century, a growing segment of women was as firmly established in the
factories as men. These women workers were "as fully proletarian, as
stable in the factory, as it was possible to be in tsarist Russia." Glickman
argues that while women had fewer skills and less *stazh* than men, they
also had weaker ties to the village. By certain criteria, women workers
could thus be considered even more "proletarian" in their identities than
their male counterparts.[14]

During World War I, women's share of the labor force jumped significantly as women replaced men who were mobilized for the army. Shkaratan
estimates that 20 percent of the industrial working class was drafted into
the army and that by 1917 fully half of all workers were "new" to the
factories.[15] According to the 1918 census, women's share of industrial
jobs increased from 31.4 percent in 1913 to 45 percent in 1918. Their
percentage increased in every industry, though their gains were greatest
in the traditionally male metal industry, where their share tripled.[16] While
many women did first enter factories during the war years, they were not

[13] Rose Glickman, *Russian Factory Women: Workplace and Society, 1880–1914* (Berkeley,
      Calif.: University of California Press, 1984), 74–75, 76; Shkaratan, 229, 192.
[14] See discussion in Glickman, 84–104.   [15] Shkaratan, 219–20.
[16] G. Serebrennikov, "Zhenskii Trud v SSSR za 15 Let," *Voprosy truda*, 1932, nos. 11–12:
      59, 60. The 1918 census covered thirty-one *guberniias* in European Russia. Serebren-
      nikov offers figures for 1913, 1917, and 1920, all years unavailable in *Trud v SSSR*.

necessarily new to the cities or even, in terms of their social origins, new to the working class. Many of these women may have been servants, low-waged, nonindustrial workers, or the wives or daughters of workers. Contrary to Bolshevik thinking at the time, "changes in the social and gender composition and consciousness of the working class did not necessarily constitute deproletarianization," write Lewis Siegelbaum and Ronald Suny.[17]

After the Bolsheviks took Russia out of the war in 1918, women were laid off in all branches of industry, but their level of participation remained high. The Red Army soon remobilized soldiers and workers, who would not return to the cities until the end of the civil war, in 1920. At this time, women had a substantial presence in almost every branch of industry, though industry as a whole was still markedly segregated by gender. Women's share was strongest in the cotton industry (64 percent) and weakest in metal (15 percent). Their participation in other industries fell somewhere between these "female" and "male" poles: they constituted 41 percent of the workforce in paper processing, 32 percent in the chemical industry, and 18 percent in lumber.[18]

After the civil war, women's presence in industry fell sharply as demobilized soldiers returned to the cities and reclaimed their former jobs. In the spring of 1921, the Party adopted the New Economic Policy (NEP), a set of measures that mandated wages in place of rations, introduced a new system of cost accounting in the factories, and sharply decreased state spending on social services such as child care and communal dining halls. Many unprofitable enterprises were forced to close. Narpit (the Union of Public Dining and Dormitory Workers) fed thousands of workers at state expense throughout the civil war but lost a significant number of its mostly female staff after the war. Shkaratan claims that more than quarter of the industrial workforce (or about 260,000 people) was fired and replaced by *kadrovye* workers returning from the army or the countryside.[19] Unemployment soared, and a large percentage of the workers who found themselves on the street were women. Serebrennikov, a labor economist, argued that prejudice against female labor played a big role in the steady drop in women's share of certain industries. He blamed both the leaders of the Commissariat of Labor (NKT) and the unions for the "devaluation of women."[20]

---

[17] Shkaratan, 247, quoting material from the 1918 census. Shkaratan argues that a sufficient layer of *kadrovye* workers remained in the factories to account for the workers' support for the Bolsheviks. On the question of class consciousness, see also Diane Koenker, "Urbanization and Deurbanization in the Russian Revolution and the Civil War," *Journal of Modern History* 57 (1985): 424–50; Siegelbaum and Suny, "Class Backwards?," 15.

[18] Serebrennikov, 60.

[19] Shkaratan, 257. This figure covers the industries under VSNKh (the Supreme Council of the National Economy).

[20] Serebrennikov, 60–62.

Table 1.1. *Women workers in large-scale industry in the USSR, 1923–1930 (January 1)*

Year	Number of women	Percentage women
1923	423,200	29.5
1924	425,900	27.5
1925	513,200	28.8
1926	643,600	28.4
1927	673,800	28.4
1928	725,900	28.6
1929	804,000	28.8
1930	885,000	28.4

Source: *Trud v SSSR. Statisticheskii spravochnik* (Moscow: TsUNKhU Gosplana, 1936), 91.[21]

By 1928, women's overall share of industrial jobs stood at 28.6 percent, where it remained even after the adoption and implementation of the first five-year plan. Their share of industry as a whole remained almost unchanged from 1926 to 1930. Table 1.1 shows that women's share of industrial jobs remained fairly constant even as their absolute numbers rose steadily. By 1928, the state had succeeded in rebuilding the industries shattered by years of war. Output attained prewar levels as existing capital stock reached its full capacity for production. Between 1923 and 1930, the number of women in large-scale industry more than doubled, from 423,200 to 885,000.

Sex Segregation in Industry

The reconstruction of industry in the 1920s drew larger numbers of women into the labor force but failed to provide opportunities for women in traditionally "male" industries. Between 1923 and 1928, women's share of every industry, with the exception of cotton, linen, sewing, shoes, and food, dropped considerably. The losses were greatest in the traditionally "male" industries of coal mining, iron ore, and ferrous metallurgy (see Table 1.2). This resulted in an overall drop in women's share of industrial jobs. The larger pattern of deployment showed that women were losing representation in heavy industry and gaining a somewhat greater

[21] The term "large-scale industry" covers mechanized enterprises with no less than sixteen workers, apprentices, and service personnel, and no less than thirty in nonmechanized enterprises. See *Trud v SSSR. Statisticheskii spravochnik* (Moscow: TsUNKhU Gosplana, 1936), 363.

Table 1.2. *Women workers in the main branches of industry in the USSR, 1923–1928 (January 1), including apprentices*

Industrial branch	1923		1925		1926		1927		1928	
	Number	Percent	Number	Percent	Number	Percent	Number	Percent	Number	Percent
Electrostations	N/A	N/A	1,200	6.1	600	3.6	700	3.8	600	3.3
Coal mining	23,200	13.6	15,500	9.7	16,500	8.4	20,600	8.1	19,300	7.6
Oil extraction	1,100[a]	3.0[a]	1,400	3.0	100	0.2	200	0.5	100	0.3
Iron ore	800[a]	10.1[a]	1,200	10.8	1,400	7.0	1,200	6.4	1,300	5.8
Chemicals	6,500	20.9	6,000	14.4	6,400	13.6	6,600	14.5	7,200	14.6
Cement	700	16.2	600	8.5	1,300	8.2	1,700	8.8	1,900	9.8
Ferrous metallurgy	11,100	13.5	12,000	11.0	11,800	7.7	11,700	6.8	10,900	6.1
Machine building and metalwork	35,800	13.4	29,100	9.6	36,100	9.0	37,600	9.2	40,200	8.8
Lumber and plywood	7,600	18.1	7,200	14.6	6,700	13.2	10,000	15.5	11,500	16.6
Paper	6,400	31.0	6,600	24.7	7,800	24.9	8,000	24.9	7,800	25.1
Printing	10,700	24.7	12,300	20.5	14,400	20.9	12,400	20.5	12,800	21.2
Cotton fabric	133,700	59.9	207,700	59.9	276,100	60.6	284,600	61.2	300,600	61.9
Linen	35,000	60.8	41,300	58.4	50,700	61.9	61,000	63.4	59,600	64.4
Wool	28,400	49.3	30,900	47.0	32,700	48.0	31,400	48.8	33,000	49.2
Leather and fur	5,000	15.4	3,500	11.2	3,600	10.5	3,700	11.2	4,200	12.2
Sewing	N/A	N/A	14,400	58.2	15,700	63.8	16,600	63.6	27,400	64.3
Shoes	3,500	26.9	4,100	23.2	5,300	28.9	6,400	30.7	7,900	29.8
Food	32,500	23.8	43,400	25.9	61,200	25.3	57,700	26.7	63,500	26.3
Total	342,000		444,700		548,400		572,100		609,800	

[a] 1924.
Source: *Trud v SSSR*, 99, 106, 114, 120, 127, 134, 142, 150, 161, 168, 176, 184, 192, 199, 207, 215, 223, 230. These numbers include workers and apprentices only.[22]

22 The yearly totals given for women in industry in table 1.1 differ from those in table 1.2 because the former includes some branches of production not included the latter, such as industrial cooperatives, smaller factories, and subsidiary industries in agriculture, construction, and trade. See *Trud v SSSR*, 369, for an explanation.

Table 1.3. *Distribution of women workers in industry, 1923 and 1928 (January 1), percent*

Industrial branch	1923	1928
Electrostations	N/A	0.09
Coal mining	6.7	3.0
Oil extraction	0.3[a]	0.01
Iron ore	0.2[a]	0.2
Chemicals	1.9	1.1
Cement	0.2	0.3
Ferrous metallurgy	3.2	1.8
Machine building and metalwork	10.4	6.6
Lumber and plywood	2.2	1.9
Paper	1.8	1.3
Printing	3.1	2.1
Cotton fabric	39.0	49.2
Linen	10.2	9.7
Wool	8.3	5.4
Leather and fur	1.4	0.7
Sewing	N/A	4.5
Shoes	1.0	1.3
Food	9.5	10.4
Total	100.9	99.6

[a] 1924.
Source: Figures derived from Table 1.2.

share in light industry. Many feminist analysts and activists were concerned that the pattern of NEP was a portent for the future. Women stood to gain little from the five-year plan's investment in and expansion of heavy industry if they were to be increasingly concentrated in undercapitalized light industries. By the end of NEP, in 1928, the number of women in large-scale industry in the USSR – 725,900 – was almost the same as it had been in 1913 (723,900).[23] Overall, labor policy during the NEP years strengthened the traditional patterns of gender segregation that had existed before the war. Women who joined the labor force during NEP tended to enter the industries long dominated by women: textiles and sewing.

By the end of NEP, the textile industries (cotton, linen, and sewing) not only contained a majority of women within their workforces but also employed the majority of women workers overall. Out of a total of 609,800 women working in industry in 1928, almost two thirds worked in textiles (see Table 1.3). The remainder was scattered in small pockets throughout various industries, with no particularly heavy concentrations. Of the total number of women employed in industry, 10.4 percent worked

---

[23] For the 1913 figure, see Glickman, 83. On women's labor-force participation between 1917 and 1928, see Melanie Ilic, *Women Workers in the Soviet Interwar Economy: From "Protection" to "Equality"* (London: Macmillan, 1999), 27–42.

in food, 6.6 percent in machine building and metalwork, 3 percent in mining, and 2.1 percent in printing. Table 1.3 demonstrates that gender segregation within industry intensified between 1923 and 1928. The percentage of all women working in coal mining, oil extraction, chemicals, ferrous metallurgy, machine building and metalwork, lumber and plywood, paper, printing, wool, and leather and fur decreased. At the same time, a larger percentage of the female industrial workforce was concentrated in cotton (rising from 39 to 49.2 percent). Women were less evenly distributed across branches of industry and more heavily clustered in the traditionally "female" sectors. If the distribution pattern of women across industries represents the job opportunities available to them, the changes that occurred between 1923 and 1928 indicate a decrease in opportunity. Thus both women's gains and their losses in the workforce during NEP helped to reassert the traditional gender balance in industry, whereby women were increasingly concentrated in textiles and other light industry, and men in metal and heavy industry. Despite the Bolsheviks' commitment to women's equality, the economic policies of NEP actually strengthened gender divisions in industry, reversing the trend toward women's participation in heavy industry that had begun after 1900 and accelerated during the war years.[24]

Skill and Wages

If the policies of NEP reinforced the vertical segregation of industry by branch, they also neglected to redress the horizontal segregation by skill and wage that existed within each branch. Throughout the 1920s, women remained in the lowest-paid and least-skilled jobs in every industry. By 1925, about half of all male industrial workers held skilled jobs, compared to only 13 percent of women (see Table 1.4). Women working in textiles and tobacco had somewhat greater opportunities for advancement, but those in traditionally male industries, such as metal and mining, had almost no chance for promotion and held virtually no skilled positions. In rubber and matches, sectors of the chemical industry, for example, about 5 percent of male workers were engaged in skilled work, compared to only .1 percent of female workers. In the chemical industry as a whole,

---

[24] These patterns were not exclusive to the Soviet Union. The sex segregation of Soviet industry was quite similar to that in other advanced industrial countries, including Germany. In the Soviet Union and Germany, women held virtually identical shares of many industrial branches, with a heavy concentration in sewing and textiles and a smaller presence in heavy industry. Yet Soviet women held a larger share of metallurgy, machine production, chemicals, construction, and lumber than their German counterparts. Thus, while Soviet industry was clearly segregated, the divisions were even more marked in Germany. See GARF, f. 5515, o. 13, d. 6, "Doklad o Sostoianii Zhenskogo Truda," 31 ob.

Table 1.4. *Industrial workers by gender and skill, May 1925 (percent)[a]*

	Skilled	Semiskilled	Unskilled	Total number
Men	49.5	30.9	19.5	280,013
Women	13.2	41.4	45.2	60,561

[a]Includes workers in coal mining, metallurgy, machine building, printing, porcelain, glass, matches, and tobacco only.
Source: A. G. Rashin, *Zhenskii trud v SSSR* (Moscow: Voprosy Truda, 1928), 12.

only .3 percent of women were in skilled positions, compared to 7 percent of men.[25]

Occupying less skilled positions, women also made less money than men, earning about 64 percent of the male wage in 1927.[26] Women were concentrated in the lowest-paid, least-skilled jobs in every industry. In 1926, 21 percent of male workers throughout the country were paid less than forty rubles a month, compared to fully 65 percent of the women. While the differences between male and female wages were most exaggerated in the metal industry – where 22 percent of the women but only 3 percent of the men earned less than forty rubles a month – wage disparities existed in textiles as well.[27]

A lack of skill and training was, however, not the only factor depressing women's wages. Women at the same skill level as men were paid less. Unskilled women consistently earned less than unskilled men in every industry (see Table 1.5). In branches ranging from tobacco to metallurgy, unskilled women made between 67 and 85 percent of the unskilled male wage. These statistics suggest that women received lower wages simply because they were women.

The "Peculiar Character" of Female Unemployment

Unemployment was a serious problem for women through the NEP years. Women's inability to support themselves and their children during NEP made a mockery of the independence granted by the new Family Codes

[25] GARF, f. 5451, o. 15, d. 362, "O Vnedrenii Zhenskogo Truda v Narodnoe Khoziaistvo v 1931," 155.

[26] A. G. Rashin, *Zhenskii trud v SSSR* (Moscow: Voprosy Truda, 1928), 39. Their lower wages were not the result of working fewer hours; see pp. 39, 48.

[27] Figures for metal are based on wages in 1928. GARF, f. 5515, o. 13, d. 6, "Rabota NKT po Uluchsheniiu Uslovii Zhenskogo Truda," 14.

Table 1.5. *Daily wages of unskilled workers, in rubles,*
March 1928

Industrial branch	Male wage	Female wage	Percent of male wage earned
Southern metallurgy	2.07	1.60	77
Urals metallurgy	1.75	1.28	73
Cotton	2.04	1.51	74
Shoes	2.56	1.71	67
Tobacco	2.90	2.47	85
Rubber	4.25	3.29	77

Source: N. V., "K Voprosy o Planirovanii Zarplaty," *Voprosy truda,*
1929, nos. 3–4: 45.

Table 1.6. *Unemployed men and women in Russia,*
1927–1930 (January 1)

Year	Total unemployed	Number of men	Number of women	Percentage women
1927	916,928	481,387	435,541	47.5
1928	985,375	546,883	438,492	44.5
1929	1,130,210	597,881	532,329	47.1
1930	620,297	281,615	338,682	54.6

Source: GARF, f. 6983, o. 1, d. 159, p. 343 ob.[29]

of 1918 and 1926 and severely undermined the prospects for women's
emancipation. Female unemployment contributed to the large numbers
of homeless street children (*besprizorniki*) and the reemergence of prostitution. Broken, ragged streetwalkers told desperate tales of layoffs from
one job after another.[28] The number of unemployed men and women increased steadily toward the end of the 1920s, reaching a high of 1,130,210
in 1929. Yet the move toward rapid industrialization affected male and
female job seekers differently. Women were hired more slowly than men.
Between 1929 and 1930, the number of unemployed women dropped by
36 percent, while the number of unemployed men fell 53 percent. As a
result, women figured ever more prominently in the ranks of the unemployed: 44.5 percent in 1928, 47.1 percent in 1929, and 54.6 percent in
1930 (Table 1.6).

[28] Goldman, *Women, the State and Revolution*, 101–43.
[29] GARF, f. 5515, o. 13, d. 6, p. 40, offers the same figures for women. Figures provided
in f. 5515, o. 13, d. 5, p. 3 ob give lower numbers for all unemployed: 1927: 858,370;
1928: 785,537; 1929: 876,073; 1930: 620,429.

Table 1.7. *Distribution of unemployed women by skill in Russia, 1927–1929 (January 1)*

Year	Industrial		Intellectual		Unskilled	
	Number	Percent	Number	Percent	Number	Percent
1927	64,042	14	97,407	21.4	384,386	62.5
1928	44,816	10.3	119,274	27.2	252,405	58.8
1929	53,524	10.1	123,460	23.2	332,427	62.5

Source: GARF, f. 5515, o. 13, d. 6, p. 40. Based on information from 172 labor exchanges.

The feminization of the unemployed was widely noted by planners as well as by labor and Party officials. Stalin observed at the sixteenth Party Congress, in June 1930, that women and teens comprised the "great majority" of unemployed registered in the labor exchanges.[30] Numerous officials in NKT commented upon the "peculiar character" of female unemployment. Although industry was growing, and male unemployment decreasing, female unemployment continued to rise. After examining the data, the NKT staffers forecasted that in the future "the unemployed would consist entirely of women."[31]

Most labor analysts attributed the growing share of women among the unemployed not to gender but to skill, or the lack thereof. Industry demanded skilled and semiskilled workers first, so women with fewer skills were ignored in favor of skilled men. Gender was a coincidental marker, they insisted, not a cause. This argument appeared in almost every government analysis of female unemployment, and though it was partially true, it omitted any analysis of discrimination. It assumed that if men and women had possessed equal levels of skill, women would have been absorbed into the labor force as quickly as men. It was true that women had fewer skills: in 1929, for example, only 10 percent of unemployed women possessed some industrial skills, compared to about 18 percent of men.[32] Table 1.7 shows that the majority of unemployed women registered in the labor exchanges had no skills. These women most likely had some prior work experience (and thus were able to register).

[30] I. Stalin, "Politicheskii Otchet Tsentral'nogo Komiteta XVI S"ezdu VKP (b) Doklad i Zakliuchitel'noe Slovo," in *Voprosy leninizma* (Moscow, Leningrad: Gosudarstvennoe Sotsial'no-Ekonomicheskoe Izdatel'stvo, 1931), 725.

[31] GARF, f. 5515, o. 13, d. 5, "Piatiletkii Plan Vnedreniia Zhenskogo Truda v Narodnoe Khoziaistvo, RSFSR," 3 ob.

[32] See table 1.8 for the number and percentage of unemployed women with industrial skills. For men, GARF, f. 5515, o. 13, d. 5, p. 3 ob., notes that there were 162,681 unemployed workers with industrial skills in 1929. Subtracting 53,524 skilled women, this leaves 109,157 unemployed men with industrial skills, or 18 percent of all unemployed men.

Table 1.8. *Skilled and semiskilled unemployed men and women in Russia, 1927–1930 (January 1)*

Year	Total	Men	Women	Percentage women
1927	162,185	104,610	57,575	35
1928	143,951	93,569	50,382	35
1929	162,681	100,700	61,981	38
1930	134,446	78,248	56,198	42

Source: Calculations drawn from figures provided in GARF, f. 5515, o. 13, d. 5, p. 3 ob.

Many unskilled women in need of work were housewives or peasants who had never worked for wages. In the Moscow region in 1930, for example, almost half of the unemployed women had never held a waged job. Of those who had worked for wages, 70 percent had worked either as servants or in unskilled positions, and 20 percent had worked outside of industry. Only 10 percent had held industrial jobs. Moreover, of the women who had worked in industry, most had been laid off from the textile and sewing industries, both targeted by the first five-year plan for low investment and growth. Thus even the small number of women who possessed some industrial experience came from declining industries.[33] Former servants, peasants, charwomen, seamstresses, service workers, and even textile workers were not considered desirable candidates for industrial jobs, either by plant managers or by the labor exchanges that registered the unemployed and sent them to fill positions. Thus women's opportunities to work were narrowed not only by a lack of skills but also by the legacy of sex segregation of industry and the lowly positions they had held in the past.

The lack of skills was not the sole explanation for the ever-growing proportion of women to men among the unemployed. Table 1.8 shows that even skilled and semiskilled women were not hired as quickly as men, suggesting that gender as well as skill figured prominently in hiring decisions. Between 1927 and 1930, women's share among the skilled and semiskilled unemployed increased significantly, from 35 to 42 percent. While the number of unemployed skilled and semiskilled men dropped by 25 percent, the number of women in these same categories fell by only 2 percent. Even women who brought needed skills to the labor market took longer to be rehired than men. Additional data on the unskilled suggest a similar pattern: unskilled men were routinely favored over unskilled women. In Moscow in 1928, women strongly predominated over

---

[33]   GARF, f. 6983, o. 1, d. 159, "O Rabote Zheninspektorov," 345 ob.

men among the unskilled unemployed. Fully 59 percent of the unskilled unemployed were women, suggesting that unskilled men were more readily hired.[34] At every level of skill, from the lowest to the highest, men were hired more quickly than women.

Discrimination or prejudice against female labor, initially discounted by official reports, played a significant role in determining women's employment prospects. The labor exchanges often cooperated with managers to ensure that men rather than women were sent to fill vacant positions. In the Stalinskii region (*okrug*), for example, women constituted about 30 percent of the unemployed but only 4 percent of the workers selected by the labor exchanges to fill positions. Managers often requested in writing that the labor exchanges send them men rather than women. Male workers displayed similar prejudices. A worker and Party member in the Vetka mine explained, "Not only is it not necessary to promote women to skilled jobs, but in general, they should not work as long as there are men without work." He went on to proclaim a principle that was widely shared: "When there are no more unemployed men, then [women] can begin to work."[35] NKT officials recognized that managers were not blind to the gender of job seekers. Although women's lack of skills diminished their opportunities, "the sluggishness of managers and technical personnel, and bad attitudes toward female labor motivated by women's maternity" were also critical. Many managers regarded the generous Soviet maternity provisions as impediments to efficiency and maximum cost accounting, and considered female labor inferior to male. Women were frequently assigned to poorly functioning machines and placed at lower job grades than men even when they had equal skills.[36]

In discussions about unemployment, women's "lack of skills" was the most often cited explanation for their unemployment. Analysts wielded the phrase so often and with so little reflection that it came to seem almost like a sex-linked characteristic. "Female" was largely synonymous with "unskilled." The very opportunity to acquire skills was itself, however, determined by gender. Both managers and male workers were tremendously resistant to permitting women to enter apprenticeships, training programs, or skilled jobs. In Ivanovo-Voznesensk, the administration refused to accept girls into apprenticeships (*podmastery*). Often the factory committees themselves were an obstacle to women's advancement. In the Leninskii factory in Rostov, for instance, the factory committee stated that it was pointless to try to improve women's skills because all women were

34   GARF, f. 5515, o. 13, d. 6, "Rabota NKT RSFSR po Uluchsheniiu Uslovii Zhenskogo Truda," 16 ob.
35   Cherevadskaia, "Trud i Byt Rabotnits," *Kommunistka*, 1928, no. 6: 61.
36   GARF, f. 5515, o. 13, d. 6, "Doklad o Sostoianii Zhenskogo Truda NKT RSFSR," 36.

illiterate.[37] In reality, persistent, pervasive discrimination played a critical role in women's lack of skills. The old adage "first fired, last hired" aptly described women's experience during NEP and at the beginning of the first five-year plan.

Fears of "Backward Women"

The Party made several efforts during NEP to eliminate discrimination, to stop the growth of unemployment among women, and to involve women in production. It tried to halt the trend toward female firings at its Thirteenth Congress, in 1924, by passing a resolution that stated, "The preservation of the female labor force in production has a political significance."[38] While the resolution in principle elevated female labor above economic utility, it had little effect in practice. The upper levels of the Party were not willing to battle the representatives of industry and labor in the context of high unemployment among *kadrovye* male workers. Little changed until the late fall of 1930, when the country was gripped by a massive labor shortage. Although women complained about their exclusion from the first five-year plan, the Party was concerned in 1928–1929 less with women's industrial prospects than with their resistance to collectivization. In November 1928, the Central Committee issued a decree entitled "The Tasks of Party Work among Women Workers and Peasants." The Central Committee stated that women should be involved in the first five-year plan, but it defined that involvement primarily as a show of support for the larger program of industrialization and collectivization. The Central Committee expressed anxiety that "class enemies" would "turn the mass of backward women against the state." Noting that women were poorly represented in leadership positions, it instructed local leaders to promote women more aggressively and to permit women's activists to participate more fully in political discussion and decision making.

In terms of its recommendations for labor, however, the Central Committee's decree was quite limited. It encouraged women to enter industry, particularly machine building, a new and rapidly growing field, as well as leather, timber, and lumber, industries in which women were not strongly represented. Yet it did not address either the sex segregation of industry or the effect on women of the first five-year plan's investment strategy. Rather, it endorsed the "maximum use" of women in the traditionally female industries of sewing, food, and textiles, and in the paper

[37] GARF, f. 6983, o. 1, d. 159, "O Rabote Zheninspektorov," 344; f. 5451, o. 15, d. 362, "O Vnedrenii Zhenskogo Truda v Narodnoe Khoziaistvo v 1931," 156.
[38] Serebrennikov, 61.

and chemical industries, retail trade, the soviet administration, and transport. It urged fuller employment of women in above-ground operations around the mines but upheld the prohibition on their working underground. It called for the creation of more, lower-cost day-care centers and other social services that would free women to enter the workforce, but it made no mention of the high levels of female unemployment.[39]

In the early summer of 1929, the Central Committee published a second decree, "On Work among Women Workers and Peasants," which repeated many of the same concerns.[40] One official Soviet history written in 1984 claimed that this decree provided a powerful stimulus to involve women in industrial production.[41] This would appear to be an exaggeration: the decree's instructions regarding female labor were almost identical to those issued the previous November. Once again, the Central Committee called for "decisive and mass promotion of women workers and peasants to leading work" and encouraged the Party's local women's departments, personnel departments, unions, and economic organs to train and promote women. It also reiterated the need for the deployment of women in the same industries and sectors that had been singled out in the first decree.

The main concern of this second decree, however – a concern voiced even more strongly than before – was that "class enemies" might manipulate "backward women." Thousands of peasant women had actively resisted the campaigns for collectivization and grain collection, and urban women were becoming increasingly disgruntled about food shortages, rising prices, and falling wages. In Party parlance, "the most backward layer of working women is helping the anti-Soviet element." The main purpose of the decree was to refocus the attention of the Zhenotdel (women's department of the Party) away from women's issues and onto the mobilization of support for the Party's program. The Central Committee ordered the Zhenotdel to organize women workers around the first five-year plan by reducing absenteeism and increasing productivity. Beyond its admission that many peasant women had turned actively against collectivization, and its brief mention of heavy industry, the decree was almost an exact replica of its predecessor in November.

The unions responded halfheartedly to the Central Committee's decree. Union officials convened to discuss it and resolved to develop a plan within two months to involve women in industry, to assess their needs for day care and other services, and to set quotas for their enrollment in a variety of training programs.[42] They failed, however, to follow

[39] RTsKhIDNI, f. 17, o. 10, d. 490, "Postanovlenie TsK VKP(b)," 57–65.
[40] "Ob Ocherednykh Zadachakh Partii po Rabote Sredi Rabotnits i Krest'ianok," *Kommunistka*, 1929, no. 14: 43–48. The decree was dated June 15, 1929.
[41] See *Sovetskie zhenshchiny i profsoiuzy* (Moscow: Profizdat, 1984), 44.
[42] "Zhenskii Trud – v Proizvodstvo," *Trud*, July 12, 1929, p. 4.

up on these resolutions. The decree also spurred VTsSPS (the All-Union Central Council of Trade Unions) and NKT to send out a circular to their local unions and departments. Echoing the Central Committee's call for a "broader involvement of women in all branches of industry," the circular criticized the decrease in women's share in industrial employment, their rapidly increasing share in unemployment, the lack of industrial training for women, and the insufficiencies of day care, laundries, and public dining halls. It reiterated the basic message of the Party decree, calling for greater participation by women in mechanical shops, machine production, transport, chemicals, leather, and lumber, and for the placement of as many women as possible in the traditional female industries of sewing, textile, paper, and food.

In an attempt at reform, the circular prohibited managers and labor exchanges from engaging in the widespread practices of firing women and replacing them with men, and of discriminating against women in hiring. It advised managers that women who had been laid off from established factories were to be rehired, if at all possible, by new enterprises. The unions were charged with maintaining women's current share of the industrial workforce at all costs, and with taking a more active role in preventing discrimination by managers and in the labor exchanges. They were also instructed to establish evening courses to help women increase their skills and to begin training them in construction, a sector in which labor shortages already threatened. Quotas were set for women in all training courses.[43] Yet the circular, like the earlier Central Committee decrees, had little real effect on the behavior of local officials. Managers continued to fire women, the labor exchanges kept on sending men rather than women out for jobs, and the unions remained indifferent, if not hostile, to women's issues.

By September 1929, the unemployment situation for women had become so painful that SNK (the Council of People's Commissars), the leading government body, ordered NKT to ensure that single women with infants were not laid off from their jobs and to give priority in training courses to unemployed and single women with small children. SNK took these measures in the hope of decreasing the numbers of women prostituting themselves on the streets to earn a living.[44] Aleksandra Artiukhina, the head of the Zhenotdel, noted in October that the Party needed to make fewer speeches and take more action to help women workers. The promotion of women, she said, was proceeding with "extraordinarily great sluggishness" and was never regarded as an issue in its own right. "We do not give the promotion of women separate attention from that of men,"

---

[43] "Ofitsial'nyi Otdel. Ob Usilenii Vovlecheniia Zhenskogo Truda v Proizvodstvo. Tsirkular TsSPS, NKT SSSR No. 168 ot Iiulia 1929 g.," *Trud*, August 4, 1929, p. 4.
[44] "Bor'ba s Prostitutsiei – Postanovlenie SNK RSFSR," *Trud*, September 4, 1929, p. 2.

Artiukina explained. "We consider both men and women 'in general.' But this 'in general' is not correct. We must give attention to women workers, *batrachki* [landless peasant women], and peasants not 'in general' but in particular."[45] Her plea was heard but largely unheeded. VTsSPS had declared an official moratorium on special work among women, and apart from the Zhenotdel itself, there was no other organization to monitor policy on women in industry and other branches of the economy. In early December 1929, the Central Committee issued yet another decree, which noted angrily that little had been done by VTsSPS or the commissariats to develop the training courses for women that the CC had ordered the previous summer. The Central Committee demanded that these courses begin no later than December 10, giving the commissariats and VTsSPS less than two weeks to fulfill its earlier instructions.[46] Yet even this decree did little to jolt either NKT or the unions out of their customary apathy toward women.

Guarding the Gates to the Working Class

As the problem of female unemployment grew more acute, the Party was split by a variety of conflicting interests. Even as the demands of industry for labor grew more insistent, the Party still feared that the working class would be undermined by "foreign elements." Its concern over the purity of the working class and the perceived need to guard its composition against peasants and other groups hobbled the Party's attempts to broaden opportunities for women and, ultimately, rendered it unable to meet the demands of industry in a timely fashion. The Party's unending stream of decrees and instructions regarding the labor market expressed the anxiety that peasants were "sneaking" and "oozing" into the ranks of the proletariat. At war with the peasantry over collectivization, the Party was clearly terrified that peasant attitudes toward the regime would undermine its last, remaining bulwark of support among industrial workers. These fears became a great obstacle to the Party's ability to respond quickly and flexibly to the changing demands of industry, the demonstrated inadequacy of the labor exchanges, and the plight of women.

Labor exchanges were established throughout the country after the civil war, in the spring of 1922. Until 1925, they served a dual function for the unemployed: workers could register there both for work and

---

[45]   RTsKhIDNI, f. 17, o. 10, d. 490, "Ocherednye Zadachi Partii po Rabote Sredi Zhenshchin v SSSR. Doklad na Zasedanii Moskovskogo Partaktiva," 37, 44.

[46]   "O Seti Kursov po Podgotovke Rabotnits k Postupleniiu vo VTUZy, Tekhnikumy i Rabfaki v TsK VKP (b)," *Trud,* December 1, 1929, p. 2.

for unemployment benefits. All hiring was conducted through labor exchanges, creating a critical distinction between the registered and unregistered unemployed. The former were awarded a monetary stipend along with the chance to get work; the latter were eligible for neither a stipend nor a job. The labor exchanges held a monopoly on the labor market, controlling access to available jobs and distributing them among their own "registered" unemployed. In order to register, an applicant had to have prior experience (*stazh*) as a worker. This rule eliminated all those who had never worked for wages, such as peasants and housewives, from the ranks of the "official" unemployed. Many women – widows, divorcees, and single mothers – found themselves at the mercy of this system. They were unable to get work or qualify for unemployment compensation because they had never before worked for wages. Although desperate to work, they were not considered officially "unemployed."[47]

The unions, eager to protect the prerogatives of their members, wholeheartedly endorsed this policy.[48] VTsSPS stressed the need to protect union members against "nonproletarian elements" at the Eighth Trade Union Congress, in December 1928, stating: "In the country of the dictatorship of the proletariat, where the unions are the basis of Soviet power, where membership in the unions establishes a series of privileges over the nonlaboring, unorganized element, this inevitably creates the preconditions for the penetration of the unions by nonproletarian elements." VTsSPS sharply counterposed the interests of its own members against those of the nonunionized unemployed, complaining that peasants, or "streams of superfluous labor from the countryside," were pushing union members out of their jobs in seasonal industries such as construction, timber, and mining. VTsSPS concluded, "Only [those] individuals for whom waged labor is the basic source of existence will be accepted as members of the unions."[49] The resolution was clearly aimed at excluding peasants, but it also left unresolved the painful paradox of work for women who had never previously worked for wages. Waged labor was dependent on union membership, but union membership was dependent on having a job.

---

[47] It was and is still impossible to receive unemployment benefits in many industrialized countries without previous employment. In the Soviet Union, however, the labor exchanges controlled employment as well as benefits.

[48] After 1925, peasant migrants to the city were granted the same right as urban workers to register at the exchange, and employers gained more control over hiring, though the exchanges still controlled unemployment compensation. For an excellent summary and discussion of the role of the labor exchanges in the 1920s, see William Chase, *Workers, Society, and the Soviet State: Labor and Life in Moscow, 1918–1929* (Chicago: University of Illinois Press, 1990), 137–49.

[49] *Rezoliutsii VIII Vsesoiuznogo s"ezda professional'nykh soiuzov* (Moscow: Knigoizdatel'stvo VTsSPS, 1929), 34.

By 1929, the labor exchanges, which had never been particularly effective in linking workers with available jobs, were struggling to match the new demands of industry to the registered unemployed and the growing numbers of rural migrants in search of work. A wave of peasants fleeing collectivization and grain procurement flooded the labor exchanges in the fall of 1929. Unemployment continued to increase despite the growing demand for labor. By August 1929, almost 1.3 million people were registered in the labor exchanges throughout the USSR; of these, 60 percent were unskilled, one third were seeking work for the first time, and 44 percent were women.[50] In Russia in 1930, women constituted nearly 55 percent of the unemployed (see table 1.6). The labor exchanges, swamped by unskilled peasants and urban women, had no way of training workers or distributing them among the various construction sites and enterprises. NKT and the unions responded by taking measures designed to maintain their precarious control over employment and to protect older cadres of workers by excluding new job seekers. Although these initiatives may have helped to protect the privileges of older workers, they did nothing to meet the growing demands of industry for labor or to help the vast numbers of poor people in need of work.

Addressing the Congress of Planners in September 1929, G. D. Veinberg, the secretary of VTsSPS, announced that both the unions and the labor exchanges were losing control of the labor force. Veinberg, anxious to protect the privileges of established workers, was particularly troubled that the social composition of the working class was being undermined by an influx of peasants. Eager to get workers quickly and cheaply, managers were bypassing the labor exchanges and hiring peasants in place of unemployed workers or their family members. Because the managers were politically indifferent to the social composition of the working class, they "treated these new enrollments very lightly." According to Veinberg, the labor exchanges were filled with the "pretend unemployed," declassed elements who were not really interested in working. Veinberg's call for a purge of the unemployment rolls elicited an enthusiastic response from G. M. Krzhizhanovskii, the head of Gosplan (the State Planning Commission), who yelled back from the floor, "It's about time!"[51]

A month later, in October, VTsSPS took a firm stand against the flood of new job seekers. It called on the unions to organize the labor market in order "to protect the interests of the older cadres of workers." The labor exchanges were "clogged," it charged, by "foreign, declassed elements who are not really unemployed." VTsSPS claimed that up to 30 percent of the

[50] "O Roste Kadrov Rabochego Klassa, Sostoianii Bezrabotnitsy i Meropriiatiiakh k ee Oslableniia. Postanovlenie TsK VKP (b)," *Trud,* December 12, 1929, p. 2.
[51] "Kontrol'nye Tsifry Budut Vypolneny," *Trud,* September 27, 1929, p. 2. The Party was likewise very concerned about the "pretend unemployed" (*mnimo-bezrabotnye*).

people registered with the labor exchanges were "nonlaboring, declassed elements or people who have never worked for wages." VTsSPS instructed the unions to take a more active role in "regulating the labor market" and ordered the labor exchanges to expel the women, peasants, and "foreign, declassed elements" who inflated the unemployment figures.[52] *Trud,* the national union newspaper, supported VTsSPS. It, too, urged the labor exchanges to narrow their definition of "unemployed" to include only "the real unemployed with definite labor experience [*stazh*]." Noting that the factories had become "revolving doors" and that people were using jobs in public dining halls, agriculture, construction, and the sugar industry as gateways to industrial employment, *Trud* demanded an end "to the infiltration of industry by unorganized and, in particular, socially harmful and hostile groups." The labor exchanges, clearly unable to cope under the circumstances, would have to be reorganized to assume the new responsibilities of training, managing, and directing the labor force.[53]

The unions thus reacted to the new changes in the economy by reviving an older, exclusionary defense of their membership. This policy, which was successful in reducing the appearance, if not the reality, of unemployment, failed to address the growing labor shortage or the needs of women, peasants, and young people in search of jobs. The Women's Inspectorate of NKT responded angrily, pointing out that the sharp drop in the number of unemployed women between 1929 and 1930 (from 532,329 to 338,682) was due to the purge of the labor exchanges, not to increased hiring. In other words, the drop in the "official" numbers of unemployed was a sham: the actual number of women in search of work remained the same.[54] The unions, focused as they were on protecting the privileges of older workers against the perceived threat of newcomers, did nothing to expand employment opportunities for women.

On the local level, the labor exchanges were finding it more and more difficult to operate within the older exclusionary policy. A group from the Workers' and Peasants' Inspectorate (Rabkrin) visited several labor exchanges in October and noted that "the lack of order leads the unemployed either to nervousness or to disgust." Arguments, fights, and scandals erupted between the unemployed and the staffs of the exchanges. Long lines at every window made registration difficult. A "secondhand market" in jobs flourished amid the chaos and the crowds as managers in need of workers sent scouts over to the exchanges to pull likely-looking prospects out of the lines. Chronic problems of communication bedeviled both the managers and the exchanges. Managers' requests for workers

[52] "Ocherednye Zadachi Profsoiuzov. Iz Materialov Podgotovitel'noi Komissii Prezidiuma VTsSPS," *Trud,* October 31, 1929, pp. 3–4.
[53] "Problema Kadrov i Bor'ba s Bezrabotnitsiei," *Trud,* December 10, 1929, p. 1.
[54] GARF, f. 6983, o. 1, d. 159, "O Rabote Zheninspektorov," 345–45 ob.

sometimes went unanswered for weeks; when, frustrated, they repeated their initial requests, the labor exchanges would mistakenly send several groups to fill the same jobs. Some workers were sent back to the same managers who had laid them off, while others were directed, in large groups, to jobs that did not even exist. Managers routinely inflated their demands for labor in the hope of having their real needs filled. The exchanges, wise to this trick, were never sure how many workers were actually required.[55]

The inability of the labor exchanges to satisfy the needs either of managers or of the unemployed prompted NKT to consider a series of suggestions for their reorganization. In November 1929, Romanov, the commissar of labor, issued a proposal to subdivide the labor exchanges into separate departments devoted to unemployment registration, training, and distribution of the labor force. Two weeks later, the staff of NKT's labor-market department (*otdel rynka truda*) met to develop a plan. The NKT officials argued that the labor exchanges would function more efficiently if registration of the unemployed was separated from the training and dispatching of workers. They hoped in this way to eliminate the long lines, the chaos, and the quarrels at the exchanges and to pay more attention to the neglected work of training and deploying workers to meet the growing demands of the economy.[56]

One month later, in December, the Central Committee issued a decree establishing new labor-market councils under the direction of NKT, staffed by representatives from various enterprises and the unions. The councils were to provide a crucial link between the enterprises and the labor exchanges, assessing the need for labor in every workplace and conveying this information to the exchanges. The decree also restricted the hiring rights of managers, who were forbidden to lay off older workers and replace them with low-waged peasants. Managers were ordered to plan their needs for labor by including their projected demands within every larger economic and technical plan they drafted. Finally, the Central Committee sought to block the most common entry points into the working class. The nonindustrial unions, including sugar, Narpit, and construction, were told to tighten up their requirements for membership and purge their ranks of "foreign elements." Nervously guarding the gates to the working class, the Party attempted to maintain some control over the jostling crowds of new workers in search of jobs. The Central Committee also ordered the labor exchanges to stiffen their eligibility requirements. Only those who had previously worked for wages and were "genuinely interested" in finding work were to receive unemployment compensation.

[55] GARF, f. 5515, o. 24, d. 262, "RKI SSSR, Gruppa Ratsionalizatsii Gosapparata," 84.
[56] GARF, f. 5515, o. 24, d. 262, "Instruktsiia Narodnogo Komissariata Truda RSFSR ot Noiabr 1929 'O Rabote Birzh Truda,'" 41–46, "Protokol Soveshchanie Otdela Rynka Truda NKT SSSR," 94–207.

(The CC did not provide any guidelines for verifying "genuine interest.") The decree also increased the length of time a person needed to work (*stazh*) in order to qualify for compensation. The only exceptions to the new rules were the children of workers and *sluzhashchie* (white-collar workers) who were already registered as unemployed. Those who had never worked for wages, primarily women and peasants, were to be permitted to register for work but not for unemployment compensation. They were not, however, to be sent to work in industry but were to be assigned instead to low-paid, less-desirable jobs in public dining or in urban kitchen gardens. The labor exchanges were instructed to remove from the list of the unemployed any person who refused work, and to purge their ranks of "foreign and hooligan elements." The older cadres of industrial unemployed were to be protected against newcomers through the denial of access to industrial jobs and to unemployment compensation. Confident that the government could regain control of the labor market through proper administration, the Central Committee indicated in its decree that NKT was to develop a plan for training a skilled labor force. The Commissariat of Enlightenment, the Supreme Council of the National Economy (VSNKh), and VTsSPS were to plan target figures for the labor needs of every branch of industry, including new industries such as automobile and tractor manufacturing. Gosplan and NKT, meanwhile, were to develop training courses both within and outside the factories. They were instructed to plan an increase in the share of women in every industrial branch and to strengthen women's participation in the construction industry, which was already experiencing a marked labor shortage.[57]

The CC's decree revealed that the Party still hoped to maintain control over the labor market by improving the labor exchanges, tightening its oversight of managers, and excluding peasants. Echoing the same fears voiced earlier by the unions and NKT, the CC noted that thousands of new workers were taking advantage of labor shortages in public dining and in construction to enter the workforce, obtain union credentials, and either register as unemployed, in order to receive benefits, or enter higher-paying jobs in industry. The nonindustrial unions had been "transformed into a conduit" into industry by "socially foreign and enemy elements" and "unorganized strata." The Central Committee was more sensitive to industry's demand for labor than either the unions or NKT, but it, too, was anxious to put the brakes on peasant labor. Its term "unorganized strata" referred to peasants and women who had never worked for wages, while "socially foreign and enemy elements" denoted peasants fleeing collectivization as well as shopkeepers, artisans, middlemen, factory owners,

---

[57] "O Roste Kadrov Rabochego Klassa, Sostoianii Bezrabotnitsy i Meropriiatiiakh k ee Oslableniiu. Postanovlenie TsK VKP (b)," *Trud*, December 10, 1929, p. 2.

traders, and other small businessmen dispossessed by the elimination of NEP. The Central Committee was also sharply critical of NKT's failure to manage and direct the labor force. Managers were bypassing the labor exchanges and hiring peasants directly from the countryside as "temporary workers." Up to 80 percent of all hiring fell into this category. Turnover within the labor force was considerable, and the demands of industry for labor were not being met. The labor exchanges were doing a poor job of managing a labor market that was increasingly unregulated and uncontrolled. The organizational mechanism for pairing workers who needed jobs with enterprises that needed labor had proved completely ineffective.

Yet the problem was not merely organizational. The Central Committee itself was still locked into an antiquated approach to labor. Its concern for preserving the privileges and, more significantly, the support of older *kadrovye* workers was in direct conflict with industry's demand for new workers. People in search of work were able to use Narpit and the construction, timber, and sugar unions as "conduits" into the workforce precisely because these sectors were desperate for labor. Managers, searching for a ready workforce, hired peasants straight from the countryside and bypassed the labor exchanges altogether. Forced to respond quickly to the changing economic situation, they were the first to perceive and to act on the incipient labor shortage. The unions, the planning and labor organizations, and the Party were slower to recognize the new needs of the economy.

The Central Committee's brief mention of women was its only concession to the need to expand the industrial working class beyond its limited boundaries of the 1920s. Although the CC recognized the existence of a labor shortage, it believed it to be confined to construction. The labor needs of industry, in its view, could still be satisfied from the pool of industrial unemployed registered with the labor exchanges; the problems in the labor market were the result not so much of a labor shortage as of poor management and coordination. Thus, apart from its concession to women, the Central Committee's decree did nothing to enlarge the ranks of the "officially unemployed" who had the right to work. On the contrary, most of its measures were aimed at limiting this group by increasing the requirements for *stazh* and purging those who had never worked for wages. Although the Central Committee attempted to improve coordination between the enterprises and the labor exchanges by creating mediating bodies, it showed little awareness of the stormy changes looming on the horizon. The economy's growing demand for labor was largely ignored. Moreover, though the CC was aware of the increasingly female and unskilled character of the unemployed, it offered no remedy for the problems of this new, nonindustrial group. Within a short time, the working class would expand enormously, yet as late as December 1929, the CC was still attempting to maintain control over the labor market through policies designed to preserve the old social composition and the purity of the working class.

Women and Labor Policy

Russian industry had always been sharply gendered both vertically, by branch, and horizontally, by skill and wage level. After 1885, however, women began to move into the workforce more rapidly, and sex segregation began to erode. This trend intensified during World War I and the civil war, as women came to fill crucial positions in industries previously dominated by men. Then, with the end of the civil war and the demobilization of the Red Army, the trend was decisively reversed. The economic policies of NEP encouraged sex segregation of the labor force and diminished women's opportunities for employment. The reconstruction of industry did not enhance opportunities for women; on the contrary, women's losses were greatest in the traditionally male industries they had entered during the war years. By the end of NEP, women had been resegregated in light industry. They were also overwhelmingly concentrated at the bottom of every industry, among the least-skilled and worst-paid workers. The introduction of the first five-year plan initially had little effect on women's presence in the labor force. By the end of the 1920s, women filled the labor exchanges, constituting an ever-growing percentage of the unemployed, and by 1930, unemployment itself had taken on a distinctly female character.

Almost all labor analysts of the late 1920s identified women's lack of skills as the main reason for their inability to get work. Yet a closer examination of the issue reveals that women suffered discrimination in hiring at every skill level. Moreover, the opportunity to acquire skills was itself premised on gender. Both skilled male workers and managers were strongly opposed to the idea of training women or placing them in skilled positions. The factories were hierarchically structured according to gender: men did the skilled work, while women worked in a janitorial capacity or in jobs demanding unskilled labor. Discrimination against female labor played as important a role in women's inability to find work as did their low levels of skill. Evidence from many sources – Party decrees, VTsSPS circulars, Zhenotdel reports, NKT documents – reveals that labor exchanges favored men over women for employment, that managers were reluctant to hire and quick to fire women, and that skilled male workers held deeply ingrained prejudices against the training and promotion of women.

While the Party was sympathetic to women's problems, it was concerned primarily with maintaining the purity of the working class. Terrified that the tiny island of support provided by older industrial workers would vanish in a sea of hostile peasants, it structured its labor policy around rigid control of the labor market. This policy, designed to screen out dispossessed peasants and NEPmen, also worked to women's disadvantage. In its attempt to preserve the purity of the working class, the Party took a rigid and fearful stance against the expansion of the labor force. By the end of 1929, the Party seemed almost paralyzed by its own rigidity, unable to respond flexibly to the rapid transformation of the economy. Caught between its fear of losing working-class support on the one hand, and managers' demands for labor and the torrent of new workers pouring into industry on the other, the Party appeared frozen, unable to mediate between the conflicting interests that demanded its attention. The definition of a worker had been contested throughout the 1920s, but in a tight labor market, the unions had been largely successful in maintaining the privileges of their members against the claims of needy peasants and women. Not until the late fall of 1930, in the face of frantic demands from industry for new sources of labor, would the Party abandon its attempt to preserve an older definition of the working class.

2

The Struggle over Working-Class Feminism

> The Zhenotdel has already ceased to be a progressive force and has become a hindrance.
>
> L. M. Kaganovich, Politburo member, 1930[1]

Throughout the 1920s, the Party's exclusionary labor policy was strongly contested by women. Many of their objections and complaints were articulated by the Zhenotdel (women's department), an organization created in 1919 by the Central Committee in response to strong pressure coming from both inside and outside the Party. The Zhenotdel struggled to broaden the definition of the working class by highlighting the problems faced by women, including unemployment, prostitution, low-waged work, and lack of skills. Although the Central Committee backed the Zhenotdel, the department's activists still came into sharp conflict with uneducated male rank-and-file Party members whose attitudes toward women did not differ substantially from those of their peasant fathers and grandfathers. From its very inception, the Zhenotdel was at loggerheads with the unions over how to organize women. Despite its difficulties, however, it represented a genuine "proletarian women's movement."[2]

[1] L. Kaganovich, "Reorganizatsiia Partapparata i Ocherednye Zadachi Partraboty," *Kommunistka*, 1930, nos. 2–3: 5.

[2] Elizabeth Wood provides the fullest treatment of the Zhenotdel's early years in *The Baba and the Comrade: Gender and Politics in Revolutionary Russia* (Bloomington, Ind.: Indiana University Press, 1997). On the Zhenotdel and the unions, see her "Class and Gender at Loggerheads in the Early Soviet State: Who Should Organize the Female Proletariat and How?," in Laura Frader and Sonya Rose, eds., *Gender and Class in Modern Europe* (Ithaca, N.Y.: Cornell University Press, 1996), 294–310. See also Carol Eubanks Hayden's "Feminism and Bolshevism: The *Zhenotdel* and the Politics of Women's Emancipation in Russia, 1917–1930" (Ph.D. diss., University of California, Berkeley, 1979), and her article "The Zhenotdel and the Bolshevik Party," *Russian History* 3, part 2 (1976): 150–73. Also see Richard Stites, *The Women's Liberation Movement in Russia: Feminism, Nihilism and Bolshevism, 1860–1930* (Princeton, N.J.: Princeton University Press, 1978), 329–45; Beatrice Farnsworth, "The Zhenotdel during the NEP" and "Socialist Feminism," in *Aleksandra Kollontai: Socialism, Feminism, and the Bolshevik*

In the period before World War I, Europe's social democratic parties, including the Bolsheviks, embraced the notions of women's equality and emancipation more wholeheartedly than any other political parties. When the Bolsheviks came to power, they immediately passed progressive legislation concerning marriage, divorce, abortion, property, illegitimacy, and equality – legislative programs that many capitalist countries have yet to adopt. They made a commitment to encompassing and far-reaching social legislation – providing for day-care centers, paid maternity leave, nursing breaks, children's food programs – that aimed to free women from domestic burdens. Yet despite the Party's social, legal, and political commitment to women's liberation, it was still strongly divided on the question of organizing women separately around issues that were specifically women's – in short, on the question of feminism. This issue created deep differences at the upper levels of the Party and, even more important, between Party leaders and local activists, between Moscow and the outlying regions. In spite of opposition, the Zhenotdel and other separate women's organizations such as the Committee to Improve the Labor and Life of Working Women (KUTB) gave a voice to working-class and peasant women through meetings, delegate assemblies, and congresses. They fought hard to include women in the plans for industrialization and were effective, however briefly, in articulating a gender perspective on state policies.[3]

In December 1927, delegates to the Fifteenth Party Congress adopted the slogan "Face toward Production." Over the next decade, this slogan came to define policy in every area of life. Stalin and his supporters purged the unions, the planning agencies, and the Party itself of "Rightists" who were seen as obstacles to the new tempos of production and the collectivization of agriculture. The very shape and structure of society were forcibly recast in what Western historians have termed "a revolution from above" and Soviet historians have called the *velikii perelom* ("great

Revolution (Palo Alto, Calif.: Stanford University Press, 1980), 284–308, 311–21; Barbara Evans Clements, "Work among Women," in *Bolshevik Feminist: The Life of Aleksandra Kollontai* (Bloomington, Ind.: University of Indiana Press, 1979), 149–77; idem, "The Utopianism of the Zhenotdel," *Slavic Review* 51, no. 3 (Fall 1992): 485–96; idem, *Bolshevik Women* (Cambridge: Cambridge University Press, 1997), 204–19, 262–79; Gail Lapidus, *Women in Soviet Society: Equality, Development, and Social Change* (Berkeley, Calif.: University of California Press, 1978), 63–73. Gregory Massell deals with the activities of the Zhenotdel in Central Asia in *The Surrogate Proletariat: Moslem Women and Revolutionary Strategies in Soviet Central Asia, 1919–1929* (Princeton, N.J.: Princeton University Press, 1974). This phrase is used by Stites, who cites "the Proletarian Women's Movement that had its dim beginnings among the textile workers and intellectuals of Petersburg in 1906" (p. 344).
3 The ideas of Soviet working-class and peasant women are accessible to historians precisely because of the published and unpublished records of the many meetings organized by the Zhenotdel and KUTB.

turning point").[4] The Zhenotdel and KUTB both served, in their time, as a counter to the ethos of "productionism." They fought to include women in industrialization on an equal basis with men and to preserve a vision of women's liberation based on the socialization of household labor. The fates of both organizations were ultimately bound up in a struggle between working-class feminism and productionism that would shape the subsequent course of Soviet industrialization.

The Struggle for a Women's Organization

The Zhenotdel was the first mass-based organization created by women to advance their own interests within a revolutionary context. Poor, laboring women had organized during the French Revolution, but primarily on behalf of their class, not their sex. France's few feminist thinkers were isolated; they lacked a mass base and they did not challenge the gender division of labor.[5] The Russian Revolution was the first to include women and their interests as an integral part of an insurgent coalition. Women not only participated actively but also, for the first time, organized themselves to advance a program for their own liberation; and they found a small but responsive audience among women in the factories and villages. The Zhenotdel itself was, in Carol Hayden's words, the result of "the determined pressure of a small group of women within the Party."[6] Their

---

[4] Historians have produced a considerable literature on the first-five-year-plan period. A brief sampling includes Eugene Zaleski, *Planning for Economic Growth, 1918–1932* (Chapel Hill, N.C.: University of North Carolina Press, 1971); R.W. Davies, *The Soviet Economy in Turmoil, 1929–1930* (Cambridge, Mass.: Harvard University Press, 1989); Sheila Fitzpatrick, ed., *Cultural Revolution in Russia, 1928–1931* (Bloomington, Ind.: University of Indiana Press, 1984), and *The Cultural Front: Power and Culture in Revolutionary Russia* (Ithaca, N.Y.: Cornell University Press, 1992); Hiroaki Kuromiya, *Stalin's Industrial Revolution: Politics and Workers, 1928–1932* (New York: Cambridge University Press, 1988); Moshe Lewin, *The Making of the Soviet System: Essays in the Social History of Interwar Russia* (New York: Pantheon, 1985); William Rosenberg and Lewis Siegelbaum, eds., *Social Dimensions of Soviet Industrialization* (Bloomington, Ind.: Indiana University Press, 1993); David Shearer, *Industry, State and Society in Stalin's Russia, 1926–1934* (Ithaca, N.Y.: Cornell University Press, 1996).

[5] Olwen Hufton, *Women and the Limits of Citizenship in the French Revolution* (Toronto: University of Toronto Press, 1992); Dominique Godineau, "Masculine and Feminine Political Practice during the French Revolution, 1793–Year III," in Harriet Applewhite, Darline Levy, eds., *Women and Politics in the Age of the Democratic Revolution* (Ann Arbor, Mich.: University of Michigan Press, 1990), 61–80.

[6] Anne Bobroff and Hayden differ strongly on why the Zhenotdel was created. Bobroff writes, "Women's sections were created as a device by which to obtain a resource, women's labor power." Hayden argues that "this view is much too simplistic," given the vast unemployment of women during NEP. See Bobroff, "The Bolsheviks and Working Women, 1905–1920," *Soviet Studies* 26, no. 4 (1974): 563; Hayden, 134, 137–38.

vision of women's emancipation became part of the legislation enacted by the Bolsheviks once they came to power.[7]

Although the Russian Revolution was the first in which women's issues featured prominently, the inclusion of women in the revolutionary coalition was never easy or comfortable. From the very beginning, the Bolsheviks regarded "feminism" – the idea of separate women's organizations designed to advance women's interests – with hostility and mistrust. They were antagonistic not only to the "bourgeois feminism" of upper-class suffragists and philanthropists but also to the feminism of women on the factory floor. Party leaders repeatedly debated the idea of creating a separate organization for women. From the Politburo to the factory cell, most Party members refused to acknowledge that male and female workers might have divergent interests, that women might need a separate organization to promote equality, or that sexual oppression was not always subject to a class solution.

Aleksandra Kollontai almost single-handedly launched the struggle to organize women separately. She was eventually joined by other highly dedicated women known as the *zhenskii aktiv,* the *zhenotdelki,* and the *bytoviki,* a women's cadre dedicated to the transformation of *byt,* or daily life. Little is known about this group, though records of the debates over the organization at the end of the 1920s suggest that most had little formal schooling and many were illiterate. The women who became involved in local assemblies organized by the Zhenotdel were predominantly peasants (59 percent), with a smaller number being workers (14 percent), white-collar workers (8 percent), and housewives (10.5 percent). Nearly one in three was totally illiterate.[8] Many Party members, women included, tended to disparage members of the Zhenotdel, considering them "politically backward" and "occupied with trivia." One woman Communist derided them as "the least qualified workers in the Party *apparat.*" At least two Party leaders noted that women, once promoted, were embarrassed by their "Zhenotdel origins."[9]

Yet the "least qualified" were also often the closest to the worlds of peasant and worker, their lack of formal education less a personal failing than a reflection of their lack of opportunity. Their leaders, too, tended to come from humble backgrounds. Aleksandra Artiukhina, the head of the

[7] Stites argues that "operational partnerships," between, for example, Aleksandra Kollontai and A. G. Goikhbarg, the jurist who drafted the first Code on Marriage, the Family and Guardianship, and Nadezhda Krupskaia and Anatoli Lunacharskii, the head of the Commissariat of Enlightenment, were instrumental in forging early policy (pp. 363, 418). See also Clements, "The Utopianism of the Zhenotdel," 496.

[8] Viktor, "Sostav Deleg: Sobranii Uluchshaetsia," *Kommunistka,* 1929, no. 12: 28–29.

[9] Z. Prishchepchik, "Zhenrabota na Krasnoi Presne," *Kommunistka,* 1928, no. 10: 24; S. Liubimova, "Bol'nye Voprosy," *Kommunistka,* 1928, no. 10: 62; L. Kaganovich, "Perestroit' Rabotu Sredi Rabotnits i Krest'ianok," *Kommunistka,* 1929, no. 14: 5; A. Artiukhina, "Povorot k Novomu," *Kommunistka,* 1929, no. 14: 10.

Zhenotdel from 1927 to 1930, was the daughter of weavers and herself began working in a textile factory at the age of twelve; she became a member of the textile union in 1909 and was arrested and deported several times. Varvara Moirova, the daughter of an Odessa laundress, became active in revolutionary politics after 1905. Klavdia Nikolaeva, an early organizer of working-class women, was born to a laundress and an unskilled worker in St. Petersburg; one of four children, she went to work at age eight. Whether known or nameless, most members of the Zhenotdel were the lowest of the low: workers in female-dominated textile factories and sewing workshops, exploited wives of soldiers, cheated widows of the villages, and landless laborers in the countryside.

The Party did little to organize women until 1905. Although the Bolsheviks supported the women's socialist clubs formed in St. Petersburg during the 1905 revolution, many were hostile to their separatist structure.[10] Kollontai tried to establish a separate organization for women workers within the Russian Social Democratic Labor Party, but her repeated requests were met with indifference. The male leadership of the Party was not interested in organizing women workers, whom it viewed as hopelessly backward, quiescent, and unresponsive. Women became more active in the mass strikes of 1905, but their new militancy did not extend to participation in the newly legalized unions, and the unions themselves refused to reach out to women, reflecting the attitudes of their male membership.[11]

In 1908, feminists organized the first All-Russian Women's Congress. Participants ranged from philanthropic aristocrats to factory workers. Kollontai pleaded with the Party to send a delegation of women workers to the congress, but the Party offered its support only belatedly, after Kollontai's organizing efforts had achieved some success. In 1909, the St. Petersburg Party committee offered its qualified support for separate organizations for women workers, but only as transitional organizations aimed at the joint organization of men and women. Even this cautiously worded resolution of support was meaningless, however, because it was never put into practice.[12] As women grew more militant after 1910, the Party began to pay more attention to them, in 1913 launching its first celebration of International Women's Day and sponsoring huge meetings on female labor. Even so, *Pravda* made it clear that the celebration was "not a concession to female separatism." *Pravda* began to feature a women's page in 1913, and a year later the Party began publishing *Rabotnitsa*, a paper for women workers. *Rabotnitsa's* first issue, however, scrupulously minimized the importance of gender, proclaiming, "Politically conscious

[10] Bobroff, 543–44.
[11] Rose Glickman, *Russian Factory Women: Workplace and Society, 1880–1914* (Berkeley, Calif.: University of California Press, 1984): 156–205.
[12] Ibid., 253, 273.

women see that contemporary society is divided into classes.... The division into men and women in their eyes has no great significance." Yet the actual experience of women workers indicated otherwise: their letters to the workers' press repeatedly recorded the hostility they encountered on the shop floor.[13]

After the February Revolution, the Petrograd Party committee resumed publication of *Rabotnitsa* (which had been shut down several years before by the police) but refused to establish a separate women's bureau. Local Party workers were opposed to the idea, and the Petrograd committee stressed that women should join factory committees, not separate women's organizations. Despite Kollontai's urging, the Party hesitated to support the thousands of soldiers' wives (*soldatki*) and laundresses who had begun to organize themselves. Finally, agitators associated with *Rabotnitsa* began to call meetings that quickly drew crowds of as many as ten thousand women. In November, the Party organized the Petrograd Conference of Working Women, with five hundred delegates representing more than eighty thousand women. According to Hayden, the conference demonstrated not only the existence and scope of a working-class women's movement but also its support for the Bolsheviks. The Bolsheviks, however, remained deeply ambivalent about the formation of separate organizations for women. Kollontai, ever persistent, suggested once again that the city Party committees form local commissions to organize women, but her suggestion was rejected.[14]

In the summer of 1918, Kollontai enlisted the help of Nikolaeva and several other women within the Party to organize a national Women's Congress. The women quickly realized that if the Party did not officially authorize and support local bureaus with designated organizers, the congress would founder on the indifference of their male comrades in the localities. After much hesitation, the Central Committee finally acceded to the women's dogged requests that it establish bureaus to select and prepare delegates. The women hoped that a small number of delegates would manage to attend, but they were not optimistic: the country was in the midst of civil war, transportation was severely disrupted, and many local Party organizations were not sympathetic to the idea of a women's congress. About forty delegates appeared the day the congress was scheduled to open. But then telegrams began pouring in from all over the country: delegates were delayed, but they were on their way. By the

---

[13]   Bobroff, 545, 546; Glickman, 275–77.

[14]   Hayden, 119–28. Hayden notes, "The Bolsheviks were thus in the odd position of organizing a special women's conference in order to propagandize against the idea of a women's organization" (p. 121). See also M. Donald, "Bolshevik Activity amongst the Working Women of Petrograd in 1917," *International Review of Social History* 27, part 2 (1982): 129–60.

time the congress opened, twelve hundred women had struggled across the war-torn country to take their seats in Moscow.[15]

At the congress, the delegates devised a tentative structure for a permanent women's organization based on local delegate assemblies and women's commissions. The assemblies would involve women in government, and the commissions would in turn organize and manage the assemblies. In September 1919, the Party approved the plan, giving the commissions special status as the women's department (Zhenotdel) under the Central Committee. The Central Committee instructed local Party committees to create their own women's departments, and regular campaigns for the election of women to delegate assemblies were planned in the towns and countryside. The *delegatki,* as they came to be known, were to rotate through the soviets and commissariats in order to learn, during a two-to-three-month term, how government actually worked. The system of delegate assemblies and local women's departments became a means for women's promotion into government and eventually produced its own *zhenskii aktiv,* a group of women committed to the education, advancement, and liberation of women.

Between 1905 and 1919, the Party radically changed its position on organizing women. This transformation, however, was not an easy one. Paralyzed by abstract definitional issues concerning separatism, the male leadership at no point took the lead in organizing women workers. At every juncture, the Party was shoved reluctantly toward change by the spontaneous militancy of women workers themselves and by the tenacious efforts of women such as Kollontai, who refused to ignore women as a constituency. The Party's leadership ultimately responded to this constituency by creating the Zhenotdel. This did little, though, to change attitudes at the middle and lower levels of the Party. As the story of the 1918 Women's Congress illustrates, local Party officials were unwilling to do anything on behalf of women without express orders from the Central Committee. Moreover, even the upper levels of the Party leadership were blinded to the powerful prejudices of male workers against women by a myth of working-class unity that had little to do with the real experiences of workers.

Transforming Life Itself

The Zhenotdel quickly became, in the words of Aleksandra Artiukhina, "a real '*univermag*'."[16] Like the *univermag,* the Soviet department store

[15] Hayden, 128–39. The account of the congress is taken from her work.
[16] *Pravda,* January 19, 1930, p. 3.

that sold all manner of goods from tools to pajamas, the Zhenotdel did a little bit of everything. Its purpose was twofold: to train cadres of women, a *zhenskii aktiv,* to enter the ranks of Party and government, and, more fundamentally, to transform the very nature and structure of daily life (*byt*). The Zhenotdel actively promoted a program for women's liberation based on women's full and equal participation in public life through the socialization of the domestic sphere. Once women's unpaid labor in the home was replaced by laundries, dining halls, and day-care centers staffed by paid workers, the family would gradually "wither away," leaving independent individuals who would be cared for in their childhood and old age by the state. People would choose their partners freely, unfettered by economic dependence or inequality.[17] Thus, in seeking to transform *byt,* the Zhenotdel aimed to change the way women and men lived their lives, organized their families, cared for their children, and divided power in every institution from the village to the state. Its vision extended far beyond the establishment of one more laundry or day-care center, to the complete reconfiguration of family life on the most intimate and daily of scales. Its goal was no less than a structural transformation of the family, women's roles, and society itself. Throughout the 1920s, the Zhenotdel struggled against great odds to realize these revolutionary aims. The adoption of the New Economic Policy in 1921 and the subsequent cutbacks in social spending, as well as the ruin of industry, the mass unemployment of women, the deep poverty of the countryside, and the orphaning of hundreds of thousands of children through war and famine all posed serious obstacles to the Zhenotdel's vision of revolutionary *byt.*[18] Moreover, male Party members at every level of the Party hierarchy – but especially at the local level – were loath to devote scarce resources to the organization's programs and goals.

According to Carol Hayden, the Party was divided, from the Zhenotdel's inception, over the purpose of the organization. Some wanted to create a *zhenskii aktiv* to serve the Party's general goals, while others felt the organization should fight for women's interests and issues. The division was apparent even in the founding purpose of the Zhenotdel: training women cadres versus transforming *byt.* In 1923, V. Golubeva, one of the organizers of the first Women's Congress, unwittingly provoked a storm within the Zhenotdel and the Party by proposing that women other than factory workers be organized through "special societies." Golubeva had devised the proposal in response to the high rate of female unemployment and the

---

[17] Wendy Goldman, *Women, the State and Revolution: Soviet Family Policy and Social Life, 1917–1936* (New York: Cambridge University Press, 1993), chap. 1. This vision also became the basis for early Bolshevik legislation on the family.

[18] Ibid., chaps. 2 and 3, on social conditions in the 1920s.

dwindling number of women in factories, but the Zhenotdel leadership and the Twelfth Party Congress roundly condemned it as motivated by feminist separatism.[19] Hayden argues that the Zhenotdel retreated further and further in the 1920s, moving from focusing on issues specific to women to concentrating on training women to enter soviet institutions. The socialization of *byt* ceased to be an end in itself and became necessary only "to achieve other aims." In Hayden's view, by 1924, the Zhenotdel had become an instrument of Party policy rather than a champion of women's interests.[20] Hayden is correct to highlight this tension but wrong to assume that it was resolved by 1924: the struggle between Party goals and women's issues in fact continued well into the 1930s. In 1927, the Zhenotdel organized the second All-Union Congress of Women Workers and Peasants, and once again large numbers of women made their way to Moscow from far corners of the land: from fishing tribes in the north, peasant villages in the south, Siberia, the Central Asian republics, factories in big cities, mines, and industrial settlements. Speaking on behalf of the women in their areas, the representatives testified to the difficult conditions they lived under and denounced the discrimination they encountered in the village *skhod,* factories, and soviets. Their concerns suggested no diminution of interest in transforming *byt,* and it was the Zhenotdel, after all, that encouraged them to return to their local areas to continue the struggle on behalf of women.[21]

The adoption of the first five-year plan actually encouraged new hopes for the transformation of *byt.* Women activists were joined by city planners, writers, and architects in imagining a world transformed by socialist industrialization.[22] At a meeting of the zhenotdel of the Moscow Party committee in 1929, Krupskaia spoke of the need to build urban housing for new workers that would incorporate common dining halls, day-care centers, and laundries. "We must think about how to build new towns and settlements," she urged, "for this is connected with the creation of new relations between men and women."[23] Iuri Larin and L. M. Sabsovich, Party leaders and strong supporters of industrialization, enthusiastically promulgated the idea of communal dwellings with collective kitchens and

---

[19] Hayden, 222–29; Farnsworth, 315–18; Wood, 170–214.
[20] Hayden, 262, 227–74. This is one of the central arguments of Hayden's dissertation.
[21] *Vsesoiuznyi s"ezd rabotnits i krest'ianok: stenograficheskii otchet* (Moscow: Izdanie TsIK Soiuza SSR, 1927). There is no evidence in the lengthy stenographic report of this mass meeting that concerns about *byt* had been preempted by other Party goals.
[22] See for example, S. Frederick Starr, "Visionary Town Planning during the Cultural Revolution," in Fitzpatrick, ed., *Cultural Revolution in Russia,* 207–40.
[23] RTsKhIDNI, f. 17, o. 10, d. 490, "Zasedanie Otdela Rabotnits MK VKP i Oblastnoi Komissii," 19, 23.

socialized child care, with children separated from adults.[24] Even after the Zhenotdel was abolished, Artiukhina and other women's activists continued to press to keep issues of *byt* at the forefront of Party goals.[25]

"Liquidationism" in the Factories and the Local Party Organizations

Although the Party officially supported the Zhenotdel, it vacillated on the issue of creating separate organizations for women, especially in factories. Loath to challenge the entrenched antifeminism of local Party and union organizations, on the one hand, and ideologically sensitive to pressure from women's activists, on the other, the Party never developed a consistent position on the question of women's organizing. It was quick to denounce "separatism" throughout the 1920s, but the Party was never clear exactly what that meant: Organizing women as a separate constituency? Or organizing around specifically women's issues? The questions replicated many of the conflicts over the purpose of the Zhenotdel itself. Moreover, if organizing women separately from men was desirable, who should be responsible for this work? A separate women's organization such as the Zhenotdel, or more general organizations, such as local Party committees, soviets, and unions?

Nor were women themselves united on these issues. A significant number of older women Communists, many "old Bolsheviks," had a negative opinion of the Zhenotdel and its work. They believed that women belonged in the same organizations as men and that the Zhenotdel was not sufficiently integrated into the larger political life of the Party.[26] Artiukhina herself admitted that many Party women felt that women should be involved in "general Party work."[27] Men commonly assumed, especially at the local level, that their female comrades would naturally take responsibility for those areas of Party work associated with social services and *byt*. Women, afraid of being marginalized, disliked having this work automatically relegated to them simply *because they were women*. This assumption replicated in the Party the same division of labor that existed in the home, and they resented it. At Party conferences, some of

---

24 Richard Stites, *Revolutionary Dreams: Utopian Vision and Experimental Life in the Russian Revolution* (Oxford: Oxford University Press, 1989), 198–222; Davies, 146–47. Davies argues that the campaign for the socialization of *byt* reached its apogee in 1929–1930.

25 A. Artiukhina, "Za Sotsialisticheskuiu Peredelku Byta," *Rabotnitsa*, 1930, no. 4: 3.

26 Kaganovich, "Perestroit' Rabotu Sredi Rabotnits i Krest'ianok," cites these attitudes on p. 5.

27 Artiukhina, "Povorot k Novomu," 8.

the strongest advocates of liquidating the Zhenotdel were actually former Zhenotdel workers who had transferred to "general" Party work.[28]

In May 1926, the organizational bureau (*orgbiuro*) of the Central Committee struck a blow against gender-based organizing in the factories by issuing a decree that shifted responsibility for organizing women workers from the *zhenproforganizator* (an organizer specially designated to work with women) to local factory committees. Many factory committees quickly complied with the decree and eliminated the position. In a survey conducted two years later, thirty-four union organizations dutifully reported that work among women had improved as a result of the decree: "Attention to work among women is stronger"; "Women have increased their participation in the general union meetings"; "More work is being done to raise the job skills of women." An independent review of the situation in the factories, however, painted a somewhat less optimistic picture. Factory committees "almost never" engaged the issues of "women's skills, working conditions, or cultural or production-oriented education." These issues were not discussed at factory or shop meetings; if they were raised at all, it was only by women workers.[29] The Central Committee itself had noted in 1927 that the elimination of specially designated women's organizers in the factories had not improved the attitudes or the work of factory committees and unions. Few women attended production meetings, and even fewer held skilled positions such as master or journeyman. In the textile unions, 33 percent of the women workers were illiterate, and a large number of the women activists were barely literate. The unions did nothing to educate women workers, many of whom were consequently drawn to anti-Semitic ideologies, evangelism, and religious sects.[30] A survey of Stalinskii *okrug* concluded, "The majority of lower union organizations have interpreted the directives to eliminate the women's organizers as a general liquidation of all work among women workers. As a result, services to them are completely insufficient." When local union officials were asked about their work with women, they responded somewhat disingenuously, "We have directives not to work among women workers and therefore we do not specifically address them."[31]

At the end of 1927, the issue of organizing women took on a sharper and more divisive edge as the Party began to mobilize its membership aggressively around rapid industrialization. A wave of what the *zhenskii*

28 E. Goreva, "Voprosy Zhenraboty na Partkonferentsii," *Kommunistka*, 1929, no. 8: 28.
29 A. Tikhomirova, "Kak Profsoiuzy Vypol'niaiut Direktivy Partii," *Kommunistka*, 1928, no. 6: 50–51.
30 Z. Prishchepchik, "Rabota Profsoiuzov Sredi Rabotnits," *Kommunistka*, 1928, no. 6: 53.
31 Cherevadskaia, "Trud i Byt Rabotnits," *Kommunistka*, 1928, no. 6: 63.

aktiv termed "liquidationism" targeted at women's organizations intensified within local Party organizations, the unions, and Party conferences. The Politburo made clear the main role of unions: they were to transform themselves from organizations designed to advance workers' interests (a function now derided as "trade unionist" and "protectionist") into "basic levers for recasting industry" and increasing production.[32] As the issue of production became central to the Party's program, local leaders were further emboldened to "liquidate" women's organizers in their midst.

Delegates to the Fifteenth Party Congress, in December 1927, criticized the Zhenotdel for duplicating the work of the Department of Agitation and Propaganda, fueling a long-standing conflict between the two organizations. The congress established rationalization committees to eliminate "parallelism," the duplication of efforts by two or more organizations. After broadly surveying the operation of Party organizations on the local level, the rationalization committees spent the first half of 1928 advising Party organizations to eliminate local zhenotdels and to transfer their work to their local departments of agitation and propaganda (agitprop) and organizational departments (orgotdel).[33] By June, the rationalization committees had swept through large sections of the country, leaving local zhenotdels in ruins.

Artiukhina argued furiously against the work of the committees, hoping to forestall further damage. She observed, "The rationalizers arrived at the Party *apparat,* noted the presence of the zhenotdel with regret, claimed 'parallelism' [the argument used by all the committees], and . . . liquidated the zhenotdel." In one region after another – Leningrad, Vladimir, Ivanovo-Voznesensk, Urals, Kostroma, Briansk, Tula, Tver, and Saratov – the rationalization committees either abolished the local zhenotdels altogether or transferred their functions to the agitprop and orgotdel. Such destruction, claimed Artiukhina, was "not accidental"; it was, rather, an expression of the deep hostility that local leaders had felt toward the zhenotdel from its inception. Appealing to the upper level of Party leadership, she angrily declared that only the Party Congress had the power to eliminate work among women. She demanded that the local zhenotdels and their staffs be restored.[34] The Central Committee did not respond to Artiukhina's demand. Instead of clarifying its stance on the role of the local zhenotdels, the Central Committee tried to mediate the conflict by promoting more women to prominent positions. In August 1928, the

[32] D. Krymskii and K. N., "Profsoiuzy na Novom Etape," *Partiinoe stroitel'stvo,* 1929, no. 2: 15.

[33] Hayden notes that the department of agitation and propaganda had already been trying to absorb the Zhenotdel for a decade (p. 351).

[34] A. Artiukhina, "'Likvidatsionnyi Zud Nuzhno Uniat'," *Kommunistka,* 1928, no. 6: 3–4.

Central Committee instructed its Personnel Department (orgraspred) and the Zhenotdel to develop a plan, within two weeks, to promote ten to twenty women Communists to leading posts. The decree stated that this marked "the beginning of an impending serious shift in the large-scale promotion of Party and non-Party women, particularly from the ranks of the workers, to leading positions in the Party, unions, and soviets."[35]

That decree, however, did little to resolve the growing tension between women's activists and local Party and union officials over the organizing of women. Even as the rationalization committees wreaked havoc on the local zhenotdels, women activists, displeased by the elimination of women's organizers in the factories, refused to let the issue die. In July 1928, delegates to the All-Union Meeting for Work among Women, a conference of the *zhenskii aktiv* in the unions, the Commissariat of Labor (NKT), and other organizations, convened to discuss the training and promotion of women and the development of social services. The delegates formally asked VTsSPS (the All-Union Central Council of Trade Unions), the coordinating and leadership body of the unions, to investigate the status of work among women in those unions that lacked special women's organizers. The *zhenskii aktiv* expected VTsSPS to present the results of its investigation at the upcoming Eighth Trade Union Congress, as part of a discussion about whether separate women's organizers were necessary.[36] Undoubtedly, they believed that the investigation would support their case for separate women's organizers by revealing the deplorable state of work among women in the factories.

Throughout the fall of 1928, a vigorous debate over separate organizations for women was waged in the pages of *Kommunistka*. In August, O. Il'ina wrote a long article about women's organizers in the textile factories, where the line between women's work and "general" Party work was particularly blurred because the union and the Party committees organized a predominantly female workforce. Il'ina argued that work in textile factories should "not be solely entrusted to women's organizers but should become the basic work of Party and union organizations," adding that the Party and unions had abdicated their responsibility by sloughing it off on local women's commissions. Moreover, she noted, even in the textile industry, there were almost no women in the leadership of the union, factory committees, the Party, or economic organs. Il'ina suggested that specially designated women's organizers would not be necessary if women were better represented in the leadership of the "general" organizations.

---

[35] "O Vydvizhenii Zhenshchin Kommunistok," *Kommunistka*, 1928, no. 8: 3. These positions included secretary of the *guberniia* Party committee, representative of the *guberniia* executive committee, chairman of the *guberniia* council of unions, and others.

[36] A. Tikhomirova, "Itogi Vsesoiuznogo Soveshchaniia po Rabote Sredi Zhenshchin," *Kommunistka*, 1928, no. 8: 65.

She implicitly posited an evolutionary organizational model to address the issues of women's oppression, in which separatism constituted a necessary but transitional phase. Initially, she explained, the Party had not given special attention to women and had rejected the idea of a separate women's organization. But eventually it had filled this gap by creating the Zhenotdel. Il'ina proposed that in the future, the Party should reintegrate women's work back into its "general" work, but only at such time as its members, at every level, demonstrated a greater awareness of and sensitivity to women's needs, and only when women held a larger share of leadership positions. At present, in her view, most local Party organizations, even those working with largely female constituencies, were not ready to assume this work. If the Party were to eliminate special women's organizers now, women would receive no attention at all. She concluded, "The current status of work among women workers in textile factories and other enterprises with a predominance of female labor will eventually result in the withering away of special forms of Party work among women, but the moment for the overall 'liquidation' of these forms has not yet arrived."[37] In other words, once Party members were capable of incorporating women's issues into their "general" work, there would no longer be a need to maintain separate women's organizations. Yet for the time being, "liquidationism" was premature: "general work" for women would be a synonym for "general neglect." Il'ina's views would soon prove tragically prophetic.

Although Il'ina took a relatively moderate position, her article provoked fierce responses from both advocates and opponents of separate organizing. Suslova responded that women were treated so poorly in factories that the unions and the Party should not even consider liquidating the local zhenotdels or other women's organizations; in her opinion, it was not yet time for liquidation even in the most advanced regions around Moscow. Bolstering her argument with figures from Baumanskii *raion,* Suslova noted that even in factories where women comprised a high percentage of the workforce, their participation in Party activity, shop bureaus, and factory committees was lower than men's. In the Zvonkov factory, for example, 75 percent of the workforce was female, yet only 5 percent of the women were Party members, in contrast to 21 percent of the men. "These figures," she explained, "indicate fairly clearly that, unfortunately, we have still not managed to raise women to the same level as men, and as a result, we cannot speak about the liquidation of special forms of work." Suslova also pointed out that many of the women workers who joined the Party had previously been members of special

[37] O. Il'ina, "O Rabote Sredi Rabotnits na Predpriiatiiakh s Preobladaniem Zhenskogo Truda," *Kommunistka,* 1928, no. 8: 11–13.

women's organizations: if the Party was truly interested in recruiting women workers, it would not eliminate the very organizations that linked it to the working class.[38] The Party's overall membership figures supported Suslova's claim: of 1,313,794 Party members in 1928, only 70,603 (5 percent) were women workers, a problematically low figure for a political party that prided itself on its egalitarian principles and working-class base.[39]

Writing in opposition to separate organizing, S. Liubimova claimed that the "liquidationist mood" that currently prevailed had been provoked by the *zhenotdelshchitsy* themselves. In a blistering attack, she charged that the *zhenskii aktiv,* "the least-qualified workers in the Party *apparat,*" responded to every criticism with an excuse: "*Nu,* if we are no good, replace us"; "*Nu,* if you know better, do it yourself"; and "It's good to talk with you, but we have our local conditions." The Zhenotdel was out of touch with workers and peasants. It did little but organize delegate meetings, and "with the exception of these meetings, its members know nothing and want to know nothing." Moreover, it was no accident that the strongest advocates of "liquidationism" were in the large proletarian regions such as Leningrad, Vladimir, Ivanovo-Voznesensk, the Urals, and Tver, where the problems of the Zhenotdel could not be blamed on male hostility. Workers and Party members there recognized that the rationalization committees were correct: the zhenotdels were simply duplicating the work of agitprop commissions. Liubimova harshly concluded, "Now is the time not to cry 'for the bitter fate of the Zhenotdel' but to take practical measures to comply with the budget and the five-year plan."[40]

Yet another writer retorted that if women's organizers were out of touch with political reality, it was because they had been systematically excluded from participation in general Party meetings. How could they be expected to understand the threat of the "right deviation" if they were not permitted to attend meetings of the *raion* Party *aktiv,* where larger political issues were discussed? Women's organizers spent their time "running to an endless number of meetings, occupied with a thousand petty details, but not thinking seriously about the basic issues of their work." Yet the *raion* Party committee gave them no help, and the unions were no better. In general, there was a "lack of sensitivity to women Communists and women workers." Women's work was considered "low status," and even women Communists did not want to do it. Clearly the factory committees, unions, and local Party organizations needed to reconsider their approach toward women.[41]

[38] Suslova, "Samolikvidatsiia Nesvoevremenna," *Kommunistka,* 1928, no. 10: 65–67.
[39] S. Smidovich, "Chistka Partii i Zhenotdely," *Kommunistka,* 1929, no. 7: 24.
[40] S. Liubimova, "Bol'nye Voprosy," *Kommunistka,* 1928, no. 10: 62–64.
[41] Prishchepchik, "Zhenrabota na Krasnoi Presne," 24–28.

When the Eighth Trade Union Congress met, in December 1928, the delegates discussed the issue of special organizing among women and crushed the hopes of the *zhenskii aktiv*. They voted to eliminate all women's organizers within the unions and to transfer their responsibilities to the unions "in general." This decision, an endorsement of the Central Committee's decree of May 1926, struck a heavy blow against future efforts to train, promote, or defend women workers on the shop floor, for it was promptly and conveniently interpreted by union officials as putting a decisive end to *all* organizing among women.[42] The unions thus stopped work among women just as the drive for rapid industrialization was beginning. Once the *zhenskii aktiv* was eliminated from the unions, there was no one left to address issues of discrimination, to advance women's interests, or to promote equality. The local union leadership complacently ignored women, confident that such neglect was sanctioned both by VTsSPS and at the very highest levels of the Party. Over the next three years, Il'ina's prediction came true: "in general" became a common euphemism among local Party and union leaders for "not at all."

Throughout the spring of 1929, a "liquidationist," antifeminist mood spread from the unions to the local Party committees. E. Goreva, a Zhenotdel leader, noted that this mood prevailed in Party conferences in many Moscow districts, including Rogozhsko-Simonovskii, where the advocates of liquidation constituted the majority, as well as Khamovnicheskii, Baumanovskii, and Krasno-Presenskii. Speakers at these conferences argued for the elimination not only of local zhenotdels but also of women's organizers in enterprises that had a predominance of female labor. Maintaining that local women's commissions had "become outdated," they explained that their work was "parallel" to that of Party organizations, duplicating efforts and creating an organizational mess. They suggested that only the delegate meetings should continue.[43]

Bab'i Bunty: Quelling Rebellion through the Zhenotdel

All through that spring of 1929, while local Party organizations in the industrial regions were discussing "liquidation," the Party faced a serious crisis in the countryside. As Party organizers stepped up their efforts to organize peasants into collective farms, peasant women rioted

[42]   GARF, f. 5451, o. 15, d. 362, "VTsK VKP (b) – Massovaia Rabota Sredi Zhenshchin," 96.
[43]   Goreva, "Voprosy Zhenraboty na Partkonferentsii," 28.

in resistance. These riots, known as *bab'i bunty*, were a spontaneous, forceful expression of peasant opposition to grain requisitioning and collectivization. Mobs of screaming, angry women, supported by men, met collective-farm organizers with force, refusing to give up their grain, socialize their seed or livestock, dispossess *"kulak"* (wealthy peasant) families, or collectivize their land.[44] Throughout the late spring and summer, *Kommunistka* warned anxiously of "backward women" led astray by *kulak* forces. Sophia Smidovich, a former leader of the Zhenotdel, noted in May that peasant women were "backing *kulaks*" and "opposing the *kolkhozs*" (collective farms). She strongly suggested that delegate meetings be deployed to promote the Party line in villages and factories. "Delegate meetings should be transformed," she wrote, "from a school of political literacy to active social units under the leadership of the Party." Women activists had to understand that delegate meetings were intended not to educate women but rather to serve as an instrument of Party policy. Delegates themselves should be used to organize women to combat "the danger of Right deviation" and to oppose attempts "to weaken the tempo of industrialization and state-farm [*sovkhoz*] or *kolkhoz* construction." She concluded that the Zhenotdel must "take a more active role in organizing peasant women to support collectivization."[45] Although the worst of the rioting would occur after the fall of 1929, the Party was sufficiently concerned by June to issue a special decree redirecting the focus of the Zhenotdel toward the countryside.

The Central Committee had not taken a clear position during the months of debate over separate organizing, but now the rebellion of peasant women compelled it to take a stand. On June 10, 1929, Lazar M. Kaganovich, a strong supporter of Stalin, a member of the Central Committee, and a recent appointee to the presidium of VTsSPS, addressed the Orgbiuro of the Central Committee and called for a broad "reconstruction" of work among women. He spoke out against "liquidationist tendencies" at the local level, declaring, "The Party must decisively put an end to this." The Zhenotdel would be preserved, but it needed to reorganize itself toward the end of mobilizing women in unions, soviets, and cooperatives around the policies of the Party. In endorsing the separate women's organization but casting it primarily as an instrument of Party policy, Kaganovich aimed to settle the debate over the purpose of the Zhenotdel. Concerned that *kulaks* had manipulated peasant women into rioting, he announced that the new role of the Zhenotdel, particularly in

---

[44] Lynne Viola, "Bab'i Bunty and Peasant Women's Protest during Collectivization," *Russian Review* 45 (1986): 23–42.

[45] S. Smidovich, "Tekushchie Zadachi Partii i Rol' Zhenaktiva," *Kommunistka*, 1929, no. 10: 9, 12–13.

the countryside, was to channel "women's activism" toward support of collectivization.[46]

Five days later, on June 15, the Central Committee published a lengthy decree, "The Tasks of the Party in Its Work among Women Workers and Peasants," elaborating on Kaganovich's address. This decree expressed the Party's anxiety over the peasant women's opposition, stating that "the most backward layer of working women are helping the anti-Soviet element in their struggle against the Party and soviets." It reiterated that the main task of the Zhenotdel was to work with this "backward layer" to lower prices, reduce absenteeism, enhance the productivity of labor, increase the harvest, and support collectivization. The decree dealt extensively with Party work in the countryside; its few references to *byt* were intended to make the larger *kolkhozs* more attractive to peasant women. Its main emphasis was on "the decisive and mass promotion of women workers and peasants into leadership," thus identifying *vydvizhenstvo* ("promotion from below") as the primary means of achieving equality. The decree also considered at some length the large number of peasant women recently elected to leading positions in rural soviets. The number of female chairmen had risen from 1 to 7 percent in the preceding elections, suggesting that the Party had intentionally advanced women candidates to challenge older, anti-*kolkhoz* peasant leaders.[47] Unfortunately, many of these women were illiterate, and the Party doubted the reliability of its own electoral success. Much of the decree was devoted to plans for teaching this new rural leadership the most basic administrative skills through literacy training and "extra instruction."[48] The Party's new role for the Zhenotdel, prompted directly by its anxiety over the *bab'i bunty*, would center on the campaign for collectivization, not on women's issues.

During the fall of 1929, public debate over the fate of the Zhenotdel subsided. Kaganovich had signaled the Central Committee's continuing support for the organization, though indicating that it was expected to play a new role. Artiukhina hopefully interpreted the Central Committee's decree as support for an expansion of the Zhenotdel: in restructuring work among women, she believed, the Central Committee was "raising it to general Party significance." She likewise predicted a more prominent role for the *zhenskii aktiv*, noting, "It is completely impermissible now, when the Party places new and difficult tasks before the Zhenotdel, that the *zhenskii aktiv* should stand on the sidelines."[49] Yet it soon became

---

[46]   Kaganovich, "Perestroit' Rabotu Sredi Rabotnits i Krest'ianok," 3–6.

[47]   The argument about the manipulation of women in the 1929 elections for the village soviets needs further investigation.

[48]   "Ob Ocherednykh Zadachakh Partii po Rabote Sredi Rabotnits i Krest'ianok," *Kommunistka*, 1929, no. 14: 43–48.

[49]   Artiukhina, "Povorot k Novomu," 7–15.

clear that local Party officials and organizers had little desire to cooperate with the organization, even in its new guise. In a speech to the Moscow Party committee in October 1929, Artiukhina called for a *krutoi povorot* ("sharp turn") in the Party's attitude toward women. She pleaded with the Party to make use of the Zhenotdel and its eight hundred thousand delegates in rural campaigns for the collection of grain. Yet activists in the countryside, engaged in a great struggle with the peasants over grain collection, ignored and derided the Zhenotdel, regarding its work as irrelevant to the "real" work of the Party. Artiukhina explained, "When comrades arrive from various organizations, we always ask, 'How is the campaign for the reelection of delegates going?' And they reply, 'What delegates? We are collecting bread now.' And we say, 'We know that you are collecting bread. But how are you using the older delegates for this? There are eight hundred thousand of them. Are you using the election of new delegates from the masses of women so that they will actively respond to the collection of grain?' 'No,' they say. 'We cannot squander our energies. We have a bread-gathering campaign, and then we'll turn our attention to this other campaign.' "[50] Artiukhina urged the Moscow Party committee to use delegate meetings of peasant women to create rural support for the Party, but local leaders were resistant, not only to women's issues but even to the inclusion of women in the Party's mass campaigns and programs.

The Liquidation of the Zhenotdel

Acting on suggestions made the previous spring by delegates to Party conferences, on January 5, 1930, the Politburo eliminated the Zhenotdel. The decision was part of a larger reorganization of the Central Committee, in which several other departments, including the Evsektsiia (Section for Jewish Affairs), the Department for Work in the Countryside, and the Statistical Department, were also dismantled. Kaganovich reported to the Central Committee that the increasing complexity of the tasks that lay before the Party leadership, in particular the development and recruitment of cadres, had prompted the reorganization. The Department of Agitation and Propaganda (Agitprop) was divided into two sections: Culture and Propaganda was to work through the Commissariat of Enlightenment to direct cultural work in print, propaganda, and cadre distribution, while Agitation and Mass Campaigns (Agitmass) was to lead campaigns involving socialist competition, elections to soviets, *kolkhoz*

---

[50] RTsKhIDNI, f. 17, o. 10, d. 490, "Ocherednye Zadachi Partii po Rabote Sredi Zhenshchin v SSSR. Doklad na Zasedanii Moskovskogo Partaktiva," 37.

contracts, labor productivity, and the collection of grain.[51] Kaganovich explained that henceforth work among women was to be subordinated to the mass campaigns already under way to industrialize and collectivize the country. The Zhenotdel would be dissolved and replaced by a women's sector within its old rival, agitmass. He noted that "in view of the fact that work among women has acquired important significance in the present period, it should be carried out by all departments of the Central Committee, and more specifically, it should be continued under the rubric of the successful mass campaigns that the Party has organized in the towns and countryside."[52] In other words, women's work was folded into "general" work, and women's issues were subsumed under the larger, and more important, campaigns for industrialization and collectivization. Although Kaganovich made token reference to the importance of work among women, he also made it clear that special women's organizers were no longer necessary: the very "significance" of women's work, according to the Politburo, compelled its transfer to "general" Party organizations.

Sensing, perhaps, that the *zhenskii aktiv* would react strongly to the liquidation of the Zhenotdel, the Politburo announced its decision circuitously. The first hint appeared in *Pravda,* in the guise of a request from women workers themselves. Beneath a prominent boldface headline, "Toward the Fundamental Restructuring of Leadership in Work among Women," a long article profiled the investigation by a women's shock-work brigade into conditions in Kharkov's factories. Not surprisingly, the brigade had uncovered an ugly state of affairs, sadly familiar to any organizer who had spent time among women in factories. Not only did women receive lower wages than men for the same work, but they were concentrated at the bottom of the pay scale, discriminated against in promotions, denied training, and subjected to endless abuse from male coworkers, foremen, and managers. Under subheadings such as "Today We Complain, Tomorrow They Fire Us," and "No One Is Interested in Us," the article repeated the standard litany of grievances voiced by women's organizers. The real purpose of the article, however, was not to showcase the brigade's findings but to publicize the conclusions it had been encouraged to draw. Under its list of remedies, the brigade declared, "Not a single organization is involved with women's work except the Zhenotdel of the Party committee. Therefore we request that the Central Committee of the Party issue a directive to include women's work in the plan of work of all the organizations."[53] In other words, without directly proposing the

---

[51]   RTsKhIDNI, f. 17, o. 3, d. 771, "Protokol 112: Zasedaniia Politbiuro TsK VKP (b)," 24–26.

[52]   Ibid., 25.

[53]   "Za Korennuiu Perestroiku Rukovodstva Rabotoi Sredi Zhenshchin," *Pravda,* January 12, 1930, p. 3.

liquidation of the Zhenotdel, the brigade uncannily echoed Kaganovich's speech to the Central Committee seven days earlier. Before any official announcement of the Politburo's decision, the careful reader of *Pravda* could thus find the requisite call from below for the Party to assume the work of the Zhenotdel, cloaked not in the antifeminist sentiments of liquidationists but in the concerns of women workers themselves. Two days later, a tiny notice appeared on the third page of *Pravda,* headed "Meeting in the Central Committee." It noted that about two hundred leading Party workers, including secretaries of *krai, oblast', okrug,* and *raion* Party committees, had met to hear Kaganovich report on the reorganization of the Central Committee.[54] *Pravda* offered no account of what Kaganovich had said, but three days later the decree "On the Reorganization of the Apparatus of the Central Committee VKP(b)" appeared on the newspaper's front page. It explained that "in view of the great tasks of the reconstruction period," it was necessary to reorganize the Central Committee. Regarding the specific fate of the Zhenotdel, it echoed the words of Kaganovich: "Since work among women workers and peasants has acquired great importance at present, it should be directed by all departments of the Central Committee. Special *agitmass* work among women should be continued under the successful mass campaigns which the Party has organized in towns and countryside."[55] The Politburo had finally made its decision public.

The following day, *Pravda* carried a long article by Artiukhina, the head of the Zhenotdel, supporting and justifying the Politburo's decision. Artiukhina attempted to interpret it as favorably as possible, stressing the importance of continuing work among women within the Party's various organizations. She proclaimed that the Politburo was raising work among women *"to a new and higher level"* and stressed that all organizations, including unions and soviets, must now be responsible for it. She urged women who had advanced in state government and in the Party apparatus to focus on women's interests and issues, to become "initiators in the establishment and advancement of questions of labor, *byt,* and culture, as well as in the promotion of women workers and peasants." Unlike Kaganovich, who had stressed the need to subsume women's issues within the larger economic campaigns for collectivization and industrialization, Artiukhina emphasized the elevation of women's issues to the level of the overall political framework. Even if the battle to maintain a separate women's organization had been lost, she refused to relinquish the importance of women's issues. She noted reprovingly that many Party activists had greeted the liquidation of the Zhenotdel with unrestrained

---

[54] "Soveshchanie v TsK VKP (b)," *Pravda,* January 14, 1930, p. 3.
[55] "O Reorganizatsii Apparata TsK VKP (b) – Postanovlenie TsK VKP (b)," *Pravda,* January 17, 1930, p. 1.

glee. A number of Party leaders had implied that it was being eliminated because it was "harmful." "There are many rumors on this subject," she wrote. "Some say, 'They have done well to liquidate the Zhenotdel. Now no one will be pestered by it anymore.'" Women Communists who were glad to see the organization abolished were mimicked by Artiukhina: "'Now I can do general work and not have anything more to do with women.'" She responded firmly to all female critics of the Zhenotdel: "It is necessary to say sharply that not a single Communist woman is freed from work among women by the decision of the Central Committee.... Now women must become even greater advocates for all issues connected with the actual liberation of the working masses of women." She urged the unions to begin thinking seriously about issues of *byt* and, more important, to act on them. She doggedly pressed the unions, the Party, and the soviets to recognize that their goal was nothing less than the socialization of household labor and the transformation of family life. This goal could not be forgotten, lost, or subsumed in mass campaigns.[56]

Artiukhina's reaction to the liquidation of the Zhenotdel and her persistent emphasis on keeping issues of *byt* at the forefront of Party work contrasted sharply with Kaganovich's understanding as printed in the final issue of *Kommunistka*. There he explained that great challenges lay ahead in the development of the economy. He noted that the Zhenotdel had played an important role in its time, primarily because it had been successful in training women to enter the Party and the government. "But precisely because of these achievements and because women themselves are beginning to work and participate actively in economic, state, and Party life as a whole," he explained patiently, "we have reached the point where the further existence of an independent Zhenotdel is inefficient." He mentioned not a word about *byt* or its transformation; rather, he reduced a decade of Zhenotdel accomplishments to a single achievement: its efficiency as a transmission belt for the promotion of individual women within the Party and state apparatus. "The Zhenotdel," he concluded, "has completed its circle of development." Women had moved up within various organizations, creating a "group that is sufficiently solid that it no longer needs special guardianship. And for further promotion and advancement, if you please, the Zhenotdel is already no longer a progressive center but a hindrance." Kaganovich thus not only ignored the chief aims of the organization through his glaring omission of issues of *byt*, but also signaled that it might not be necessary to continue promoting women in an attempt to redress gender imbalances. "It is time to begin to promote

---

[56] "Rabotu Sredi Zhenshchin Dolzhen Provodit Ves' Apparat Partii, Sovetov, Profsoiuzov," *Pravda*, January 18, 1930, p. 4. This article was republished in *Kommunistka*. See A. Artiukhina, "Zhenraboty Vesty Vsei Partiei v Tselom," *Kommunistka*, 1930, no. 2–3: 6–10. The quotes here are taken from *Kommunistka*.

women not as women but as workers – equal, adult, and developed."
Women had made so many gains that special attention was no longer
required.[57]

A week after the decision to eliminate the Zhenotdel was announced,
Kaganovich met with local Party leaders to brief them about the reorganization. Most approved of the move, but several expressed concern for the
future of work among women. Khataevich, secretary of the Middle Volga
krai committee, greeted Kaganovich's report with "great satisfaction"
and suggested that the Party might now think seriously about abolishing
women's work altogether. "In my opinion," he said, "we don't need to
create a women's sector in the Department of Mass Agitation because it
will eventually end up just like the Zhenotdel. Permit women to work in
Agitmass like any other department, but they should be concerned with *all*
work, not only women's work." Klavdia Nikolaeva, head of the organizational department of the North Caucasus *krai* committee and a leader of
the Zhenotdel, also publicly agreed with the decision, though she firmly
reprimanded Khataevich: "Comrade Khataevich is mistaken to suggest
that there should not be special women's sectors in the Department of
Agitation. I think these sectors are needed as a temporary, transitional
stage." She warned that the women's movement would benefit from the
reorganization only if Party cells became directly involved in women's
work. If this work, however, was relegated to a single women's organizer,
and the rest of the cell remained indifferent, then "the situation created
will be unsatisfactory." Like Artiukhina, she urged Party cells to take
women's issues seriously and to devote time and resources to questions
of *byt*. Rumiantsev, secretary of the Western *oblast'* committee, frankly
doubted whether Agitmass was capable of continuing the important work
done by the Zhenotdel; and Stolbova, secretary of the Kostroma *okrug*
committee, wondered how Party organizations that were known to hold
women's work in contempt could be successful in this task. Razumov, secretary of the Tatar *oblast'* committee, which operated in a predominantly
Moslem area, expressed concern that the liquidation of the Zhenotdel
would "affect the women's movement negatively." Keenly aware of the
powerlessness of women both inside and outside the Party in Moslem republics, he noted skeptically that "the strengthening of women's positions
in the mass organizations that Comrade Kaganovich referred to is still insufficient. If we cease to be involved with this work as special work in the
national republics, we will lose much." Artiukhina agreed, noting that
the Zhenotdel should be preserved in Central Asia and in those national

[57] L. Kaganovich, "Reorganizatsiia Partapparata i Ocherednye Zadachi Partraboty,"
Kommunistka, 1930, nos. 2–3: 3–5. This final issue carried a large notice to subscribers
urging them to switch to the journal *Sputnik Agitatora*, which would thenceforth cover
women's issues, among other matters.

republics where the position of women in the Party and the government was still weak.[58]

Local Party leaders and the *zhenskii aktiv* seemed confused and uncertain about what the Politburo actually intended by its decision to liquidate the Zhenotdel. Many local leaders interpreted the decision as official permission to abolish all women's work. Others, including Artiukhina and Nikolaeva, outwardly supported the decision but continued to press the Party as a whole to engage issues of *byt,* female labor, and advancement for women. A significant segment of the *zhenskii aktiv* refused outright to support the decision. Deeply embittered, they saw it as a blow struck against women's work. Many of these women had organized in factories since before the revolution; others had been given their first opportunities for literacy, political education, and advancement through the delegate meetings and organizational efforts of the Zhenotdel. If some had found, as their critics charged, a sinecure in the Zhenotdel, many more by far seemed to have found in it an epiphany. Powerfully committed to women's equality and the transformation of *byt* as fundamental tenets of the revolution, they were unwilling to accede gracefully to the liquidation of their organization. Kaganovich admitted, "We have collided with enormous opposition from those very women comrades who work in the Zhenotdel apparatus." Many Zhenotdel workers had told him, frankly and angrily, "You are ruining Party work among women."[59]

Face toward Production, Forget *Byt*

In a speech delivered to the Orgbiuro of the Central Committee in February, Kaganovich attempted to placate the restive *zhenskii aktiv.* The Zhenotdel was not being liquidated, he gently admonished; it was simply being restructured. Using the dialectical sophistry that would later become the butt of so many Soviet-era jokes, he explained that the very success of the organization "forces us to rethink the future organization of work among women," for "a good organization for one period becomes its opposite for another." In place of an organization designed to promote women's issues, he offered the incentive of upward mobility for individual women. He promised that once the "historically outdated partition between women's work and 'general' work is removed, thousands of women will advance through the unions."[60] While Kaganovich

[58] "Ne Obkhodimost' Reorganizatsii Partiinogo Apparata Vyzyvaetsia Ogromnym Uslozhneniem Zadach Partrukovodstva v Usloviiakh Rekonstruktivnogo Perioda," *Pravda,* January 19, 1930, p. 3.

[59] L. Kaganovich, "Ob Apparate TsK VKP (b)," *Partiinoe stroitel'stvo,* 1930, no. 2: 12.

[60] Ibid.

reassured the *zhenskii aktiv* that their good work would not be lost, he made it clear that it would take new forms. Women would have to relinquish their commitment to the socialization of household labor and the reorganization of domestic life in favor of a new emphasis on the Party's mass campaigns for industrialization and collectivization. But in return, they could expect large-scale upward mobility – *vydvizhenie* – within the ranks of the government, the Party, and the unions.

The Central Committee named P. Ia. Voronova, secretary of the textile workers' union, to be deputy director of Agitmass in charge of the women's sectors. Voronova, born to a working-class family in 1892, had worked in textile factories since the age of fifteen. After joining the Party in 1917, she had headed the local zhenotdel in Ivanovo-Voznesensk, a textile region, in 1919–1920. She had risen steadily in her union, becoming a member of its central committee and its secretary in 1927.[61] She did not, however, offer much leadership to the newly created women's sectors. Unsure of their purpose or function, the sectors did little work in the spring of 1930. Some of the former Zhenotdel staff who had transferred into the sectors attempted to carry on the work they had done before, but they were soon reprimanded. In the reproving words of Varvara Moirova, a former Zhenotdel leader, the women in Agitmass wrongly attempted to recreate "poor [*zakhudalye*] facsimiles of the old zhenotdels."[62] Artiukhina and others like her, still hoping that the Party as a whole would engage women's issues seriously, had not yet fully grasped the meaning of the liquidation of the Zhenotdel – the notion that the mass promotion and advancement of individual women would now replace a mass organization designed to revolutionize the lives of all women. This new direction was clarified and hardened that spring. In May, the Central Committee issued a resolution condemning as premature the drafting of "semi-fantastic" schemes for new socialized towns and dwellings. It accused enthusiasts such as Sabsovich and Larin of ignoring the need to concentrate "resources on the rapid industrialization of the country." "Only that," the resolution explained, "will create the real material conditions for a fundamental transformation of *byt*."[63]

In June, the Central Committee called a special meeting of women's sectors of Agitmass to clarify their purpose and dispel their lingering, and now inconvenient, attachment to issues of *byt*. The Central Committee announced that the new sectors were to concentrate on a single task: organizing peasant and working-class women "to aid in socialist construction

[61] "Tov. Voronova – Zaveduiushaia Zhenskim Sektoram TsK VKP (b)," *Trud*, February 8, 1930, p. 1.
[62] V. Moirova, "Rabota Sredi Zhenshchin v Perelomnyi Period," *Partiinoe stroitel'stvo*, 1930, nos. 13–14: 21.
[63] *Pravda*, May 17, 1930, as quoted in Davies, 152.

and to surmount difficulties of this construction." Many of the former *zhenskii aktiv* – old *bytoviki,* they were called – nonetheless refused to accept this single-minded focus on production. They anxiously inquired, if the women's sectors were not to lead the reorganization of *byt,* who was? In the absence of the Zhenotdel, which organization would promote the revolutionary transformation of life? Surely, they reasoned, the Party was not planning to abandon one of the most fundamental premises of the revolution. Who would support women's self-activity? asked Ashkinadze, an old Zhenotdel worker from the Ukraine. Who would support women's own efforts to create new forms of domestic life?[64] The answer, in brief, was "No one," as Moirova explained on behalf of the Central Committee. Women's sectors were not to be involved with issues of *byt* or with the promotion and advancement of women, a task that now belonged to the Department of Cadres. Moirova flatly noted, "Questions of *byt* cannot occupy a central place in mass work among women. The central issues of our agitation are those raised by the Fifteenth Party Congress." Lest anyone wonder what these were, she clearly enumerated them: to increase the tempo of economic development, to improve the quality of work, to lower prices, and to mobilize women into shock work (campaigns to increase production) and other forms of socialist competition. *Byt,* revolutionary or otherwise, was not included in the list. She criticized the past orientation of the Zhenotdel for slighting industrial production. Women workers' attention to *byt* had "interfered with their correct involvement in, for example, production meetings." Moirova's description of the women's sectors of Agitmass left no room for interpretation: "If those sectors again attempt to become involved in basic questions of *byt,* they will be committing a mistake." In towns, women's sectors were to occupy themselves primarily with production, and in the countryside, with "the tempo and quality of *kolkhoz* construction, internal discipline and mobilization, and the strengthening of collective labor customs and social responsibility." These issues were to "subordinate all others."[65]

Despite the clear change in the Party line, a considerable portion of the *zhenskii aktiv* continued to resist the new approach. Several delegates at the meeting maintained that women's sectors should keep on monitoring the advancement of women and pushing for the transformation of life. They frankly doubted that the Party "in general" could do as a good a job as the Zhenotdel had done, a view that representatives of the Central Committee considered unacceptable. Although the meeting appeared to have reached a standoff, the delegates finally adopted a compromise resolution: "In view of the great significance of the reorganization and construction of new *byt,* to ask the Central Committee for

---

[64] Moirova, "Rabota Sredi Zhenshchin v Perelomnyi Period," 22.   [65] Ibid., 22–23.

the rapid creation of an internal Party agency to provide ideological leadership for this work."[66] The old *zhenskii aktiv*, demobilized within the new women's sectors, thus registered its last collective protest with the Central Committee against the liquidation of the Zhenotdel. But if this special meeting of women's sectors gave the members of the *zhenskii aktiv* an opportunity to vent their disappointment, it failed to inspire them to organize around issues of production. The Central Committee later commented on "a certain demoralized mood among the *zhenskii aktiv*, a peculiar understanding of the decision of the Party that it was necessary to liquidate completely all specialized forms of attention and methods of work among laboring women." It noted that mass work among women had "collapsed" in soviets, unions, cooperatives, and economic organizations. Unions, in particular, had done absolutely nothing to organize the hundreds of thousands of new women entering production.[67] Just as Il'ina had warned two years before, the decision to integrate women's work into "general" work had produced only indifference, neglect, and organizational chaos.

After the Sixteenth Party Congress, in the summer of 1930, the Central Committee published a long document, "The Primary Tasks of the Sectors," in another attempt to clarify the role of women's sectors and revive their work. It reiterated that the Zhenotdel "as an independent entity" was "inefficient" under the new conditions of the reconstruction period but maintained that work among women remained necessary. Faced with the complete collapse of work among women, the Central Committee belatedly explained that liquidation did not signify "a weakening of work"; accordingly, the prevalent "mood" in local organizations "must be given a decisive rebuff." Women's sectors were needed precisely because peasants, workers, and even Party members had demonstrated "significant sluggishness" in regard to women. Yet the tasks of women's sectors had not changed. The Central Committee insisted, once again, that activists were not to become involved in "all those questions that previously occupied the Zhenotdel." Their present role was to teach women about class struggle in the transitional period and to expose the class enemy: "All political agitation should be based on the struggle for the Leninist general line, the struggle with right-wing moods of the Right opposition as the main danger and with the Left deviation." Having carefully plotted the correct path through the deviationist thicket, the Central Committee left the abstract realm of high politics to offer the women's sectors a concrete example of their duties: as a result of the shift in investment from light

---

[66] Ibid., 24.
[67] RTsKhIDNI, f. 17, o. 10, d. 490, "Ocherednye Zadachi Raboty Sektora," 78–79. This document is, unfortunately, undated, but it was written sometime after the Sixteenth Party Congress, held in June–July 1930.

to heavy industry, the women's sectors were instructed to prepare women workers for mass layoffs in the textile factories. For the women of the *zhenskii aktiv,* many of whom had begun their revolutionary careers in those same factories, no task could have carried more bitter irony than one that simultaneously attacked their old base of support and slashed the production of the clothing and other textiles so desperately needed by women and their families.

Finally, the Central Committee severely reprimanded the *zhenskii aktiv* once again for using delegate meetings as "a higher school of political literacy." The Central Committee explained that "special work" was not necessary among women who had already acquired some political education. Activists were forbidden to focus on women's issues and were commanded to work with "the ordinary as well as the most backward working women in the towns and the countryside and, in particular, in the East." Delegate meetings were to be reoriented toward "the ranks of the masses"; basic education was to center on the five-year plan and collectivization because "women workers and peasants are completely disoriented in today's complex political conditions." In this case, *disoriented* was a code word for opposition to collectivization, grain requisitioning, falling wages, and work speedup in the factories. In view of these problems, rendered in Party language as "complex political conditions," urban delegate meetings were to concentrate on popularizing the Party's relentless emphasis on production. They were to emphasize production, socialist competition, shock work, and the plan. Women's sectors were to familiarize workers in the factories with "production control figures and how to meet them." In the countryside, delegate meetings were to organize support for collectivization and labor discipline and to combat "*kulak* agitation," to which peasant women were particularly susceptible. Once again the Central Committee reiterated, "The focus of mass work should be on production." The message was unmistakable: all women's issues were to be subordinated to production, a goal construed no more broadly than the control figures adopted for each factory and *kolkhoz.*[68]

Work among Women Collapses

The attempt to substitute production goals for *byt* failed, leaving the *zhenskii aktiv* embittered at the loss of the Zhenotdel and local Party leaders uninterested in organizing women around any issue. In September 1930, the Central Committee published a decree stressing the importance of

[68] RTsKhIDNI, f. 17, o. 10, d. 490, "Ocherednye Zadachi Raboty Sektora," 68, 69, 70, 78, 73, 74, 75, 80.

delegate assemblies, the only organizational form created by the Zhenot-del that had survived the liquidation decree. The Central Committee in-structed the unions and local Party organizations to launch a mass cam-paign among women to reelect delegates – a campaign that was to be based on a series of cumbersome slogans carefully spelled out by the Central Committee: "Mobilize the Activity of Laboring Women of Town and Countryside to Fulfill the Important Political and Economic Tasks of the Party!"; "Liquidate Gaps in Industry!"; "Strengthen the Existing *Kolkhozs*, Develop New Waves for the *Kolkhoz* Movement!"; "Fulfill the Plan for Bread Collection!"; and the inimitably catchy "Better the Orga-nization for Struggle with *Kulaks* and Liquidate Them as a Class through Decisive Struggle with Petty-Bourgeois Moods Encouraged by Right Op-portunist and Trotskyist Elements!"[69] Not one of these slogans dealt with women's issues or mentioned the increasingly important role played by women in production and heavy industry. Even from the perspective of the Party's priorities, the slogans were, without exception, ill suited and poorly designed to target women's concerns or to mobilize women to sup-port the Party's push for industrialization and collectivization. A lengthy report submitted by VTsSPS to the Central Committee in 1931 noted that the entire union hierarchy – from VTsSPS itself to the *krai* council to the factory committees – had abandoned work among women over the past two years. The delegate assemblies, once the basic local bloc of the Zhenotdel, were falling apart. Local unions had widely ignored the dele-gate reelection campaign in November 1930, and both women's activists and local officials agreed that it had been a failure.[70] That failure could not be blamed solely on the slogans, which the majority of unions had simply ignored; not surprisingly, since they had been encouraged to ignore women's issues, they ignored the reelection campaign as well.

The reelection campaign was recognized by many Party officials and women's activists as a debacle. The Central Committee continued to stress the importance of delegate meetings, yet little changed through the spring and summer of 1931. In Krasnyi Putilovets, one of the oldest and most revolutionary of the metal factories, a woman activist tried to discuss "the disgusting attitudes toward the delegate meetings," but the factory committee refused to place the issue on its agenda. Elections for the dele-gate meetings dragged on for months in both Krasnyi Putilovets and the Northern Shipyards, with no organizational assistance forthcoming from local unions or Party organizations.[71] A report sent by VTsSPS to the

---

[69] GARF, f. 5451, o. 15, d. 362, "Postanovlenie TsK," 66.
[70] GARF, f. 5451, o. 15, d. 362, "VTsK, VKP (b). O Massovoi Rabote Sredi Zhenshchin Sviazan s Vnedreniem Novogo Sloia Zhenshchin v Promyshlennost'," 96.
[71] GARF, f. 5451, o. 15, d. 361, "Soveshchanie o Podgotovke Materialov Vnedreniiu Zhenskogo Truda v Proizvodstvo," 35.

Central Committee, written in the spring of 1931, recorded that refusal to support the delegate meetings was not confined to these two plants: local unions throughout the country displayed a similar apathy. The report noted, "The liquidationist mood toward delegate meetings has still not been eliminated." In many factories, delegate meetings had not been held in over two years.[72] M. Lenau, the head of the sector for mass campaigns within VTsSPS, noted that the decision to dissolve the Zhenotdel had been broadly taken "as a signal" by the unions "to liquidate all work with women." In many places, local unionists called off the delegate meetings as well, declaring with relief, "When the *baba* falls out of the carriage, the horse is better off."[73]

The liquidation of the Zhenotdel was viewed as a signal to do away with women's inspectors in NKT (the Commissariat of Labor), organizers in the factories, the women's sectors in Agitmass, and the delegate assemblies. The position of special women's inspector had been created within NKT in 1928 for several republics. Russia had ten such inspectors, and Ukraine twelve; for republics without special inspectors, the responsibility for women's work was divided among existing staff. A secret letter from Serina, the chief inspector for women's labor in NKT, to the women's sector of Agitmass complained that almost all of the inspectors had lost their jobs in the "waves of liquidation that occurred in connection with the reorganization of the organs of labor in 1930." The Workers' and Peasants' Inspectorate (Rabkrin) severely purged the departments of labor, but none of its suggested changes or reorganizations benefited female labor. In fact, Rabkrin systematically deleted the sections on female labor in every report and plan.[74] Local Party officials also neglected and ignored the new women's sectors under Agitmass, regularly assigning the least experienced Party members to "women's work," only to "promote" them within several months. Women's work was considered the least-desirable Party assignment and was given the lowest priority. The Zhenotdel's delegate assemblies also began to disintegrate, despite the Party's attempt to preserve them. In one industrial region after another – Ivanovo, Cheliabinsk, Kurgansk, Western Siberia – the vast network of meetings and assemblies, involving some forty to seventy thousand women per region, collapsed. Local union officials had little interest in organizing the regular elections on which the assemblies were based. Nonetheless, in the spring of 1932, the Central Committee attempted once again to revive them. The CC was aware that "the backward female layer" of the working class was

[72] GARF, f. 5451, o. 15, d. 362, "VTsK, VKP (b). Massovaia Rabota Sredi Zhenshchin," 100.
[73] *Trud*, February 3, 1931, p. 1.
[74] GARF, f. 6983, o. 1, d. 159, "V Zhensektor TsK VKP (b). Rabota Organov Truda v Oblasti Zhenskogo Truda," 40.

discontented. Living conditions in the cities, towns, and industrial settlements were horrendous, and workers constantly grumbled about the lack of food, the poor housing, the short rations, and the squalor. The Central Committee hoped that the delegate meetings might work to improve *byt* and to develop women's support for the industrialization drive. It noted that "a decisive change" in attitudes toward mass work among women was needed on the local level.[75] In August 1932, Shaburova, the head of the women's sectors, wrote to the CC that her study of numerous regions showed that local officials were ignoring the CC's instructions to revive the delegate meetings.[76] In 1933, Safina, the head of the sector for work among women within VTsSPS, complained that not one of the unions' central committees was working with women.[77]

Finally, in 1932, the Committee to Improve the Labor and Life of Working Women (KUTB), under the Central Executive Committee, was also eliminated, and its work transferred to women's sectors within the local soviets. KUTB was a planning body composed of representatives from various commissariats, Gosplan, and other departments. Several former Zhenotdel leaders worked within KUTB to plan women's labor-force participation. Although KUTB did not do any actual organizing work with women workers or peasants, after the elimination of the Zhenotdel, it constituted the last bastion of organized and effective feminism. Located within the soviets, it pushed nationally and locally to include women's interests in state policy. Its elimination followed the same pattern as the Zhenotdel's: calls to work "in general" as opposed to specifically with women were followed by an "enormous decrease in the number of women involved in government positions." Many of the local soviets never created the mandated women's sectors and simply stopped working on women's issues altogether. Several soviet officials explained, "Once women achieve equal rights juridically and factually, it is not necessary to do any special work."[78] The work was being done "in general" – or, from the viewpoint of women workers, not at all.

[75] RTsKhIDNI, f. 17, o. 114, d. 280, "Protokol No. 94 Zasedaniia Sekretariata TsK VKP (b) ot 15 Fevraliia 1932," 116–118; f. 17, o. 114, d. 297, "Protokol No. 108 Zasedaniia Sekretariata TsK VKP (b) ot 15 Maia 1932," 60.
[76] RTsKhIDNI, f. 17, o. 114, d. 297, "O Nevypolnenii Reshenii TsK VKP (b) o Rabote Delegatskikh Sobranii," 65.
[77] GARF, f. 5451, o. 17, d. 294, "Zav. Sektoram po Rabote Sredi Zhenshchin pri VTsSPS – Tov. Safinoi," 6.
[78] GARF, f. 3316, o. 51, d. 7, "Zadachi Sovetov v Rabote Sredi Trudiashchikhsia Zhenshchin-Rabotnits, Kolkhoznits i Krest'ianok Edinolichnits," 16–22. KUTB had been formed in 1926 as the Commission to Improve the Labor and Life of Women. In July 1930, it had become the Committee to Improve the Labor and Life of Women Workers and Peasants. Artiukhina, Baranova, Smidovich, and Moirova, all former Zhenotdel leaders, were members of KUTB's presidium in 1930.

Labor and the Liquidation of the Zhenotdel

The elimination of the Zhenotdel put an end to a broader program for women's liberation, destroying key organizational links between the Party and working-class women. The decision to eliminate the Zhenotdel was made in the name of "productionism," but it came just at a point when severe labor shortages were beginning to be felt. In October 1930, the Party called for 1.6 million women to enter the labor force. In February 1931, VTsSPS called a huge meeting of union activists to mobilize women and to change prevailing attitudes toward women workers. Many former *zhenotdelki,* now working in the women's sectors and the unions, attended the meeting. They painted a grim picture of industrial chaos, widespread turnover, and organizational collapse. Hundreds of thousands of women were entering industry, but the unions were doing nothing to combat the hostility and discrimination of managers, foremen, and male workers. Women were passed over for training and promotions and subjected to abuse when they entered "male" shops or apprenticeships. Men frequently refused to work with women, asserting that they did not belong in certain jobs or shops within the factories.

Once again, the *zhenskii aktiv* condemned the liquidation of the Zhenotdel. Gudrova, a woman shock worker in the metal industry from the Mekhanicheskii State Factory, spoke harshly about the Party and unions: "The work among women was reorganized, the Zhenotdel was liquidated, and the work drifted along. When you knock at the door of the unions, you receive the answer, 'Never!', and the same from Party organizations."[79] Radchenko, a delegate from Rostov Sel'mashstroi, a huge agricultural machine plant, also lamented the loss of the Zhenotdel. "In several places, we incorrectly eliminated our special women's organizations," he explained, "and when we transferred this work to women's *agitmassoviki,* then our *agitmassoviki* in several cases made a mess of this women's work." The Agitmass department did almost no work among women, and the unions treated them "with coldness." The managers and union officials in Radchenko's plant believed that women were incapable of doing skilled work.[80] Spivak, a delegate from eastern Siberia, described a similar situation in his area, where "sluggishness" in every economic and labor organization hampered the fulfillment of Party directives and the goals of the industrialization drive.[81] Many of the delegates complained bitterly about the unions. Chichlovskaia noted that they refused to organize women and had no idea how many women worked in factories or

[79]   GARF, f. 5451, o. 13, d. 357, "Stenogramma Vsesoiuznogo Soveshchaniia po Rabote Sredi Zhenshchin," Tom 1, 26, 27.
[80]   Ibid., 28, 31.   [81]   Ibid., 42.

what their needs were. "There is no assessment on the woman question," she declared. "Absolutely no one does this work." Chichlovskaia herself had managed, with great difficulty, to organize a meeting of women shock workers, who in turn asked that a member of the presidium of the union attend. The official had replied, " 'You, Comrade Chichlovskaia, will be there, and that's enough.' "[82]

Lisenkova, a delegate from the chemical plant Krasnyi Sormovo, expressed similar complaints. Some thirty-three hundred women labored in her factory, but no one organized them. When the issue had come up at a union meeting, the presidium had declared, " 'Give the work to Lisenkova, the *babas* all go to her, let her do it.' " When Lisenkova protested that she knew nothing about organizing women, the presidium responded, " 'It's nothing, don't worry about it.' " When she began to ask about what she should do, she discovered that "no one knew anything." She complained that women were automatically assigned to work among women whether or not they were qualified.[83]

Many delegates angrily noted that the liquidation of the Zhenotdel had exacerbated the poor treatment that women received from the unions. Ianovskaia, a delegate from the Ukraine, said regretfully, "It is painful for me to see the old Zhenotdel, for over the past year work among women has fallen apart." Gal'perina, a delegate from the North Caucasus, said, "The basic mistake of unions was that they did not understand the decision of the Party about the liquidation of the Zhenotdel. They did not understand that this meant the unions were entrusted with a greater responsibility for women's work than before." Makarova, a delegate from Siberia, said that after the liquidation of the Zhenotdel, no work was done among women for an entire year. "In 1930," she explained, "no work was done because the women's organizers were changed, four or five were replaced, and as a result all the work fell apart." Spivak agreed: "We became accustomed to the idea that if there is no Zhenotdel, there is no work among women."[84]

A few delegates were annoyed by unending recriminations over the liquidation of the Zhenotdel. Plaksina, a textile worker from Ivanovo who had worked in the Zhenotdel for many years, spoke for the Party when she announced, "This meeting was not called so we all could cry and complain about the deficiencies in our work. A number of comrades here have carried on about the Zhenotdel. I think we must look at the Zhenotdel this way: It did great work in its time, and it forged many activists from our ranks. The conclusion is that we don't need to consider the Zhenotdel as we have been doing here." Yet there were limits to Plaksina's support for the Party's decision, for later she declared that she had still not seen "a single directive from VTsSPS establishing work among

[82] Ibid., 44, 46.   [83] Ibid., 53.   [84] Ibid., 63, 68, 36, 42.

women." She argued that if organizing among women was to be effective, the unions had to take responsibility at every level.[85]

Shaburova and Voronova, the director and deputy director of the women's sectors in Agitmass, firmly addressed complaints about the Zhenotdel, repeating the Party's standard line: It had done good work, but now conditions had changed. Shaburova explained that even though the decree on liquidation had been widely misinterpreted, it had not been a mistake. Overlooking much of the testimony from delegates, she maintained that "the Party has not weakened work among women" but rather "has raised it to the highest political level." She emphasized that all of the questions that had previously occupied the Zhenotdel should now be left to mass organizations, which were concerned with this work "in general."[86] Voronova simply added – one more time – that women's sectors were to organize not around women's issues but rather around the fulfillment of the five-year plan.[87]

Naum M. Antselovich, a candidate member of the Central Committee and the chairman of the land and forest workers' union, ended the meeting with a speech that lasted almost an hour. He wasted little breath on the Zhenotdel, dismissing the organization and its history with crude contempt: "The main thing, comrades, is not that ten Zhenotdel members met and picked their noses. The main thing is mass work among women workers, work in the factories, there where women work."[88] He did not care to examine, however, the lesson suggested by the numerous delegates who had testified to the collapse of mass work in the factories. Nor did he consider the effects of liquidation on the Party's own industrial goals, on its pressing need to involve women in production, to train and promote qualified people, and to fill gaps in industries that had long been traditionally male.

The Party's new policy toward women perfectly mirrored its policy toward workers, male and female. With the adoption of the optimum variant of the five-year plan in the spring of 1929, the unions had been forced to abandon their role as "protectors" of the working class in order to become the organizational "levers" for raising production. The Party had aggressively purged all union leaders and activists who refused to accommodate themselves to this new role.[89] In place of the promotion of

[85] Ibid., 72, 75.
[86] GARF, f. 5451, o. 15, d. 358, "Stenogramma Vsesoiuznogo Soveshchaniia po Rabote Sredi Zhenshchin," Tom 2, 37, 40.
[87] GARF, f. 5451, o. 15, d. 357, "Stenogramma," Tom 1, 210 ob.   [88] Ibid., 202.
[89] Davies writes, "The need to enlist the trade unions as an obedient agent of this policy lay behind the struggle with Tomsky and his supporters. The subordinate and instrumental role of the Soviet trade unions continued throughout Stalin's lifetime and the decades beyond" (p. 65).

workers' *class interests*, the Party had substituted the wholesale promotion of individual workers (*vydvizhenie*). While thousands of individual workers were clearly served by upward mobility, this policy did nothing to advance the interests of the class *in and for itself*. The Party adopted a similar policy toward women. With the liquidation of the Zhenotdel, it renounced its commitments to remaking domestic life and to the advancement of women's interests. In place of women's issues, Kaganovich promised individual women *vydvizhenie* through the unions, the soviets, and the Party itself. Thousands of women undoubtedly benefited, but the organization that might have advanced *the interests of women as a group* was eliminated. Women's gender interests, like workers' class interests, were relentlessly subordinated to the Party's interests in production, accumulation, and investment.

Strong parallels also existed between the Party's approach to the Zhenotdel and other organizational policies of the late 1920s. Just as the Party launched a massive drive to collectivize land without being able to provide sufficient tractors to convince peasants of the material advantage of consolidation, and just as it eliminated private traders and small craftsmen without a sufficiently developed retail apparatus to replace them, so it liquidated the Zhenotdel at the very moment when it was most needed to integrate women into the factories.[90] Union and local Party leaders regarded the decision as an official sanction for their neglect and discrimination, fostering hostility toward women precisely when they were most needed in the labor force. The decision left a legacy of organizational chaos that did little to promote production. Thus, even from a productionist standpoint, the liquidation of the Zhenotdel, like the drives to collectivize and to eliminate private trading, was premature, poorly thought out, and fraught with unforeseen consequences.

Throughout the 1920s, attempts by women activists to transform *byt* conflicted constantly with the entrenched prejudices of local Party and union officials. Debates over liquidationism raged at the local level toward the end of the decade. The Central Committee did not step in to resolve these disputes until the summer of 1929, when the spread of *bab'i bunty* throughout the countryside pushed it to restructure the Zhenotdel as a mobilizing force for collectivization. Yet local officials stymied even this decision by simply refusing to work with the organization. Stripped of its focus on *byt* by the highest level of the Party and boycotted as an instrument of Party policy by the lowest level, the Zhenotdel was left

---

[90] Ibid., 77. Davies notes the same connection: "In retrospect, the analogy is obvious between the policy pursued in 1927–1929 of eliminating private trade before the socialized sector was able to replace it, and the policy pursued in 1929–1931 of collectivizing agriculture before state industry was able to supply tractors and other machinery in place of peasant horses and implements."

without a purpose. By January 1930, the Central Committee considered it expendable. The decision to eliminate the women's department was made "from above"; it was not the result of a democratic, participatory process, and it brooked no appeal. The proletarian women's movement, born in a revolution from below, met its death in the "revolution from above."

Party members and others maintained a lively interest in the transformation of *byt* throughout the first five-year plan, but the Politburo, the highest level of the Party, decisively renounced its commitment to *byt* with the liquidation of the Zhenotdel. Party leaders hammered this message home to a stubbornly reluctant *zhenskii aktiv* in every subsequent speech. New women's sectors were to concern themselves with production in factories and on *kolkhozs,* not with the transformation of life. Although the Party strongly encouraged women to enter training programs and jobs previously reserved for men, its neglect of *byt* effectively guaranteed that women would never achieve equality with men in the waged labor force. The elimination of the Zhenotdel, the delegate assemblies, the women's inspectors, women's factory organizers, and KUTB had a decisive impact on the subsequent shape of Soviet industrialization. In the absence of women's organizations, women lost the opportunity to express their grievances and their interests. The elimination of women's organizing broke the link between women in the factories and the Party, for women had no way to affect policy in the soviets or in planning organizations. Without an organization to advance their specific interests, women entered industry *samotek* – spontaneously and haphazardly. Although they did enter traditionally male industries in record-breaking numbers, Soviet industry retained both vertical and horizontal patterns of sex segregation. Women were clustered in traditionally female sectors of light industry, service, and retail trade, and they remained at the bottom of the wage scale and skill hierarchy in every industry. Their position was shaped in no small measure by the prejudices of male workers and managers and by the short-term imperatives of production. Driven by a mania for production, Stalin and his supporters successfully remade the revolution, which had encompassed so many different aspirations in 1917, in the image of rapid industrialization.

Aleksandra V. Artiukhina (1889–1969) headed the Zhenotdel from 1927 to 1930. She began working in a textile factory at age twelve, joined the Bolshevik Party in 1918, and worked as an editor of *Rabotnitsa* from 1924 to 1931. She served as head of the textile workers' union from 1934 to 1938 and during World War II directed several textile mills in Moscow. She was awarded the Order of Lenin three times during her life. She retired in 1951. Photograph taken in 1930.

3

The Gates Come Tumbling Down

Millions of women – wives and family members of workers and employees, servants, women in handicrafts and artels, landless women, poor peasants, collective farmers, eastern tribal women – this entire mass, once occupied with exhausting and dulling household labor, is now joining the great socialist construction of the country.

B. Marsheva, labor analyst, 1931

The composition of the new working class takes its shape in large measure from unused reserves in the working-class family.

Report on female labor, 1932[1]

In the spring of 1929, the Party adopted the first five-year plan. The plan, taking up three volumes and more than two thousand pages, allocated 64.5 billion rubles to investment, 78 percent of which was targeted for heavy industry and 50 percent for new construction. Adoption of the plan, in the words of one economist, was "tantamount to turning the country into a vast construction site."[2] After a decade of unemployment and exclusion, the gates to the working class came tumbling down. Almost 2.3 million people entered the waged labor force in 1930, followed by 6.3 million more in 1931. Party leaders, labor officials, and planners critically noted at the time that this mass influx of new workers occurred "*samotek,*" or independent of any state plan or policy. The building of huge new industrial complexes and hydroelectric stations such as Magnitostroi, Kuznetsstroi, and Dneprostroi drew thousands of workers.[3] Hungry town dwellers and dispossessed peasants massed at new

[1] B. Marsheva, "Zhenskii Trud v 1931 godu," *Voprosy truda*, 1931, no. 1: 40. GARF, f. 6983, o. 25, d. 986, "Itogi Vnedreniia Zhenskogo Truda v 1931–1932," 265.
[2] Eugene Zaleski, *Planning for Economic Growth in the Soviet Union, 1918–1932* (Chapel Hill, N.C.: University of North Carolina Press, 1971), 58, 61.
[3] On the building of industry, see R. W. Davies, *The Soviet Economy in Turmoil, 1929–1930* (Cambridge, Mass.: Harvard University Press, 1989); R. W. Davies, Mark Harrison, and S. G. Wheatcroft, *The Economic Transformation of the Soviet Union, 1913–1945*

construction sites and factory gates in search of work. Waves of people crashed into the towns and then receded, flooding the roads and railway stations. The Soviet labor historian O. I. Shkaratan noted that the migration was of a magnitude "never before seen in human history."[4] Not only was the movement enormous, but it also shattered previous patterns. Whereas the great majority of migrants seeking work had formerly been men, women now figured prominently among the new arrivals. Urban women, wives and daughters of male workers, were also strongly represented in the ranks of new workers. Women entered all sectors of the economy, but the largest number went into industry. Within a short time, they assumed significant roles in industries long dominated by men, transformed the gender composition of the workforce, and subverted older lines of sex segregation. Their share in the formation of the working class was unprecedented in terms of sheer numbers, rapidity of involvement, and participation in traditionally "male" heavy industries.

Why did peasant and urban women leave their villages and homes to take up the shovel, the lathe, or the drill? Who were they, and where did they come from? Were they actively recruited and directed to work by labor officials, or did they choose waged labor of their own volition? The answers to these questions lie in a tangled knot of policy and consequence, of state decisions and popular responses that linked village to town and peasants to wage earners in an escalating sequence of unplanned and unanticipated events. The process of rural dispossession, waged labor, industrialization, and urbanization that stretched over centuries in the West was compressed in the Soviet Union into a mere decade. In no country of the world did this process occur with such rapidity and intensity. Each woman's decision to become a waged worker was made individually, within particular circumstances of family and place. Yet each decision was also a response to vast collective upheavals connecting town to village. As in a car wreck involving multiple vehicles, state policy and economic consequence alternated in a series of successive collisions, each new action in turn forcing the Party and various social groups into sharp and unforeseen reactions.

Historians, confronted with such deep social and economic upheaval, have tried to attain a manageable vantage of study by dividing workers from peasants, urban life from rural, and labor policy from collectivization.

(Cambridge: Cambridge University Press, 1994); Stephen Kotkin, *Magnetic Mountain: Stalinism as a Civilization* (Berkeley and Los Angeles: University of California Press, 1995); Anne Rassweiler, *Generation of Power: The History of* Dneprostroi (New York: Oxford University Press, 1988); Hiroaki Kuromiya, *Stalin's Industrial Revolution: Politics and Workers, 1928–1932* (Cambridge: Cambridge University Press, 1988).

[4] O. I. Shkaratan, *Problemy sotsial'noi struktury rabochego klassa SSSR* (Moscow: Izdatel'stvo "Mysl'", 1971), 225–26.

The Soviet state contributed to these divisions by concealing the extent of the urban unrest that simmered in the late 1920s and 1930s in response to food shortages. As a result, the complex links between poor harvest and urban inflation, between urban social unrest and the decision to collectivize, have yet to be fully explored. Yet the formation of the Soviet working class, and in particular the unprecedented role of women in its composition, cannot be understood apart from these links.

Food Shortages, Inflation, and Collectivization

From the earliest days of Soviet power, Party leaders struggled to establish a stable balance between industrial and agricultural production. During the civil war, food detachments of workers and soldiers scoured the countryside for grain to feed the Red Army and the starving cities. With few consumer goods to trade for grain, they often forced peasants to relinquish their harvests at gunpoint. By the end of the civil war, peasants were refusing to give up their grain, reducing their sown areas, and rioting in protest, and Soviet power stood to lose its hard-won military victory to peasant hatred of the food detachments. In 1921, at Lenin's urging, the Party adopted the New Economic Policy (NEP) to address the peasants' concerns. Although NEP was highly successful in encouraging the peasants to increase their sowing and trading, the Party never fully trusted the market. The delicate balance of trade between town and countryside, between industrial and agricultural output, proved tricky to manage and maintain. Throughout the 1920s, leaders fiddled with the ratio of industrial to agricultural prices, seeking to establish an equilibrium that would yield decent wages for the urban working class, low-priced goods for the peasantry, and a stable food supply for the cities. Party leaders understood that working-class support depended on a steady supply of food, and that their own political fate rested on the well-being of the workers.

By the end of the 1920s, many Party leaders and economists recognized that the policies of NEP had reached an impasse. War damage to the existing industrial infrastructure had been repaired, but if production was to expand beyond its prewar level, capital was needed for new construction. Older existing plants and equipment were also worn out and in need of replacement. Constraints on the production of consumer goods created periodic "goods famines" throughout the 1920s. With limited industrial goods for which to trade their agricultural produce, peasants were reluctant to expand their efforts in production or marketing, preferring to either store or eat their surplus. Moreover, the small industrial base was unable to absorb the large numbers of peasants in need of supplemental waged work, and unemployment was a serious problem for workers and peasants alike. The Soviet leadership found it impossible now to obtain the foreign capital that had fueled industrial development before the revolution. The leader faced a serious economic dilemma.[5] In their view, the fate of the world's first socialist revolution hung in the balance. As pressure built, the Party split into a left and a right faction, led respectively by Evgeny Preobrazhensky and Nikolai Bukharin. Each advanced complex and opposing theoretical solutions to the twinned problems of agricultural and industrial development.

Preobrazhensky and Bukharin had initially held similar views of agriculture. In *The ABC of Communism,* an internationally popular primer that they coauthored in 1919, they shared a general commitment to large-scale communist farming on the grounds that it would "prove more productive" than individual peasant farms. Model farms staffed by trained experts and mechanics would, they believed, eventually transform Soviet farming by showing "the peasant the advantages of large-scale, collective agriculture." The two authors stressed, however, that the process should never involve force: it must be *gradual* and *voluntary,* based on education and material aid. In their words, there was "no other certain, speedy, and direct way of reaching the desired goal." Moreover, they agreed that collectivization was not on the immediate horizon; small-scale peasant farming would predominate "for a long time to come."[6]

By the late 1920s, Preobrazhensky and Bukharin had sharply diverged in their prescriptions if not in their goals. Preobrazhensky argued that by lowering the costs of industrial production, keeping the prices of consumer goods high, and setting the state price for agricultural goods relatively low, the state would be able to realize a "profit" from rural/urban exchange that could be applied to the further development of industry and the mechanization of agriculture. Bukharin strongly disagreed. Such a policy, in his view, would disrupt relations between town and country, alienate the peasantry, and re-create the tensions of the civil war years. He argued for a slower approach to capital accumulation based on increasing trade with the peasants through the production of more consumer goods. Yet before 1927, for all their differences, neither Preobrazhensky, representing the "Left" position in the Party, nor Bukharin, representing the "Right," saw mass collectivization as a solution to the state's need for capital. Both thought collectivization should be a gradual process premised on the introduction of scientific methods, mechanization, and skills. The Left in particular considered it pointless to pool peasants' meager holdings and

---

[5] Michal Reiman, *The Birth of Stalinism: The USSR on the Eve of the "Second Revolution"* (Bloomington, Ind.: Indiana University Press, 1987).

[6] Evgeny Preobrazhensky and Nikolai Bukharin, *The ABC of Communism: A Popular Explanation of the Program of the Communist Party of Russia* (Ann Arbor, Mich.: University of Michigan Press, 1966), 298, 302, 306, 311–12.

primitive implements in the absence of machinery to realize economies of scale. Moshe Lewin, the well-known historian of collectivization, notes that even the Left, which advocated a quicker tempo of industrialization, "had no intention of precipitating collectivization in the countryside. They had no overall plan."[7]

By 1928, the pressure on Party leaders began to increase. The 1928 harvest proved smaller than that of 1927, and there was a steady decrease in grain deliveries after November 1928. With each passing month, the Party leadership felt more anxious about its inability to control food supply and prices. Millions of small peasant producers, not the Party, controlled the grain market. A consequential but little-known crop failure led to famine in the Ukraine and decreased the availability of bread throughout the country. The disparity between state and free-market prices encouraged peasants to withhold grain from the state for future sale on the private market. According to Lewin, the promise of profits was so attractive that even peasants who were members of the Communist Party refused to sell to the state. As the free-market prices of grain and food began to rise, real wages began to fall, and worker unrest developed in the Donbas, Smolensk, and Ivanovo.[8] Grain supply became the most critical issue facing the Party. Working-class support, as well as means for capital investment, depended on the maintenance of a good supply of grain at low cost. Party leaders, terrified of worker dissatisfaction, took harsher measures in the countryside.

[7]   Moshe Lewin, *Russian Peasants and Soviet Power: A Study of Collectivization* (New York: W. W. Norton and Co., 1968), 152–53, 156. On the complex debates that emerged in the 1920s over industrialization, see Alexander Erlich, *The Soviet Industrialization Debate, 1924–1928* (Cambridge, Mass.: Harvard University Press, 1960). Historians have advanced a variety of explanations for collectivization, including the Bolsheviks' innate distrust of the peasantry, Stalin's personal predilection for violent solutions, and the defeat of Bukharin's views in the power struggles of the 1920s. These explanations are based largely on the internal politics of the Party and assume the leadership's firm ideological commitment to a well-defined concept of collectivization and its imposition at all costs. Social pressures, particularly workers' discontent over high food prices, have not received much attention. The linkage of agricultural policy with the needs of urban workers, however, places the Party's actions within a different context. From this vantage point, the Party's response to the peasantry in 1929 appears neither as a vicious, premeditated attack nor a well-planned effort to realize economies of scale. Collectivization, adopted in panic and implemented in haste, appears rather as a desperate solution to a perennial problem that the Party never fully mastered: how to provision the cities with food. See, for example, Robert Conquest, *The Harvest of Sorrow* (New York: Oxford University Press, 1986); Robert Tucker, "A New Stage in the Revolution," and Stephen Cohen, "The Moderate Alternative," in R. W. Daniels, ed., *The Stalin Revolution: Foundations of the Totalitarian State* (Toronto: D. C. Heath and Co., 1990). Moshe Lewin demonstrates the importance of contingency and improvisation in the decision to collectivize, and Michal Reiman emphasizes the relationship between high Party politics and the social and economic crises of the late NEP.

[8]   See, for example, Jeffrey Rossman on worker protest in the Ivanovo region, "Worker Resistance under Stalin: Class and Gender in the Textile Mills of the Ivanovo Industrial Region, 1928–1932" (Ph.D. diss., University of California, Berkeley, 1997).

In the winter of 1928–1929, the state began applying coercive meth-ods to extract grain from the Urals, Volga, and Siberian regions. Rykov, the chairman of SNK USSR (the Council of People's Commissars), told Siberian officials in January 1929, "Look at the scurvy in Pskov, the hunger in the Ukraine, and the shortages felt everywhere by workers. Yet you come and tell me that the figures for grain collection should not be raised."[9] Middle and prosperous peasants (*kulaks*) alike were threat-ened with fines for hoarding, punishment for "speculation," confiscation of their belongings, and imprisonment for refusing to deliver grain to the state. Yet such harsh methods did little but embitter the peasantry toward the Party. By the spring of 1929, the procurement campaign was 20 percent below the previous year. As frightened peasants decreased their sown areas, many Party leaders wearied of the uncertainties inherent in haggling with millions of small producers each season. They concluded that collectivization would solve the chronic problem of state procure-ments by reorganizing agriculture along industrial lines, increasing pro-ductivity through mechanization, and permitting the state greater control over production, procurement, and distribution. Stalin believed that the very future of socialism in the Soviet Union hung in the balance, depen-dent on the Bolsheviks' ability to deliver grain to the cities. He wrote privately to Molotov, "Grain procurement this year will provide the basis for everything we're doing – if we foul up here, everything will be wiped out."[10] Stalin began pushing hard to revise the original, more gradual plans for collectivization.

In June 1929, the Party stepped up its efforts to gain control of the grain supply by launching a campaign to collectivize. Over the summer, activists moved to collectivize entire areas through mass or *sploshnaia* collectivization. Party leaders began intense preparations for procure-ments in the fall, setting targets 50 percent higher than the previous year. Stalin insisted that even collective farms were hiding grain from the state in the hope of selling it more profitably on the free market. He called for the arrest and deportation of grain "speculators" and the prosecu-tion of state purchasers who engaged in competition.[11] Force produced results: despite a poorer harvest, the targets were met by December. Stalin

---

[9]   Quoted by Mark Tauger in "Grain Crisis or Famine? The Ukrainian State Commission for Aid to Crop Failure Victims and the Ukrainian Famine of 1928–1929," in Donald Raleigh, ed., *Provincial Landscapes: Local Dimensions of Soviet Power* (Pittsburgh: University of Pittsburgh Press, forthcoming). Tauger focuses on the little-known famine in the Ukraine in 1928, arguing that it helped push the Party toward collectivization.

[10] Lars Lih, Oleg Naumov, and Oleg Khlevniuk, eds., *Stalin's Letters to Molotov* (New Haven, Conn.: Yale University Press, 1995), 169. The editors argue that Stalin saw collectivization as a way of avoiding endless confrontations with the peasantry and the continuing use of emergency measures (p. 38).

[11] See Politburo decree, "On Grain Procurement," August 15, 1929, reprinted in Lih et al., eds., *Stalin's Letters to Molotov*, 166–67 and 165–66.

wrote privately, "If we can beat this grain thing, then we'll prevail in everything, both in domestic and [in] foreign policies." The state now fully embraced collectivization as a solution to the grain crisis.[12] In December, Stalin announced a new policy aimed at the "liquidation of the *kulaks* as a class." Chaos reigned in the countryside as peasants refused to enter the collective farms and slaughtered their livestock in protest. Thousands of *kulaks* and their families, along with middle peasants, were arrested and deported. The campaign to collectivize agriculture did not, however, solve the shortages of grain, vegetables, fruits, meats, and dairy products in the towns, cities, and industrial settlements. Prices in the free or private peasant markets rose precipitously, often doubling and tripling the cost of certain items. Collectivization, initially aimed at guaranteeing a stable grain supply, defusing workers' protests, and promoting a high rate of industrial investment, proved to be a dismal failure as agricultural production plummeted. Shortages haunted both urban and rural areas. Food prices, reflecting the chaos in the countryside, continued to rise. Peasants fled from the countryside to the towns, only to discover, along with workers, that the male wage was no longer sufficient to cover the basic food needs of a family.

Inflation and the Fall in Real Wages

By 1929, workers were experiencing a serious crisis in provisioning. Shortages led to rising prices, and real wages fell. The Party introduced bread rationing in February 1929 in an attempt to guarantee workers and their families food, to halt speculation, and to offset the declining purchasing power of the wage. In December 1930, the state created priority lists that provided higher rations for workers than for other segments of the population, including dependents. Rationing was gradually extended from bread to other items, including sugar, meat, butter, and tea. Although rationing ensured a basic minimum for workers, it did not address the problem of shortages. In many workers' cooperatives, there was simply nothing to buy, so workers were still forced to acquire much of their food

---

[12] Lih et al., eds., *Stalin's Letters to Molotov*, 175. This brief chronology of collectivization is drawn from Lewin, 371–507. See also Michal Reiman and R. W. Davies, *The Socialist Offensive: The Collectivization of Soviet Agriculture, 1929–1930* (Cambridge, Mass.: Harvard University Press, 1980); Lynne Viola, *Best Sons of the Fatherland: Workers in the Vanguard of Soviet Collectivization* (New York: Oxford University Press, 1987), and *Peasant Rebels under Stalin: Collectivization and the Culture of Peasant Resistance* (New York: Oxford University Press, 1999); Sheila Fitzpatrick, *Stalin's Peasants: Resistance and Survival in the Russian Village after Collectivization* (New York: Oxford University Press, 1994).

in private markets, where high prices severely undercut their wages.[13] Many women took jobs in an effort to switch their ration status from dependent to worker.

Planners initially aimed to *increase* real wages during the first five-year plan, based on a planned decrease in prices and an anticipated increase in the productivity of labor. VSNKh (Supreme Council of the National Economy) planners expected production to increase by 168 percent; other planners, even more optimistic, put the figure at 200 percent. Such projections called for labor productivity almost to double and for agricultural prices to fall relative to industrial prices. The state also intended to take over a larger share of the retail sector, thereby diminishing the role of private trade and its high prices. The Eighth Trade Union Congress pledged in January 1929 that average real wages for industrial workers would rise by 50 percent during the first five-year plan. It expected to see "yearly raises" and vowed to protect the wage by ensuring lower prices and market regulation.[14] VSNKh claimed that nominal wages would rise by 36 percent, and real wages by 56 percent. Workers would thus increase their purchasing power not simply by bringing home a bigger paycheck but also through substantial decreases in the cost of food and consumer goods. Each ruble earned would buy more than before. Prices, as represented by the budget index or market basket of food and goods required by an average family, were expected to decrease in 1928–1929 by 14 percent over the previous year. These gains would be passed along to the workers in the form of cheaper, better products and an increase in purchasing power.[15]

Throughout the spring and summer of 1929, planners pored over these statistics, fine-tuning an abstract equilibrium among the size of the labor force, the productivity of labor, production costs, and prices. One economist suggested as early as January 1929, however, that the increase projected by VSNKh for real wages was unrealistic. He noted that the budget index and retail prices for agricultural goods were not decreasing. If prices did not come down, workers' real wages would not increase by 50 percent unless VSNKh agreed to increase nominal wages at least 35 to 40 percent over their 1927–1928 level.[16] In other words, if the state did not start paying workers enough to cover the rise in prices, real wages would drop. By fall, this small warning had the ring of prophecy

[13] On the history and politics of rationing, see Elena Osokina, *Ierarkhiia potrebleniia. O zhizni liudei v usloviiakh stalinskogo snabzheniia, 1928–1935 gg.* (Moscow: Izdatel'stvo MGOU, 1993).
[14] "Rezoliutsiia VIII Vsesoiuznogo S"ezda Profsoiuzov," *Trud,* January 13, 1929, p. 3.
[15] Pavel Ioffe, "Osnovye Voprosy Truda v Kontrol'nykh Tsifrakh Piatiletnogo Promyshlennogo Plana," *Trud,* January 1, 1929, p. 2.
[16] Ibid.

as the situation assumed crisis proportions. The unplanned rise in prices made a mockery of the planners' aims to increase real wages during the first five-year plan. The abstract debate over productivity and prices was swept away in an unexpected hurricane of price increases. No amount of statistical tinkering could rescue the falling wage.

During the first two years of the five-year plan, both retail and wholesale prices rose. VSNKh planned a 3 percent drop in prices, but prices actually rose by 5 percent. According to the plan, state procurement prices, or the price paid by the state to the peasants for goods, were supposed to remain the same in 1928–1929 as in the previous year. In fact, the state was forced to increase prices considerably beyond the planned level in order to procure food (see Table 3.1). The increase in procurement prices was in turn passed along to urban consumers. The state paid a hefty 20 percent more for grain in 1928–1929 than it had the year before, and officials were anxious not to increase procurement prices for grain or animal products again in 1929–1930. Yet prices rose significantly again. The peasantry thus played havoc with the plan both in 1928–1929 and the following year. The attempt at mass collectivization in the summer and fall of 1929 only made matters worse: by 1929–1930, the price of butter and eggs had risen sharply, reflecting the mass slaughter of animals by peasants as a protest against collectivization and harsh procurement measures. Procurement prices for butter and eggs rose steeply during the first two years of the five-year plan, easily outstripping projections. In every area, the prices paid by the state were higher than planned: 9 percent higher for grain, 7 percent higher for meat, 20 percent for butter, and 44 percent for eggs. Consumer prices in the state sector rose as well, reflecting the increase in procurement prices.

Prices for consumers on the free market rose even more steeply. As the amount of available produce shrank, peasant sellers and middlemen ratcheted up the price of food. Between 1927–1928 and 1929–1930, the general price index rose 219.3 percent, bread prices rose 327.5 percent, vegetables 63.3 percent, meat 152.2 percent, and milk 138.5 percent. The highest price increases occurred in the East, in the Urals and Siberia, but prices also rose in the central districts. By 1930, cattle production had fallen 10 percent below the 1916 level, sheep production almost 15 percent, and pig production 40 percent. Overall, there was a greater than 70 percent reduction in the amount of meat for sale to consumers.[17] Increases in prices hit workers throughout the country, with the heaviest impact being felt in the Urals, Donbas, Kharkov, and Sverdlovsk industrial regions. Workers' daily diets suffered accordingly. They ate less flour, fish, meat, milk, butter, eggs, and fat. As meager compensation for the huge

---

[17] "Povyshenie Real'noi Zarplaty – Osnovnaia Zadacha Potrebkooperatsii," *Trud*, July 24, 1930, p. 2.

Table 3.1. *State procurement prices, planned and actual*

Type of goods	Planned prices			Actual prices		
	1928–1929 as percent of 1927–1928	1929–1930 as percent of 1928–1929	For two years of five-year plan	1928–1929 as percent of 1927–1928	1929–1930 as percent of 1928–1929	For two years of five-year plan
General index	107.4	100	107.4	111.2	103.3	114.9
Grain	114.0	100	114.0	119.6	103.0	123.2
Animal products:	102.1	100	102.1	107.2	105.5	113.1
Meat	100	100	100	103.0	103.7	106.8
Butter	108.0	100	108.0	116.9	109.7	128.2
Eggs	100	100	100	114.8	125.5	144.1

Source: A. Averbukh, "Tseny i Real'nye Dokhody Naseleniia," *Na planovom fronte*, 1930, nos. 15–16: 23.

reduction in protein, fat, and dairy products, they ate 3 percent more potatoes and vegetables and 50 percent more rye bread. Between 1929 and 1932, the consumption of meats, dairy, and fats dropped between 45 and 55 percent. Workers lived on dry rye bread and potatoes, a few seasonal vegetables (cabbage, onions, and carrots), and canned fish.[18] In Proletarian Labor, a wool spinning factory in Moscow, one woman worker complained, "They are decreasing the bread ration. They will not give out meat. They feed the workers on bony fish and send the ham to the Kremlin." Another declared, "The Bolsheviks have brought us to the point where soon everyone will croak from hunger." Many workers were hungry and malnourished. Riots, work stoppages, wildcat strikes, and grumbling convulsed factories everywhere. In some areas, workers' bodies were actually bloated from hunger. Party leaders received regular reports on workers' moods from informers inside the factories.[19] The situation in the cities served as a sharp and ever-present reminder of the need to control pricing and the food supply.

In September 1929, Veinberg, the secretary of VTsSPS (the All-Union Central Council of Trade Unions), spoke before a congress of planners about the "insufficient growth in real wages." He noted the great difficulties in supplying workers with vegetables, meat, and milk. VTsSPS received a steady stream of complaints from industrial settlements around the country about the lack of food.[20] Almost a year later, in May 1930, the plenum of VTsSPS acknowledged that there had been no improvement because the planned increase in real wages had never materialized.[21] In the summer of 1930, Party leaders announced that real wages had risen 39 percent *since 1913,* but they were silent about the wage record of the past two years.[22] Although they publicly touted this increase as an

---

[18]   GARF, f. 5515, o. 17, d. 185, "Srednemesiachnoe Priobretenie Produktov Pitaniia i Predmetov Shirokogo Potrebleniia Semeinymi Rabochim Promyshlennosti v Srednem na Dushu po SSSR," 29. In 1929–1930, workers consumed 17 percent less meat and suet, 14 percent less butter and eggs, and 18 percent less sugar than the previous year. They also ate less bread and margarine, substituting potatoes, fish, vegetables, and milk. Workers ate even more poorly in 1931. They consumed 12 percent less rye flour, 29 percent less wheat flour, 9 percent less wheat bread, 28 percent less meat, 49 percent less suet, 9 percent less fish, 22 percent less milk, 28 percent less butter, 58 percent less margarine, and 35 percent fewer eggs than they did in 1930. See A. Averbukh, "Tseny i Real'nye Dokhody Naseleniia," *Na planovom fronte,* 1930, nos. 15–16: 24, 26. For an extended discussion of the overall decrease in workers' living standards, see John Barber, "The Standard of Living of Soviet Industrial Workers, 1928–1941," unpublished paper.
[19]   GARF, f. 5451, o. 43, d. 13, "Signal'naia Svodka No. 3," 21; f. 5451, o. 43, d. 30, "V Sekretnuiu Chast' VTsSPS," 131.
[20]   "Kontrol'nye Tsifry Budut Vypolneny," *Trud,* September 27, 1929, p. 2.
[21]   "Mobilizovat' Sily na Bor'bu za Povyshenie Real'noi Zarplatu," *Trud,* May 18, 1930, p. 18.
[22]   "Zadachi Profsoiuzov v Rekonstruktivnyi Period," *Trud,* May 21, 1930, p. 1; "Zarabotnaia Plata ot XV do XVI S"ezda," *Trud,* July 10, 1930, p. 2.

achievement, the grim reduction in workers' consumption of all basic foodstuffs told a different tale. The budget index, or price of an average market basket, had increased by 126 percent over the index for 1913.[23]

It is difficult to determine how far real wages fell during the first five-year plan. Workers' budgets were based on a combination of rations, free-market and state-subsidized items, and heavily subsidized meals served in factories, schools, and other institutions. Solomon Shwarz has estimated that real wages fell 40 percent among all workers and 50 percent among industrial workers during the first five-year plan. Eugene Zaleski maintains that they fell more than 50 percent by 1932, continued to fall until 1934, and made a slow recovery between 1935 and 1938. Yet even in 1937, the official Soviet estimate placed real wages at only 66 percent of their 1928 level. According to Shwarz, living standards could not have dropped any further after 1931 without causing "a complete disintegration of economic life."[24]

In April 1929, Party leaders removed Tomsky as head of the trade unions and denounced "rightists" within the Party and the unions. The new task of the unions and the press was to "face toward production." Journalists, union leaders, and planners did not publicly calculate how far real wages had fallen, though they referred elliptically to "extreme strains in provisioning," "insufficient growth," "shortcomings or gaps [*proryvy*] in the plan," and "unhealthy moods among the workers due to the lack of food." They noted that "class sabotage by *kulaks* had a negative impact on real wages."[25] Strievsky, a union official, told Moscow unionists in September 1929 that real wages had "not grown" that year, especially in relation to food prices. He delicately suggested that real wages might rise if the state would lower prices to 1927 levels.[26] He implied, in other words, that the state should absorb the high cost of agricultural produce and not pass it on to urban consumers. Although Strievsky did not explicitly mention a decrease in real wages, his pointed reference to

[23] "Povyshenie Real'noi Zarplaty – v Opasnosti," *Trud*, May 28, 1930, p. 4.
[24] Solomon Shwarz, *Labor in the Soviet Union* (New York: Praeger, 1951), 139–64; Janet Chapman, *Real Wages in Soviet Russia since 1928* (Cambridge, Mass.: Harvard University Press, 1963); Zaleski, *Planning for Economic Growth in the Soviet Union*, 392; R. W. Davies, *The Soviet Economy in Turmoil*, 304–9. Sarah Davies, *Popular Opinion in Stalin's Russia: Terror, Propaganda, and Dissent, 1934–1941* (Cambridge: Cambridge University Press, 1997), discusses the reaction of workers to the fall in living standards on pp. 23–48.
[25] See, for example, "Rezoliutsiia VIII Vsesoiuznogo S"ezda Profsoiuzov," *Trud*, January 13, 1929, p. 3; "Kontrol'nye Tsifry Budut Vypolneny," *Trud*, September 27, 1929, p. 2; "Sotsialisticheskoe Stroitel'stvo i Zadachi Profsoiuzov," *Trud*, November 24, 1929, p. 2; V. Bunimovich, "Piatletka i Real'nyi Uroven' Zarplaty," *Na planovom fronte*, 1930, no. 7: 24; A. Averbukh, "Tseny i Real'nye Dokhody Naseleniia," *Na planovom fronte*, 1930, nos. 15–16: 27.
[26] "Ocherednye Zadachi Profsoiuzov Moskovskoi Oblasti," *Trud*, September 7, 1929, p. 5.

1927 (when prices had been cut by 10 percent) suggested that the steep price increases of the past two years had painfully reduced workers' living standards. Prices continued to rise through the fall of 1929 both in state cooperative stores and on the private market. In December, Gosplan (the State Planning Commission) boldly announced, with the endorsement of the Central Committee, that real wages would rise by 12 percent in 1930. Union leaders did not speak out directly on behalf of the workers, but they tried to call attention to the gap between promise and reality. In the early spring of 1930, VTsSPS organized fifty thousand workers into brigades and charged them with canvassing the country to verify Gosplan's planned increase. The verdict: it had "come to naught." In May, VTsSPS conceded that "real wages have remained at last year's level": there had been no increase.[27] Planners acknowledged that any increase in real wages depended on price stabilization.[28]

Socializing Retail Trade

Although the food crisis was itself the product of a harsh approach to procurements, it paradoxically made it almost impossible to go back to the freer policies of NEP. Once force had created fear and uncertainty among the peasants, a return to private farming and marketing threatened even greater shortages. Yet if the Party was to retain its working-class support, it had to halt the fall in living standards. Several strategies were possible. G. L. Piatakov, the chairman of Gosbank, proposed that the state import more raw materials for consumer goods, increase output overall, and stop exports of butter, eggs, meat, and other foods.[29] Several union officials alluded to the possibility of printing more money and raising nominal wages to cover the rising cost of food. Although these leaders had opposed the course advocated earlier by Bukharin, their suggestions were strongly reminiscent of the program offered by the "Right opposition." Stalin rejected them. Importing consumer goods and curtailing exports would have depleted the capital available for industrialization, while raising nominal wages would have channeled money through the workers into the hands of private traders and market-oriented peasants, strengthening the very groups the Party was seeking to control. The Commissariat of

[27] "Direktivy o Povyshenii Real'noi Zarplaty ne Vypolniaiutsia," *Trud*, March 15, 1930, p. 3; "V Bor'be za Real'nuiu Zarplatu Nuzhny Novye Tempy," *Trud*, March 5, 1930, p. 1; "Mobilizovat' Sily na Bor'bu za Povyshenie Real'noi Zarplatu," *Trud*, May 18, 1930, p. 1.

[28] "Direktiva o Povyshenii Real'noi Zarabotnoi Platy Dolzhna Byt' Polnost'iu Osushchestvlena," *Trud*, December 13, 1929, p. 1; "Real'naia Zarplata – v Tsentr Vnimaniia," *Trud*, December 15, 1929, p. 1.

[29] Lih et al., eds., *Stalin's Letters to Molotov*, 188–89.

Labor (NKT) stressed that real wages could not be increased "simply by raising nominal wages"; *prices* had to come down. The leadership identified prices as the key to stabilizing living standards and the wage.

Yet as long as prices reflected free-market supply, they would remain high. If the state was to keep prices artificially low, the free market had to be drastically curtailed. In the fall of 1929, the Party concluded that the key to lowering prices was "squeezing out the private trader." In the words of one planner, who called for the socialized sector to meet 95 percent of workers' needs by 1930, workers' standard of living "had to be freed from the private sector."[30] The state struggled to get control over prices by expanding the state system of provisioning, narrowing the free market, and eliminating the private trader and "speculator." Yet this countermove quickly spawned a host of new difficulties as the state tried to replace a lively, well-entrenched system of private trade with its own inadequate and poorly organized retail apparatus. The hasty attempt to substitute state cooperatives for private trade led to further chaos and disruption. The new cooperative stores were badly organized: glutted with some goods and desperately short of others, they exacerbated shortages, created long lines, and promoted abuses in the state sector. Many goods were permanently *"defisit,"* and cooperative workers as well as consumers were strongly tempted to divert state goods to private markets and bazaars for resale at steeper prices. The Party's attempt to stamp out private trade and to dominate the retail sector served, at least in the short run, to intensify rather than alleviate the crisis.

The difference between state and private prices was considerable and steadily widening. In 1927–1928, there was a 23 percent difference in the price of agricultural goods; in 1928–1929, the difference was 55 percent, and in 1929–1930, it was 99 percent. That is to say, by 1930, prices in the private market were double those in the state stores. Private traders not only charged higher prices but also controlled a considerable portion of the retail trade. In 1928–1930, workers bought approximately one quarter of their food on the private market.[31] They purchased more than half of their potatoes and milk, almost one quarter of their butter, 18 percent of their vegetables, 16 percent of their eggs, and 14 percent of their meat and suet from private traders and got their bread, margarine, and fish from the state. In some cities the private-market percentages were even greater.[32] In the industrial towns, private traders provided workers with

[30] "Real'naia Zarplata i Smotr Rabochii Kooperatsii," *Trud,* December 22, 1929, p. 1; "Bor'ba za Real'naiu Zarabotnaiu Zarplatu," *Trud,* April 13, 1930, p. 3.
[31] V. Bunimovich, "Piatiletka i Real'nyi Uroven' Zarplaty," *Na planovom fronte,* 1930, no. 7: 24–25.
[32] GARF, f. 5515, o. 17, d. 185, "Protsent Priobreteniia v Chastnoi Torgovli Semeinymi Rabochimi Promyshlennosti Otdel'nykh Produktov Pitaniia i Predmetov Shirokogo Potrebleniia s Srednem po SSSR v 1930," 32.

50 to 60 percent of their flour and 50 to 90 percent of their vegetables and dairy products.[33] The Party dubbed private traders "speculators," "*kulaks,*" and "privateers" and targeted them as the main culprits behind the fall of real wages. Planners and trade-union leaders publicly concurred: the only way to raise real wages was to wipe out private trade and expand the socialized sector.[34]

Stamping out the stubborn, ubiquitous impulse to turn shortage into profit, however, proved almost as difficult as creating a network of clean, efficient, low-priced, and well-stocked state stores. The cooperatives experienced a myriad of problems, beginning with the lack of an efficient distribution network that could match supply with demand. In the Ukraine, potatoes were so scarce in some areas that they cost more than the highest-quality fruit. In Kharkov, people stood in line for more than four hours to buy potatoes, while nearby, mountains of potatoes rotted in railroad cars. Shortages provoked grumbling, long lines, even riots. Workers' wives lined up all day and all night to buy apples in Grishin; they brought along pillows and blankets and slept in the streets.[35] Most cooperative stores did not sell bread, and people were forced to line up for hours at a few distribution points. In Stalingrad, the cooperatives had nothing at all to sell because only a fraction of their delivery contracts were fulfilled. Suppliers offered helpless excuses about "objective conditions" in the countryside, and desperate workers banded together in a "self-supply system" to scour the countryside for food. In Samara, where basic food prices increased faster than anywhere else, food shortages created a riot among workers on the eve of the October Revolution holiday. After rumors circulated that no potatoes would be given out following the holiday, people thronged to the state stores to stock up. As workers waited in lines all night to get their potatoes, union leaders fretted that they would not appear the next day for the demonstration. The potatoes turned out to be useless for cooking – mere eyes, tiny, no more than a centimeter in diameter – and there were no other vegetables to be had in the entire city. In Astrakhan, the budget index for food jumped 50 percent between 1928 and 1929. There were sharp price increases in the cooperatives as well. Astrakhan, the "fish capital" of the country, had no fish. Here, too, trouble threatened on the eve of the October holidays, when workers were unable to buy bread because they were busy standing in line to receive new ration books. In the Donbas, an "entire catalog of cooperative plagues" thrived, including "bungling, confusion, abuse, and

---

[33]   "Real'naia Zarplata – V Tsentr Vnimaniia," *Trud*, December 15, 1929, p. 1.

[34]   V. Bunimovich, "Obespechit' Real'nuiu Zarabotnuiu Platu," *Na planovom fronte*, 1930, no. 2: 21–24; "Profsoiuzy i Kontrol'nye Tsifry na 1929–1930 god.," *Trud*, August 30, 1929, p. 1.

[35]   "V Poloborota i Potrebiteliu," *Trud*, September 7, 1929, p. 7.

rude, vulgar treatment of customers." In Stalino, the "miners' capital," the stores were relatively well provisioned but so few and far between that workers on the Don River side had to travel to a neighboring town to buy even a spool of thread. The lines to enter the tiny stores in workers' settlements were "unimaginable," "a daily, constant phenomenon." Whole shops of women left the factories at once to stand in line. Sales clerks were rude and offensive. After one cooperative advertised that thread would be available the next day, people stood in line all night; when the store opened, three hundred people were waiting at the door. The clerks posted a small announcement that no thread was available, and the crowd dispersed, cursing. Three hours later, the store began selling thread.[36]

Under conditions of deprivation and shortage, everyone became a "speculator." The high prices commanded by goods outside the state sector prompted sellers and buyers alike to resort to the market for resale at inflated prices. Cooperative employees devised a variety of ingenious scams. They recycled or resold the ration coupons they received from customers, intensifying demand for a limited stock of goods. They diverted food for resale on the private market and hid the losses by manipulating the number of coupons, which served as receipts. They sold goods to customers without coupons and pocketed the money. They substituted low- for high-quality items, sold merchandise at fantastic prices, and skimmed stock for their own use or for resale. They even developed connections with private traders, the very scourge the cooperative movement aimed to eliminate. Often a fresh shipment to the cooperative was barely unloaded before it turned up for sale on the private market. All of these scams profited individuals but led, in turn, to ever-greater shortages by further reducing the stock of goods available to consumers at affordable prices.[37]

Shortages summoned private traders as if by magic, calling forth the very creatures who created greater shortages. Such traders thrived on shortages, stepping in when goods could not be obtained through government orders and even facilitating trade between one state agency and another. They procured rare items such as varnish, paint, soap, glass, and dye from state factories and sold them back to state agencies, albeit at markups of up to 2,000 percent. In the pharmaceutical trade, they

---

[36] "Vrediteli Real'noi Zarabotnoi Zarplaty," "Ovoshchnaia Partizanshchina," and "Revoliutsii ne Pomogut!," in *Trud*, December 5, 1929, p. 3; "Na Bor'bu za Povyshenie Real'noi Zarplaty Vmeste s Brigadami VTsSPS Vystupaiut Massy," *Trud*, January 12, 1930, p. 2; "Rabochee Snabzhenie – Osnova Povysheniia Real'noi Zarplaty," *Trud*, March 17, 1930, p. 3; "Povyshenie Real'noi Zarplaty," *Trud*, February 7, 1930, p. 4.

[37] "Na Bor'bu za Real'naia Zarplata," *Trud*, January 8, 1930, p. 2; "Povyshenie Real'noi Zarplaty," *Trud*, February 7, 1930, p. 4.

sold medicine to regions that lacked state stores. Shortages and poverty transformed people of every social class into potential traders who grimly calculated the resale value of every commodity on the private market. Even workers turned into "speculators" at the prospect of earning a few rubles. Hungry workers scammed to get milk for overage "children" and continued to use the coupons of dead family members to acquire food. When a large shipment of felt boots (*valenki*) appeared in the cooperative stores at nine rubles a pair, an "aggressive, loud, violent" mob of workers stormed the stores. By evening, not a single pair of boots was left. The next morning, however, a full assortment appeared for resale in the bazaar at twenty rubles a pair, a 122 percent markup by workers desperate to supplement their wages.[38]

The food situation in urban areas became so dire that the Party launched a policy to produce food within the cities. The press began a noisy campaign to encourage workers to plant vegetable gardens outside the towns. VTsSPS suggested that gardens around the industrial centers could cover 80 percent of workers' food needs; when workers in Dnepropetrovsk complained about food shortages to Shvernik, the head of VTsSPS, he urged them to plant cucumbers and cabbage and pickle their own produce. "Stop waiting for food to be delivered to you," he told the members of the local unions, the factory committees, and the town soviet. The new watchword was industrial self-sufficiency, but "industrial kitchen gardens" were not particularly successful. After working all day, workers, unionists, and cooperative-store clerks were singularly unenthusiastic about having to grow their own food. Cooperative leaders initially refused, announcing, "We are not in the business of creating suburban farms." The campaign soon deteriorated into petty municipal quarrels over garden-plot allotments. In Vladimir, the town soviet, the department of communal services, the communal trust, the land administration, the cooperatives, the local state farm, the collective of unemployed, and even the managers of the town jail argued heatedly over land assignments, and "as a result, not a single organization did any practical work." Moreover, the kitchen gardens replicated the problems of the collective farms: no one knew where to plant, monies did not materialize, and there were no seeds. Urban workers were placed in the absurd position of having to beg their local state and collective farms for the seeds and tools they needed to grow their own food. But it appeared that there were no seeds to be had, even at the local state farms. By the end of May 1930, only 25 percent of the land that had been earmarked around the industrial centers for

---

[38] "Na Bor'bu za Povyshenie Real'noi Zarplaty Vmeste s Brigadami VTsSPS Vystupaiut Massy," *Trud*, January 12, 1930, p. 2; "Sistema Raspredeleniia Tovarov i Real'naia Zarplata Rabochikh," *Trud*, January 19, 1930, p. 2; "Chastnik Zhivuch, Potomu Chto Zhivuchi Blagodetali," *Trud*, January 14, 1930, p. 4.

kitchen gardens had been assigned to specific organizations, and even less was under cultivation.[39]

The Party meanwhile blamed the food shortages on cooperative employees – "foreign people, bureaucrats, and dealers" – and urged a "militant purge" of the co-ops.[40] The unions, prohibited from agitating for nominal increases, a strategy anathematized as "narrow shop and trade-unionist tendencies," were instead deployed to stabilize real wages by monitoring price trends in the cooperative stores.[41] The unions organized thousands of workers throughout the country into brigades to check prices, uncover abuses, and guarantee supplies. Cooperatives in Saratov, for example, had raised meat prices 760 percent. Another cooperative bought a shipment of tomatoes for 291 rubles and sold it for 1,162 rubles. There were similar markups on potatoes, apples, and fruit. In Leningrad, cooperative employees marked up goods whenever they were moved from one counter to another. The attempt to control retail prices by driving out "speculators" (a loose category that embraced peasants, middlemen, cooperative employees, and even state purchasing agents and collective-farm directors) quickly deteriorated into arrests, show trials, and violence. Stalin instructed Molotov to purge the finance and Gosbank bureaucracies, to "definitely shoot two or three dozen wreckers from these *apparaty,* including several dozen common cashiers," and to execute "a whole group of wreckers in the meat industry." In September, OGPU (the Political Police) discovered a wrecking organization in food supply aimed at creating "hunger in the country." Forty-eight "wreckers" were shot to serve as an example to others.[42] Yet under conditions of extreme shortage, even capital punishment was not a sufficient deterrent to scam, diversions, and trade. And honesty at the retail counter could not create food from scarcity.

As prices rose and the value of the wage plummeted, women in urban and working-class families began searching for jobs to offset their falling standard of living. NKT planners officially explained women's decisions "primarily as a display of their desire for industrialization" and "their

39 "Sotsialisticheskoe Stroitel'stvo i Zadachi Profsoiuzov," *Trud*, November 24, 1929, p. 2; "V Bor'be za Real'nuiu Zarplatu Nuzhny Novye Tempy," *Trud*, March 5, 1930, p. 1; "Povyshenie Real'noi Zarplaty – v Opasnosti," *Trud*, May 28, 1930, p. 4; "Rabochie Tsentry – v Kol'sto Ogorodov," *Trud*, March 15, 1930, p. 3; "Mobilizovat' Sily na Bor'bu za Povyshenie Real'noi Zarplaty," *Trud*, May 18, 1930, p. 1.
40 "Povyshenie Real'noi Zarplaty," *Trud*, February 7, 1930, p. 4.
41 Zadachi Profsoiuzov v Period Rekonstruktsii," *Trud*, November 23, 1929, p. 2; "O Merakh po Obespecheniiu Real'noi Zarplaty. Tsirkuliar NKT SSSR," *Trud*, January 9, 1930, p. 4; V. Bunimovich, "Obespechit' Real'nuiu Zarabotnuiu Platu," *Na planovom fronte,* 1930, no. 2: 23; "Bystrei i Reshitel'nei Dobyvat'sia Povysheniia Real'noi Zarplatnoi Platy," *Trud*, January 15, 1930, p. 1.
42 Lih et al., eds., *Stalin's Letters to Molotov,* 200, 193–194. See *Trud*, September 22 and 25, 1930.

aim to be included directly in general socialist construction."[43] While many women may have been drawn by a desire to build socialism, they were also pushed by a crisis in urban food supply – a crisis created by harsh methods of grain procurement in the countryside. By 1928, workers and peasants alike were swept up in a whirling vortex of policy and consequence. Decreasing harvests led to growing shortages and urban unrest. Panicked Party leaders took emergency measures in the countryside, which in turn frightened peasants into decreasing production and marketing. As economic problems reached a crisis point, many Party leaders were convinced of the need to take control of agricultural production and pricing. The hasty attempt to collectivize and to eliminate private trade, however, only exacerbated the crisis. As prices rose and real wages fell, women entered the workforce in an attempt to maintain their families' standard of living through access to wages and higher rations. The wife of a sewing worker, for example, received a ration of only one hundred grams of bread, which, in the words of one husband, was tantamount to "slow death."[44] A family with children or dependent elderly could not live on one wage alone. Women began streaming into the workforce almost a full year before the Party targeted them as a key reserve of labor in the late fall of 1930. Food shortages, high prices, and hunger, only later boosted by a strong ideological campaign to involve women, gave the new Soviet working class its unique gender composition.

Women and the Composition of the New Working Class

Party leaders and planners initially lacked any comprehensive statistical knowledge of the transformation in the labor force. By the summer of 1930, they realized that certain sectors of the economy were desperately short of workers, but the reports fired off by the frantic managers of construction sites and factories were fragmentary and provided inadequate data from which to develop an overall picture of the economy. Neither Gosplan nor VSNKh had proved accurate in plotting or predicting the growth or composition of the labor force. The statistical projections of the five-year plan had underestimated the changes in size. In January 1929, VSNKh had estimated that the number of women workers in industry would increase by 793,000 during the first five-year plan. This figure, when matched against the actual increase of 1,268,000, was well

---

[43] GARF, f. 5515, o. 13, d. 18, "Ob'iasnitel'nye Zapiski o Plane Zhenskogo Truda v 1932," 7.
[44] GARF, f. 5451, o. 43, d. 30, "V Sekretnuiu Chast'," 131.

Table 3.2. *Workers and* sluzhashchie *(white-collar employees) in the national economy, 1929–1933 (January 1)*

Year	Total workers	Number of men	Number of women	Percentage women
1929	11,873,000	N/A	N/A	N/A
1930	13,333,800	9,743,300	3,590,500	26.9
1931	15,602,200	11,405,200	4,197,000	26.9
1932	21,923,400	15,916,400	6,007,000	27.4
1933	22,649,200	15,741,200	6,908,000	30.5

Source: *Zhenshchina v SSSR. Statisticheskii shornik* (Moscow: Soiuzorguchet, TsUNKhU, 1937), 51.[46]

off target.[45] The Party did not address the magnitude of the transformation until the fall of 1930, when it finally decreed the end of unemployment, pushed NKT into active recruiting, and launched a campaign to pull 1.6 million women into the labor force. By this time, however, the transformation of the working class, in terms of its size, age, experience, and gender composition, was already well under way.

During the first five-year plan (1929–1932), almost 10.8 million people entered the waged labor force (Table 3.2). The number of waged workers and employees almost doubled, from 11.9 million in 1929 to 22.6 million in 1933. As the economy expanded, the number of women in the workforce grew more rapidly than the number of men, but women's share of all jobs did not begin to increase until 1932.

Table 3.3 shows the number of workers entering the economy each year. The largest increase, 8.6 million, occurred in 1930 and 1931. Over 600,000 women entered the labor force in 1930, followed by 1.8 million in 1931 and 900,000 in 1932. After 1930, women figured ever more prominently among incoming workers. In 1932, men left the labor force as women entered; 100 percent of incoming workers were women.

During the first five-year plan, almost every sector of the economy expanded rapidly. Between 1929 and 1933, the number of workers employed in industry, the largest sector, more than doubled, as did the number in

[45] For VSNKh's prediction, see GARF, f. 6983, o. 1, d. 159, "Materialy 5 Letnemu Planu Zhenskogo Truda," 79. For the actual number, see table 3.5.

[46] These figures are identical to those on *Trud v SSSR. Statisticheskii spravochnik* (Moscow: TsUNkhU Gosplana, 1936), 25. In both sources, the figures for 1929 and 1930 are annual averages, while those for the remaining years are numbers as of January 1. To derive a January 1 figure for 1929 and 1930, I added the annual average for the given year and the previous year and divided by 2. This permitted a more precise calculation of the yearly increase in workers. I am indebted to R. W. Davies for this suggestion. The annual average for 1929 for all workers was 12,147,000, and for 1930, 14,520,600.

Table 3.3. *Workers and* sluzhashchie *entering the
national economy, 1929–1932*

Year	Total	Number of men	Number of women	Percentage women
1929	1,460,800	N/A	N/A	N/A
1930	2,268,400	1,661,900	606,500	26.7
1931	6,321,200	4,511,200	1,810,000	28.6
1932	725,800	−175,200	901,000	100.0

Source: Derived from table 3.2. No breakdown by sex is available
for 1929 due to the inability to calculate January 1 figures.

transport. Other sectors grew even more rapidly: the number of workers increased more than threefold in construction and communications
and more than ninefold in socialized, or public, dining. Every sector of
the national economy increased its labor force, with the exception of
small industry and domestic service/day labor. In 1929, the largest number of waged workers were employed in industry, followed by agriculture,
transport, state administration, construction, enlightenment, and domestic service/day labor. By the end of the first five-year plan, in 1932, the
overall distribution of the waged labor force had shifted to reflect the great
building projects then under way. Industry and agriculture remained the
largest employers, followed by construction, transport, state administration, and trade. Among the more striking changes were the growth of the
retail trade sector and the decline of domestic service and day labor. As the
state curtailed private trade and assumed greater control of distribution,
it employed increasing numbers of workers, including many women, to
staff its cooperative and state stores. The numbers employed in domestic
service and day labor, once important sources of wages for women and
poor peasants, shrank as servants found better jobs in other sectors and
peasants in rural areas moved into collective and state farms.[47]

For women, the shifts in the economy between 1929 and 1933 were
even more dramatic (see Table 3.4). Industry remained the largest employer of women but increased its share from 28.4 percent of all working
women in 1929 to 32 percent in January 1933. The number of women rose
in every sector, with the exception of domestic service/day labor, which lost
248,000 women. Domestic service, the second-largest employer of women
in 1929, had steadily shrunk to become the smallest by 1933, when it
employed a mere 3 percent of women. The second-largest employer of

[47] "Dinamika Sredne-Godovoi Chislennosti Rabochikh i Sluzhashchikh po Otrasliam
Narodnogo Khoziaistva," "Srednaia Godovaia Chislennost' Rabochikh i Sluzhashchikh
po Otrasliam Narodnogo Khoziaistva za 1923/24–1935 gg.," *Trud v SSSR*, 12–13,
10–11.

Table 3.4. *Women in the main branches of the national economy,*
1929–1932

Sector	1929	1930	1931	1932	1933
Industry	939,000	1,236,000	1,440,000	2,043,000	2,207,000
Construction	64,000	156,000	189,000	380,000	437,000
Agriculture	441,000	425,000	221,000	394,000	508,000
Transport	104,000	146,000	173,000	243,000	322,000
Trade	97,000	179,000	233,000	374,000	432,000
Socialized dining	37,000	100,000	172,000	301,000	354,000
Enlightenment	439,000	482,000	514,000	692,000	790,000
Health	283,000	320,000	358,000	426,000	466,000
State administration	239,000	332,000	373,000	475,000	510,000
Domestic service/day labor	527,000	312,000	283,000	279,000	241,000
Total	3,304,000	3,877,000	4,197,000	6,007,000	6,908,000

Source: "Chislennost' Zhenshchin po Otrasliam Narodnogo Khoziaistva v 1929–1935 gg,"
Trud v SSSR, 25. Data for 1929 and 1930 are given as the annual average, while data for
1931–1933 are as of January 1. This accounts for the differences between figures in Tables
3.2 and 3.4 for total female employment in 1929 and 1930. Table 3.4 includes all employees
in each sector, not just workers.

women in 1933 was enlightenment, a sector encompassing education, day
care, and social services. Agriculture was replaced by state administration
as the third-largest employer. Construction employed a greater share of
all working women, expanding from 2 to 6 percent, as did trade (from 3
to 6 percent).

How did women's employment patterns during the expansion of the
first five-year plan compare with those of men? Did men and women
entering the labor force follow roughly the same trajectories? Table 3.5
shows the sectors of the economy that incoming workers, both men and
women, entered between 1929 and 1933. Comparing men and women,
we see that more men entered the waged labor force: 5.5 million men, as
against 3 million women.[48] Of these new wage earners, a greater percentage of women than of men entered industry: 40.9 percent compared to
31.8 percent. Incoming women workers thus contributed a larger share
of their number to the making of the industrial proletariat, the group
most extolled in Soviet society. The largest group of workers, among men
and women, entered industry, and the second-largest, construction. The
employment patterns here were the same. Yet after these two largest employers, the patterns of incoming men and women diverged. A much larger
group of men than of women entered transport (the third-largest draw
for men), while women took more white-collar jobs in enlightenment,

[48] These figures cover men and women who entered the main sectors of the economy shown
in table 3.5. The actual numbers of incoming workers in all sectors was 10.7 million.

Table 3.5. *Distribution of workers entering the national economy (by gender and sector), 1929–1933*

Sector	Number of men entering	Percentage of all men entering the labor force	Number of women entering	Percentage of all women entering the labor force
Industry	1,764,000	31.8	1,268,000	40.9
Construction	1,444,000	26.0	373,000	12.0
Agriculture	457,000	8.2	67,000	2.1
Transport	815,000	14.7	218,000	7.0
Trade	437,000	7.8	335,000	10.8
Socialized dining	140,000	2.5	317,000	10.2
Enlightenment	248,000	4.4	351,000	11.3
Health	37,000	0.6	183,000	5.9
State administration	299,000	5.3	271,000	8.7
Domestic service/day labor	−102,000	−1.8	−286,000	−9.2
Total	5,539,000	99.5	3,097,000	99.7

Source: Figures for incoming workers have been calculated on the basis of "Chislennost' Zhenshchin po Otrasliam Narodnogo Khoziaistva v 1929–1935 gg.," *Trud v SSSR. Statisticheskii spravochnik* (Moscow: TsUNKhU Gosplana, 1936), 25, using the annual average figures for 1929 and January 1 figures for 1933. Although these are the main sectors of the economy, they do not cover all incoming workers.

socialized dining, and trade. Only 14.7 percent of men entered these sectors, in contrast to 32.3 percent of women. Both sexes fled day labor and domestic service. Overall, the deployment of large numbers of new workers undercut older lines of gender segregation even as it established new ones. The new influx of women during the first five-year plan began to feminize sectors such as socialized dining, enlightenment, health, and state administration, but it also created a more even balance between the sexes in industry and construction.

Women in Industry

The first five-year plan initially had only a modest impact on work opportunities for women. In fact, despite overall economic growth, unemployment among women actually increased. One labor analyst, B. Marsheva, critical of the five-year plan's effect on women, noted that women were moving into the labor force "at a snail's pace." The number of women entering industry in 1929 did not increase significantly over the number for the previous year, and between 1929 and 1930, women's share of industry in fact decreased slightly. Marsheva explained that this "impermissible drop" was the result of women's "weak involvement in heavy industry."[49] As the state shifted more resources to the development of heavy industry, women's share of industrial jobs shrank. Women industrial workers were also hurt by contractions in the cotton industry, which lost 115,400 workers (58,600 of whom were women) between 1929 and 1931, and in the food industry.[50] These contractions in industries with a strong female presence added to the stubborn level of unemployment among women. Women also lost jobs in the tobacco industry, prompting some critics to charge that managers were purposely forcing women out of production in certain male-dominated shops.[51]

Many women's activists were disappointed at first with the five-year plan, the high level of female unemployment, and women's decreasing share of industrial jobs. A report issued in April 1930 by the Women's Inspectorate, a short-lived attempt within NKT to monitor conditions for women in the factories, revealed that despite efforts to strengthen women's participation in industry, progress remained "insufficient." The inspectors referred once again to women's lack of skills, but they also indicated that "the sluggishness of the economic organs and the technical personnel in the enterprises, coupled with a negative attitude toward female labor," were critical factors. The report noted that managers and foremen deliberately placed women on malfunctioning machines, paid them lower wages than men working in the same jobs, denied them entrance into apprenticeships that would train them for skilled work, refused to hire them if they were pregnant, and threatened them with criminal sanctions if they concealed pregnancies.[52] VTsSPS attributed women's slow absorption into industry to "existing prejudices of the economic organs against female labor."[53]

Yet the fears of the women's activists proved unfounded. The number of women in industry increased dramatically in 1930 and 1931 (Tables 3.6 and 3.7 show the growth of industrial workers). During the first five-year plan, 2.3 million workers entered industry, 1.3 million of them men and 1 million women. In 1930, the number of women in industry increased by almost one third. Almost five times as many women workers entered

---

[49] B. Marsheva, "Zhenskii Trud v 1931 godu," *Voprosy truda*, 1931, no. 1: 32, 33.
[50] *Trud v SSSR*, 184, 230. The food industry also laid off 30,300 workers between 1929 and 1930, 6,300 of whom were women.
[51] F. Vinnik, "Bezrabotnitsa Sredi Zhenshchin u Pishchevikov," *Voprosy truda*, 1929, no. 2: 119–21. Vinnik concludes that these charges were not true.
[52] GARF, f. 6983, o. 1, d. 159, "O Rabote Zheninspektorov," 342 ob. On Soviet maternity legislation, see Melanie Ilic, *Women Workers in the Soviet Interwar Economy: From "Protection" to "Equality"* (London: Macmillan, 1999), 57–77. Similar problems existed in Cuba due to generous maternity benefits; see Lois Smith and Alfred Padua, *Sex and Revolution: Women in Socialist Cuba* (New York: Oxford University Press, 1996), 127.
[53] GARF, f. 5451, o. 15, d. 362, "Tezisy k Dokladu o Vovlechenii Zhenskogo Truda v Narodnoe Khoziaistvo v 1931," 118. See *Trud v SSSR*, 106, 142, for figures.

Table 3.6. *Workers in large-scale industry, 1928–1932 (January 1)*

Year	All workers	Men	Women	Percentage women
1928	2,531,900	1,806,000	725,900	28.6
1929	2,788,700	1,984,700	804,000	28.8
1930	3,116,200	2,231,200	885,000	28.4
1931	4,256,400	2,984,900	1,271,500	29.8
1932	5,271,300	3,535,900	1,735,400	32.9
1933	5,139,700	3,313,500	1,826,200	35.5

Source: "Chislennost' Personala na 1 Ianvaria 1923–1936 gg.," *Trud v SSSR*, 91. These numbers include workers and apprentices only.

Table 3.7. *Workers entering large-scale industry, 1928–1932*

Year	Total	Men	Women	Percentage women
1928	256,800	178,700	78,100	30.4
1929	327,500	246,500	81,000	24.7
1930	1,140,200	753,700	386,500	33.8
1931	1,014,900	551,000	463,900	45.7
1932	−131,600	−222,400	90,800	100

Source: Derived from "Chislennost' Personala na 1 Ianvaria 1923–1933 gg.," *Trud v SSSR*, 91. Workers and apprentices only are included here.

industry in 1930 as in 1929. Women also constituted a growing share of industrial workers, from 28.6 to 35.5 percent between 1928 and 1933.

Women figured even more prominently among newly hired industrial workers. Table 3.7 shows the yearly increase in industrial workers and the percentage of women among them. In 1930, 386,500 women entered industry, followed by 463,900 in 1931. The largest increases, for both sexes, occurred in these two years. In 1932, the industrial labor force contracted, losing 222,400 men but only 131,600 workers overall: women continued to be hired even as men were leaving, partially offsetting the overall loss. That year, incoming women workers represented the sole source of growth for the industrial working class.

The large number of new women workers had a considerable impact on the vertical sex segregation by branch that had characterized industry earlier in the 1920s. Table 3.8 indicates that during the first five-year plan, between 1929 and 1933, women increased their share of every branch of industry. The rapid expansion of heavy industry created new opportunities, enabling women to establish a significant presence in industries previously dominated by men. By 1933, new industries such as

Table 3.8. *Women workers in the main branches of large-scale industry, 1929 and 1933 (January 1), including apprentices*

Industrial branch	1929 Number of women workers	1929 Percentage of workforce women	1933 Number of women workers	1933 Percentage of workforce women
Electrostations	500	2.5	7,500	14.2
Coal mining	21,100	7.7	74,300	17.4
Oil extraction	100	0.3	2,400	5.1
Iron ore	1,700	6.3	7,500	19.2
Chemicals	8,800	14.9	47,900	28.3
Cement	2,000	10.0	8,100	24.3
Ferrous metallurgy	14,100	7.1	63,100	21.1
Machine building and metalwork	44,600	8.8	325,200	23.2
Lumber and plywood	14,000	18.3	58,100	31.9
Paper	7,500	23.8	14,300	32.4
Printing	12,700	21.9	35,700	46.0
Cotton fabric	322,000	62.5	305,100	68.4
Linen	58,900	65.2	44,500	67.9
Wool	34,600	49.4	50,200	59.8
Leather and fur	5,600	12.8	31,000	43.5
Sewing	40,800	63.8	170,600	81.3
Shoes	12,500	30.9	49,200	53.7
Food	68,400	26.2	157,900	35.5
Total	669,900		1,452,600	

Source: *Trud v SSSR*, compiled from tables on pp. 99, 106, 114, 120, 127, 134, 142, 150, 161, 168, 176, 184, 192, 199, 207, 215, 223, 230, and 237. This includes workers and apprentices in the main branches of industry. The totals for 1929 and 1933 are less than the total number of industrial workers and apprentices in industry in these years.

machine building and electrostations, as well as older industries with new and expanding branches, including chemicals, metallurgy, and mining, all contained substantial percentages of women among their workers. The percentage of women among workers increased almost sixfold in electrostations, almost tripled in machine building and metalwork, and more than doubled in mining. In the coal-mining industry, underground jobs were opened to women in 1931, and women replaced men in many jobs above ground. The opportunity to work in the pits, which paid better than above-ground work, was given to those women who had the greatest seniority, and their numbers multiplied rapidly. In ten mines surveyed in May 1931, there were only 401 women underground (3.2 percent of the total underground workforce) and 12,637 women working above ground. By February 1932, there were 2,355 women underground (11.5 percent of underground workers) and 20,065 women above. The number of women underground had increased more than fivefold. There were similar increases in other mines as well.[54]

Table 3.8 also shows that as the percentage of women in traditionally "male" industries grew, the traditionally "female" industries – cotton, linen, wool, and sewing – became even more intensely feminized. The percentage of women among sewing workers, for example, leapt from 63.8 to 81.3 percent. Cotton and linen, the only two branches to lose workers overall, also became even more distinctly "female," while printing, a previously "male" industry, approached gender equilibrium. By 1933, 44 percent of printing workers were women, as 3,300 men left the industry and 23,000 women entered.[55] Male workers fled textiles, sewing, and printing for higher wages in heavy industry. A male worker who left a cotton factory, for example, did not seek skilled work as a spinner or weaver elsewhere; instead, he typically sought a job in heavy industry, as an unskilled apprentice or a mechanic, for there the wage of an unskilled worker was higher than that of a skilled worker in light industry.[56] Gender segregation thus lessened in some industries, as a wider range of opportunities became available to women, but intensified in others that were already heavily female. The larger shift in sex segregation was thus created not only by the expansion of opportunities for women but also by men's abandonment of light for heavy industry, and by women's replacement of them.

Which industrial branches did incoming workers, male and female, enter during the first five-year plan? Table 3.9 shows where incoming workers, men and women, found jobs. The trend toward gender segregation, so pronounced during NEP, was decisively undermined by incoming workers. For the first time since the civil war, the majority of new women workers did not enter traditionally female industries. Machine building, a relatively new industry, expanded enormously, offering opportunities to both male and female workers. The largest groups of new workers among both sexes, 60.7 percent of men and 36 percent of women, took jobs in this branch. After machine building, the second-largest group of women entered sewing, a traditionally female industry. No workers entered cotton or linen, and men also bypassed printing and wool. The branches that attracted the most workers, in order of their importance, were machine building, sewing, food, and coal mining for women, and machine building, coal mining, food, and chemicals for men. Except in sewing, which drew women but not men, the patterns of male and female deployment were similar. Gender differences were not completely eliminated by the explosion in numbers and new patterns of deployment, but they were substantially undermined. The new and newly expanded industries

---

[54]   GARF, f. 5451, o. 16, d. 557, "Informsvodka," 28.
[55]   *Trud v SSSR*, 176.
[56]   Z. Mokhov, "Rost Tekuchesti Rabochei Sily v 1929/30 g.," *Voprosy truda*, 1930, no. 6: 22.

Table 3.9. *Main branches of industry entered by workers between 1929 and 1933 (January 1), by gender*

Industrial branch	Number of women entering	Percentage of all women entering industry	Number of men entering	Percentage of all men entering industry
Electrostations	7,000	0.8	26,000	2.5
Coal mining	53,200	6.8	98,600	9.6
Oil extraction	2,300	0.3	11,900	1.1
Iron ore	5,800	0.7	6,400	0.6
Chemicals	39,100	5.0	71,100	6.9
Cement	6,100	0.7	7,300	0.7
Ferrous metallurgy	49,000	6.2	50,400	4.9
Machine building and metalwork	280,600	36.0	617,100	60.3
Lumber and plywood	44,100	5.6	61,000	5.9
Paper	6,800	0.8	5,900	0.5
Printing	23,000	2.9	−3,300	−0.3
Cotton	−16,900	−2.1	−52,700	−5.1
Linen	−14,400	−1.8	−10,400	−1.0
Wool	15,600	2.0	−1,600	−0.1
Leather and fur	25,400	3.2	2,300	0.2
Sewing	129,800	16.6	16,000	1.5
Shoes	36,700	4.7	14,400	1.4
Food	89,500	11.4	94,700	9.2
Total	779,700	99.8	1,015,100	99.6

Source: *Trud v SSSR*, compiled from tables on pp. 99, 106, 114, 120, 127, 134, 142, 150, 161, 168, 176, 184, 192, 199, 207, 215, 223, 230, and 237.

were critical in this process. A larger percentage of new female industrial workers than male (6.2 versus 4.9 percent) entered ferrous metallurgy, for example. If we look at the distribution of women workers over the industrial branches, we can see the effect of the new patterns of deployment. Between 1929 and 1933, the concentration of women in textiles was reduced, and their numbers were spread more evenly throughout the various branches. In 1929, 61 percent of all women workers held jobs in cotton, linen, and wool; by 1933, the figure was down to 27 percent. The most striking shift was in machine building, which went from employing only 6 percent of all women workers in 1929 to employing 22 percent in 1933.[57]

In both industry and the larger economy, expansion produced a paradox, intensifying the feminization of traditionally female branches and sectors even as it undermined rigid lines of gender segregation. New opportunities opened up for women in sectors previously dominated by men,

[57] These statistics are derived from data provided in table 3.8.

at the same time that men fled from the service sector to industry and from light to heavy branches of industry. In the larger economy, the sectors of socialized dining, enlightenment, health, and state administration became more feminized just as women gained a greater share in industry. The same process was replicated within industry itself. Cotton, linen, wool, and sewing – the "female" branches – became yet more feminized even as record numbers of women moved into heavy industry, taking jobs in machine building, metallurgy, and mining. The traditionally "female" industries came to employ a greater percentage of women, but women workers overall were no longer so intensely clustered in those industries. New patterns of deployment created new patterns of employment. Leather/fur and printing, two branches with small percentages of women before 1929, also became increasingly feminized. Thus, from the perspective of women workers, industrialization had both positive and negative consequences. For women coming into the waged labor force, a broader array of work was available. At the same time, new, highly feminized preserves were created in the retail and service sectors and in the industrial branches of cotton, linen, wool, and sewing. Older women workers in undercapitalized, stagnating industries such as textiles now found their workplaces becoming increasingly female. The first five-year plan did not serve these workers very well: by 1933, the patterns of gender segregation within the economy had shifted considerably, but segregation itself had not disappeared.

Who Were the New Women Workers?

Many historians of Soviet industrialization have emphasized the importance of the peasantry in the formation of the new working class. Historically, throughout industrialized and industrializing nations, the working class has grown out of the dispossessed, impoverished, and desperate ranks of the peasantry. The process in the Soviet Union was not dissimilar, though it was marked by two outstanding exceptions. Between 1929 and 1935, women constituted a significant and unprecedented source of waged labor: 37 percent of all newly hired waged workers and fully 50 percent of those entering industry were women. Moreover, data suggest that a considerable number of these women – initially more than one in three – came from working-class families.[58]

The majority of new workers of both sexes during the first five-year plan were from peasant backgrounds. This was true not only in seasonal

---

[58] *Trud v SSSR*, calculated from pp. 10, 25, and 91. Data on class background are based on workers entering industry in 1931.

industries such as peat and timber but also in mining, coal, cement/ ceramics, basic chemicals, ferrous metallurgy, and food.[59] Between 1928 and 1932, approximately 12 million people moved from village to town. Many peasants had previously left the countryside on *otkhod,* a long-standing and regular pattern of temporary outmigration. In certain areas, peasants traveled from their villages to work in the same industries year after year. They retained their share in the land, contributed their wages to the household, and left their families behind.[60] The line between *otkhod* and permanent migration became blurred, however, amid the great outmigration of the first five-year plan, the high turnover of the labor force, and the chaos of collectivization. Many peasants who planned to take only a temporary leave from their villages never returned; others moved back and forth between countryside and city. The first great peasant departures occurred in the spring of 1929 in tandem with collectivization. The anxiety felt by union officials over the increasing numbers of peasants in the workforce was prompted in large part by this first wave. Still other peasants were forcibly deported, deprived of citizenship rights, and sentenced to corrective labor alongside waged workers in construction, timber, and industry. Mass deportations of *"kulaks"* lasted until March 1930, when Stalin published his article "Dizzy with Success," calling a temporary halt to repressive measures.[61] A study of twenty-two large Russian towns showed that at least half as many people left as arrived in 1932. In Stalingrad, for example, approximately 104,500 people arrived as 53,000 left. In many towns – Tomsk, Orenburg, Astrakhan, Saratov, Iaroslavl, Ivanovo – the numbers of those leaving reached 70 to 80 percent of those arriving. Yet amid the accretion and loss of population, the towns grew, increasing their numbers by 90 percent in 1930 and an additional 56 percent in 1931. In almost every town, women constituted between 40 and 50 percent of the new arrivals in 1931. And they proved just as mobile as men, making up between 40 and 50 percent of those who left the towns as well. Overall,

---

59 Goltsman, "Sostav Novykh Rabochikh," *Udarnik,* 1932, nos. 3–4: 61–64.
60 Male *otkhodniki* outnumbered their female counterparts until the late nineteenth century. On prerevolutionary *otkhodnichestvo,* see Robert Johnson, *Peasant and Proletarian: The Working Class of Moscow in the Late Nineteenth Century* (Leicester: Leicester University Press, 1979); Barbara Engel, *Between the Fields and the City: Women, Work, and Family in Russia, 1861–1914* (New York: Cambridge University Press, 1994).
61 Fitzpatrick, *Stalin's Peasants,* 80–83, and idem, "The Great Departure: Rural-Urban Migration in the Soviet Union, 1929–1933," in William Rosenberg and Lewis Siegelbaum, eds., *Social Dimensions of Soviet Industrialization* (Bloomington, Ind.: Indiana University Press, 1993), 17–19. At the time, labor analysts claimed that the majority of peasants who entered waged labor were either collective farmers or poor or middle individual farmers (*edinolichniki*). Fitzpatrick estimates that two out of three were *kulaks.* It is difficult to ascertain the social backgrounds of the new peasant workers because both the Party and the peasants themselves had a strong interest in concealment. The Party was committed to keeping former *kulaks* out of industry, and the peasants were anxious to present "proper" class credentials.

for every 100 men arriving in the towns, there were 66 women in 1932, 67 in 1933, and 64 in 1934.[62] Traditional regional patterns also shifted, overrun by those fleeing collectivization. The numbers of *otkhodniki,* both male and female, surged in regions of *sploshnaia,* or mass collectivization, including the Central Black Earth, North Caucasus, and Middle Volga regions. In areas with long-standing traditions of *otkhod* but lower rates of collectivization, such as the Moscow, Western, and Ivanovo regions, the numbers did not increase so dramatically. Yet women's share of *otkhodnichestvo* rose in every area except the Lower Volga district. It more than doubled in the Leningrad, Western, Urals, Ivanovo-Voznesensk, and Middle Volga regions. New construction sites such as Magnitostroi made *otkhod* a new and attractive option for women in areas of poor agriculture. By 1931, women comprised about 30 percent of all *otkhodniki* in the Urals, the North Caucasus, and the Lower Volga.[63]

Peasant women thus figured prominently among new workers, but there was a significant percentage of urban women as well. The latter constituted a distinct group among the incoming workers, one that has been largely ignored by labor historians but that recomposed and transformed the Soviet working class. If we compare new male and female workers, we find that among women, a much larger percentage came from working-class backgrounds. In industry, 52 percent of new women workers came from working-class families, in contrast to 36 percent of men. In construction, transport, trade, and socialized dining, a lower percentage of both sexes came from working-class families, but the relationship between women and men remained roughly the same: more women than men were from the working class.[64] Women workers in general retained fewer ties to the village: 39 percent of men entering industry had ties to the countryside, but only 16 percent of women did. In construction, a larger percentage of both sexes had such ties, but here, too, the percentage of women with ties was smaller than that of men. The rural ties of both sexes were weakest among transport workers, but among women in transport, they barely existed: only 3 percent of new women transport workers had rural ties, suggesting that the vast majority came from working-class families with long-established histories of waged labor.[65]

---

[62] RGAE, f. 1562, o. 20. d. 25, pp. 5, 6, 17. See *Trud v SSSR,* on the ratio of female to male migrants for 1932–1934 (p. 8).

[63] GARF, f. 3316, o. 25, d. 986, "Itogi Vnedreniia Zhenskogo Truda v Narodnoe Khoziaistvo v 1931 godu i Plan na 1932 g.," "Ob'iasnitel'naia Zapiska k Balansu Narodnogo Khoziaistvo SSSR na 1932 god," 84, 77–78.

[64] GARF, f. 6983, o. 25, d. 968, "Itogi Vnedreniia Zhenskogo Truda v 1931–1932 g.," 264–65. Data from VTsSPS are for the first half of 1931.

[65] Goltsman, 61–64, 68. The majority of new workers, both peasant and urban, had no previous experience in waged labor. Among new union members in the Moscow region in 1931, for example, fully 89 percent had never worked for wages. Most of these new union members were very young: 58.1 percent in industry were under the age of twenty-two.

Table 3.10. *Social origins of men and women entering unions in the second half of 1931 (percent)*

Region	Gender	Occupation of father					
		Worker	Peasant	White-collar	Handicrafts	Trade	Other
Moscow	Male	36.3	49.0	9.3	3.1	0.2	2.1
	Female	43.9	35.5	17.0	2.1	0.2	1.3
Leningrad	Male	26.5	59.9	10.0	2.5	0.2	0.9
	Female	37.4	41.0	18.0	2.3	0.2	1.1
Ivanovo	Male	36.3	53.0	7.2	2.4	0.2	0.9
	Female	45.3	41.1	10.4	1.6	0.2	1.4
Tatariia	Male	26.0	62.2	7.1	4.2	0.1	0.4
	Female	31.0	55.4	9.1	3.8	0.1	0.4
Kazakiia	Male	25.9	66.9	3.0	3.2	—	1.0
	Female	32.5	47.7	14.9	2.6	0.2	3.1
Belorussia	Male	30.3	47.6	8.2	10.6	0.3	3.0
	Female	42.2	31.4	12.3	9.1	0.3	4.7

Source: RTsKhIDNI, f. 17, o. 10, d. 496, p. 27.

Table 3.10 underscores the differences between new male and female workers and the importance of urban, working-class women in class recomposition. In every region, a larger percentage of women than of men came from working-class families. In the regions of Moscow, Ivanovo, and Belorussia, over 40 percent of new women workers had working-class fathers; less than half of the women in every region (with the exception of Tatariia) had peasant fathers. Among men, however, the largest group came from peasant families.

Labor officials were pleased that a high percentage of new working women came from "proletarian elements of working-class families," noting that as a group, their social composition was "significantly better" than that of their male counterparts.[66] Yet they were not entirely satisfied by the "very variegated" character of the new women, either. Labor officials maintained a clear hierarchy of the sources of labor: wives and daughters of workers were the "better part," followed by female collective farmers and then poor, landless, and middle peasants. They were concerned that new women workers, too, were contaminated by "declassed and foreign elements" such as former traders, declassed *kulaks,* and other "former" people who had been deprived of full citizenship (*lishentsy*). Officials worried that new workers were generally less reliable than the prerevolutionary, industrial proletariat: they did not value work, display steady work habits, or understand the need to sacrifice for socialism.[67]

[66] GARF, f. 3316, o. 26, d. 986, "Itogi Vnedreniia Zhenskogo Truda v Narodnoe Khoziaistvo v 1931 godu i Plan na 1932 g.," 83 ob–84.
[67] "Vovlechenie v Proizvodstvo Zhen i Docherei Rabochikh," *Trud*, January 18, 1931, p. 2.

Although the women were more likely than the men to be from urban, wage-earning families, most had never worked before. Among women entering industry in the Moscow region in early 1931, only 27 percent had any experience in waged work (compared to 33 percent among men). By the second half of the same year, even fewer had former work experience. Of the women new to waged labor, 24 percent were former students, 14 percent housewives, and 11 percent peasants.[68] An earlier study in 1930 had noted that 5 percent of new workers were former servants who had left domestic service for better-paying jobs. Housewives who took jobs tended to be older than other new women workers: more than 80 percent were twenty-four or older, and 50 percent were over thirty. About one third had prior experience in waged work, mostly in factories. Their age profile suggested that many married women dropped out of the workforce when their children were young and returned when they entered school.[69] A study in the Dinamo factory in 1931 underscored that women's participation in the labor force was shaped by motherhood. The great majority of women in the factory were either under twenty-two (38 percent) or over thirty (32 percent); less than one third were between those ages. Their age distribution contrasted sharply with that of the men, 41 percent of whom were clustered in the middle group. Most of the male and female workers in Dinamo were new: 63 percent of women and 70 percent of men had worked there for less than a year. Yet almost twice as many women as men (22 versus 10 percent) had been at the factory for more than five years. A larger percentage of women thus had greater seniority (*stazh*). Many studies showed that women were less likely than men to leave one job for another, and female turnover rates were consistently lower than male.[70]

The overwhelming majority of new union members were literate. The highest rates of illiteracy for both men and women were in the regions of Tatariia, Kazakiia, and Belorussia. In the Moscow, Leningrad, and Ivanovo regions, over 90 percent of men and women demonstrated some literacy. Soviet schools were highly effective in teaching basic skills to working-class and peasant children: literacy rates among women union members had risen from 44 percent in 1918 to 94 percent by 1931. Yet new women workers in industry and construction in the Moscow region still lagged behind men, with almost twice their percentage of illiteracy. Illiteracy was most prevalent among both sexes in construction, a seasonal sector that employed many peasant migrants.[71]

[68]   RTsKhIDNI, f. 17, o. 10, d. 496, p. 26.
[69]   G. Serebrennikov, "Zhenskii Trud v Sotsialisticheskom Stroitel'stve," *Udarnik*, 1932, no. 10: 27; Goltsman, 69.
[70]   GARF, f. 5451, o. 16, d. 557, "Akt," 65.
[71]   RTsKhIDNI, f. 17, o. 10, d. 496, pp. 28, 30; Goltsman, 69.

"Most Profitable for the State": Women and Capital Accumulation

Planners frankly admitted that they had not directed the explosive growth and transformation of the working class. NKT struggled to master an unruly expansion that it barely apprehended; in fact, NKT officials complained throughout 1931 that their recruitment efforts had been a failure and that the labor market was chaotic and beyond state control. Women went to work "outside the concrete, planned actions of leading managers and unions," in the words of one planner, "as a result of massive desire."[72] What was it that provoked such "massive desire" among peasant and working-class women alike? The Party's ideological appeals to build a new socialist society and the availability of new jobs and opportunities undoubtedly figured into women's choices. Yet the massive influx cannot be fully understood apart from the economic crisis of the first five-year plan. As the price of food skyrocketed and the male wage covered less of the family's basic needs, women entered the workforce to make up the difference. Every woman undoubtedly faced a grim calculus familiar from village life: the ratio of workers to "eaters." The fewer earners and the more dependents, the poorer a family would be. In the early 1930s, Ivan Voronin, a sewing worker, supported a wife and six children on his wages. The family lived in a cold, dark, damp cellar. The only piece of furniture in the tiny room, which measured four square meters, was a broken box that served as a bed for the entire family. The children, aged eleven, nine, six, four, two, and one, were dirty and bloated from malnutrition. Ivan was also bloated and sick. When Party activists came across the Voronins, they had eaten nothing but a dog over the past few days and were just consuming the last of its hide. The activists found a room for the family, placed the children in school and day care (where they would be fed), and, most important, got Ivan's wife a job in a factory.[73] The Voronins were among the poorest of workers, in part because the family included so many young children who needed food and their mother's care at home. Yet statistics show that during the first five-year plan every family was ruled by the ratio of dependents to earners, which steadily dropped from 2.46 to 1.59 dependents for every provider between 1927 and 1935.[74] One government report noted that expenses per person in workers' families increased 73 percent in this period, while individual salaries increased

---

[72] A. Isaev, "Ispol'zovanie Zhenskikh Trudovykh Resursov vo Vtoroi Piatiletke," *Voprosy profdvizheniia*, 1934, no. 1: 57; Serebrennikov, 27.
[73] GARF, f. 5451, o. 43, d. 30, "V Sekretnuiu Chast' VTsSPS," 131 ob.
[74] Shwarz, 145; Y. S. Borisova, L. S. Gaponenko, A. I. Kotelents, and V. S. Lelchuk, *Outline History of the Soviet Working Class* (Moscow: Progress Publishers, 1973), 200.

only 43 percent.[75] Other estimates suggest that real wages fell by half and that even the addition of a second earner may not have sufficed to maintain a family's standard of living.

The public discussion over the fall in real wages was veiled. Planners, Party leaders, and union officials admitted that real wages had not increased and that workers suffered terribly because of food shortages and poor provisioning, but they never openly revealed how far real wages had fallen. Yet planners were keenly aware of the ways in which women's entrance into the workforce alleviated the worst effects of the fall in real wages. Two incomes instead of one made it possible to maintain a working-class family above starvation levels, even if the purchasing power of the wage fell by half. In essence, women's wages supplied what inflation wiped out. Numerous planners alluded to the fact that women's wages enhanced the "well-being of the working-class family," and some even conceded that any increase in the general standard of living of the working class in 1929–1930 was the result of other family members' entering the workforce.[76] Additional income within the family helped offset the painful cuts created by inflation, creating the illusion of a better standard of living for the family as a whole without an increase in real wages.

From the state's perspective, women's entrance into the labor force provided numerous benefits. It helped to compensate for falling wages, to cushion losses in the standard of living, and to defuse workers' protests. The employment of women who were already lodged in towns ensured that no additional monies would have to be spent on housing. In 1929, Veinberg, the secretary of VTsSPS, demanded that the wives and children of workers be hired first; this, he explained, would "improve the social composition of the working class" as well as the family's standard of living.[77] The employment of working-class women would halt labor turnover, buttress "the basic cadres of the proletariat," counterbalance the poor work habits of new peasant workers, and strengthen the Party's political base. Beyond its benefits for the family, women's entrance into the workforce was also enormously beneficial to the state.

By the end of the first five-year plan, NKT still considered urban women a key labor reserve and thus an important element in its plans for labor. NKT projected that 1.5 million women would enter the waged labor force in 1932, constituting 44.4 percent of all incoming workers. More than one half of these women were expected to come from urban areas – housewives, teenagers, and others – and only seventy-five thousand directly from the village. The planners pointed out that peasant women required

[75] GARF, f. 6983, o. 25, d. 968, "Itogi Vnedreniia Zhenskogo Truda v 1931–1932 g.," 264.
[76] Bunimovich, 24; Averbukh, 27.
[77] "Kontrol'nye Tsifry Budut Vypolneny," *Trud*, September 27, 1929, p. 2.

housing and other services; urban women were thus vastly preferable.[78] And NKT maintained its preference for urban women over peasants into the second five-year plan. In 1934, A. Isaev, a member of NKT's labor-market department, noted that the dependents of waged workers were "still the most profitable for the state." No additional outlay had to be made for housing or services, and "from the point of view of labor discipline and a socialist attitude toward work, the members of working-class families constitute the most satisfactory material."[79]

Most important, women played a critical role in capital accumulation. Inflation and the fall in real wages allowed the state to employ two workers for the price of one. Whereas a man's wages had once been sufficient to cover the basic costs of rearing a family, beginning in 1929, a family needed at least two wages to maintain itself. The state realized the output of two workers for the price of one and could plow the "profit," or surplus value, back into industrialization. Women, due to their strategic placement within the working-class family, made an enormous contribution to capital accumulation and investment in industrialization. Planners did not intentionally create inflation, but from the state's perspective, a better strategy could scarcely have been designed to slash real wages, attract women into the workforce, and squeeze desperately needed capital from the labor of the working class.

[78] GARF, f. 5515, o. 13, d. 18, "Ob'iasnitel'nye Zapiski," 9–10.
[79] Isaev, 55.

Workers and their families arriving at the railroad station in Magnitogorsk in search of jobs at the new metallurgical complex, then still under construction. 1931.

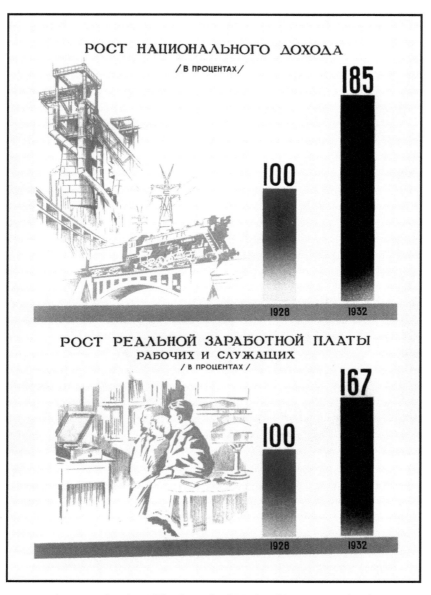

A poster showing "The Growth of National Income" and "The
Growth of Real Wages" during the first five-year plan. The lower graph
pictures a well-dressed family at home with a lamp, a table and
tablecloth, a book, and a phonograph, all symbols of the new
working-class prosperity promised by industrialization.

Temporary housing for workers on the construction site of the Kuznets metallurgical complex in Novokuznetsk. New workers on construction sites and in towns often lacked even the most rudimentary housing, furniture, and domestic comforts. 1930.

4

From Exclusion to Recruitment

We must broaden the circle of registration of the unemployed to include those who have not had the right to register with the organs of labor up to this time.   Decree on registration, May 10, 1930[1]

We need to spend the minimum on housing to guarantee the maximum tempo of industrialization. This can be done only if we maximize the labor resources of the present urban population and those in the new towns. This means the maximum involvement of women.

L. Sabsovich, planner, 1930[2]

Throughout 1930 and 1931, labor officials struggled to apprehend and gain control of the vast changes taking place in the economy. Employees in the labor exchanges (*birzhi truda*) stood in the front line of the transformation, desperately trying to create order out of chaos. Caught between the insistent demands of managers for labor and the hordes of incoming workers on the one hand, and an increasingly obsolete labor policy on the other, they were largely ineffective in their efforts to direct and deploy the labor force. As labor shortages rapidly replaced unemployment, the state was forced to replace a policy based on exclusion with a scheme for recruitment. The Commissariat of Labor (NKT) was confronted with the new and difficult tasks of understanding, directing, and mastering the roiling waves of movement and migration stirred up by collectivization, the socialization of retail trade, and industrialization. Thousands of peasants fleeing collectivization jostled dispossessed NEPmen, the hungry wives of workers, and unemployed young people in the crowded, dirty labor exchanges. Thousands more were hired directly at the factory gates by managers in need of workers. But if the

---

[1] GARF, f. 5515, o. 33, d. 11, "V Sovet Narodnykh Komissarov Soiuza SSSR," 18.
[2] L. Sabsovich, "Rost Gorodskogo Naseleniia i Sotsialisticheskaia Rekonstruktsiia Byta," *Na trudovom fronte*, 1930, no. 5: 29. Hereafter cited as *NTF*.

gates were already tumbling down, what, then, was the role of the gate-keepers?

In the 1920s, NKT had neither possessed nor needed an arm for the recruitment of labor. The labor exchanges were filled with job seekers from the towns and countryside as a steady stream of peasant migrants, prompted by rural overpopulation and family need, came to the cities of their own volition in search of waged work. In the words of the labor historian A. M. Panfilova, "The stream of labor from countryside to town in the 1920s occurred in significant measure *samotek,* or spontaneously."[3] In fact, amid conditions of high unemployment, NKT tightly controlled hiring to ensure that unemployed union members would receive priority over women, young people, and peasants who had never worked for wages. The state sought to screen the latter groups from entering the working class, not to recruit them.

In the late spring of 1930, planners perceived that in certain economic sectors, the problem of unemployment was rapidly being superseded by a new crisis: labor shortage. The transition from the persistent and nagging unemployment of NEP to labor shortage was startling and unexpected. It occurred unevenly, taking hold in certain sectors and regions and bypassing others. Moreover, the labor exchanges were still filled with thousands of unemployed people, including skilled workers awaiting jobs in their trades. As the labor shortage widened and intensified during the summer and into the fall, Party leaders and labor officials struggled to develop a new labor policy to meet the changing needs of the economy. The older labor policy, based on priority for unemployed industrial workers and tight screening of new job seekers, was useless in the face of a labor shortage and effectively prevented the leadership from acting flexibly and quickly to address new issues. Between 1929 and 1931, millions of new workers poured into the labor force *samotek* and independent of directives from above. Within a short time, the labor force was transformed as new workers doubled its ranks and radically altered its gender and social composition. Party leaders and planners, however, had a poor grasp of the changes sweeping construction sites, lumber camps, railroads, and factories throughout the country. The planners' projections for labor, so carefully developed in 1929, now floated away like so many useless bits of flotsam in a crashing wave of unimaginable size. Over the next two years, planners struggled to apprehend these changes and to master a labor market that had burst all bounds of expectation, regulation, and control.

---

[3]   A. M. Panfilova, *Formirovanie rabochego klassa SSSR v gody pervoi piatiletki, 1928–1932* (Moscow: Izdatel'stvo Moskovskogo Universiteta, 1964), 17.

Shifting Paradigms: Unemployment or Labor Shortage?

The possibility of an imminent labor shortage had seemed unlikely in 1929. In fact, when Party leaders approved the optimum variant of the first five-year plan in the spring of that year, they believed that the rate of industrialization required to eliminate unemployment was entirely out of reach; they were resigned to living with it for many more years.[4] In September 1929, Veinberg, secretary of VTsSPS (the All-Union Central Council of Trade Unions), announced that the number of workers was expected to increase a mere 6 to 7 percent in 1929–1930. E. Bronshtein, one of the key planners for female labor, noted as late as that fall that "a known segment of the Party" was beset with "pessimism and panic" over the seeming intractability of unemployment. Although Bronshtein himself took a more sanguine view, many "skeptics and doubters" were convinced that unemployment was becoming an "economic catastrophe," and Party members at every level "painted unemployment in extraordinarily gloomy colors." Moreover, planners in both NKT and VTsSPS doubted that the five-year plan would alleviate the situation. Although Gosplan argued that the five-year plan would produce a 50 percent decrease in unemployment, planners in NKT and VTsSPS insisted that the state would be lucky to maintain unemployment rates at 1928–1929 levels. Not even the most optimistic of the planners foresaw a labor shortage or a doubling in the numbers of workers. Bronshtein, remarking on "the reigning pessimism among us," specifically suggested that "the deeply rooted pessimism in NKT" would "take much time to disappear."[5] Up through the spring of 1930, Party leaders and planners seemed confident that the demand for labor could be met by the experienced cadres of skilled and semiskilled unemployed workers registered in the labor exchanges.

The first complaints about NKT's inability to meet industry's demand for labor were heard in the fall of 1929. The planner Emelian Kviring was among the first to note publicly the emergence of a curious phenomenon. Although there were more than 1 million unemployed people registered in labor exchanges nationwide, in some areas there were shortages of both skilled and unskilled labor. The construction industry alone was unable to fill some fifty thousand jobs. A planned economy was based on the principle that unemployed workers would be matched with available

---

[4] R. W. Davies, *The Soviet Economy in Turmoil, 1929–1930* (Cambridge, Mass.: Harvard University Press, 1989), 66.

[5] E. Bronshtein, "Pravyi Pessimizm Bezrabotnitsa i Regulirovanie Rynka Truda," *Na planovom fronte*, 1929, no. 1: 34–37, and "Eshche o Pravom Pessimizme v Voprosakh Bezrabotnitsy," *Na planovom fronte*, 1929, no. 6: 30–35.

jobs, yet how could the state ensure that a shortage of labor in one area would be filled by a glut from another? Kviring conceded that NKT was not doing a very good job of "organizing the labor force" or deploying the unemployed to fill the demand for labor. The simultaneous existence of unemployment and labor shortage posed the challenge of training and distributing workers as well as matching skilled workers with proper jobs. As Kviring pointed out, there were only 230,000 experienced industrial workers left among the 1.1 million unemployed who were registered with the labor exchanges and received regular unemployment stipends or insurance from the bureau of social insurance (*kassa sotsstrakha*). Noting that this group could be expected to dwindle even further in the near future, Kviring questioned whether there were "sufficient reserves" of experienced workers to meet the projected demand of the five-year plan. He concluded that NKT had to train workers better and match them more accurately to the changing needs of the economy.[6]

Despite these changing needs and the clear limitations of a labor policy based on exclusion, however, Party leaders and planners were slow to develop a new approach. Early attempts to plan and recruit a labor force to coincide with the needs of industry were tentative and largely ineffective. In November 1929, the Council of People's Commissars (SNK) instructed NKT and VSNKh (the Supreme Council of the National Economy) to draft a comprehensive plan, broken down by quartile, region, industry, and skill, for supplying labor to the economy. Planners in VSNKh requested that all managers of enterprises complete forms specifying their anticipated needs for labor. The forms were drawn up and dutifully sent out, but VSNKh was unable to get its own managers to return them.[7] NKT, bedeviled by a similar lack of information from local enterprises, also had difficulty determining the need for labor in various sectors of the economy.

The reorganization of the labor exchanges and the creation of labor-market councils in the fall of 1929 did not help NKT get a clearer sense of the demand for labor. Despite the participation of representatives from both NKT and the enterprises, the labor-market councils were unable to gather the necessary statistics. Part of the problem, NKT officials complained, was that VSNKh had failed to provide either a plan or figures on the labor force in the factories and on the new construction sites. In late winter, NKT impatiently censured VSNKh and announced it would work out its own plan. Thereafter the two organizations worked at cross purposes, and while each found it convenient to blame the other for the delays in planning, neither was able to master the new situation. NKT, despite its lack of statistics, was beginning to realize that the registered

---

[6]   Em. Kviring, "Rabochii Rezerv i Bezrabotnitsa," *Na planovom fronte*, 1929, no. 1: 37.
[7]   R. W. Davies, *The Soviet Economy in Turmoil*, 281.

unemployed might not be able to meet the new demands for labor. Recognizing that new sources of labor might be necessary, but hesitant as always to "dilute" the working class with peasants, it vowed to study the use of nationalities, the Jewish poor of Belorussia and the Ukraine, and women.[8]

As the labor shortage intensified throughout the spring and summer of 1930, Party and NKT leaders struggled to make sense of the new situation. Slowly, labor officials began to shift from a paradigm based on "guarding the gates" of the working class to active recruiting. The first step in this process was a growing mistrust of the unemployed. In March, NKT sent out a circular to all of its local departments warning that many unemployed who were dismissed, purged, or sent to work from one labor exchange simply reregistered in another, as did workers who were dissatisfied with their job assignments. If the labor exchanges were to halt the turnover of labor in the factories, they had to exercise greater control over the circulation of labor. NKT urged the labor exchanges to begin marking the documents (*talony*) they gave workers with the reasons for their dismissal from previous jobs. Workers had to be stopped from shopping for jobs in one exchange after another.[9]

As NKT's awareness of the labor shortage deepened, its impatience with the unemployed increased. If labor shortages existed in certain areas, the unemployed could not claim state support; they were "unworthy" of state expenditure. In April, NKT sent a circular to all the labor exchanges and social insurance departments, noting that though demands for skilled workers were increasing, there were still "hundreds of thousands of unemployed on the rolls of the labor exchanges who need work." Although some could not work because they had no skills, many others simply preferred collecting unemployment stipends to working. The circular impatiently explained, "We are currently spending money on people who are not going to work or who refuse to work." Up to 30 percent of the unemployed refused to respond to job summonses. These people, in NKT's view, were shirkers. NKT urged the labor exchanges and social insurance departments to coordinate their activities so they could eliminate payments to people who refused work, and shift funds for the unemployed into training.[10]

By the spring of 1930, labor shortages had become acute in coal mining and construction, both seasonal industries dependent on peasant migrant labor. Labor experts in NKT came to the startling realization that for the

8   GARF, f. 5515, o. 24, d. 262, "Proekt Postanovleniia Kollegii NKT SSSR," 10.
9   GARF, f. 5515, o. 24, d. 262, "Narkomtruda Vsem Soiuznym Resp.," 63–65.
10 GARF, f. 5515, o. 24, d. 262, "Tsirkuliarno o Poriadke Naznacheniia i Vyplaty Posobiia po Bezrabotnitse na Osobe Postanovleniia NKT SSSR ot Marta 1930 g.," 49, and "Postanovlenie NKT," in "Novyi Poriadok Naznacheniia i Vyplaty Posobii po Bezrabotnitse." This pamphlet, published in Moscow by Gostrudizdat in 1930, is included in its entirety in this *delo*. Except for its first page, however, it is not numbered.

first time since the inception of NEP, there were shortages of *unskilled* as well as skilled labor. Yet apart from introducing punitive measures to purge "shirkers" from the rolls of the labor exchanges, NKT was still unable to unravel the riddle of unemployment and labor shortage. A variety of proposals for recruiting were advanced and discarded by Party officials and labor experts. The state considered using prisoners in construction and timber, people deprived of voting rights, seasonal workers from the new collective farms, *kulaks* expelled from the collective farms to special settlements, landless peasants, volunteer workers, and demobilized soldiers. But none of these ideas was implemented immediately.[11]

In May, the state took its first step toward broadening the group of people who were eligible for jobs beyond union members. New legislation expanded the categories of people permitted to register to include divorced wives of workers, widows, women who had left the labor force to raise children, *sluzhashchie* (white-collar workers), invalids, craftsmen and their children, *batraks* (landless peasants), and many smaller groups.[12] The new list targeted urban inhabitants and drew heavily on unemployed women in search of work. *Rabotnitsa*, a journal for women workers that actively promoted the interests of unemployed women, strongly endorsed the legislation. Diverging from its usual appeals for skilled workers, the journal noted that unskilled ones were needed now as well and that the pool of unemployed was rapidly dwindling.[13] Yet the state's attempts to solve the labor shortage were still more passive than active. It relaxed the stringent criteria used by the labor exchanges to include new categories of job seekers, but it did not actively solicit workers to meet specific labor shortages. It opened the gates slightly to those waiting outside, allowing urban women and the children of the urban employed to slip in, but it still did not make the leap from gatekeeper to recruiter. Its basic approach to managing the labor force did not change.

Delegates to the Sixteenth Party Congress, in June 1930, seemed oblivious to the growing demand for labor and devoted almost no discussion to women or other new sources of labor. Much of the congress was taken up with criticism of Tomsky and "the Right wing" within the unions. N. M. Shvernik delivered a lengthy report on the tasks of the unions, stressing the need to develop heavy industry and fulfill the five-year plan in four years. He harshly criticized "the opportunistic leadership" of VTsSPS

[11] GARF, f. 5515, o. 33, d. 11, pp. 18, 35–38, 88; f. 5515, o. 33, d. 12, pp. 16–18, 23; and R. W. Davies, *The Soviet Economy in Turmoil*, 282.
[12] GARF, f. 5515, o. 33, d. 11, "Postanovlenie o Registratsii v Organakh Truda Lits Ishchushchikh Truda, i Napravlenii ikh na Rabotu, TsIK i SNK (SSSR)," 19–22; "Bezrabotnitsa v SSSR Umen'shilas' Na 38 Prots.," *Trud*, May 11, 1930, p. 4.
[13] M. Gal'perin, "Uskorit' Utverzhdenie Zakona o Priniatii na Uchet Birzh Truda Odinokikh Zhenshchin," *Rabotnitsa*, 1930, no. 21: 19.

for its refusal to take on "new tasks" and its stubborn advocacy of the "protective" rather than the "productive" duties of the unions. He urged the unions to assume a new role in disciplining the working class to achieve high tempos of production through the organization of socialist competition and shock work. But even as Shvernik spoke about the role of the unions, his statistical projections on membership revealed his limited awareness of the changes in the size and composition of the working class. He announced to his fellow delegates that 330,000 mostly skilled workers were expected to enter industry in 1930–1931, a figure dwarfed by the massive number of largely unskilled workers flooding industry at the very moment of his speech. Moreover, he did not once refer to women, even though record numbers of women were then swelling the ranks of the working class in industry and construction. Shvernik simply reiterated the prevailing but increasingly outdated wisdom about the labor market. While he did note that unemployment was coming to an end, he once again stressed the need for skilled workers.[14]

Stalin touched briefly on the contradiction between persistent unemployment and the labor shortage in his concluding speech. He accused NKT and VTsSPS of creating "a big mess." According to their own figures, there were approximately 1 million unemployed in the country, mostly unskilled women and teenagers, yet the labor exchanges were unable to meet 80 percent of the requests for labor from factory managers. "How do we make sense of this mess?" Stalin bluntly demanded. He answered obliquely: "In any case, it is clear that these unemployed do not compose either a reserve or even a permanent army of unemployed for our industry."[15] Stalin, like NKT's leaders, was still operating under the assumption that industry did not need unskilled labor. The warning, if not the remedy, was clear: the pool of "employable" unemployed was rapidly disappearing, and NKT and VTsSPS were failing to provide industry with the skilled labor force it needed. Stalin, to his credit, recognized the contradiction. But beyond his rather muddled summary, he provided little in the way of policy. He, too, seemed to think that neither women nor peasants could be a reliable labor force. He offered no suggestions for recruiting workers or matching them with the demands of local industry and construction. In its concluding resolutions to the congress, the Party referred in passing to "the growing role of women and youth in production," but it was concerned mainly with its own lack of influence among peasant women. Shaken by the *bab'i bunty* (women's riots) against

---

[14] *XVI s"ezd vsesoiuznogo kommunisticheskoi partii (b). Stenograficheskii otchet* (Moscow and Leningrad: Gosudarstvennoe Izdatel'stvo, 1930), 645, 648–49, 655, 658.

[15] I. Stalin, "Politicheskii Otchet Tsentral'nogo Komiteta XVI S"ezdu VKP (b) Doklad i Zakliuchitel'noe Slovo," *Voprosy leninizma* (Moscow and Leningrad: Gosudarstvennoe Sotsial'no-Ekonomicheskoe Izdatel'stvo, 1931), 725–26.

collectivization, the Party sought to neutralize peasant women's hostility toward the regime. Among the many resolutions emphasizing the role of socialist competition and shock work, the congress once again reiterated the requisite formulation on "drawing women into production and training and retraining them in different types of schools and courses."[16] Yet this resolution did not differ from hundreds of others passed in the 1920s. The Party, riveted by the purge of the Right, shaken by the resistance to collectivization, and anxious to preserve its proletarian base in the cities, seemed unable to read or respond to the rapidly shifting labor market.

Improvising a Response

Through the summer and fall of 1930, the Party's response to the intensifying demand for labor consisted in the passage of a series of short-term, limited measures improvised in response to immediate crises. By May, the timber industry was experiencing "extraordinary difficulties." The ports of Leningrad and Arkhangelsk were short twenty-five thousand stevedores to load timber for export. Syrtsov, the head of the Council of People's Commissars (SNK) and a member of the Council of Labor and Defense (STO), a key economic planning agency, sent a frantic letter to Uglanov, the head of NKT (USSR), instructing him to disregard the priority lists used in the labor exchanges and quickly marshal a labor force. STO made plans immediately to provision Leningrad with extra food and to construct barracks for the new workers.[17] The industrialization drive depended on capital from exports, and bottlenecks in the ports put all of that at risk. The shortage of stevedores thus merited the attention of the highest government officials. Yet this was crisis management, not a model for managing a labor force. Many other enterprises and sectors appealed to the state for similar intervention. Requests for labor poured in from all the port cities and the defense industry. Enterprises were short of timber workers, skilled workers, dockworkers, and stevedores. The defense factories were furious with the construction sites for "stealing" their workers. One note explained, "The position with regard to labor in the defense factories at present is catastrophic."[18]

Narpit (the Union of Public Dining and Dormitory Workers), which was responsible for feeding thousands of workers on newly cleared construction sites, meanwhile struggled to fill its own crippling labor shortage.

---

[16]   *XVI s"ezd vsesoiuznogo kommunisticheskoi partii (b)*, 715, 738.

[17]   GARF, f. 5515, o. 33, d. 11, "Osoboupolnomochennyi Soveta Truda i Oborony po Drovolesozagatovkam i Lesoeksporu," 24.

[18]   GARF, f. 5515, o. 33, d. 12, "Direktory Zavoda No. 60," 162–64; "Sluzhebnaia Zapiska," 177; "NKTruda RSFSR i SSSR," 179; "Zaveduiushchim Otdelam Truda," 184; "Mobilizatsionno-Planovomu Upravleniiu VSNKh SSSR," 187.

Thousands of workers on huge new industrial construction sites such as Magnitostroi, Kuznetsstroi, Avtostroi, and Bereznikikhimstroi were living in tents, flimsy barracks, and holes in the ground, eating their meals in hastily built public dining halls. In 1929, the Central Committee had disapprovingly singled out Narpit as a key entry point through which "declassed elements" could infiltrate the working class. By the summer of 1930, Narpit had become a key exit point as well. Peasants fleeing collectivization frequently took jobs in public dining halls and then moved quickly into better, higher-paid jobs in construction or even production. Narpit was desperate for workers. In July, NKT expressly targeted housewives as an untapped reserve of labor and drafted a decree to recruit workers' wives to work in the dining halls. The unemployed who had once filled these low, poorly paid positions had already found other jobs; if new workers could be drawn from the wives of better-paid industrial workers, NKT believed that turnover in the working class as a whole might decrease.

In early July, the Social Life Sector (Sotsial'nyi Bytovyi Sektor) of VTsSPS met to discuss the deployment of workers' wives in the dining halls. Vaisfal'd, a member of the Central Committee of Narpit, explained that staff turnover had gotten so bad as to interfere with service. One small dining hall with a staff of 53, for example, had employed 250 different workers over the course of a single year. Such turnover rates were not uncommon. "It is impossible to work like this," Vaisfal'd complained. He noted that on large new construction sites such as Kuznetsstroi, there were thousands of workers in need of shelter. If new workers from the labor exchanges were sent to work in the dining halls on these sites, they would only intensify the competition for housing. "In order not to create a crisis," Vaisfal'd explained, "we need to hire the wives of workers who already have housing." Narpit jobs should henceforth be offered not to the unemployed but rather to politically active wives of workers in transport and industry or to housewives with at least two years' former work experience. Narpit set up an organization to recruit actively among housewives, but its efforts were stymied by proponents of the outdated labor policy, such as Isaev, a prominent member of NKT, who objected that the wives of workers might preempt jobs that should rightly go to registered unemployed women. (Neither Narpit nor NKT officials questioned the assumption that only women should work in the dining halls.) Amid the severe labor shortage, members of the two organizations continued to bicker over who should be given first priority for lousy jobs that most workers now rejected anyway at the first opportunity.[19] Still

[19] GARF, f. 5515, o. 13, d. 17, "Zasedanie Sotsial'nogo-Bytovogo Sektora VTsSPS," 1–2; f. 5515, o. 33, d. 12, "TsK Professional'nogo Soiuza Rabochikh Narodnogo Pitaniia i Obshchizhitii SSSR," 86–86 ob.

worried about controlling entrance to the working class, neither Narpit nor NKT recognized that the balance of power in the labor market had already shifted from the labor exchanges to the workers themselves. Industry's exploding demand for labor was rapidly making a mockery of their carefully constructed priority lists and classifications.

By midsummer, NKT had developed a more realistic assessment of the situation. In July, Romanov, the commissar of labor (Russia), explained to representatives of the local labor departments that over the past year the labor market had changed dramatically. There were no skilled workers left in the labor exchanges, and fully 70 percent of the registered unemployed were now women. Local labor departments therefore had to assume responsibility for training a new workforce. Moreover, he rebuked the labor exchanges for sending women to work in unskilled jobs requiring heavy physical labor. Women, he instructed, were to be sent where they belonged: to the white-collar service sector in health, Narpit, retail sales, and the state bureaucracy, as well as "industries where female labor can be used correctly." NKT planners had recently drafted a "Five-Year Plan for Female Labor," which was never published, but Romanov echoed its recommendations in his instructions to the local labor departments. Soon after the Sixteenth Party Congress, NKT launched some training programs for those seasonal industries suffering from the greatest labor shortages, and developed plans to supply the construction and lumber industries with workers.[20]

These efforts, however, were insufficient. By September, the labor shortage had produced serious bottlenecks in the economy. Machine parts, raw materials, and produce piled up before storefronts, on sidewalks, on railroad sidings, on construction sites, and at factory gates. Desperately needed rail cars and trucks stood idle, waiting for workers to load or unload them. Perishable foodstuffs lay rotting in huge piles throughout the country. The raw materials and machine parts stacked up at sidings created stoppages in those sectors of the economy that were dependent on their delivery. NKT responded harshly, with new, draconian instructions directed toward the unemployed. Everyone registered with the labor exchanges, regardless of his or her skill or training, was to be mobilized for loading and unloading. Anyone who refused work without good reason was immediately to be deprived of benefits and deleted from the rolls. Managers were forbidden to use loaders for any other work. Women were to be deployed equally with men but assigned to lighter work. NKT ordered the local labor organs to prepare medical reports on every worker listed in the exchanges to determine whether he or she was physically capable of work. The organs of labor were urged to prosecute

[20] "Problema Ispol'zovaniia Zhenskogo Truda," *Trud*, July 14, 1930, p. 6.

anyone – whether manager, labor recruiter, or worker – who encouraged loaders to leave their jobs for other positions. More important, the labor exchanges lost their exclusive right to control hiring, due to the severe labor shortages at local sites throughout the country. Managers were permitted to transfer workers from one region to another and to hire independent of the exchanges if NKT could not meet their demands for labor.[21] NKT, acknowledging its own inability to solve the crisis, ceded power temporarily to local managers. There was no discussion about which workers were properly qualified to receive jobs loading and unloading goods. At this point, NKT no longer cared whom managers hired: any hands, peasant or female, would do.

By October, new shortages of labor were crippling the construction industry as well. Zimichev, the head of the construction union, noted in his keynote speech to the Eighth All-Union Congress of Construction Workers that the industry now faced a shortage of three hundred thousand workers, a sixfold increase over the previous year. No unemployed workers remained in the labor exchanges to take these jobs. The crisis was now full-blown. Although leaders of the Party, the unions, Gosplan, VSNKh, and NKT had all drifted through the spring and summer seemingly oblivious to the changes in the economy, everyone now blamed NKT for failing to anticipate the crisis. Zimichev, for example, accused NKT of blocking the construction union's earlier demands for more workers. He noted that for more than a year, he had been locked in a battle over statistics with NKT, struggling to train 150,000 more workers than NKT's paltry target of fifty thousand permitted. In fact, NKT had not even succeeded in reaching its own goal: only twelve thousand construction workers had actually been trained. Several of NKT's attempts to provide training ended in dismal failure. In the winter, the agency brought a hundred landless peasants to Moscow to learn construction trades, but neither food nor housing could be found for them. Dumped in a freezing shelter, men and women together, the peasants were so disgusted by the situation that they demanded to be sent home.[22] Zimichev, desperate for new sources of labor, now turned to women. "One of the most basic sources of additional construction workers," he announced, "is female labor. Unfortunately, we have only one hundred thousand women [in the union]. This figure is insignificant. We must use the labor of women as broadly as possible."[23] Thus the union leaders in the less skilled sectors of the economy – Narpit, loading, and construction – were the first to turn to women

[21] "O Merakh po Obespecheniiu Rabochei Siloi Pogruzo-Razgruzochnykh Rabot v Osennem Periode, 1930–1931 goda," *Trud*, September 13, 1930, p. 4.
[22] GARF, f. 5515, o. 33, d. 12, "Vypiska. Vsesoiuznyi Professional'nyi Soiuz Stroitel'nykh Rabochikh. Moskovskii Gubotdel," 23–24.
[23] "Podgotovit 350 Tysiach Stroitelei," *Trud*, October 10, 1930, p. 3.

as an important labor reserve. Searching for new ways to meet the crisis, they responded by attempting to hire the wives of workers as quickly as possible. The shortages in loading and construction were portents of a larger crisis, but the Party was still paralyzed by an older paradigm whose first tenet was to maintain the pure proletarian character of the working class. Romanov, the commissar of labor, noted that many Party leaders were panicking at the realization that the basic cadres of the working class "were all washed up."[24]

Policy on the Front Lines: The Labor Exchanges

By early fall, NKT had become the official scapegoat for the government's failure to address the labor crisis. VSNKh's failure to provide adequate statistics, Gosplan's inaccurate assessments of growth, the Party's own blindness to changing economic conditions were all conveniently overlooked. On September 3, the Central Committee sent out a circular criticizing the organs of labor for their "bureaucratic attitudes." It noted reprovingly that despite the labor shortage, there were approximately 1 million people still registered in the labor exchanges and soaking up millions of rubles. The circular strongly chastised NKT, but it offered little in the way of new policy.[25] Clearly, the labor exchanges were supposed to address the new needs of the economy, but neither the leadership of NKT nor the Party itself pointed them in a new direction or provided a clear set of instructions.

As the labor shortages intensified through the late summer and fall, officials in the labor exchanges were gripped by a rising sense of panic. With no direction forthcoming from NKT, labor exchanges in a number of cities began to act independently to address the crisis, establishing a patchwork of local regulations that differed widely from place to place. In October, NKT called a meeting of representatives from various departments and key labor exchanges to review how the exchanges had responded to the Central Committee's September critique.[26] Anxious to forestall further criticism, the representatives tried to stress the positive measures they had taken, but they also honestly acknowledged the confusion, lack of central authority, and vacillation that prevailed in labor exchanges throughout the country. Officials in the exchanges were trapped by an outdated labor

---

[24] GARF, f. 6983, o. 1, d. 159, "Rol' Organov Truda v Sotsialisticheskom Stroitel'stve," 26–30.

[25] GARF, f. 5515, o. 17, d. 23b, "Soveshchanie pri NKT SSSR Sovmestno s Zaveduiush-chimi Birzh Truda po Voprosu o Proverke Vypolneniia TsK Partii ot 3-go Sentiabria 1930," 2.

[26] Ibid., 2–75.

policy that offered no method for controlling or delivering a labor force. The central question of the meeting, posed by the chairman in her open-ing remarks, was how the labor exchanges could meet the new needs of the economy, distribute a labor force to areas of shortage, prevent labor turnover, train more skilled workers, and control the labor market. In her words, "If up to now the labor exchanges have been means for passive registration, what sort of measures are needed so that they can become organs to plan and provision the labor market with a labor force?"[27] The labor exchanges needed to limit and control the mobility of workers, direct them to areas of shortage, and compel them to work under diffi-cult conditions. In other words, they needed the power to eliminate the free-labor market. One representative noted, "If up to now we have been concerned only with sending the unemployed from the labor exchanges to work, then now the questions are how to organize the labor force, how to provision a labor force, how to plan distribution. In these areas, our work is extraordinarily poor." Several representatives observed that the labor exchanges could not halt turnover without having sole control over hiring. Workers should be able to get work only through the exchange, they suggested; this monopoly would give the exchanges the power to punish and thus to control, as workers who left their jobs without per-mission or who were fired due to disciplinary infractions could be refused further work.[28]

At present, however, managers, unions, and workers all colluded to undermine control by the labor exchanges. Managers hired "from the gate" because they could not get labor from the exchanges, and workers bypassed the exchanges because they could be easily hired "from the gate." Workers could also turn to their unions if they did not want to go through the exchanges. Thus rendered impotent by the independent actions of managers, workers, and unions, the exchanges were unable to deliver workers to areas that needed them or to halt the massive turnover that was interfering with production and construction throughout the country. Workers moved freely from one exchange to another, registering for new job assignments in the hope of securing better wages, housing, or working conditions.

Representatives pointed out the endless obstacles to coordinating the supply of and demand for labor. Managers routinely inflated their requests for workers. Biriukov, the head of the construction workers' section of the Moscow labor exchanges, explained, "A manager needs fifty, but he says he needs a hundred. Therefore we cannot talk about the large numbers of unfulfilled demands, we can talk only about unsatisfied requests." He noted that when the labor exchanges did manage to fill a request in its

[27] Ibid., 2.   [28] Ibid., 56, 5.

entirety, workers often returned to the exchanges because they could not find housing. Managers in the timber industry, for example, provided housing for only 15 percent of the thousands of workers they contracted for and hired. One representative remarked, "Life conditions there are very wretched, wages are low, and, clearly, turnover is very great." In other cases, managers laid off workers once they met their own monthly or quarterly production targets. These workers bounced back and forth between the factories and the exchanges. Neither fully employed nor unemployed, they muddied the statistical dimensions of unemployment, making it difficult to assess the size of the labor reserve. The labor exchanges, too, contributed to the problem of accurately assessing demand: overwhelmed by new job seekers, they sometimes sent large groups of workers to jobs without first bothering to register them, omitting paperwork and records in the interest of efficiency. Biriukov admitted, "We work stealthily." If labor was to be planned, it had to be carefully coordinated with production, a task that seemed almost insurmountable at this early, unpredictable stage of industrial growth.[29]

Several representatives expressed frustration at the absence of any central policy to guide the transformation from passive registration to active planning and control. The local organs of labor, they observed, were operating without "a legislative base." Mordukhovich, a representative of NKT, argued that older labor legislation rendered it impossible to gain control of the labor force; as a result, he said, "redistribution is still at a dead halt." Fialkov, the head of the Bureau of Registration in the Central Labor Exchange, testified that many labor exchanges were afraid to take action without explicit instructions from NKT. And employees in the labor exchanges regularly complained that they "receive no leadership in this new situation." According to one representative, the labor exchanges were "completely entangled by the old legislation, and the organs of labor are unable to cut through it." He summed up, "We are actually operating, legally and in practice, on legislation from 1922 to 1927. There are no other laws regulating the work of the labor exchanges. In 1929, this legislation was tossed into the garbage because no one could live with it."[30]

In the absence of central legislation, the major labor exchanges in the larger cities had begun to make their own policy. In Leningrad, for instance, the labor exchanges had broadened the right to register for a job to include anyone who had not been deprived of voting rights. In April, they began registering anyone who had lived in Leningrad for a minimum of three months. In May, they permitted all skilled and handicraft (*kustar*) workers, regardless of where they lived, to register. In June, they opened the exchanges to women, sending more than fifty-four thousand unskilled

[29]   Ibid., 58–59, 68, 13.   [30]   Ibid., 41, 63, 66–67.

women to work in various sectors of industry. On their own initiative, the Leningrad exchanges began an aggressive "regendering" program. Male and female job applicants were processed separately, with men being sent to industry and women to state stores, cooperatives, and local rail transportation. Flouting older laws guaranteeing workers a job in accordance with their training, the Leningrad exchanges instituted new, punitive rules in an attempt to control the labor force. Anyone who turned down a job assignment for any reason was promptly removed from the registration list and denied further work. In an attempt to halt turnover and to establish sole control over hiring and distribution, the Leningrad exchanges prohibited managers from hiring "from the gate." When managers ignored the prohibition and continued to hire independently, the Leningrad labor department took them to court. The exchanges forbade local social insurance offices to give out unemployment insurance, cut off aid to the able-bodied unemployed, and sent everyone out to work immediately after registering. Workers from ailing industries such as sewing, textiles, and leather were no longer permitted to wait for their old jobs to reopen; cut off from aid, these skilled, mostly female workers were promptly sent off to fill a severe shortage of stevedores.[31]

Most labor exchanges, however, were less decisive in their actions. In Moscow, for example, the exchanges were much slower to take the initiative. In response to the Central Committee's criticism in September, some exchanges expanded the list of those permitted to register, but many were unsure how to proceed further. Confusion reigned. Vashkevich, an official in one of the large Moscow exchanges, noted that he had never seen any instruction from NKT on broadening the circle of registration. "If they published this order, why wasn't it passed on to the labor departments?" he demanded angrily. Zhukrov, the head of the Moscow labor exchange, commented that the rolls were "horribly blocked up [*strashno zasoreny*]." Outside of the major cities, the system of registration had broken down completely; all hiring now occurred *samotek*, or spontaneously. When some labor exchanges tried to broaden their criteria for registration, a flood of new applicants overwhelmed them. Their employees could not cope even with the relatively simple task of registration. Fialkov, the head of the Bureau of Registration, complained that NKT had refused to issue national guidelines for broadening the registration criteria. He had repeatedly requested that handicraft workers be included, but NKT was unwilling to act, despite pressing shortages of skilled labor. Some exchanges went ahead and registered these people anyway; others hesitated to make such a move without instructions from above. As requests for skilled labor mounted, heated arguments broke out over what

[31] Ibid., 20–24.

to do. According to Fialkov, not only had NKT failed to redistribute the labor force, but it was barely able to handle the transfer of excess workers from one factory to another.[32]

Who Were the Unemployed?

As the labor exchanges struggled to forge new policies, they began to question the presence of the registered unemployed. Were "the unemployed" workers in need of jobs, a reliable reserve of labor, or "shirkers" who refused to work? Nobody seemed to know. The very fact of labor shortages called the current definition of unemployment into question. Exchanges simultaneously purged their rolls and broadened the right to register, two seemingly contradictory activities that reflected the larger entwined phenomena of unemployment and labor shortage. Some officials questioned whether unemployment even existed: did the names on the rolls represent real people in need of jobs? Ivanov, a representative from a Moscow labor exchange, noted, "Here we have fourteen thousand unemployed, and in Leningrad, fifteen thousand. Do they exist, or don't they? And if we have thirty thousand unemployed on our hands, why can't we find anyone to load and unload potatoes and vegetables?" Zhukrov, the head of the Moscow labor exchange, maintained that the registrants were real people, but he argued that they did not constitute a reserve of labor. For a variety of reasons – lack of skills, mental or physical disability, and pregnancy – they were useless to the managers of Moscow's enterprises. Stalin had expressed similar reservations at the Sixteenth Party Congress.[33]

The experiences of Moscow's labor exchanges seemed to confirm the assertion that most of the remaining registered unemployed were not able-bodied workers in search of jobs. In early fall, the Moscow labor exchanges purged 24,774 people from the rolls, leaving 7,260 registered unemployed, who were then summoned to the labor exchange to receive work assignments. Only 3,132 answered the summons. Zhukrov speculated that the remaining 4,128 were either dead or vanished souls, fictive names masking cheaters who were receiving illegal benefits, or "double dippers" who had found work but still collected stipends. The head of the Bureau of Registration, Fialkov, succinctly summed up the situation: "The problem is that we are now crying that we have no unemployment and cannot fill requests for labor, but at the same time, we cite figures for the unemployed. Not one organization is investigating this group of unemployed that we currently have in the labor exchanges."[34]

[32] Ibid., 55, 32, 33, 38, 41–42.   [33] Ibid., 56, 3–4.   [34] Ibid., 3–7, 39.

The labor exchanges also vacillated over how to treat skilled workers who could not find work in their own towns but were needed in other regions. These workers were understandably reluctant to leave a comfortable dwelling in a city or town for an unheated barracks or tent on a construction site. Did skilled workers qualify as "unemployed" if there was work for them elsewhere? A representative named Fominykh noted that often there was a shortage of workers with certain skills in one area and an excess of such workers in exchanges in other areas. Shaking his head, he ruefully remarked, "This is the kind of absurdity we have now: a month ago, we had about five hundred plumbers registered in the Moscow labor exchange at the same time that Magnitostroi was being choked by a shortage of these people and was not able to lay down the water lines that were holding back the tempo of construction. They began to recruit people from all ends of the union, but no one went to the labor exchanges to compel these people to go to work." Fominykh was concerned that the labor exchanges lacked the power to compel workers to go where they were needed or to work outside their trades. Fialkov insisted impatiently that the figures from Moscow were simply "impermissible." If factories across the country were desperate for skilled metalworkers, he demanded, "how is it possible to say that we have a thousand unemployed metal workers?" Both Fominykh and Fialkov expressed a concern common among employees of the labor exchanges: If they were to plan and distribute a labor force, they needed the power to dispatch workers to areas of labor shortage. Workers' mobility had to be controlled to meet the needs of the economy rather than the needs of the individual. Fialkov concluded, "There should not be any experienced workers left in the labor exchanges at all. They should all be at work. These are simply rolling stones [*letuny*]. Today they are here, and tomorrow at another factory. This is not a reserve."[35]

But what did constitute a "real" reserve of labor? Did unskilled women or peasants count? Just as the officials running the labor exchanges struggled to redefine "unemployment," they also sought to redefine its flip side – namely, the "working class." Not surprisingly, after years of "guarding the gates," the labor exchanges were biased against potential workers who were not already part of the "hereditary, skilled, male proletariat." One representative who attended the meeting was furious that so many peasants flocked to the Moscow exchanges in search of work: "They come here from the countryside, we put them all on the rolls, and they all stand around in the exchange." He also expressed disgust with workers who left their jobs: "Indeed, they come from Kharkov, Kiev, Nizhnii Novgorod, from the Donbas mines. And all of them say, 'Put me on the rolls.'" He

[35] Ibid., 54, 39.

noted angrily that none of them had permission slips (*spravki*) allowing them to leave their former jobs, and if the labor exchanges refused to register them, they simply scurried off to their unions, which promptly sent them to new jobs. He exclaimed, "If a year ago someone had suggested that we take the sort of person we are taking now, I would have called him an opportunist." Prejudice against both women and peasants ran high, though some officials expressed a marginal preference for urban women. Mordukhovich, the NKT representative, remarked disapprovingly that though the wives of workers were excluded from production, "we have opened the door to all elements from the countryside, who work in town for about a year and get a union card in their pocket." Other representatives, however, took an equally negative and unpromising view of unemployed women, confirming women's long-standing suspicion that male officials in the exchanges discriminated against them. According to one official in the Zamoskvoretskii exchange in Moscow, unemployed women did not constitute a reserve labor force (or any sort of labor force, for that matter) because they were all sick or pregnant. "What kind of manager would take a pregnant labor force?" he asked indignantly. "They work three to four months, then they get laid off, and the manager writes to send fifteen or twenty more workers. This benefits no one."[36]

Throughout 1930, as the crisis intensified, the "labor market" spun wildly out of control. Without central directives, the labor exchanges were unable to solve the labor problem on their own. They lacked the power to change legislation, to control mobility, to coordinate the supply of labor with demand, or to dispatch and deliver workers to areas of labor shortage. With managers, unions, and workers all acting at cross purposes, the labor exchanges were not even able to assess how many workers were needed by a given enterprise. Despite elaborate projections and plans, there was no regulation of the labor market. The labor exchanges struggled to make the transition from "gatekeeping" to planning, but by the fall of 1930, it was clear that the new situation had overwhelmed them.

Smashing the Old Paradigm: Women as a Key Reserve of Labor

On October 9, the government finally responded to the labor crisis. NKT issued a terse decree announcing that unemployment, the scourge of NEP, had been eliminated and replaced by a labor shortage. The labor exchanges were ordered to stop all unemployment benefits immediately and send all those still registered as unemployed to work. First priority in hiring

[36]   Ibid., 52, 55, 29.

was to be given to the registered unemployed, but if work was not available in their trade, they were to be sent to other jobs. Any refusal to work that was not corroborated by a medical certificate would lead to expulsion from the exchange.[37] Two days later, the Moscow labor exchange announced that its list of unemployed had shrunk from 8,500 to 177 people. Its budget for unemployment compensation was to be converted into a fund earmarked for the training and retraining of workers. Not a single kopeck more would be spent on the unemployed.[38] Almost overnight, the term "those who refuse to work" replaced "unemployed."

On October 20, the Central Committee officially announced "the full liquidation of unemployment in the Soviet Union." In a lengthy decree, it called for hundreds of thousands of new workers to enter the workforce, explaining that the "most important economic and political task" currently before NKT was the elimination of bottlenecks that were holding up new construction. The Central Committee commanded NKT to develop a plan within twenty days to train more than 1.3 million workers to enter industry in 1931. The CC moved quickly to expand the labor pool registered in the exchanges. Family members, teenage children, and widows of workers and *sluzhashchie*; workers in handicraft cooperatives; the children of independent craftsmen; and landless peasants (*batraks*), poor peasants (*bedniaks*), and *kolkhozniki* were all encouraged to register with the labor exchanges, regardless of their previous work experience. New workers were to be drawn from the ranks of urban housewives and teenagers as well as poor peasants and *kolkhozniki*. Registration now entitled workers to a job only, not to unemployment compensation. NKT was instructed to send every job seeker out to work within ten days. Anyone who refused to work would be struck from the rolls.

The Central Committee heavily criticized NKT even as it expanded its powers. It blamed the agency for its "extreme clumsiness and lack of planning," its failure to provide a skilled labor force for critical branches of heavy industry, construction, and transport, its "Right opportunism," and its waste of millions of rubles on "the so-called unemployed." It censured NKT's staff for its "extremely unsatisfactory" record. Other, presumably more efficient Party members were being assigned to NKT to ensure its proper direction. Yet in an effort to strengthen government control over the labor force, the Central Committee also gave NKT the right to transfer skilled workers to critical sectors such as coal mining, ferrous metallurgy, transport, and large capital construction. In fact, this was more a mandate than a right: the CC voiced the vague threat that any administrator who

---

[37] "V Strane Sovetov Net Bezrabotnitsy – Postanovlenie Narkomtruda," *Trud*, October 11, 1930, p. 1.
[38] "Ni Odnoi Kopeiki Posobiia Otkazuvaiushchimsia ot Raboty," *Trud*, October 12, 1930, p. 1.

interfered with the transfer of skilled workers "would be held responsible." Finally, in an attempt to stem the massive turnover of workers and relieve the shortage of labor, the Central Committee declared a moratorium on the promotion of workers into management. Workers who excelled in production were to be rewarded with housing, schooling, and vacations. Any worker who stayed in mining, construction, transport, or the textile, chemical, and machine-building industries for two years or more would receive extra pay or vacation time. The Central Committee ordered Gosplan, NKT, VSNKh, and VTsSPS to eliminate wage inequalities and irregularities among regions, and even within the same jobs, by the beginning of the new year. All "socially foreign elements," including declassed NEPmen and *kulaks,* were to be expelled from the labor force.[39]

Within two weeks of its decree, in November 1930, the Party launched a mass campaign to mobilize women into the labor force. *Trud,* the country's labor newspaper, announced the campaign with a front-page headline: "A Million Women to the Workbench and the Machine."[40] NKT, VSNKh, VTsSPS, Gosplan, and the commissariats of Enlightenment and Health were to recruit the wives of workers and provide every factory and industrial site with a female workforce. Women were to compose fully 50 percent of all new workers.[41] On December 18, the government took an additional series of actions to encourage women to enter the labor force. SNK and the Central Executive Committee (CEC) issued a decree instructing NKT to give family members of workers first priority for jobs in industry and transport. The decree emphasized the decision to rely on urban women rather than peasants to meet the labor shortage. Proclaiming "the full liquidation of unemployment," it stressed NKT's obligation to meet the needs of industry. Managers were reminded that they could hire only through the labor organs, not independently. Thus the Central Committee's decree of September, which had expanded managers' authority to hire loaders in the face of severe shortages, was rescinded.[42] This new decree strengthened the labor exchanges and shored up their rapidly dwindling control over the workforce.

In December 1930 and January 1931, SNK and the CEC attempted a bold reorganization of NKT. The state transformed the labor exchanges, which were no longer needed as unemployment centers, into cadre departments and gave them responsibility for actively recruiting labor, planning

---

[39] "O Meropriiatiiakh po Planovomu Obespecheniiu Narodnogo Khoziaistva Rabochei Siloi i Bor'be s Tekuchest'iu," *Trud,* October 22, 1930, p. 1; B. Marsheva, "Zhenskii Trud v 1931 godu," *Voprosy truda,* 1931, no. 1: 37.

[40] "Million Zhenshchin k Stankam i Mashinam," *Trud,* November 6, 1930, p. 1.

[41] "Zhenshchina na Zavod, k Stanku," *Trud,* November 16, 1930, p. 2; "Rabochie – 'Na Zapas,'" *Trud,* November 17, 1930, p. 1.

[42] "Dobit'sia Planogo Raspredeleniia i Ispol'zovaniia Rabochei Sil'e," *Trud,* December 18, 1930, p. 1.

the labor force, controlling the distribution of skilled labor, and dispatching job seekers to industries in need of labor. Managers were responsible for sending the labor departments their yearly and quarterly plans for labor, and the labor departments, in turn, were responsible for finding new sources of labor to cover their needs. People in search of work were to report to the cadre department, which would find them a job within three days. The cadre departments also had the right to sentence any worker who refused a job or who repeatedly appeared in the cadre department seeking a new job to six months' compulsory labor for being a "malicious disorganizer." The state challenged NKT to expand its role by searching for new sources of labor within the families of urban workers and collective farmers and redistributing skilled workers to important industries. Most important, NKT was to counter "the spontaneous moods of the economic organizations" – in other words, the growing tendency on the part of managers to hire their own workers. The state emphasized again that managers were not permitted to hire workers; *job seekers could be hired only through the organs of labor.*[43] After a year of rapid change, worsening labor shortages, and massive mobility among millions of old and new workers, the state had finally come to recognize that its policy of protecting the working class from infiltration by women, peasants, and youth had become a serious obstacle to industrial growth. SNK and the CEC aimed to reorganize and change the task of the labor exchanges from "gatekeeping" to active recruiting and planning. The new cadre departments would replace the labor exchanges and broaden their role significantly beyond the unsuccessful labor-market councils.

Recruiting Women: "Bring Your Wife to Work!"

The new system dissolved into chaos almost immediately. Local workplaces failed to send in their reports, leaving NKT with no information on their needs. Innocent workers who left sites because there was no housing for them were deemed "malicious disorganizers" and sentenced to compulsory labor. The cadre departments were crowded with workers, and the three-day limit went widely unenforced.[44] Throughout the spring of 1931, NKT struggled frantically to gain some control over the labor force. The deputy commissar of labor, I. A. Kraval', noted in a speech to VTsSPS staff that though supplying the economy with a labor force was one of the most

---

43 "Postanovlenie TsIK i Sovnarkoma SSSR o Poriadke Nauma i Raspredeleniia Rabochei Sil'e i o Bor'be s Tekuchest'iu," *Trud*, December 18, 1930, p. 1; "Dokladnaia Zapiska Upravleniia Snabzheniia Kadrami Narkomtruda SSSR v Kollegiiu ob Obespechenii Narodnogo Khoziaistva Rabochei Siloi," in *Industrializatsiia SSSR, 1929–1932. Dokumenty i materialy* (Moscow: Izdatel'stvo "Nauka," 1970), 418–20.

44 Ibid., 419–23.

important tasks of 1931, the recruiting organizations were extremely ineffective. He conceded, "It is necessary to say that of all the various apparatuses we have, the weakest and the most careless of the supply apparatuses
is neither the executive committees nor the unions, but the apparatus for
recruiting a labor force."[45] But despite the deputy's newly placed emphasis
on the recruitment and organizing of the labor force, NKT had scant success. Managers, acutely short of workers, hired "*na zapas,*" or whoever
was "at hand." Directly flouting the government decrees of December and
January, which had given NKT sole control over hiring, managers hired
anyone who showed up at the factory gates. Hundreds of thousands of
women and peasants, eager to work, bypassed the cadre departments entirely. The pervasive need for workers turned managers into criminals,
and cadre departments into superfluous organizations.

One critic, summing up the record of the cadre departments, remarked
that though they were no longer called labor exchanges, their role remained the same. They had simply continued their old practice of registering people in need of work and sending them out to jobs. They had done
nothing to develop a labor force and match it with the new needs of industry, nothing to recruit workers or mobilize untapped reserves of female
labor. Not even highly skilled workers, in demand throughout the country, were transferred to key industries. The new cadre departments had
no idea which regions or enterprises were experiencing labor shortages,
or what sort of workers they needed; they seemed incapable of coordinating even the simplest match between skill and demand. They proved
unable to cope not only with their new tasks of planning and recruitment but also with their old job of processing the enormous backlog of
workers waiting for jobs. In Moscow, the cadre department failed to find
jobs even for metalworkers, doctors, teachers, and other skilled applicants who languished on the unemployment rolls. Swamped by demands
from workplaces, the administrative staff flatly refused to process further
requests for labor. Communication between the cadre department and
the economic organs broke down completely amid mutual accusations
and recriminations. Brandishing a recent decree urging the labor organs
to work "in a planned and systematic fashion," the Moscow cadre department justified its refusal to process new requests with the assertion
that workers would be provided in "a planned manner." One observer
concluded, "A worse example of bureaucratism and distortion of the directives of the Party and state would be difficult to imagine." There were
similar scenarios in other places.[46]

[45] "V 1931 godu Narodnomu Khoziaistvu SSSR Potrebuetsia 3.5 ml. Novykh Rabochikh,"
Trud, January 28, 1931, p. 2.
[46] N. Shastin, "Upravleniia Kadrami – Ne Birzhi Truda," *NTF*, 1931, no. 20: 12–13.

The labor exchanges, now operating as "cadre departments," were accustomed to acting as gatekeepers to the working class. Using established priority lists, they had always determined which job seekers would have an opportunity to apply for the privilege of a union job. Yet under conditions of explosive economic expansion, elaborately planned priority lists of workers had become an anachronism. The old habits of the labor exchanges, based on the allocation of work according to seniority and skill, prevented the rapid deployment of labor. Unsure how to organize recruitment or training, inadequately informed as to the needs of the localities, and overwhelmed by job seekers and demands for labor, the cadre departments were unable to make the critical transition from local suppliers of the urban unemployed to national providers of a recruited labor force.

As it became increasingly clear that NKT could not respond to the needs of industry, the state began shifting control over hiring to managers. On March 3, 1931, the Council of Labor and Defense (STO), a central planning organization, issued a decree transferring the task of recruiting workers from NKT to the economic organs. The intention behind the move was not entirely clear, and it did little to impose order on the chaotic situation. The decree outlined a complex division of responsibility for labor recruitment among various organizations. NKT was to supervise and allocate local recruitment among the various economic organs and plan the distribution of workers; the economic organs would be responsible for direct recruitment of workers. NKT would cede responsibility for direct hiring to the economic organs but would continue to play an important role in planning the labor force and supervising recruitment.[47]

Through the spring and summer of 1931, NKT focused on identifying new sources of labor and methods of mobilization. Building on the campaign first launched in the fall of 1930 to bring women into the labor pool, it targeted the wives and daughters of workers. A ready-made workforce, these women did not need to be recruited from far away, housed, or acclimatized to the discipline of waged labor. NKT hoped that by recruiting women who lived close to the factories, it could stem the massive turnover resulting from workers' leaving in search of housing. With some workplaces experiencing up to 250 percent turnover per year, urban women might stabilize the situation. On March 28, NKT sent a letter to its local labor departments, ordering them to recruit the wives of workers into the same plants as their husbands. The aim was to reduce turnover, raise wages in the family, and create "socially-valued and

[47] "Do Kontsa Vytratit' 'Sistem u Samoteka' v Organizatsii Otkhodnichestva," *NTF*, 1930, nos. 23–24: 20.

stable cadres of women workers."[48] Yet the local departments of labor were unable to deal with even the relatively simple task of recruiting a captive audience. On April 10, the leaders of NKT met to discuss the issue of women workers. They concluded that "the organs of labor have not given this work the necessary attention and have not taken measures to realize the plan." Nevertheless, women were streaming into the labor force independent of any plan: "In reality, the involvement of women is proceeding *samotek*." Critical of their own labor departments, NKT officials noted that managers, VSNKh, the Commissariat of Enlightenment, and the Commissariat of Provisioning had likewise failed to encourage women's entrance into the workforce.[49]

NKT soon recognized that its local labor departments were incapable of recruiting even wives and daughters. Following the protocol earlier established by the Council for Labor and Defense, it proposed that managers assume this task, giving them the limited right to bypass the local organs of labor in hiring women who were related to workers with three or more years of seniority.[50] NKT hoped that if managers had the authority to hire the wives and daughters of workers, they would be able to tap into an immediately accessible reserve of labor. In mid-May, VTsSPS prepared a lengthy document for the Orgbiuro of the Central Committee, in which it concluded that both NKT and VSNKh had done a poor job of involving women in the workforce. It seconded NKT's suggestion that the main responsibility for recruiting women be transferred to the local workplaces themselves.[51] In reality, the power to recruit labor was becoming increasingly decentralized, moving from NKT to the economic organs to the enterprises and then finally to the managers themselves. Yet officially, at least, the issue of power was still unresolved. "We have this unhealthy phenomenon," Samoilov, a representative of VTsSPS, noted in May 1931. "Gaps in industry are filled with the wives of workers, and gaps in the state apparatus and cultural sector with the wives of white-collar employees [*sluzhashchie*]. These divisions are not correct either politically or practically." Although Samoilov spoke out against the practice of "bringing one's wife to work," managers were in fact encouraged to meet labor shortages in precisely this way.[52] One advocate of NKT charged in the summer 1931 that even though the labor departments were doing a lousy

48   GARF, f. 6983, o. 1, d. 165, "Tsirkuliarnoe Pis'mo Vsem Oblastnym i Kraevym Otdelam Truda i NKT Avtonomnykh Respublik," 78.
49   G. Ritov, "Sotsialisticheskaia Industriia Dolzhna Poluchit' ne Menee 1,600,0000 Novykh Rabotnits," *NTF*, 1931, no. 18: 3. See the report on this meeting in "V Tsentral'nykh Organakh Truda," *NTF*, 1931, no. 14: 18.
50   GARF, f. 5451, o. 15, d. 362, "Orgbiuro TsK VKP (b)," 83–84.   51   Ibid., 101.
52   GARF, f. 6983, o. 1, d. 165, "Zasedaniia Komiteta po Uluchsheniiu Truda i Byta Rabotnits i Krest'ianok pri Prezidiuma VTsIK," 48 ob.

job, it was "an opportunistic invention" to claim that NKT was no longer responsible for recruiting.[53]

As the state shifted the job of recruiting to managers, the purpose of the cadre departments became ever more obscure. One critic urged NKT to reorganize the cadre departments yet again because they had become useless. They did little to recruit among the families of workers already established at a plant or site. They did nothing to create *byt* institutions so women could go to work. And worst of all, their actions abetted labor turnover by providing workers with the opportunity to register repeatedly. The cadre departments in Kharkov, for example, reregistered hundreds of dissatisfied workers and sent them off to new jobs. Workers sent to one machine-building plant were disgusted by the conditions they found there and returned en masse to the cadre department, where they were dispatched to new jobs. Labeling these workers "self-seekers, rolling stones, absence mongers, and disorganizers," the critic recommended that the cadre departments keep records of workers who repeatedly moved from job to job.[54] The cadre departments, initially designed to prevent labor turnover, had instead become a new source of mobility. Other critics questioned the very purpose of these departments. One queried, "There is no unemployment, but there are still unemployed. Who are they? They are people who do not want to work." He noted that there were still crowds of people, young and old, in the Moscow cadre department. These were workers who either had been fired or simply did not want to work. When a brigade of four foundry workers organized by the newspaper *Na trudovom fronte* checked the Moscow cadre department in May 1931, they found seventeen thousand people on the rolls. Their review categorized 50 percent of these as "self-seekers and idlers." Many workers remained registered even after they were employed. The cadre department was shamed into sending nine hundred people per day off to work; by the time the brigade had finished its investigation, not a single unemployed person was left. The brigade concluded that cadre departments were unnecessary. Both their tasks – distributing workers and registering them for work – were "done in vain," for the cadre departments were used mainly by "chronic idlers." In the foundry workers' view, "Honest workers can always find work. The administration of cadres does not administer cadres." The brigade noted that it was an open secret that managers were recruiting labor themselves, and that "the role of the cadre departments has been reduced to a formal registration of hire, which task is done in reality, legally or illegally, by the enterprises themselves." The cadre departments had become "a superfluous bureaucratic turnpike on

[53] A. Fridrikh, "Po-Novomu Rabotat', Po-Novomu Rykovodit'," *NTF*, 1931, no. 19: 3–4.
[54] N. Shastin, "Upravleniia Kadrami – ne Birzhi Truda," *NTF*, 1931, no. 20: 12–13.

the road to supplementing the labor force," a nuisance that managers simply avoided. Although many managers were pushing to eliminate the cadre departments altogether, the brigade suggested that they be retained as a planning organization to ascertain demand and supply.[55]

By the end of May 1931, NKT at last concluded that the cadre departments were not capable of supplying the economy with a labor force. Despite various recommendations, their efforts had proved more of a hindrance than a help. In a final decree legalizing an already widespread practice, NKT and SNK announced the elimination of compulsory hiring through the organs of labor and significantly broadened the rights of managers to recruit and hire their own workers. Henceforth, urban workers would be recruited directly by managers of the enterprises. The state also severely curtailed the number of cadre departments. Only those in large industrial centers would remain open; in other areas, the local departments of labor were to establish special sectors to guarantee enterprises a workforce.[56] This was the third major reorganization NKT had undergone in less than eighteen months in the attempt to plan and provide industry with a workforce. From the labor-market councils in late 1929, through the transformation of the labor exchanges into cadre departments in January 1930, and finally to the elimination of all but a few cadre departments in May 1931, NKT had repeatedly endeavored to create an organization capable of supplying industry with workers. By late spring, the state finally admitted defeat, recognizing that under conditions of severe labor shortage, any centralized effort to plan and deploy workers was almost surely doomed to failure.

Reports through the summer indicated that hundreds of thousands of women were streaming into the workforce, largely on their own initiative. As one skeptic asserted, it had nothing to with state planning. "It would be a mistake," he wrote "to look for an explanation in the initiatives of the economic or social organizations. All occurs *samotek*." As every published and unpublished report from the localities noted, organizational efforts to recruit women, even workers' wives, remained ineffectual. Only a few large recruitment drives were organized, and these were not always led by Party, labor, or economic organizations. Women in mining communities, for example, organized themselves, going from door to door and signing up housewives to enter the mines, with no help from the Party, the unions, or NKT.[57]

If the local state and Party organizations failed to follow through on the campaign to involve women in the workforce, how did women find jobs?

[55] "Ne Tolkuchka, a Planovoe Raspredelenie Rabochei Sily," *NTF*, 1931, no. 19: 7–8.
[56] "Dokladnaia Zapiska," in *Industrializatsiia SSSR*, 423.
[57] Ritov, "Sotsialisticheskaia Industriia Dolzhna Poluchit' ne Menee 1,600,000 Novykh Rabotnits," 3–5.

Some managers took NKT's advice and attempted to recruit women by launching "bring your wife to work" campaigns. The director of AMO, a machine-building factory in Moscow, posted signs in all the shops reading "Comrade shock workers: Tell your wives that enrollment in the factory is open to women! Call them to work at the bench!"[58] When the Northern Shipyards experienced a severe labor shortage, managers began recruiting dockworkers' wives, students in working-class neighborhoods, and unemployed women in workers' housing. In Krasnyi Putilovets, managers gave job applications to workers in certain shops and told them to sign up their wives, daughters, and relatives.[59] In Sovetskaia Zvezda, the factory committee made a special effort to recruit women by developing contracts with the local housing authorities.

Recruiting family members of workers required little effort, yet many managers did not even bother to try. Rather, the process of recruitment occurred *samotek*: workers brought female relatives to work, and women appeared at factory gates and construction sites. Preliminary and fragmentary data from the Leningrad region showed that women entered industry independent of the efforts of local authorities. Large numbers of women entered every branch of the economy – with more than twenty-eight thousand going into industry – in the first six months of 1931. A report sent by the Leningrad Executive Committee to the Russian Central Executive Committee noted that by July, women's share of industry (41.1 percent) had surpassed the control target (38.6 percent) set earlier. Yet according to the report, "The control figures were met in the first half of 1931 *samotek*." Women were hired because there was not a single able-bodied man left in the labor exchanges. Although reserves of male labor were exhausted, neither the department of labor, nor the regional economic organs, nor the district soviet knew how many potentially employable women lived in the Leningrad region.[60]

Chaos and disorganization likewise prevailed on the large construction sites. In Magnitogorsk, a huge iron and steel complex, about half of the workers on site had arrived *samotek*. Waves of people rolled in and receded: between October 1930 and July 1931, 79,000 workers arrived on the site, and 56,000 left. Although there were an estimated 15,000 unemployed women on hand, there was no planned recruitment of women. About 8,000 had no children and could have gone to work immediately. The system of food distribution was so bad, however, that women often stayed out of work in order to stand in line. One inspector explained, "Women stand in line at the food cooperatives from morning to night. If

58 N. Kal'ma, "Tysiachi Kilovatt Zhenskoi Energii," *NTF*, 1932, no. 7: 10.
59 S. Modestov, "Ot Slov k Delu," *NTF*, 1931, no. 18: 12–13.
60 GARF, f. 6983, o. 1, d. 165, "V Prezidium VTsIK," 4–5 ob.

a wife did not stay home, her husband would go hungry."[61] In mining, women began working underground in the pits at the beginning of 1931. A year later, 2,355 women, or 11.7 percent of the female workforce, were working underground. Yet here, too, the initiative came from women themselves. In the Makeevskii district, for example, women eager to earn higher wages petitioned the mine administration to allow them to work underground. Despite severe labor shortages in mining, labor officials did little to recruit women.[62]

NKT's attempts to recruit peasants through contracts between local labor departments and managers of collective farms were also largely unsuccessful. Throughout 1930, industrial managers were forbidden to visit the collective farms to recruit individual workers. In February 1931, Kolkhoztsentr (the Union of Agricultural Collectives) and NKT signed an agreement arranging for peasants to work in industry in exchange for mutual help between collective farms and workplaces, but the decree was never implemented. When labor recruiters visited the collective farms, they met with strong resistance on the part of the farm managers. Anxious to retain control over "their" peasants and fearful of their own labor shortage, they tried to bar NKT representatives from the collective farms and in some cases even threatened to arrest them if they turned up. They also took punitive measures against those peasants who left the collective farms, deducting up to 50 percent of their wages from their seasonal jobs. On March 3, NKT, Kolkhoztsentr, the Commissariat of Land, and VSNKh all signed an agreement to direct "unneeded" workers on collective farms to seasonal work, but it had little effect: apparently the farm managers "needed" all their workers. After the Council of Labor and Defense transferred all recruiting to the enterprises on the basis of individual labor contracts, Kolkhoztsentr moved quickly to annul all existing contracts and to eliminate recruiting. It ordered the collective-farm unions to stop providing statistics on the availability of farm labor. Kolkhoztsentr concluded that the collective farms should have nothing further to do with recruiting: henceforth, recruiters could contract with individual peasants.[63] The lines were thus drawn between agriculture and industry in the battle over labor. In March, SNK retaliated against collective-farm managers by forbidding them to restrain or obstruct peasants who wanted to leave the farms to work in industry or construction.

[61] GARF, f. 5515, o. 17, d. 65, "Na Urale Ne Vse Blagopoluchno," 18–19. See also Stephen Kotkin, *Magnetic Mountain: Stalinism as a Civilization* (Berkeley, Calif.: University of California Press, 1995), 72–105, 223–24.
[62] GARF, f. 5451, o. 16, d. 557, "Informsvodka," 30–31; Likhterev, "Rabotnitsa Dolzhna Zavoevat' Gornuiu Promyshlennost'," *NTF*, 1931, nos. 8–9: 17.
[63] "Do Kontsa Vytravit' 'Sistem u Samoteka' v Organizatsii Otkhodnichestva," *NTF*, 1931, nos. 23–24: 20.

Labor shortages persisted, however, despite the peasants' official freedom of movement. By the spring of 1931, there were severe shortages in all leading sectors of industry, including metal, machine building, chemicals, coal mining, iron ore, and construction. Many of the largest and most important building sites were functioning with fewer than half the number of construction workers they required. A. M. Panfilova, a Soviet labor historian, has noted that NKT "did a very poor job of organizing the labor force and planning its deployment. It could not adjust to its new tasks."[64] And still NKT continued to be stymied by the outright resistance of collective-farm managers. In July, it ordered the collective and state farms to provide figures on the rural population. In many areas, including the Central Black Earth region, the order was completely ignored.[65] Collective farms in the Leningrad region meanwhile refused to give up a single peasant to the timber industry, which was desperately short of woodcutters and floaters. Sawmill managers expected fourteen hundred peasants to arrive for work, but not a single one showed up. One collective-farm union slapped the following restrictions on seasonal work: no more than 25 percent of the men would be permitted to leave the farm, no women would be considered, peasants would be released only at the beginning of haymaking, and everyone must work locally.[66] Recruitment of the peasantry, especially for seasonal industries, was not working out as planned. The needs of the economy, according to all reports, were not being met according to plan, though the labor market was not quite "free," either. Large trusts, sectors, factories, construction sites, and collective farms battled fiercely over labor, attempting to hold on to workers through a variety of promises, inducements, blandishments, and repressive measures.

NKT, meanwhile, chastened by the failure of its cadre departments and the difficulties it had experienced in recruiting peasants, began to press the enterprises to recruit urban women more aggressively through contracts with local housing authorities.[67] In the early fall, it instructed managers to exploit the extensive system of housing cooperatives, which managed buildings throughout the cities, to identify and mobilize women. Every workplace would be linked to one or more nearby housing cooperatives, which would deliver a specified number of women to the workplace. In exchange, the workplace would provide funds, materials, and equipment so that the cooperatives could construct day-care centers, dining halls, laundries, and other services to enable housewives to go to work. NKT sent instructions to the cooperatives, unions, and local labor

---

64 Panfilova, pp. 12–50, offers an excellent overview of recruitment among the peasantry.
65 S. Orlova, "Nado Nailuchshim Obrazom Naladit' Uchet Trudovykh Resursov," *NTF*, 1931, no. 34: 5.
66 "Kak Ne Nado Organizovat' Otkhodichestvo," *NTF*, 1931, nos. 26–27: 7.
67 Trubnik, "1,600,000 Zhenshchin v Proizvodstvo v Kontsu 1931," *NTF*, 1931, no. 28: 8.

departments, urging them to implement these contracts immediately. The instructions noted that the labor shortage had become "so severe that enterprises are forced to search for a labor force from thousands of kilometers away, at the same time that the towns have a fairly significant cadre – housewives, working-class family members – of unused labor." Sensitive to the decrease in real wages, NKT added that the recruitment of women would have the further benefit of raising the income of the working-class family.[68] In August, NKT issued a decree noting that the Party's decision to involve 1.5 million women in the workforce was being fulfilled "with impermissible weakness." There were still no plans for various branches of industry, no review to verify that directives were being implemented. NKT suggested that special personnel be designated within the departments of labor to ensure women's involvement.[69] NKT, VSNKh, VTsSPS, and the Association of Housing Cooperatives (ZhAKT) sent out a circular rebuking their local organs for doing nothing to draw women into the labor force. Aiming to send housewives to work, it instructed housing cooperatives to bypass local labor and cadre departments by establishing labor contracts directly with local enterprises. Every enterprise would inform the housing co-ops of its needs, and the co-ops would in turn recruit the required number of housewives. Each housing cooperative would maintain ties with several enterprises and assume responsibility for supplying them with female workers.[70] Once again, NKT's plan proved impracticable: the contracts obligated plant managers to allocate scarce funds to day care and other services, a concession most managers were reluctant to make. Denied that quid pro quo, housing officials, offered little help with recruitment. Few contracts were concluded, and in the opinion of one observer, women continued to enter the labor force "mostly *samotek*."[71]

Reports of poor coordination, chaos, and interagency conflicts persisted. At a meeting of the sector of industrial cadres of VTsSPS in September, a representative of the Central Housing Union (Tsentrozhilsoiuz) complained that no one apart from the officials of the housing cooperatives was doing anything to recruit women. Work among women was "going very poorly." The housing cooperatives had succeeded, for example, in mobilizing five thousand women into the workforce in the Urals, but NKT had remained stubbornly unhelpful. In Kazan, the housing cooperatives had mobilized two hundred housewives, but the labor department

[68]   GARF, f. 5515, o. 17, d. 687, "Narkomtrud SSSR, VSNKh SSSR, VTsSPS, Tsentrozhilsoiuz," 249–249 ob. For a prototype contract, see "Tipovoi Dogovor Mezhdu Zavodupravleniem i Pravleniem ZhAKT'a," 243.
[69]   GARF, f. 5451, o. 15, d. 363, "Postanovlenie Kollegii NKT SSSR," 21.
[70]   GARF, f. 5451, o. 15, d. 362, "Vsem Organam Truda," 140–41.
[71]   I. B——n, "Zhenshchinu – Na Proizvodstvo," *Na fronte industrializatsii*, 1932, nos. 5–6: 7–8.

had arrogantly responded, "We don't need them now. Send them when we ask." A representative from NKT apologized on behalf of her organization for the blunder in Kazan, but she noted that the cooperatives were supposed to notify the labor department before they began recruiting women. There was clearly a lack of coordination on the local level. Another representative at the meeting remarked that the incident in Kazan was typical; such things occurred throughout the country. Several Party leaders, clearly unaware of the earlier circular, questioned whether housing cooperatives should be mobilizing women at all.[72] From top to bottom, from the center to the local level, severe problems of coordination, motivation, and organization plagued every attempt to draft women into the workforce. At the end of September, VTsSPS held a meeting to review the results of the campaign. Safina, a member of the Sector of Mass Work under VTsSPS, gathered and analyzed reports from local areas. On the basis of this information, she concluded that the unions, with few exceptions, had done no work to popularize the decisions of the All-Union Meeting for Work among Women, held the previous February. "There is no system, and no plan," she said. "Work proceeds *samotek*."[73]

"Free" Market or Planned Deployment?

During the first five-year plan, the Party was forced to give up its attachment to an exclusionary labor policy and respond in new ways to a widespread labor shortage. These years were marked by fierce and troubling contradictions: exclusion versus recruitment, unemployment versus labor shortage, control versus chaos. Until October 1930, the Party still held to an older model of the working class. Policy was predicated on the need to protect the privileges of industrial workers, fear of "nonproletarian elements," low regard for the unskilled, and apathy toward women. These tenets all proved to be serious obstacles to the Party's ability to respond to the unexpectedly powerful demands for new labor. Fearful that the transformation of the working class would undermine their base of support, Party leaders hesitated to relinquish control over entrance into its ranks. They deeply distrusted peasants and others who had never worked for wages, and that view was largely validated by the peasants' own response to collectivization. Sheila Fitzpatrick estimates that one out of every three peasants who entered the workforce during the first five-year plan left the countryside as a result of dekulakization. These individuals nursed "bitter feelings" toward Soviet power, and the Party regarded

[72] GARF, f. 5451, o. 15, d. 361, "Soveshchanie pri Sektore Promkadrov VTsSPS po Voprosu o Vnedrenii Zhenskogo Truda v Promyshlennost'," 40–54.
[73] GARF, f. 5451, o. 15, d. 363, "Itogi Vnedrenie Zhenskogo Truda v Promyshlennost' za 1-oe Polugodie 1931," 18.

them as "a new class of hidden enemies." In Fitzpatrick's words, "The great peasant exodus to town ... was also a paranoid nightmare come true."[74]

The old policy paradigm was finally shattered by the Party's announcement, in October 1930, that unemployment had been eliminated and superseded by a labor shortage. Yet by the time the Party acted, the labor force was already being transformed from below as millions of new workers sought jobs. Policy served to ratify and further these changes, but ultimately it did not initiate, shape, or control them. By the time the Party launched its campaign to hire women, the labor market, already swollen beyond all expectations, had overrun the flimsy controls of an outdated labor policy and was verging on anarchy. The organized campaigns to recruit women (through housing cooperatives) and peasants (through collective farms) faced numerous obstacles. Neither could be deemed a success in meeting industry's voracious demands for labor. Although Party leaders tried to adapt their labor policy to the new demands of industrialization, their efforts proved slow and ineffective. The Party turned to urban women as a major reserve in November 1930 not only for economic reasons but also because it feared the "unreliable" peasantry. Leaders and planners spoke repeatedly of the need to shore up the proletarian composition of the towns and to stem the draining of services by millions of newly arriving peasants.

Another unexpected consequence of industrialization, recognized only belatedly by planners and Party leaders, was industry's need for unskilled and semiskilled labor. With no help from NKT, industrial managers hired hundreds of thousands of unskilled, inexperienced workers – women and men – and provided them with effective training on the job. Although male skilled workers were hired before women, the threat of labor exchanges peopled permanently by unskilled women proved in the end to be baseless. Operating on an older model based on craft skills, Party leaders, planners, and labor officials did not fully comprehend the transformative nature of the industrial revolution they themselves had launched. They continued to insist on industry's inability to absorb the unskilled even as hundreds of thousands of new workers were finding jobs. These workers, concentrated on massive construction sites, in logging camps, factories, shipyards, shops, and railroads, formed a new Soviet working class. Pushed forward by the great human upheaval and dispersal of collectivization and industrialization, this working class was created by forces unleashed, but largely uncontrolled, from above.

---

[74]   Sheila Fitzpatrick, "The Great Departure: Rural-Urban Migration in the Soviet Union, 1929–33," in William Rosenberg and Lewis Siegelbaum, eds., *Social Dimensions of Soviet Industrialization* (Bloomington, Ind.: Indiana University Press, 1993), 34.

A village meeting to recruit new workers for Magnitogorsk. 1931.

Construction of ore and coke bunkers for a blast furnace for the Azovstal' (Azov steel) factory in the Ukrainian town of Mariupol. 1932.

Construction at Serp i Molot (Hammer and Sickle), one of Moscow's largest metallurgical complexes. 1932.

5

"The Five-Year Plan for Women": Planning Above, Counterplanning Below

> The fulfillment of the plan in 1931 and the following years demands a series of maneuvers from the labor force: a group of men must leave work, and women must replace them. Men, after retraining in their positions, will be sent to jobs that would be harmful to the female organism.
>
> S. Gimmel'farb, labor economist, 1931[1]

In the summer of 1930, as hundreds of thousands of unemployed workers, peasants, and women poured through the tumbled gates to the working class, planners quietly tucked away a set of elaborate blueprints for the deployment of women in the files of the Commissariat of Labor (NKT), the State Planning Commission (Gosplan), and the Council of People's Commissars (SNK). The plans, redrafted many times, had resulted in a final, detailed document entitled "The Five-Year Plan for Female Labor." Never published or publicly discussed, this plan had emerged from countless meetings of NKT, Gosplan, the Committee to Improve the Labor and Life of Women (KUTB), and other commissariats and departments throughout the spring and summer of 1930. Planners based their plan for female labor on intensive research into Soviet industry in 1930. Surveying the advances of rationalization and mechanization in various industries, they set target figures and training quotas for women throughout the economy, specifying their numbers and placement in various sectors, industries, shops, and jobs.

The plans, preserved in the State Archive of the Russian Federation (GARF), are fully revealed and analyzed for the first time in this chapter. Although they had an important impact on the configuration and composition of the Soviet labor force, few labor historians have even been aware of their existence. Solomon Shwarz referred to them briefly in his well-known book *Labor in the Soviet Union*, but he was never actually

---

[1] S. Gimmel'farb, "Likvidatsiia Bezrabotitsy v SSSR i Problema Kadrov," *Problemy ekonomiki*, 1931, nos. 4–5: 45.

143

able to read them. He noted that they were sketchily outlined by their coauthor, E. Bronshtein, only after World War II.[2]

The plans were intended not to open up opportunities for women on an equal basis with men, or even to send them to work in those sectors of greatest labor shortage, but rather to deploy them rapidly by reserving for them specially designated areas and jobs. In effect, they *"regendered," or resegregated by gender, the entire economy from above.* Large groups of women, rather than individuals, could thus be moved en masse into positions vacated by men or created by industrialization. The plans were premised on the idea of sex integration through segregation, a seeming paradox that promoted an overall increase in women's share of the labor force while maintaining carefully defined boundaries for their deployment. The line between men's and women's work would thus be redrawn but not erased.

The planners' strategy of integration through segregation was not entirely unwelcome to women's activists in the planning process. Baranova, the head of KUTB, and Serina, a prominent member of NKT, pushed hard to include women in the larger five-year plan. They were not averse to a strategy aimed at moving large numbers of women into the workforce. The plans also encouraged feminist brigades to enter the factories to determine which jobs were suitable for women. The "small-scale planning" of the brigades replicated at the local or factory level the larger, central strategy to regender jobs, shops, and sectors. Local factory activists challenged managers with "counterplans" from below, commanding them to "regender" certain positions and open them to women. Although the "Five-Year Plan for Female Labor" was never enacted as legislation, it became the basis for several important decrees and the Party's subsequent strategy toward female labor. Most important, the combination of these two processes – large- and small-scale planning – was responsible in great measure for the subsequent shape of the Soviet labor force. Many lines of sex segregation that were first planned in 1930 have survived, surprisingly intact, to this day. Women retail clerks, service personnel, streetcar drivers, plasterers, and turners, as well as the women in all-female factory shops and in thousands of other jobs and sectors today, all unknowingly owe their place to the five-year plan for female labor.

The Struggle to Include Women in the First Five-Year Plan

Women's activists (*zhenskii aktiv*) in unions, NKT, and the Party were dissatisfied with the five-year plan's failure to include women from the very

[2] Solomon Shwarz, *Labor in the Soviet Union* (New York: Praeger, 1951), 69–71.

beginning of the planning process, in 1928. They believed that the plan, which ignored women entirely, needed to include them in its projected expansion of the labor force. Their frustration grew as they watched the planners focus ever more narrowly on heavy industry, a male-dominated sector. Initially, both women's activists and labor experts criticized the five-year plan for favoring heavy industry. One expert on female labor worried that the plan's disproportionate investment in that sector would further undermine women's share in production. Critical of the plan's priorities, she argued that "the stable position of women's labor is possible only under a general storming of *all* [Soviet] industry."[3] Other economists noted with apprehension that Gosplan's proposed link between wages and productivity would hurt women, who were concentrated in more backward, less productive industries; if salary differentials between light and heavy industry widened, women would lag even further behind men. The plan's critics argued that investment should be redistributed and priorities adjusted so that all workers would benefit equally from industrialization. Some planners suggested that the surplus generated by greater productivity and investment might be distributed fairly among all workers, and not just handed over to the more skilled in priority industries.[4] Baranova angrily pointed out at a meeting in 1930 that the five-year plan "did not say a single word about female labor." Her comments made it clear that women's activists had hoped for a more detailed plan of inclusion since 1928: "When we noted this [exclusion], it was already too late," she explained. "The control figures were set. Two years passed, and nothing was done to include women."[5]

The state had, in fact, made some early efforts in this direction. In March 1929, SNK issued a decree instructing NKT USSR to incorporate a section on women's labor and *byt* in the first five-year plan.[6] NKT, however, failed to comply. In November 1929, an interdepartmental commission was set up with the express purpose of including women in labor planning. Bronshtein, from Gosplan; Marsheva, a well-known expert on female labor from NKT; and representatives from VTsSPS (the All-Union Central Council of Trade Unions), VSNKh (the Supreme Council of the National Economy), and the Commissariats of Land and Transport met to work out a "five-year plan for female labor." They quickly

[3] B. Marsheva, "Problema Zhenskogo Truda v Sovremmenykh Usloviiakh," *Voprosy truda,* 1929, no. 2: 40.
[4] F. Vinnik, "O Planirovanii Zarabotnoi Platy," *Voprosy truda,* 1929, no. 1: 49–50; F. Bulkin, "Leningradskie Soiuzy i Zarabotnaia Plata v Piatiletke," *Trud,* October 14, 1928.
[5] GARF, f. 6983, o. 1, d. 159, "Protokol No. 15. Zasedanie Prezidiuma Komiteta VTsIK po Uluchsheniiu Truda i Byta Rabotnits i Krest'ianok," 271.
[6] GARF, f. 3316, o. 22, d. 941, "Sovet Truda i Oborony. Gosudarstvennaia Planovaia Komissiia. Gosplan SSSR v SNK." This decree is mentioned in the exchange between Gosplan and SNK, p. 20.

concluded that they needed more information on women in the labor force and asked VSNKh and the Commissariat of Transport to prepare reports on mechanization, training, and skill among women workers. VSNKh was also to report back shortly on the possibility of placing more women in the metal and electrical industries, and VTsSPS was to contact its member unions and ask them to prepare similar studies on the potential role of women within their own industries. The commission met again less than two weeks later to review recommendations from VSNKh and the Commissariat of Transport, but it received no information from the unions. With its fact-finding mission at a halt, the commission evidently abandoned its short-lived effort at planning.[7]

As the commission was supposed to be hammering out its five-year plan for female labor, NKT Russia was also attempting to draft a plan to serve the Russian Republic. Almost two months later, in January 1930, KUTB sent a curt note to NKT asking for an immediate update on its work. Romanov, the head of NKT Russia, responded that no further planning for Russia was possible because Gosplan and NKT (USSR), which were responsible for producing the all-union plan, had refused to do anything until April.[8] Once again, all plans disappeared into the black hole of bureaucracy. Another month passed, and then Uglanov, the head of NKT USSR, complained to Gosplan that it could not possibly work out a plan before April because it had not received the necessary data in "a timely manner." Uglanov requested that Gosplan grant him an extension until April or May.[9] Fifteen days later, in late February, Bronshtein and Shmidt, members of Gosplan, indignantly complained to SNK that NKT had already been granted too many extensions: the commissariat had been asked to include women in its plan over a year ago, in March 1929, and still it had done nothing. The deadline was then extended to March 1, 1930. Now NKT announced that it needed another extension, until April. Despite Gosplan's "significant help," NKT had not managed to produce a plan. Bronshtein and Shmidt wrote angrily, "Gosplan considers it impossible to extend the deadline any further and requests NKT to present its report no later than March 15."[10] March 15 passed with no plan. Toward the end of that month, the Central Executive Committee bowed

[7] GARF, f. 3316, o. 22, d. 941, "Protokol No. 1. Zasedaniia Mezhduvedomstvennoi Komissii po Prorabotke 5 – Letnogo Plana po Zhenskomu Trudu," and "Protokol No. 2. Zasedaniia Mezhduvedomstvennoi Komissii po Sostavleniiu 5-ti Letnim Plane po Zhenskomu Trudu," 7–5, 15. This entire *delo* is numbered backward.

[8] GARF, f. 3316, o. 22, d. 941, "Spravka," and "RSFSR. Narodnyi Komissariat Truda," 16, 17.

[9] GARF, f. 3316, o. 22, d. 941, "Narodnyi Komissariat Truda SSSR v Gosplan SSSR," 19.

[10] GARF, f. 3316, o. 22, d. 941, "Sovet Truda i Oborony. Gosudarstvennaia Planovaia Komissiia. Gosplan SSSR," 20.

to the inevitable and voted to delay presentation of a five-year plan for female labor until the middle of April.[11] Once again, the deadline passed without a plan.

Finally, on May 3, 1930, the presidium of Gosplan USSR met to hear Bronshtein, a Gosplan representative, and Shvartz, a representative of NKT USSR, present a plan for women's labor. Titled "Perspectives on Female Labor," it was approved by the presidium. Drafted mainly by Gosplan, it was soon widely circulated among the unions, the Institute for the Protection of Labor, VSNKh, Tsentrosoiuz (the All-Union Central Union of Consumer Societies), various commissariats, and KUTB.[12] Although the plan had been in the making for over a year, it was surprisingly vague. The planners lacked current data on women in the labor force and were uncertain about what effect the larger five-year plan had had on women thus far. The document had a perfunctory, even obligatory quality, perhaps reflecting, the reluctance the planners had felt in drafting it.

Gosplan's "Perspectives on Female Labor"

"Perspectives on Female Labor," the first planning document to focus specifically on women workers and industrialization, was aimed neither at meeting a labor shortage nor at filling specific gaps in the industrial workforce.[13] In fact, the planners consciously sought to include women for "political" rather than "economic" reasons and seemed unperturbed by the labor shortage. Women's share of the number of unemployed had reached politically embarrassing levels: 684,670 women, or 55 percent of the total, were unemployed by October 1929.[14] Many women's activists believed that women were not sharing in the growth generated by the five-year plan. "Perspectives on Female Labor" was intended not only to put women back to work but also to address their mounting resentment at exclusion. Surveying the role of women in the economy, Gosplan reported that urban women represented a significant reserve of unused labor power. The planners noted, however, that many branches of industry, including machine building, mining, metal, and leather and fur, were either "inaccessible or barely accessible to women." Gosplan held to the prevailing wisdom that women's "lack of culture [*nekulturnost'*] and low level of skills," not discrimination, constituted the main

11 GARF, f. 3316, o. 22, d. 941, "Protokol No. 34. Zasedaniia Sekretariata TsIK SSSR," 21.
12 GARF, f. 3316, o. 22, d. 941, "Kopiia," 40.
13 GARF, f. 6983, o. 1, d. 159, "Perspektivy Zhenskogo Truda," 322–36. Another copy can be found in GARF, f. 3316, o. 22, d. 941, pp. 38–33 (numbered backward).
14 B. Marsheva, "Voprosy Zhenskogo Truda," *Okhrana truda*, 1930, no. 3: 2.

obstacle to their employment. Yet Gosplan accepted the critique made
by women's activists at the beginning of the five-year plan: if women
were to retain their share of the industrial workforce, they would have to
move into the traditionally male industries targeted for investment and
growth.

The plan included elaborate statistical charts plotting the future share
and number of women in every industry and branch of the economy.
The plan predicted, for example, that industry would employ 1.4 million women (33.5 percent of the industrial workforce) by the end of
1932. Later statistics showed that the plan had underestimated the numbers but was on target on the percentage: in January 1933, 2.2 million
women made up 34.5 percent of the industrial workforce. The plan's main
emphasis was on moving women into heavy industry and more skilled
work. It called for a doubling of their participation in heavy industry,
from 10.3 to 20.2 percent, and while it posited an increased demand for
workers in light industry, it expected most of the increase in women's
share in the larger workforce to result from their move into heavy industry, particularly metal. It advocated greater representation of women in
skilled and semiskilled occupations in agriculture, setting a target figure
of six hundred thousand *traktoristki* (female tractor drivers). Concluding
that mechanization, automation, and the rebuilding of shattered industries opened up new possibilities for women, it recommended that more
women enter agriculture, industry, construction, transport, state administration, and trade – in other words, every branch of the economy. In
the planners' view, "significant shifts in regard to female labor" were
imminent.[15]

Gosplan's decision to designate specific numbers of women to various
sectors was based on its underlying assumptions about the needs of the
economy, male prejudices, and women's skills. Among these, Gosplan was
perhaps least clear about the needs of the economy. It noted that its "very
rough" projections were based on calculations that VSNKh had failed to
complete. The authors of the plan were sensitive to male prejudices against
female labor and hesitated to place women in certain sectors, such as local transport, chauffeuring, and shipyard loading. They also bowed to
"established tradition," noting that "women's labor has rarely been used
on railroads and almost never on water." The planners seemed not so
much concerned about physiological differences between the sexes as
unwilling to challenge traditional prejudices too vigorously. Although
they recognized that women were physically weaker than men, they did
not hesitate to set high targets for women as loaders and stevedores in

[15]   GARF, f. 6983, 0. 1, d. 159, "Perspektivy Zhenskogo Truda," 323, 331, in comparison
         with *Trud v SSSR. Statisticheskii Spravochnik* (Moscow; TsUNKhU Gosplana SSSR,
         1936), 25.

overland transport, as surface workers around the mines, and as agricultural laborers, all jobs that required backbreaking work.[16]

More important, the document was the first to advance the strategy of deploying women by redesignating entire sectors of the economy as "female," or what amounted to a process of "regendering" from above. Although the plan opened with a quote from Lenin about women's liberation, the planners did not seek to equalize opportunity for women; rather, they aimed to create opportunity through *resegregation*. They did not view sex segregation as their primary concern and did not seek to provide equal opportunity to women in every branch. On the contrary, they believed that women could be deployed most effectively through the practice of reserving certain job categories and sectors for them, either primarily or exclusively. Justifying this sweeping strategy on the grounds of labor efficiency, they recommended transferring men from lighter, less physically taxing jobs into heavy industry and replacing them with women. Men were to be moved out of white-collar and service jobs such as secretary, accountant, and conductor into *"muzhskie,"* or male professions. The entire service and white-collar sector of the economy, including communications, trade, and state administration, was to be staffed primarily by women.

Having identified those areas of industry and the economy that were "best suited" for women's labor, Gosplan moved aggressively to establish quotas for training women. Fully one third of all places in training courses and programs were to be reserved for women. Here, too, the idea of equal opportunity was superseded by an emphasis on the rapid, planned deployment of women. Although the quota system was established to ensure women's participation and to boost their share of skilled jobs, it did not always operate to their advantage. Women comprised only 5 percent of engineers and highly trained specialists, for example, but Gosplan did "not foresee the possibility of significant increase" in such professions. The planners expected engineers and specialists to come from the ranks of skilled workers, a group that was overwhelmingly male.

The plan also contained a rough design for the development of *byt* or "life/service" institutions aimed at freeing women from cooking, housework, and child care. The plans for communal dining were especially ambitious. Gosplan projected that by the end of the period covered by the five-year plan, fully half of the urban population would eat all its meals in public dining halls. The private kitchen and the housewife cook would be rendered obsolete. Hot meals, requiring preparation and ingredients, would be served in schools, factories, and workplaces by Narpit (the Union of Public Dining and Dormitory Workers). Sharply reducing the demand for the retail sale of food, the plan would transform the entire

[16] GARF, f. 6983, o. 1, d. 159, "Perspektivy Zhenskogo Truda," 325, 326.

food distribution network. The number of nonworking housewives was expected to drop by 15 percent, despite an enormous increase in the urban population.[17]

Gosplan presented its report to KUTB on May 15, 1930. KUTB, one of the few organizations to focus exclusively on women after the liquidation of the Zhenotdel, was organized under the Central Executive Committee of the Congress of Soviets. Many ex-Zhenotdel activists found their way into this agency, whose representatives became the strongest and most consistent advocates of including women in the national plans for economic development. Representatives to KUTB noted approvingly that Gosplan's report finally provided "a basis for broadening women's labor." Still, members voiced several reservations. Some pointed out that more information was needed on women workers in both industry and agriculture. Others emphasized that managers and economic officials had a long history of ignoring women; the plan, they said, could not succeed without broad support among workers and strong follow-up mechanisms to ensure its fulfillment.[18] Despite these caveats, KUTB members voted unanimously in favor of the plan, lauding its completion as "a fact of great importance" for women. They quickly created a commission to revise it and to bring the new version before SNK for its legislative approval. Stressing that the plan was long overdue, KUTB noted the lackadaisical attitude harbored toward women at both the state and local levels. Worried that the plan might be ignored, KUTB requested that SNK instruct the localities on how to implement it in industry, and give KUTB the authority to oversee its implementation.[19] The involvement of women in industry, as opposed to trade or service, was clearly a top priority of KUTB.

On June 24, Baranova, the head of KUTB, sent an angry report to the Central Executive Committee, summarizing the lack of progress on the plan. Baranova, frustrated by and impatient at the state's seeming inability to implement the plan, complained that the planning agencies, both central and local, moved at "too slow a tempo." The training of women had "lagged seriously behind the demands" of the economy, "insufficient attention" was being given to the promotion of women, and little was being done to establish *byt* services. Baranova warned that this "sluggish" approach to women's involvement in production posed "a serious threat to socialist construction" and called for a "basic turning point [*perelom*]

[17] Ibid., 322–28.
[18] GARF, f. 6983, o. 1, d. 159, "Predlozheniia Komiteta po Uluchsheniiu Truda i Byta Zhenshchin pri TsIK Soiuza SSR," 321, 314, 315.
[19] GARF, f. 3316, o. 22, d. 941, "V SNK SSSR, Gosplan SSSR, NKT SSSR," and "Protokol Zasedaniia Komissii po Prorabotke Proekta Predlozhenii Gosplana i NKT SSSR o Perspektivakh Primeneniia Zhenskogo Truda," 69, 64.

in the activities of the various commissariats." She summed up the official attitude toward women in harsh terms: "The main reason for these insufficiencies is the undervaluation of the role of working women, who compose half the laboring population of the USSR." She demanded that the Central Executive Committee force the various government agencies to cooperate.[20]

Once again, KUTB would be severely disappointed. Not only did the Central Executive Committee take no action to hasten the plan's implementation, but SNK met the very next day to scuttle Gosplan's draft. On June 25, SNK reviewed the plan at a meeting chaired by Riazanov, a representative of the Central Committee. Riazanov declared it "unsatisfactory" and "inexpedient." The representatives from Gosplan and NKT protested. The plan had "great political significance," they said: even if it was not economically viable, it would serve to placate the women's activists and KUTB. But in the end, SNK bowed to the wishes of the Central Committee, resolving to send the plan back to Gosplan and NKT for further work and more specific figures, with the revised version to be brought back to the Council for Labor and Defense (STO) within two months.[21] The attempt to include women within the larger five-year plan had been torpedoed yet again. Still, KUTB, despite this latest setback, did not give up. On August 3, it sent an impatient note to SNK, demanding to know "immediately" what had happened to the plan for women's labor. It noted, "We have not heard anything further about the progress of this business since June 25."[22] On August 14, SNK responded by passing a lengthy decree that summed up the resolution of its June 25 meeting: Gosplan and NKT were to work out a new plan for female labor, with particular attention to how women could be used in 1930–1931.[23] With 1930 already half over, everyone was sent back to the drawing board.

NKT's "Five-Year Plan for Female Labor in Russia"

Even as Gosplan and NKT were struggling to devise a plan for women at the all-union level, planners in NKT Russia were drafting a plan for the Russian Republic entitled "A Five-Year Plan for Female Labor in the

[20] GARF, f. 6983, o. 1, d. 159, "Provoditsiia Oprosom Prezidiuma Komiteta po Uluchsheniiu Truda i Byta Rabotnits i Krest'ianok pri Prezidiume TsIK SSSR," 268–69.
[21] GARF, f. 3361, o. 22, d. 941, "Protokol N. 36/374 (po SNK). Zasedanie SNK SSSR," "Spravka k Zasedaniiu TsK," 71, 73.
[22] GARF, f. 3316, o. 22, d. 941, "V Upravlenie Delami SNKoma SSSR," 72.
[23] GARF, f. 3316, o. 22, d. 941, "Postanovlenie No. 322," 74.

Economy." Although the central recommendations were similar to those spelled out in Gosplan's all-union version, NKT's plan was more detailed and comprehensive. Whereas Gosplan offered a "political" justification for employing women, NKT provided a new and powerful economic rationale. While Gosplan made vague mention of "imminent shifts" in the economy, NKT was the first to recognize that the most "imminent" of these was a serious labor shortage.[24] Based on a demographic analysis, the plan warned that the increased tempo of industrialization, the shrinking pool of unemployed workers, and losses suffered in World War I and the civil war were all contributing factors in the dwindling reserves of labor. NKT concluded, "We can project a sharp slowdown in the increase of the able-bodied population for the second five-year plan." The country would soon face a considerable gap between its demand for labor, which was projected to grow by 50 percent, and the numerical strength of its working class, which was expected to increase naturally by only 15 percent by the end of 1932. Female labor, in NKT's view, would fill the gap: "The involvement of women in production is the most vital economic necessity because only here can we find a serious additional source of labor."[25]

NKT also supplied a persuasive economic justification for urban women's employment, based on the costs of housing, education, and municipal and social services. Unlike peasants, urban women would not place additional strain on the state's budget for the construction of new services. NKT's planners projected a demand for five to six million new permanent waged workers. The construction of housing, schools, baths, clubs, laundries, and other services was expected to cost the towns at least 6 million rubles (which was itself an absurdly conservative estimate). If urban women filled half the demand for labor, the government could "economize by several million rubles." NKT planners estimated that two million out of the approximately three million dependents within the working-class urban population could enter the labor force. They stated unequivocally, "These figures should define our relations to women and to the five-year plan."[26]

NKT made its case for female labor in class rather than gender terms, playing on the widely voiced fear that the hereditary industrial proletariat,

---

[24]   GARF, f. 5515, o. 13, d. 5, "Piatiletnii Plan Vnedreniia Zhenskogo Truda v Narodnoe Khoziaistvo RSFSR," 3–22 ob. The document is undated, but it uses statistics from the first quartile of 1930, suggesting that it was written sometime after April and before the end of the second quartile, in August. *Sovetskie Zhenshchiny i Profsouizy* (Moscow: Profizdat, 1984) notes that it was first drafted in the beginning of 1930 but does not give a specific date (p. 44). A fuller version of the same plan can be found in GARF, f. 6983, o. 1, d. 159, pp. 189–255. Hereafter cited as "Piatiletnii Plan RSFSR."

[25]   GARF, f. 5515, o. 13, d. 5, "Piatiletnii Plan RSFSR," 4 ob, 5.

[26]   GARF, f. 5515, o. 13, d. 5, "Piatiletnii Plan RSFSR," 5.

the most reliable social base of the Party, was drowning in a sea of peasant migrants. Women's entrance into the workforce would serve not only to "proletarianize" urban women but also to "proletarianize the towns." Planners believed that the percentage of urban men who were workers would rise very little by the end of the first five-year plan, though they anticipated that the percentage would almost double among women. Thus the main increase of workers within the towns' population would be attributable to women's entrance into the labor force. The proletarianization of the towns would in turn create a broader social base of support for the policies of the Party and the state. "The involvement of women," the planners maintained, "will create a basis for socially homogeneous towns," new "forges of communist fighters against class enemies."[27] Their reasoning reflected the embattled state of the Party, its deep anxieties over the changing composition of the working class, and the growing peasant influence on the towns, industry, and the working class itself. Urban working-class women would provide a badly needed bulwark against a flood of peasants. NKT's arguments, couched in class rather than gender terms, eschewed appeals to the political importance of women's liberation. Its call to reproletarianize the towns was guaranteed to speak to a Party locked in a bitter struggle with the peasantry over collectivization and the collection of grain.

Although NKT's plan was more comprehensive than Gosplan's, it, too, failed to grasp fully the increase in the size of the working class. NKT planners, one group that might be expected to have up-to-date labor statistics, still considered the problem of female unemployment intractable. Even full implementation of their plan would not alter this unpleasant fact. They maintained that, "the involvement of women in industry, transport, and construction will not have a decisive impact in curtailing unemployment."[28] There were only two solutions to female unemployment, they insisted: raising women's skill levels and creating exclusive preserves for women's labor. Their plan set impressive targets for increasing women's skills in every industry, including metalwork, machine building, and other branches in which women were traditionally underrepresented.[29] The planners did not assume, however, that

---

[27] GARF, f. 6983, o. 1, d. 159, "Piatiletnii Plan RSFSR," 249. See David Hoffman, *Peasant Metropolis: Social Identities in Moscow, 1929–1941* (Ithaca, N.Y.: Cornell University Press, 1994), on the influence of peasant culture.

[28] GARF, f. 6983, o. 1, d. 159, "Piatiletnii Plan RSFSR," 228.

[29] "Skilled" work refers to jobs requiring one and a half to three years of training, and "semiskilled," three months to one and a half years of training. In the metal and machine-building industries, for example, the plan projected increases in women's share of skilled work from 2.2 to 16.1 and from 1.9 to 12.2 percent, respectively, by 1932–1933. Much higher increases were projected for the food industry, where women's share of skilled labor was expected to jump from 2.0 to 29.8 percent.

opportunity alone would ensure women's participation, so they set high quotas for training and apprenticeships in every branch of industry, including those branches long considered "male." Even higher quotas were established for women trainees in "female" industries and for enrollees in shorter courses for semiskilled positions. Although the quotas for training in heavy industry were lower than those in textiles, food, and clothing, they nonetheless represented a considerable advance over women's previous participation.[30] The plan set the highest quotas for training in industries that were already dominated by women – textiles and food – followed by new and rapidly expanding industries such as rubber, chemical pharmaceuticals, machine building, and mining.[31] The expansion of women's share of skilled positions, unlike a simple increase in their numbers, directly threatened men's dominance through a corresponding reduction of the male share. Although this greater participation by women was to be accompanied by a vast increase in the number of available jobs, quotas challenged the notion that skilled work was a male preserve, as they aggressively aimed to expand the representation of women in jobs from which they had previously been excluded.[32] If successful, NKT's plan would radically alter men's exclusive claim to skilled work, as well as the gender composition of the most privileged stratum of workers.

Like Gosplan's all-union version, NKT's plan for Russia strongly endorsed the strategic regendering of the economy from above. It argued that women should be deployed in low-skilled positions in state administration, retail trade, and local transportation in order to free men to enter industry. It emphasized the need for women in construction, a largely seasonal industry dominated by part-time workers from the countryside, explaining, "The enormous demand in this area is impossible to satisfy without significant numbers of women." Elaborating more fully on previous divisions, NKT's plan provided long lists of jobs in which women would gradually replace men. The lists, running to several pages, covered low-level, white-collar jobs in government as well as sales and service positions: women were to become secretaries, stenographers, copyists, registry

[30] GARF, f. 5515, o. 13, d. 5, "Piatiletnii Plan RSFSR," 9 ob–10, 10 ob. Sixteen percent of the apprenticeships in mining, 18 percent in oil, 22 percent in machine building, 15 percent in metals, 37 percent in construction, and 64 percent in paraffin/wax, all industries in which women were poorly represented, were set aside for women in 1930–1931. High percentages of apprenticeships were also reserved for women in food (67 percent), clothing and toiletries (43 percent), porcelain (68 percent), textiles (37 percent), and chemical pharmaceuticals (47 percent). In the shorter courses for semiskilled jobs, the quotas were even higher: 90 percent in textiles, 85 percent in rubber, 20 percent in machine production, 36 percent in timber, 16 percent in blooming mills, and 12 percent in ferrous metal.
[31] Ibid., 10.   [32] Ibid., 7 ob, 8 ob, 9.

and archive personnel, cashiers, accountants, bookkeepers, timekeepers, store and warehouse workers, ticket inspectors, inventory checkers, and directors of dining halls, day-care centers, and schools; retail clerks in bakeries, groceries, liquor stores, confectioneries, and tobacco shops and at clothing, shoe, stationery, toy, and cosmetic counters; conductors on trains, trams, and buses; waiters, stamp affixers, coat checkers, doorkeepers, porters, movie-house personnel, switchmen, post-office and telegraph workers, hairdressers, dining-hall cooks and servers, buffet workers, hospital and ward inspectors, elevator operators, and weighers, among many other things.[33] For the first time, planners presented certain jobs not as likely possibilities for female employment, but rather as the exclusive preserve of women. Men had previously occupied many of these jobs, especially in government service. They eventually became bastions of female labor and remain so to this day.

The planners also recognized that once women entered the workforce, day-care centers and other services were required to replace their labor in the home. They maintained that the socialization of *byt,* of "the most vulgar and slavelike work of the household," was "one of the decisive preconditions of economic liberation and involvement in social production and productive work." But while they affirmed these arguments in principle, they were vastly less optimistic about realizing them in practice, and their projections were less certain here than for employment and training. The plan aimed to serve three meals a day in public dining halls to 90 percent of workers and 75 percent of their families on the new industrial sites, and to 70 percent of the total urban population. These figures were similar to those proposed by Gosplan. In addition, the plan called for nearly a tenfold increase in the number of child-care centers, from 76,200 to 723,000; the creation of more than ten million children's rooms and playgrounds; and the installation of enough laundries to serve 70 percent of the urban population.

This astonishing program, however, was accompanied by a critical financial caveat. In the planners' view, these figures could meet popular demand *if* the state would provide the financing. The statistical projections for *byt,* unlike those for labor or training, were speculative, guided by a sense of social need rather than by economic feasibility. The planners were not hopeful about the state's financing such initiatives, cautiously noting, "At the current time, maximum means must be devoted to industrialization, to the development of tractors, combines, and seeding machines to aid the social recasting of the countryside. It is impossible to

---

[33] GARF, f. 6983, o. 1, d. 159, "Piatiletnii Plan RSFSR," 229–30. These are commonly called "pink-collar" jobs in America because they are so often filled by women.

provide more than a minimum for the realization of the socialization of *byt.*" NKT planners recognized that if women were to enter the waged labor force, the "minimum must be significant," but they also knew that resources were limited and that the socialization of *byt* was not one of the state's investment priorities.[34] The main goal of the five-year plan for female labor was to meet the demands of industry, not to liberate women. The principled commitment to women's liberation that had resonated so clearly throughout the 1920s, and that still echoed faintly in Gosplan's version, was absent here.[35]

NKT's plan was production-oriented in every respect. Even its approach to the disparity between male and female wages was based on the needs of industry rather than the principle of equality. In 1929, women had earned 68 percent of the male wage, and even less than that in male-dominated industries. Planners reasoned that women tended to leave the workforce after marriage because they earned less than their husbands. Viewing wage equality as a device rather than a principle, they argued that greater equality would reduce turnover and bolster industry's retention rates with respect to women.[36] If the needs of production coincided with women's liberation, so much the better. A productionist ethos also guided NKT's planners in the deployment of new women workers. Unlike Gosplan's earlier version, which had set quotas to expand opportunity for women in a five-year plan favoring heavy industry, NKT's plan specified training quotas that were carefully tailored to meet industrial demand, not designed to promote equality or even equal opportunity. The planners aimed to train more women for skilled work in industries in which women already predominated, as well as in new or rapidly expanding fields. They gave women a foothold in industries that had been primarily male but did not extend their opportunities there as strongly as they did in new or predominantly female industries. Moreover, the planners did not hesitate to reserve large sectors of the economy filled with low-skilled, low-waged service positions exclusively for women. As they encouraged women to enter industries and skilled jobs previously reserved for men, they also created a new service sector of "female jobs" that would eventually become the poorly paid preserve of women. Taken in its entirety, the document was productionist rather than principled, guided as it was in all matters, and most particularly on the issue of *byt,* by a sharp awareness of cost accounting and effectiveness.

---

[34]   GARF, f. 5515, o. 13, d. 5, "Piatiletnii Plan RSFSR," 3, 21 ob, 22 ob.

[35]   See the discussions of *byt* in Wendy Goldman, *Women, the State and Revolution: Family Policy and Social Life, 1917–1936* (New York: Cambridge University Press, 1993).

[36]   GARF, f. 5515, o. 13, d. 5, "Piatiletnii Plan RSFSR," 10 ob.

Debating the Plan for Russia

Throughout May and June of 1930, representatives from NKT, KUTB, Narpit, Gosplan, and several other commissariats met to discuss NKT's plan. Repeated invitations were sent to VTsSPS as well as the unions of water transport, leather, health care, metal, food, printing, construction, chemicals, and sewing, but the unions, indifferent to women's issues, chose not to participate. KUTB encouraged planners to emphasize women's participation in heavy industry, particularly mining, metallurgy, and machine production, the very branches that had excluded women after the civil war. It also pushed to expand their involvement in chemicals, paper, and food and in industries such as leather and lumber, where women's labor was "justified but insufficient." Still concerned about the high level of female unemployment, KUTB cared less about potential new lines of sex segregation than about creating jobs. Stressing the "political" significance of women's employment as part of a larger commitment to female economic independence, KUTB pressed Gosplan and NKT to gather more data on women, to set higher targets, and to ensure compliance. Highly critical of the planning organs, VSNKh, and central and local organizations, KUTB angrily charged that "the issue of female labor has not found any reflection in the five-year plan up to this time" due to those agencies' "extreme slowness" and "complete lack of work."[37]

Representatives attending the meetings were dissatisfied with the plan's lack of specificity, complaining that it failed to provide figures for women in agriculture, at the district level, and in the national republics. Others defended the plan, noting that specific projections could not be developed without information from factories, labor exchanges, construction sites, and other local organizations. One representative from Gosplan asked his colleagues to lower their expectations. He reminded them that the five-year plan for the entire economy was still being revised and that without precise production figures for various branches of industry, it was impossible to plan women's participation.[38]

Only a few representatives objected to the strategy of introducing more women into the labor force by regendering the economy. A Gosplan representative reported that his department did not agree with the strategy of replacing men with women: "I consider that this idea is unsuitable and scarcely in accordance with the interests of the economy," he asserted. Baranova, the head of KUTB, strongly objected, speaking on behalf of women. "We must render justice," she declared. "Our main task is to

---

37 GARF, f. 6983, o. 1, d. 159, "Rezoliutsiia," 285–285 ob.
38 GARF, f. 6983, o. 1, d. 159, "Protokol Zasedaniia Sotskul't Sektsii Gosplana RSFSR Sovmestno s Drugimi Vedomstvami," 266.

involve women in production." She criticized the plan's deployment of women in low-level service and white-collar jobs within the state administration. "There is no need to write about soviet institutions [state administration]," she said. "We should note that despite the Party's decrees, women are still underrepresented in heavy industry. And here, even the guidelines in NKT's plan say little about the large-scale involvement of women in these industries." She urged the planners to abandon the idea of reserving service and clerical jobs for women and to concentrate instead on getting them into heavy industry. Kosheleva, a representative from the miners' union, supported Baranova's suggestion and advocated raising the target figures for women in mining. "This miserly percent is insufficient," she declared. If more women were to be encouraged to enter the mining industry, which was mostly located outside of towns, then high quotas, active recruitment, and "the forced application of female labor" would be necessary.

Others, however, endorsed the creation of specific jobs and sectors for women. Vaisfal'd, a representative of Narpit, argued that the strategy of replacing men with women had been quite successful over the past two years; a similar process could occur in other sectors, he insisted, "without victims." He proposed that women should staff all new positions in public dining halls.[39] Several representatives called for an even sharper regendering of the workforce, based on physiological differences between the sexes. One member of Gosplan explained, "We have many men who are sitting in jobs that do not require physical strength. Moreover, we do not have enough labor in general, and enough labor in industry in particular." Jobs currently held by men but not requiring a man's strength should be filled exclusively by women.[40]

The assumptions about men's physical superiority provoked angry responses from several women, who noted with bitter irony that women's supposed "weakness" was frequently used to keep them out of skilled, mechanized positions and to consign them to heavy, unskilled labor. Women had voiced similar concerns throughout the 1920s. Ignat'eva, representing the Moscow soviet, noted that the current prohibition against women in the mines excluded them from the more mechanized work underground and consigned them to pushing heavy wagons above ground. Baranova agreed: under the guise of protection, women were actually given heavier work. She noted sharply, "Up to now, women in this industry have done the most difficult, most unskilled work above ground. As far as underground mechanized work, we have some nonsense that

---

[39] GARF, f. 6983, o. 1, d. 159, "Protokol No. 15. Zasedanie Prezidiuma Komiteta VTsIK po Uluchsheniiu Truda i Byta Rabotnits i Krest'ianok," 270, 271 ob, 270 ob.

[40] GARF, f. 6983, o. 1, d. 159, "Protokol Zasedaniia Sotskul't Sektsii Gosplana RSFSR Sovmestno s Drugimi Vedomstvami," 265–67.

says this is harmful for women. Not long ago, I personally visited the mines. At the end of the workday, I saw women staggering from terrible exhaustion from lifting heavy wagon loads." She urged NKT to reconsider the legislation forbidding women to work underground.[41]

Still representatives cited the practical difficulties of implementing NKT's plan. Petrenko, a representative of the railroad workers, noted a twofold problem: the leaders of his union were uninterested in hiring women, and managers were openly hostile. "Managers show every kind of resistance," he reported. "They even throw dust in our eyes, saying that a woman needs very special skills to be a conductor." "What do you think?" he asked in mock disbelief. "What kind of skills do you need to go from one railroad car to another with a flashlight and ask for tickets!" Baranova remarked that male workers as well as managers were resistant to the idea of placing women in skilled jobs and often actively tried to drive them out. "If something happens to the tractor of a [male] *traktorist*," she said, "and he needs to move it, the *muzhiki* [male peasants] will help him. But if such a crisis happens to a [female] *traktoristka,* then we see a revolting scene: the men gather around her, roaring with laughter, and say, 'You went into this work, deal with it yourself.' " Other representatives angrily pointed out that many unions had declined the invitation to participate in this meeting.[42]

Although several representatives praised NKT for its efforts, Baranova impatiently criticized the government for its failure to move quickly enough on the issue of female labor. "We have already been talking a long time," she said. "Since the first days of the revolution. More than once we have made resolutions, but they all remain on paper. We have still not managed to deal with these questions. One could say we are limping on both legs." She noted angrily that the five-year plan for the entire economy nowhere mentioned female labor, and that NKT had managed to produce only "a rough draft that still needs refining." Baranova expressed the frustration that many women's activists felt about promises made but not kept. The meeting ended with a decision to appoint a commission to develop recommendations for submission to the Council of People's Commissars (SNK), and a resolution to censure the unions for treating the five-year plan for female labor "very negligently." Despite objections on the part of several of their number to the resegregation of retail trade,

---

41 GARF, f. 6983, o. 1, d. 159, "Protokol No. 15. Zasedanie Prezidiuma Komiteta VTsIK po Uluchsheniiu Truda i Byta Rabotnits i Krest'ianok," 270–71. Melanie Ilic, *Women Workers in the Soviet Interwar Economy: From "Protection" to "Equality"* (London: Macmillan, 1999), 149–69, notes that while the 1918 Labor Code contained a prohibition against underground work for women, this provision was never fully enforced. A tiny number of women worked underground in the 1920s; their number increased beginning in 1931, and the prohibition was finally lifted in 1940.
42 GARF, f. 6983, o. 1, d. 159, "Protokol No. 15," 270 ob, 271.

state administration, the service industry, and local transportation, the representatives fully approved NKT's proposal on June 16, 1930.[43] By midsummer, NKT had moved to enact the plan, drafting a decree in support of the plan to submit to SNK Russia for its legislative approval. The draft decree underscored the impending labor shortage: only women, it maintained, could relieve "the strained state of both the urban and rural labor markets." Although various representatives from Gosplan and KUTB had objected to the resegregation of the labor force, the plan was based on this strategy. Positions within the lower and middle levels of the state administration, wholesale and retail trade, and Narpit were "to be filled basically at the expense of women." Men were to be transferred into jobs from which women were legally barred. Control figures for female labor were to be met by means of "the uninterrupted substitution of women for men." NKT would prepare a specific index of positions that were to be occupied exclusively by women.[44]

The All-Union Plan

Late that summer, at the all-union level, planners at NKT and Gosplan complied with SNK's August 14 decree that they research the factories in order to uncover the statistics, conditions, and opportunities for female labor.[45] The new all-union version, entitled "Material for a Five-Year Plan for Female Labor," was bound and printed for government circulation in pamphlet form.[46] Once again, the planners tried to develop a comprehensive and acceptable blueprint for involving women in the economy. This time, however, they gathered information on women workers at the local level and carefully studied the effects of new forms of mechanization and rationalization in different industries. The planners noted that they had faced "insuperable difficulties" from the outset: there were almost no statistics on women at the national, regional, or local levels, and production targets for industry were constantly being revised upward. Planning women's participation was literally like trying to hit a moving "target." The planners admitted that they had based their work on inadequate sources, patching together spotty local statistics, recent experiments with

---

43 Ibid., 271, 271 ob.
44 GARF, f. 5515, o. 13, d. 5, "Postanovlenie Sovnarkom RSFSR. O Piatiletnem Plane Zhenskogo Truda," 2–2 ob. There are many versions of this draft decree. See also GARF, f. 6983, o. 1, d. 159, pp. 187–88, 262–64, 288, 346–48.
45 GARF, f. 6983, d. 1, o. 159, "Postanovlenie No. 322 Soveta Narodnykh Komissarov Soiuza SSR," 114.
46 GARF, f. 6983, d. 1, o. 159, "Materialy 5 Letnemu Planu Zhenskogo Truda. Doklad Narodnogo Komissariata Truda SSSR Sovetu Narodnykh Komissarov SSSR," 79–118 ob.

mechanization, research on occupational health, information garnered from Russia's wartime experience with female labor, and even data from capitalist countries. Meeting with factory managers, union and NKT officials, and specialists from the Institute for the Protection of Labor, they tried to determine which jobs were suitable for women. Despite all its problems, the plan was the first to be based on real research, and it offered new and startling insights about women and industrialization.

The planners recognized for the first time that industrialization was transforming skilled work. A new stratum of semiskilled jobs, requiring no more than one to three months of training, was rapidly emerging in place of older skilled jobs, which had required lengthy apprenticeships. In the paper industry, for example, new rag-sorting machines had been introduced. Unskilled, mostly female rag sorters were laid off, and men were placed on the new machines. The planners suggested that women replace men and also fill other auxiliary positions in transport, repair, and construction. In the food industry, the planners noted sharp gender segregation in branches such as wine and flour, which employed less than 5 percent women, as well as in confectionery, tobacco, and conserves, where women comprised up to 65 percent of employees. The mechanization of many hand operations, such as bottling, promised more opportunities for women in mechanized, semiskilled jobs. In the chemical industry, too, mechanization seemed to be the key to expanding women's roles both within and beyond the traditionally female sectors of matches, rubber, and pharmaceuticals. For the first time, planners now abandoned the prevailing wisdom, which held that women's low level of skills and education barred them from an industrial labor force in need of skilled workers, and argued instead that women could be hired in newly mechanized jobs. The share of women in unskilled jobs would remain large, they explained, but women should also be encouraged to enter more skilled and semiskilled positions. The plan's targets were similar to Gosplan's, calling for 1.4 million women in industry by 1933, or 35.7 percent of the industrial workforce. Slightly more women were projected to enter light rather than heavy industry, but as in Gosplan's version, the main increase in women's share would come as a result of their participation in heavy industry.

The all-union plan, like earlier variants, offered recommendations based on a regendering strategy, but its specifications for industry were new and highly detailed. In metal, for example, it proposed that women take 30 to 50 percent of the machines ("benches") given to new workers in mechanical shops. In mining, all men working above ground were to be replaced by women, including those in highly skilled positions. The plan urged greater female involvement in iron-ore mining, which took place on the surface, and in oil drilling, an almost entirely male occupation. In lumber, it advocated increasing women's share at all skill levels and replacing men with women at box-making and woodworking machines. In leather, it recommended almost 100 percent replacement of men by women in many shops, including haberdashery, shoes, fur, feathers and down, and brushes. It projected that women would fill 80 percent of the jobs in sewing and 90 percent of those in textiles, leaving only a small group of men to work on the heavier linen looms and at the chemically hazardous boiling cauldrons. A new, wide array of jobs in construction were to be opened to women, from plastering, painting, tiling, slating, and stove repair to joining, fitting, cabinetmaking, concrete pouring, and glazing. The plan contained more than twenty pages of job lists covering every industry, specifying by skill level what percentage of new workers should be female. Basing its strategy on the development of mass-production, semiskilled, mechanized jobs, the plan foresaw new opportunities for women in the expansion of public dining halls, industry, transport, and construction. Targeting specific jobs, shops, and sectors as potentially "female," it gave much greater specificity to Gosplan's initial variant. A draft decree prepared the plan for affirmation by SNK, but it was never enacted. The draft placed the regendering strategy at the heart of "the broad application of female labor" and "the most rational use of female resources." It recognized for the first time the potential inherent in mechanization and "the efficiency of redistributing the labor force by transferring men from easier to more difficult work and replacing them with women, particularly in those areas of production where rationalization led to the layoffs of many working women."[47]

The planners had devoted a great deal of study, time, and effort through the summer to crafting a five-year plan for women's labor. They had drafted three versions, each more deeply researched and sophisticated than the last. With each successive draft, they developed a clearer economic rationale for employing women, and a better understanding of the economy. The final, all-union version of the plan demonstrated a firm grasp of the transformations wrought by industrialization in every branch of industry. Newly conversant with rag-picking and box-sorting machinery, the planners were able to inject a confident specificity into their projections and recommendations. Yet neither the Russian nor the all-union version was enacted. Despite resolutions by KUTB to bring the drafts "before the masses for broad discussion," no version ever appeared in the newspapers, women's or labor journals, or pamphlets for a public audience. Managers made no attempt to implement their measures. And after August, there was no more discussion of the plans. Even KUTB fell silent.

---

47   GARF, f. 6983, o. 1, d. 159, "Postanovlenie Soveta Narodnykh Komissarov Soiuza SSR, 'O Piatiletnem Plane Zhenskogo Truda,'" 316–18. This document is not dated.

By August 1930, serious labor shortages were being reported in various sectors of the economy. Timber, construction, and public dining halls were all desperately short of workers. The only organization to take independent action on the issue of female labor was the Leningrad soviet. In September, the presidium of the soviet ordered every workplace in the city to develop, within a month, its own plan for bringing women into the workforce.[48] In compelling every enterprise to review its jobs and identify those suitable for women, the soviet was following the strategies laid out by Gosplan and NKT. Yet managers throughout the city widely ignored the soviet's decree.

On October 20, 1930, the Party finally stopped the policy of drift and declared an end to unemployment. Within two weeks, it launched a highly publicized campaign to mobilize women into the labor force. The Party's official recognition of the labor shortage and the need to employ women propelled VSNKh, NKT, and Gosplan back into action. Seeking to move large numbers of women into the workforce as rapidly as possible, planners retrieved various versions of their "female labor" plans and compiled a long list of jobs that were to be filled either primarily or exclusively by women. Covering fifteen pages, the lists carved out entire sectors of the economy and industry as preserves of female labor.[49]

Counterplanning from Below: Feminism in the Factories

The Central Committee's October decree not only spurred NKT to resurrect its plans for women but also sparked a bacchanalia of "small planning" from below. Various organizations, including the Leningrad Executive Committee, KUTB, and Gosplan, began sending small brigades into the largest factories to determine which jobs could be set aside for women. The brigades, often staffed by women's activists, met with overwhelming hostility from managers, factory committees, and male workers. Undaunted, they made detailed surveys of female labor in the factories. They reviewed every job not prohibited to women by law and drew up comprehensive lists of jobs in which women could replace men. The surveys offered the first statistical profile of female labor on the local level, as well as brutally frank descriptions of managerial attitudes toward women. The sexist remarks of managers and workers alike were

48 GARF, f. 6983, o. 1, d. 165, "Vsem Predpriiatiiam i Uchrezhdeniiam v Mesiachnyi Srok Vnedreniia Zhenskogo Truda v Proizvodstvo, Torgovye Organizatsii, Tramvai i pr., Vydeliv Otveststvennoe za Kontrol' Vypolneniia Oznachennogo Plana Litso," as cited in "Zhenskii Trud v Promyshlennosti," 135 ob.
49 GARF, f. 6983, o. 1, d. 159, "Postanovlenie Soveta Narodnykh Komissarov," 55–63.

widely repeated, finding their way from the brigades' initial reports into Party policy documents and the popular press. The reports strongly indicated that if women were to enter production in large numbers, managers would have to change their attitudes. The brigades' vivid descriptions of workplace discrimination helped launch a mass campaign to eliminate negative stereotypes about female labor.

In Leningrad, representatives from the local branch of KUTB, the labor department, the soviet, and the city's neighborhoods met throughout late October and November to gather and discuss data from various workplaces. They dispatched brigades to thirty-two different enterprises, including Elektropribor, cooperatives, tramparks, and the printing plants, Tipografiia Volotsarskogo and Sokolov Tipografiia. They quickly discovered that the September directive from the Leningrad soviet, ordering every workplace to develop a plan for women's labor, had never reached the shop floors. In an "overwhelming number of cases, practically nothing was done."[50] Angry at the failure of managers to obey the soviet's decree, representatives to the meetings vowed to hold them accountable before the Leningrad Soviet of the Economy (Lensovnarkhoz). They pushed the Leningrad soviet to adopt a plan to involve women, mobilize worker-journalists in the factories to publicize their efforts, and gather statistics on female labor.[51]

Counterplanning at once began to spread throughout the country. Brigade members from Leningrad traveled to Moscow to set the process in motion on the national level. The KUTB, under the leadership of VSNKh, sent out four brigades to research the largest factories in the country. They visited Krasnyi Putilovets, the Stalin plant, and Elektrosila in Leningrad; spent time at the Borets factory, Krasnyi Proletarii, Elektrozavod, the Podol'skii sewing-machine plant, and the Kolomenskii plant in the Moscow region; and forwarded questionnaires to Kharkov Elektromash, Rostovsel'mash, the glass factory Vosstanie, and the first lumber factory of Moslesprom. The questionnaire asked for detailed information on women: the number employed and their percentage of the workforce, job assignments, plans for production and labor, *byt* services, training, productivity and turnover, and jobs in which women could replace men. Reviewing the completed questionnaires, the brigades concluded that "the information gathered must be considered unsatisfactory" because managers knew so little about the women in their factories. Many

---

[50]   GARF, f. 6983, o. 1, d. 165, "Vyvody i Predlozheniia po Rabote Brigad po Vnedreniiu Zhenskogo Truda v Proizvodstvo," 155–56.

[51]   GARF, f. 6983, o. 1, d. 165, "Soveshchanie po Voprosu o Vnedrenii Zhenskogo Truda ot 22/X/30," 163; "Soveshchanie pri Komiteta UTB Lenoblispolkoma i Lensoveta po Voprosu ob Organizatsii Rabot po Vnedreniiu Zhenskogo Truda v Proizvodstvo," 157–58, 161–62.

managers could not even say how many women they employed.[52] Still, despite the abysmal data, the brigades were able by mid-November to prepare reports on the factories, with specific recommendations about jobs, skills, and training. Many suggestions grew out of lengthy conversations with workers. Although some managers were cooperative, many others were unwilling to become involved in the planning process, and in several instances workers and managers actively tried to sabotage the brigades. In Marti, the workers refused to carry out their instructions to designate jobs for women. In Zavod Kooperator, the shop heads called a halt to a meeting the brigade had organized for workers, announcing that they would not hire women or discuss the issue any further. In Krasnyi Putilovets, Russia's largest, oldest, and most revolutionary metal factory, the director took the issue of female labor off the agenda of a production meeting and declared that he was finished with the whole business. When the brigade suggested that he hire three thousand women, he flatly refused.[53]

The main findings of the brigades contradicted a decade's received wisdom about women and labor. The brigades argued that prejudice against female labor, not women's lack of skills, was the main obstacle to their employment. They uncovered significant differences between managers in old factories and those in new ones. The electrical industry, for example, was a comparatively new branch that had expanded greatly under the first five-year plan and employed a high percentage of women. In contrast, older factories with long-established traditions, such as Krasnyi; Putilovets, the Stalin plant, Krasnyi Proletarii, and Borets, had smaller percentages of women and were more hostile toward the idea of hiring them for production jobs. And there were also important variations among factories within the same industry. At the new electrical factory Elektrozavod, for instance, women comprised 30 percent of the workforce and held in a wide variety of jobs. At the older Elektrosila, however, they comprised only 19 percent and were more restricted.[54] Attitudes even differed among shops within the same factory. At Elektrozavod, a relatively open factory within a more open industry, a tour through the shops quickly revealed what the aggregate statistics hid: women were segregated by shop and by job. Between August and October 1930, more than a thousand women were hired on at Elektrozavod, coming to constitute 30 percent of the workforce. The number of all workers increased by 88 percent in 1930, while the number of women more than doubled. Yet despite these overall gains, women were clustered primarily in three departments: the

[52] GARF, f. 6983, o. 1, d. 165, "Soveshchanie Brigad Obsledovaniiu Sostoianiia Rabot po Vnedreniiu Zhenskogo Truda v Proizvodstvo," 135.
[53] Ibid., 160.   [54] Ibid., 136–136 ob.

lamp department, where they held 73 percent of the jobs; the tungsten department, where they held slightly more than 50 percent; and autos and tractors, where they held about 25 percent. The mechanical department did not employ a single woman, and other specialized shops had very few. Patterns in other electrical plants were similar. Thus even in factories whose overall statistics indicated a greater "openness" to female labor, closer research disclosed segregation by shop.[55]

The research of the brigades was exhaustive, and their recommendations were highly specific. Following the same strategy of integration through segregation proposed by Gosplan and NKT, they aimed to identify certain shops and jobs as "female." If successful, this strategy would decrease the appearance of sex segregation at the industry-wide level while maintaining or even increasing the prevalence of the practice within the factories themselves. Women would expand their share of most industries, thus undercutting the sharp division between "male" and "female" branches, but the shops would remain strongly segregated. Sex segregation would continue, albeit in a masked form. In Elektrozavod, for example, the brigade focused on getting women into the transformer, lamp, and experimental research departments. In the Krasnyi Proletarii machine production plant, the brigade suggested that the drilling, electrical, crane, paint, storehouse, and automated and semiautomated spindle shops become exclusively female. They recommended that at least ten other shops hire up to 75 percent women and provided a list of forty-nine skilled jobs that should be either half or wholly filled by women in 1931.[56]

The brigades noted that newer shops, like newer industries, offered women particularly good hiring opportunities. The brigade in the Krasnyi Putilovets metal plant carefully reviewed the possibilities for female employment in thirty-five shops employing almost twenty thousand workers. The plant had recently transformed its shipbuilding sector to tractor production, and it planned to open a number of new, highly mechanized shops in 1931. The brigade noted that the tractor department alone could employ up to three thousand women – meaning that the number of women in the factory could be doubled simply by placing them all in one shop! Working closely with the brigade, the staff of the factory's engineering and technical department prepared a list of skilled jobs in which significant numbers of women could be employed, including turner, milling machine operator, and driller. By working on a shop-by-shop basis, the brigade considerably increased the percentages of women initially targeted for hire by the factory administration. The brigades also advocated aggressive and sweeping replacement of men by women wherever possible. After a painstaking review of every job in the Borets factory, the brigade

[55]   Ibid., 137.   [56]   Ibid., 139 ob–140, 138 ob–139.

concluded that up to 23 percent of the men could be replaced by women. In Rostov Sel'mashstroi, an agricultural machine building plant, the brigade recommended replacing twenty-six hundred men with women. In the Stalin plant, the factory committee was persuaded to replace men with women in at least fifteen jobs that cut across shop and departmental lines: milling machine cutter, polisher, presser, uncoiler, inspector, bolter, crane operator, instrument mechanic, and many others. The brigade's recommendations affected thousands of workers.[57]

The brigades' detailed surveys provided an unprecedented view of industrialization at the factory level, and their conclusions put forward new perspectives. First, they strongly reinforced the ideas about skill and gender advanced in NKT's all-union plan. Once on the shop floor, the brigades, too, realized that increasing mechanization of the labor process was opening many new semiskilled jobs to women. Managerial attitudes, not lack of skills, constituted the greatest deterent to women's employment. Second, the brigades gave specific meaning to the concept of regendering departments, shops, and jobs. They noted with complete frankness, "Under current conditions, our sharp shortages in the workforce present colossal maneuvering possibilities for redistributing the labor force and, primarily, for replacing men with women, with the aim of sending men to more difficult work." Mechanization, in their view, created the possibility of a complete reconfiguration of the labor force.[58]

Throughout November and December, Gosplan and KUTB promoted a nationwide effort to include women in the labor force. They urged city soviets, local departments of labor, factories, and local planning organizations to appoint their own brigades to enter the factories and develop plans for 1931. Working directly at the local level, they gathered information that had eluded the central planners in Moscow.[59] Gosplan noted that though few workplaces had entered women in the control figures for 1930–1931, the decision to move the beginning of the economic year from September to January would permit a new round of planning to correct this oversight. It urged every workplace, including trade and transport, to begin adding women to the labor force or using them to replace men. Workers' brigades were to draft specific plans for every workplace and send them to Gosplan as soon as possible; a detailed questionnaire on female labor was provided by the agency to guide their work.[60] Thirty

---

[57] Ibid., 139–139 ob, 140 ob–141.   [58] Ibid., 141.
[59] See replies from the Ivanovo and German Volga soviets in GARF, f. 6983, o. 1, d. 165, "V Komissiiu VTsIK po Uluchsheniiu Truda i Byta Rabotnits i Krest'ianok," and "VTsIK Komitetu Uluchsheniia Truda i Byta Zhenshchin," 201, 184.
[60] GARF, f. 6983, o. 1, d. 165, "Vsem Komitetam po Uluchsheniiu Truda i Byta Rabotnits i Krest'ianok pri TsIK'akh ASSR, Oblastnykh i Kraevykh Ispolnitel'nykh Komitetakh," and "Vsem Respublikam i Oblastnym Planovym Komissiiam i Organam NKT," 206–8.

additional factories also received special notification that they needed to develop plans for including women.[61] Gosplan sent telegrams to the soviets in six major cities, advising them to familiarize themselves with the questionnaire that had been distributed to factories in their areas.[62] Throughout the late winter and spring of 1931, completed questionnaires would arrive in Moscow from the localities.[63]

In the late fall of 1930, KUTB compiled the material gathered thus far by the brigades and presented a lengthy report to the All-Union and Russian Central Executive Committees. It noted that the reserves of unemployed had disappeared and that new sources of labor, "primarily female labor above all," were consequently needed for industry. There were six million housewives in the towns alone. KUTB sharply criticized managers, charging that they had "not given the necessary attention" to the question of female labor, lacked plans to train and hire women, and had failed to establish *byt* services. Soviet workplaces were hostile toward female workers, even though they demonstrated higher productivity and lower turnover than males. Factory managers refused to cooperate with the brigades, officials had "criminally ignored" the decree of the Leningrad soviet, and male workers flaunted the "classic formula": "We don't need *babas*."[64] The KUTB report concluded with a series of concrete suggestions. VSNKh and every workplace manager were to include a category for female labor in all subsequent plans. Unions and factory committees were to put the issue of female labor on their agendas. VSNKh and NKT were to take a census of unemployed women in workers' families. NKT, the unions, and managers were to transfer men out of jobs that could be performed by women and replace them with the wives and daughters of workers. Every workplace was to draft a plan for *byt* services; central planners were to create plans for the largest and most important enterprises. Gosplan, NKT, and VSNKh were to collect more data on absence, turnover, child care, labor discipline, and productivity among women. Local and regional Party organizations were to mobilize women into production, and local economic organs were to deliver reports on their areas to the Orgbiuro of the Central Committee. Finally, VTsSPS and the Press Sector of the Central Committee were to develop a broad campaign in the

---

[61]   GARF, f. 6983, o. 1, d. 165, "Spisok Predpriiatii," 217.

[62]   GARF, f. 6983, o. 1, d. 165, "Telegramma," 211–16.

[63]   GARF, f. 6983, o. 1, d. 165, "V Komitet po Uluchsheniiu Truda i Byta Rabotnits i Krest'ianok pri Prezidiume VTsIK" and "Bytovoi Komissii pri Prezidiume VTsIKa." The Crimean KUTB, for example, responded, "We have informed the labor exchanges of the need to hire the wives and dependents of workers. NKT will work out how to replace men with women" (pp. 149–52). See reports from Russia and other republics, pp. 84–102.

[64]   GARF, f. 6983, o. 1, d. 165, "O Planovom Vovlechenii Zhenskogo Truda v Promyshlennost'," 165–74.

popular press to involve women in production.[65] KUTB's recommendations aimed to put female labor on the agenda of every labor, economic, planning, and Party organization, both central and local.

From Small- to Large-Scale Planning: Regendering by Decree

At the higher levels of the state, implementation of NKT's long list of jobs reserved primarily or exclusively for women was stalled. In October 1930, NKT had asked the Scientific Institute for the Protection of Labor to review the list within six months. The institute, rattled by NKT's willingness to carve up the economy so rapidly, warned that due to a shortage of time and expertise, "we cannot exclude the possibility of an increase in occupation-related illnesses in certain jobs in which women will be broadly employed." The institute cautioned that many jobs on the list had never been studied to determine if they were safe for women.[66] The agency did not have the power to stop NKT's broad regendering efforts, but it noted that the headlong rush to involve women in industry might be hazardous to their health.

By November, the women's sectors under the Department for Mass Campaigns were tired of waiting. Declaring that NKT's foot-dragging violated the Central Committee's October decree, they deemed the list inadequate: "The list shows that the study of this question has received too little attention." Moreover, six months was too long to wait for expert opinions. They demanded that the institute engage the issue of female labor immediately and develop an expanded list within six weeks, not six months. Like KUTB, the women's sectors had absorbed many former Zhenotdel activists, who had heard too many broken promises. They had little patience for protective labor legislation that kept women out of work. They noted that the commissariats of Labor, Health, and Enlightenment all "need a strong shove to get them off the dead halt they've been at until now in terms of involving women in production." They vowed to monitor the labor exchanges to prevent them from sending skilled women "to dirty unskilled work" and "repeating other stupid mistakes." The women's sectors also criticized NKT for its past failure to involve women, and for its "exceptionally clumsy and sluggish work." According to the women's sectors, KUTB was the only organization that had made an honest effort to involve women in production.[67]

[65] GARF, f. 6983, o. 1, d. 165, "Vyvody i Predlozheniia po Dokladu KUTB TsIK Soiuza SSR i VTsIK o Planovom Vovlechenii Zhenshchin v Proizvodstvo," 176–79.
[66] GARF, f. 6983, o. 1, d. 159, "V NKT RSFSR," 4.
[67] "Million Zhenshchin k Stankam i Mashinam," *Trud*, November 6, 1930, p. 1.

When the All-Union Meeting on Labor was convened on November 14, attendees urged NKT to publish a list of jobs to be filled primarily by women.[68] Once again NKT was publicly flayed for its "exceptional sluggishness." Delegates to the meeting harshly criticized the economic organs and unions for their failure to meet industry's demand for labor and ordered them to "decisively reconstruct their work" with women. Beginning with the wives of workers, NKT, VSNKh, VTsSPS, Gosplan, and the commissariats of Enlightenment and Health were to develop plans to provide every factory and industrial site with a female workforce. Women were to compose fully 50 percent of all new workers.[69]

At the end of November, KUTB met again with representatives from NKT, VTsSPS, Gosplan, and several unions to discuss the work of the brigades. The representatives urged NKT (Russia and USSR) to publish the lists of jobs developed in October. They agreed that the brigades would conclude their research by December 5.[70] Drawing on the brigades' work, KUTB pressured the central organs to draw up nationwide guidelines for regendering the workforce. Three days later, NKT Russia sent KUTB its list. It had been approved by every union, with the exception of the sewing workers, who feared that if jobs in their area were reserved exclusively for women, it would make hiring impossible. KUTB in turn passed the list on to the Department for Mass Campaigns under the Central Committee, where Shaburova, a former Zhenotdel leader, reviewed it.[71]

Within less than a week, the government moved to designate large blocks of jobs as "female." On December 8, 1930, SNK published a decree listing the trades and positions that were to be staffed either primarily or exclusively by women. The decree, prepared by NKT, explained that mechanization in production and transportation created new opportunities for women. The use of female labor would free "significant cadres of the [male] labor force for areas in which women are not physically capable of being employed." In mining, for example, all surface jobs, including mechanic, electrical technician, machinist, wagon coupler, crane operator, conductor on electrical trains, equipment manager, coal pourer and dryer, and switch worker on the rail lines, were to be filled *primarily* by women. Many of these jobs, such as wagon coupler and coal pourer, required considerable strength. Others, such as railroad switcher and equipment manager, demanded a high level of sobriety and responsibility. In the chemical

[68] "Net Bezrabotitsy – Ne Dolzhno Byt' Vykhodnykh Posobii," *Trud*, November 15, 1930, p. 1.
[69] "Zhenshchina na Zavod, k Stanku," *Trud*, November 16, 1930, p. 2; "Rabochie – 'Na Zapas,'" *Trud*, November 17, 1930, p. 1.
[70] GARF, f. 6983, o. 1, d. 165, "Soveshchanie Prezidiuma Komiteta TsIK Soiuza SSR po Uluchsheniiu Truda i Byta Rabotnits i Krest'ianok," 200–200 ob.
[71] GARF, f. 6983, o. 1, d. 159, "V Komissiiu po Uluchsheniiu Truda i Byta Rabotnits i Krest'ianok pri VTsIK," "Spisok," and "V TsK VKP (b)," 1, 2, 53.

industry, women were to replace most men in rubber, paints, dyes, matches, glass, and porcelain – sectors that had always employed a large percentage of women anyway – and all men in soap and perfumes. In the paper industry, the long list of jobs reserved primarily for women included gluer, cardboard sorter, paper roller, cutter, smoother, box maker, and weigher. Most of the designated jobs required some training but not a high level of skill.

SNK's decree also set aside many jobs *exclusively* for women. In the metal and electrical industries, thirteen jobs, ranging from coil winder to apprentice mechanic, were reserved for women only. Almost all office jobs, including stenographer, secretary, office staffer, low-level statistician, bookkeeper, clerk, typist, and telephonist, were to be filled only by women, as were certain positions in education and food service, among them store, day-care center, school, and dining hall director and inspector. Some of these jobs, such as clerk and bookkeeper, had been held mostly by men prior to the revolution. The vast majority of retail sales positions were also given over exclusively to women, mandating female retail clerks in clothing, tobacco, cosmetics, toys, wine, food, candy, bread, hosiery, shoes, dishes, and writing supplies. An entire sector of poorly paid, low-level jobs known collectively as lower service personnel (*mladshii obsluzhivaiushchii personal,* or MOP) was also henceforth to be the sole domain of women: coatroom attendant, theater ticket taker, train and tram conductor, postal and telegraph worker, watchman, courier, hairdresser, cook, buffet worker, hospital aide, chambermaid, laundress, dishwasher, film splicer, floor washer and cleaner, table waiter, pharmacist, and stretcher carrier. These jobs rapidly became the doubtful privilege of women only. SNK's list was taken directly from the unpublished plans earlier developed by NKT and Gosplan, augmented by the suggestions of the brigades. The list was republished by NKT Russia on January 16, 1931.[72]

The jobs selected for women by SNK fell into several categories. Many were in new industries that either were developed or significantly expanded during the first five-year plan. Created by new technical innovations and demanding new and unfamiliar skills, these jobs were in the electrical, chemical, and mining industries. The decision to train women for them did not challenge long-standing male prerogatives. Other female-only jobs, such as day-care and school director, store and equipment manager,

---

[72] These lists of jobs were initially developed by NKT during the summer and fall of 1930. See for example, GARF, f. 5515, o. 13, d. 12, "Tezisy k Dokladu o Vovlechenii Zhenskogo Truda v Narodnoe Khoziaistvo v 1931 godu," 15–35; GARF, f. 6983, o. 1, d. 159, "Postanovlenie Soveta Narodnykh Komissarov RSFSR," 55–70; "800,000 Zhenshchin – K Stanku," *Trud,* December 28, 1930, p. 3. The list was republished by NKT (RSFSR) on January 16, 1931. See, GARF, f. 5451, o. 15, d. 362, "Postanovlenie No. 5," 103–4.

inspector, railroad switcher, bookkeeper, and supervisor, required basic arithmetical and literacy skills as well as a high level of personal responsibility, honesty, and sobriety, qualities that were assumed to be more developed among women. Finally, SNK's December 8 decree recommended that women replace men wherever protective legislation did not directly prohibit their employment. Men were to be transferred to heavy labor that women were either legally or physically unable to perform.

SNK's December 8 decree insisted on a radical redivision of the workforce. While it aimed to move women into the labor force as rapidly as possible, it had several unforeseen consequences. It led to mass dismissals of men who were already skilled at particular jobs in order to make way for unskilled women. In an economy desperately short of skilled labor, deskilling men did not make for the most efficient use of workers' training. It also promoted deep hostility between men and women workers, as men angrily vacated positions now reserved for women. And it provoked at least one NKT official, E. S. Serina, formerly chief inspector for women's labor under NKT, to argue against the idea that certain jobs should be set aside for women.[73]

SNK's sweeping move to introduce women into waged labor en masse by regendering the labor force was the culmination of a complex and interactive process of planning from both above and below. The process began in the spring of 1930 with Gosplan's and NKT's initial drafts. These plans, discussed and refined by representatives of unions, social-service organizations, and, most important, KUTB, achieved greater specificity with each new revision. The final version, NKT's all-union plan, showed a much surer grasp than earlier drafts of the opportunities created for women by mechanization in every industry. Yet the central plans, however insightful and ultimately well crafted, quickly dropped out of sight, as if written for the desk drawer. They were never enacted, published, or publicly discussed. The labor shortage, however, accomplished what KUTB's principled commitment to women's inclusion could not. After the Central Committee decreed an end to unemployment in October 1930, the locus of planning shifted from the central organs to local brigades, from the all-union aggregate to the factory, from above to below. The strategy of sending female brigades into the factories was first developed in Leningrad but soon spread to Moscow and the rest of the country. As organized by KUTB, the strategy proved brilliantly effective. Gathering information in a workably small unit – the factory – the brigades were able to provide detailed surveys on a shop-by-shop, job-by-job basis. They raised the percentage targets for female participation through discussions

[73] GARF, f. 5515, o. 13, d. 18, "Ot NKT SSSR. K SNK RSFSR," 17.

of particular jobs, and their highly specific understanding of shop-floor realities enabled them to make concrete suggestions to managers and central organizations. Such suggestions were much harder to ignore than the vague directives from the center. Their work brought the issue of female labor into the shop.

The brigades' research was also instrumental in changing experts' opinion about industry's long-standing failure to include women in the labor force. Throughout the 1920s, labor experts had maintained that women's inability to find work was the result of their lack of skills: industry, they patiently explained, needed *skilled* labor. This formula, repeated like a mantra, found its way into almost every analysis of women and the labor force. It was invoked with even greater frequency in the late 1920s, when women's share of unemployment began to rise to politically embarrassing proportions. The formula, while true in one sense, prevented investigation into other causes of women's exclusion, most important among which was discrimination. Women were the last to be hired and the first to be fired; their lack of skills was only part of a greater problem. Greeted by a blast of managerial hostility, the brigades placed discrimination at the forefront, insisting that plenty of jobs would be suitable for women if managers would only hire them. Their conclusions were a far cry from those contained in Gosplan's first version of the plan, which focused on "women's lack of culture and low level of skills."[74] The brigades, observing the emergence of new strata of semiskilled jobs, broke the link between women's exclusion and their lack of skills by proclaiming that jobs existed and that women could be trained to do them. Unlike the central plans, which were unknown to the wider public, the experiences of the brigades were highlighted in the labor press. Long articles were written about specific factories; the hostile remarks of managers were quoted repeatedly and eventually incorporated into a larger campaign to involve women. Both the brigades' research and their recommendations received a great deal of publicity and were used, in turn, by the central organs to support nationwide measures related to female labor. Finally, the work of the brigades and KUTB spurred NKT and other planners back into action at the highest state level. Incorporating material from the local level that identified specific jobs women could do, NKT published its own all-union lists. "Small planning" thus helped revive the process of "big planning." Between May and December 1930, the interaction between large- and small-scale planning came full circle as SNK at last approved the long lists of jobs reserved primarily or exclusively for women. The lists, which had their origins in

---

[74] GARF, f. 6983, o. 1, d. 159, "Perspektivy Zhenskogo Truda," 323.

Gosplan's earliest attempts to regender the workforce, became the law of the land.

Large- and Small-Scale Planning: The Feminist Impulse in Regendering

From the very outset of the planning process, there were two warring impulses at work in the project to involve women: productionism and feminism. Although the two were not always mutually exclusive, they came into conflict as planners sought to devise a strategy for including women. Large-scale planning, the work of male experts in Gosplan and NKT, was identified mainly with a productionist ethos that sought to move large numbers of women into the labor force; these planners were not concerned with the overall problem of sex segregation. Small-scale planning, in contrast, was the work of mostly female brigades. Their mandate legitimated their mission: to smash open the gates to good production jobs in industries that had traditionally been closed to women. KUTB pushed both types of planning in its impatience to develop a program that would succeed in bringing women into production. The agency was involved with large-scale planning primarily as a critic, constantly pressing the planners to achieve greater specificity at the local level. It was closely identified with the strategy of small-scale planning through the work of the brigades. Here, bypassing NKT and Gosplan, it became a significant force in the planning process. Both small- and large-scale planners aimed to get more women into the labor force, but this common aim did not obscure their differences over precisely *where* those women should work.

A few feminist critics in KUTB, NKT, and Gosplan voiced objections to the larger plans almost from the beginning. They were opposed to the identification of the service sector, unskilled bureaucratic jobs, and the retail trade as "female," sensing that such a classification would create new, low-paid ghettos of women workers. They did not object, however, to the strategy of regendering per se. They were excited about the possibility of opening up "male" production jobs in heavy industry to women, and they were never averse to the notion of reserving such jobs exclusively for women. In deploying women, they wanted to keep the emphasis on industry, and particularly heavy industry, the most favored, best-paid sector of the economy. For their part, the large-scale planners in NKT and Gosplan appeared to have no scruples about reserving certain low-paid sectors of the economy for women. Their main aim was to move as many women as possible into the labor force in the shortest time, freeing men for "heavier," but also better-paid, work. They were not concerned about segregating women workers in less favored sectors. Their plans laid out enormous and exclusive preserves for women in retail sales, janitorial and scrub labor, office and clerical work, and the service sector. These jobs, requiring few skills and offering minimum pay, quickly developed a strong identity as "women's work," an identity that has survived to the present. The central planners also sought to open up traditionally "male" industries to women, but here, too, their aim was not to create equality or even equality of opportunity. The inroads that women made into skilled industrial work were largely in areas that were new and expanding. Women were openly steered into jobs, specialties, and even entire sectors that were reserved either primarily or exclusively for them. The central planners thus created a greater set of possibilities for women, but at the same time, they reinforced rather than diminished the identification of certain jobs as "male" or "female."

The feminist fear that women would be isolated in white-collar and service jobs had little effect on the central plans. By the fall of 1930, the centers of women's activism – the Zhenotdel, the women's factory organizers, and the women's sectors under Agitmass – had been either eliminated or reoriented toward Party goals. The women activists in KUTB and the brigades were not strong enough to counter the central planners' strategy. With the liquidation of the Zhenotdel, women lost their main advocacy group and their most radical voice. The largely uncontested decision to promote women's involvement through sex segregation was a result of this void. KUTB was so anxious for Gosplan and NKT to take action on female unemployment that it was not willing to jeopardize the planning process by questioning the decision of which jobs would be opened to women.

The brigades, however, as small-scale planners, embodied what remained of the feminist critique in their exclusive and aggressive focus on industry. Ignoring the state administration and service sectors altogether, they marched directly into factories in male-dominated industries and carved out new places for women. Although they, too, adopted a regendering strategy, it had a very different impetus and focus. In shop after shop, they opened up to women jobs that had previously been the exclusive preserve of men. Although many of these jobs would henceforth become "female," the brigades believed, with some justification, that they were creating opportunities that had never existed before for women. The resistance of managers, foremen, and male workers reinforced their sense that they were not resegregating women but fighting new battles for equality on the shop floor. The strategy of regendering was thus put into practice differently from above and below. The central planners concentrated on redividing the entire economy by gender and establishing new, low-waged "female" sectors. The brigades, in contrast, emphasized opening up industrial sectors that had traditionally been closed to women.

The regendering strategy used by both large- and small-scale planners had profound implications for women's place in the labor force. It helped to move women into the labor force en masse, but it did not advance the idea of gender equality. Even when new opportunities opened up for women in heavy industry, the jobs remained largely segregated by sex. Moreover, the creation of a mainly female, low-waged service sector had its origins in the plans initially developed by NKT and Gosplan in the late spring of 1930. Thus the very strategy of moving women into the labor force, to give them economic autonomy and independence, staked its strength, efficiency, and success on the deliberate drawing of the boldest, sharpest lines ever to delineate "male" and "female" work.

A group of record-setting women workers (*udarnitsy*) in mining. 1931.

A male member of the Komsomol (Communist Party Youth
Organization) teaches metalworking to a young female collective
farmer. Note the girl's homemade bast sandals. 1930.

Dasiuk and Ianovskaia, two record-setting concrete workers on the construction site of the Dnieper River dam, in the Ukraine. 1932.

6

Planning and Chaos:
The Struggle for Control

We have, even now, no methodology for accounting for women or cal-
culating the demand for them.

G. Ritov, labor expert, summer 1931[1]

There is no system and no plan. Work proceeds *samotek*.

Safina, Department for Mass Campaigns, VTsSPS, fall 1931[2]

In the Leningrad electrical factory, Elektroapparat, the "door to the production shop was closed to women." They could always be found out-
doors, however, hauling heavy loads in the freezing, dirty yard that sur-
rounded the factory. Male workers joked that the yard was "the women's
shop."   Reporter, 1931[3]

By the beginning of 1931, the state had developed extensive plans for
involving women in the labor force. NKT (the Commissariat of Labor)
and Gosplan had drafted a five-year plan for female labor, the Party had
launched a campaign to employ 1.6 million women, the government had
published long lists of jobs reserved primarily or exclusively for women,
and women's brigades had visited factories throughout the country to
determine which jobs women could fill. Yet all of these plans, lists, and
recommendations still existed only on paper. For the central authorities
and KUTB (the Committee to Improve the Labor and Life of Women),
the key question in 1931 was how to move plans from paper to reality.
Were they successful in this task? *Could* central planners in Moscow hope
to create meaningful target figures for regional and local areas, coordinate national and local targets, get the cooperation of local authorities,

[1] G. Ritov, "Sotsialisticheskaia Industriia Dolzhna Poluchit' ne Menee 1,600,000 Novykh
Rabotnits," *Na trudovom fronte*, 1931, no. 18: 3. Hereafter cited as *NTF*.

[2] GARF, f. 5451, o. 15, d. 363, "Itogi Vnedreniia Zhenskogo Truda v Promyshlennost' za
1-oe Polugodie 1931," 18.

[3] K. Silin, "Samodury Meshaiut Vnedreniiu Zhenskogo Truda," *Na fronte industrializatsii*,
1931, nos. 17–18: 49. Hereafter cited as *NFI*.

179

establish an effective chain of command, and ensure that managers followed the regendering strategy?

The British state was the first to attempt to collect information about its working classes. Marx himself remarked upon this process of information gathering at the factory level. Government officials were interested in the basic elements of structure and composition, such as the number of people in the factories and their attendance habits, skill levels, and social backgrounds. Dipesh Chakrabarty, contrasting the British and Indian states in a study of the Calcutta jute industry, noted that in India, the "conditions for working-class knowledge" did not exist. Whatever flicker of interest the Indian state might have possessed was extinguished by factory foremen, who proved singularly incapable of providing even the most rudimentary statistics about their workers. They did not know, for example, how many people they employed, who worked where, or who did what. In short, they had no system of accounting for labor.[4]

The Soviet state's relationship to its labor force during the first five-year plan combined features both British and Indian. British in its aspirations, Indian in its operations, the Soviet state aimed not only to collect statistics but also to plan, scientifically and purposively, every input and output in the development of industry. Capital investment, raw materials, machinery, production, labor, and even the gender stratification of the workforce were to be meticulously outlined in plans at every level. From the master national plan to its local factory variants, every worker was to be accounted for. Yet planning, the vaunted antithesis to the anarchy of the free market, demanded a developed and reliable "apparatus" of knowledge at every level, from the central government to the local workplace. This apparatus, developed over decades, if not centuries, under capitalism, originated in the need to discipline the worker to the requirements of production: attendance, timeliness, steady work, measurable productivity. Such systematic means of collecting data were lacking, however, in the Soviet Union, where central planners were drawing up sophisticated plans even as plant managers were struggling to create basic attendance records. At every level of the state, from the regions to the districts to the factories, Moscow's reach exceeded its grasp. Until 1932, Soviet local officials, like their Indian counterparts, were both unwilling and unable to provide even the most basic information needed by the state.

As the planning juggernaut spun its way into 1931, generating ever greater showers of statistical sparks, a struggle for control developed among central planners and authorities, KUTB, and local officials and

4   Dipesh Chakrabarty, "Conditions for Knowledge of Working-Class Conditions: Employers, Government and the Jute Workers of Calcutta, 1890–1940," in Gayatri Spivak and Ranajit Guha, eds., *Selected Subaltern Studies* (New York: Oxford University Press, 1988).

managers. KUTB, an organized expression of women's interests, played a significant role in pushing for implementation of the plans. Allying itself with central Party and state authorities who were also anxious to subordinate the localities to central state power, KUTB wielded the plans for women's labor as an instrument to bend the localities to the state's will. KUTB officials believed that local plans were the key to transforming local realities. If local officials could be forced to develop clear target figures, they could be held accountable. For the women of KUTB, who had been endlessly frustrated by the state's apathy with respect to women's issues, detailed local planning was the means to local compliance and implementation.

From Moscow to the Factory: Planning at the Local Level

For the central authorities, the first step in implementing the plans for female labor was to determine how to deploy the large number of women who were projected to enter the labor force in 1931. In January 1931, the Central Executive Committee (CEC) ordered NKT to plan the deployment of 1.6 million new women workers, providing detailed statistical breakdowns by region, industry, factory, and even job. NKT's calculations would, it was hoped, bring the scattered regions of the country into Moscow's firmly fixed orbit of command.[5] Moreover, if local officials and managers were to implement plans for women, they would need a much greater degree of specificity. The five-year plans initially developed by NKT and Gosplan had to be broken down by year, and national figures had to be divided up into regions, provinces, and districts. The local officials responsible for implementing a plan could do little without having target figures tailored to the industries and factories in their areas. NKT thus began working on two projects simultaneously: planning the deployment of 1.6 million new women workers and developing regional control figures for 1931.

In February, the Russian CEC demanded an even more exacting level of detail, charging NKT with ensuring that every factory and each state and collective farm develop its own plan for female labor by March 8, International Women's Day. The planning juggernaut was whirling now in ever larger circles, sweeping up even the smallest economic units in its path. For NKT, planning at this microlevel posed special challenges, requiring close

---

[5] *Resheniia partii i pravitel'stva po khoziaistvennym voprosam, 1929–1940*, tom 2 (Moscow: Izdatel'stvo Politicheskoi Literatury, 1967), 253–54; GARF, f. 6983, o. 1, d. 165, "Narodnyi Komissariat Truda RSFSR," 84–92.

coordination with regional targets as well as detailed knowledge of every workplace. To these ends, NKT was to mobilize its local labor departments to gather statistics on women workers, assess demands for labor within the workplaces, and set target figures for women's participation in every locality. Using these statistics, the local labor departments would then assist the enterprises in developing workable plans.[6] The labor departments were critical to the process, as they would generate the statistics, compile them, and create the plans. The assignment itself was curiously circular. The local labor departments had no independent method of assessing demand without receiving information from local managers. Thus, in practice, the labor departments were instructed first to find out from the managers how many women worked in their plants and how many more they needed, and then to convert the managers' own assessments into a district plan. The local plan would essentially be an aggregation of managerial requirements for labor. Yet was aggregation the same as planning? This process would produce control figures, but it negated the very principle of central planning, which rested on guiding direction from above rather than an expression of demand from below.[7]

Unfortunately, even simple aggregation was beyond the reach of local officials. The March 8 deadline came and went, but the vast majority of managers failed to produce plans for women's labor. Not only did managers come up short, but NKT itself seemed unable to compile workable target figures for women's participation at the regional or district levels. In March, Gogoleva, a member of the mass-campaign sector of VTsSPS (the All-Union Central Council of Trade Unions), complained that NKT still had not set control figures for women's participation at the district (*raion*) level. NKT planners had a weak grasp of regional demands for labor and thus did not know where to send job seekers. They could not find reliable statistics at the local level. Gogoleva angrily noted that local labor organizations considered the inclusion of women to be someone else's problem.[8] Even NKT's own labor departments refused to respond to its requests, failing to gather local statistics or develop even the sketchiest of plans.

Also in March, Baranova, the head of KUTB, fired off an irate letter to Romanov, the head of NKT, about the local labor departments. Baranova had received information from many regions, including East Siberian, Western, and Lower Volga, that regional and district labor departments were disregarding central directives to involve women in production.

[6]   GARF, f. 6983, o. 1, d. 165, "Protokol No. 11 Zasedaniia Komiteta po Uluchsheniiu Truda i Byta Rabotnits i Krest'ianok pri Prezidiume VTsIK," 69 ob. The decree is mentioned in this meeting.
[7]   Kenneth Straus, in his *Factory and Community in Stalin's Russia* (Pittsburgh: University of Pittsburgh Press, 1997), makes a similar observation (p. 68).
[8]   M. G., "Ot Slova k Delu," *NTF*, 1931, nos. 8–9: 15.

Representatives from local branches of KUTB reported that the reason there were no statistics for women at the local level was that no one had bothered to collect them. Stymied by the inaction of the local labor departments, the local KUTBs could not carry out their work. Baranova told Romanov that he must force his local departments to engage the issue of women's labor and provide the statistics needed for planning. She tartly requested that he inform her as to how he planned to rectify the situation.[9] Romanov responded to Baranova's sharp rebuke: on March 28, NKT sent an impatient letter to all of its local labor departments, repeating the order to compile statistics on the number of women in every industrial branch, enterprise, and training course in their jurisdiction. Based on their assessments of the demand for labor in 1931, they were to establish local plans for women's participation in industry.[10]

NKT, hobbled by the lack of statistics from the localities, was more successful at the regional level. On March 26, NKT sent KUTB a copy of its target figures for 1931, broken down by industrial branch and region (*oblast, krai*). These figures were important because they both reflected and determined opportunities for women. The control figures were an "objective" assessment of industry's demand for labor, but they also constituted a blueprint for where and in what numbers female job seekers would be deployed. Would women be sent to the service sector and light industry or to better-paying jobs in heavy industry? According to its regional figures, NKT located the greatest demand for women in heavy industry: 50 percent of new women workers in Ivanova, a textile region, and fully 90 percent in the Urals, a new center of steel and metallurgy, were projected to enter heavy industry. The industrial branches targeted to employ the largest numbers of women were machine production, timber, electrical, building materials, ferrous metallurgy, and automobiles.[11] NKT put the main demand for women in the newest industries, including machine production, autos, and electrical, as well as in rapidly expanding branches such as timber and building materials.

NKT also developed a national plan for the 1.6 million women projected to enter the labor force. The target number punctuated headlines and articles throughout the press, but the Party never specified which sectors of the economy were expected to absorb these women. Differing interpretations abounded. Some writers took the call to mean "1,600,000 women *to the bench*" – in other words, to skilled industrial jobs. Others

9 GARF, f. 6983, o. 1, d. 165, "V Narkomtrud RSFSR t. Romanovu," 79.
10 GARF, f. 6983, o. 1, d. 165, "Tsirkuliarnoe Pis'mo Vsem Oblastnym i Kraevym Otdelam Truda i NKT Avtonomnykh Respublik," 78.
11 GARF, f. 6983, o. 1, d. 165, "Narodnyi Komissariat Truda RSFSR," 84–102. The figures also covered Karelia, the Tatar Republic, the Western region, Moscow, Mongolia, Ivanova, Nizhegorod, Bashkiria, Crimea, Siberia, and the Volga.

posited that the women would enter all forms of waged labor, including jobs in retail sales, clerical work, and construction. NKT's plan offered a fairly conservative interpretation, setting a balance between industry and other sectors. Only 284,000 women were targeted to enter large-scale industry; another 274,000 would go into construction, and 26,000 into transport, for a total of 584,000. The remaining one million women, the vast majority, were expected to enter seasonal industries. By allocating the majority of women to this category, NKT retreated from the more ambitious goal of involving women in industry or even in permanent waged labor. This was also the least concrete part of the plan – not surprisingly, since NKT lacked even a shred of data about women's participation in seasonal industries in 1930. Moreover, seasonal industries such as timber, mining, and peat tended to employ peasants, yet NKT estimated that most new women workers would come from urban, working-class families. Lumber camps and peat bogs were unlikely destinations for urban, working-class housewives. Only 90,000 women (less than 6 percent of the total) were expected to enter skilled jobs; the overwhelming majority would be enrolled either in short-term training courses within the factories, to prepare them for low-skilled and semiskilled jobs in mass production, or in NKT-sponsored courses for construction jobs, where they would learn to be plasterers, concrete workers, painters, and so on. Overall, NKT calculated that women would meet approximately 50 to 60 percent of industry's labor demand, thus constituting more than half of the new industrial working class.[12]

KUTB officials met on April 27 with representatives from NKT, Gosplan, and other commissariats and organizations to discuss NKT's regional and industrial targets and its proposed deployment of the 1.6 million women. The discussion quickly deteriorated into yet another round of frustrations, criticisms, and complaints. Several representatives questioned whether the regional figures were based on sufficient data. Others demanded that NKT review the activities of its local labor departments, which were widely perceived as obstacles to the hiring of women. Markus, a highly regarded expert on female labor from Gosplan, noted that no one had followed up the work of the brigades to ascertain whether managers had implemented their instructions. Vafina, a representative of the women's sector in Bashkiria, cautioned that without follow-up, "all the local plans stay on paper." Overall, the KUTB representatives expressed disappointment in NKT's work. The agency had missed the March 8 deadline set by the CEC back in February to create a plan for

---

[12]   GARF, f. 6983, o. 1, d. 165, "Protokol No. 11 Zasedaniia Komiteta po Uluchsheniiu Truda i Byta Rabotnits i Krest'ianok pri Prezidiume VTsIK," 69–70. The plan was presented at this meeting.

every farm and factory. Its regional figures for female labor in industry were not specific, and its lack of data from the localities compromised its ability to plan. Its labor departments manifested "a complete lack of attention" to female labor. The training and hiring of women were occurring *samotek,* or independent of any plan. KUTB recommended that NKT return to the drawing board to rework both its regional statistics and its national figures for the deployment of the 1.6 million women. Concerned that managers were disregarding the regendering lists and using women as unskilled labor, KUTB ordered NKT to take the job lists into every workplace by the end of May, for discussion among workers and managers. Over the next two months, NKT was to ensure that the plans for female labor and training were strictly adhered to in factories and on construction sites. KUTB, fed up with the endless delays, resolved to bring NKT's failures to the attention of the CEC.[13] KUTB's dissatisfaction was not shared, however, by SNK (the Council of People's Commissars), the highest state body. Three days after the meeting, on April 30, SNK overrode KUTB's instructions and affirmed NKT's plan for deploying 1.6 million women.[14] Its guidelines would henceforth provide direction for the allocation of women workers. Four months into 1931, the state had finally succeeded in adopting a national plan for how to deploy women that year.

KUTB was frustrated by the state's lack of control over the labor force. While hundreds of thousands of women were entering industry, they were being deployed by managers and foremen who had no interest in regendering jobs or training women. On May 16, KUTB leaders met with a large group of representatives from the Commissariat of Health (NKZdrav), the Commissariat of Land (NKZem), the Union of Agricultural Collectives (Kolkhoztsentr), Gosplan, and other organizations to hear a report from NKT on the training of women. Once again, the meeting offered an opportunity for KUTB officials to express their dissatisfaction with NKT's slow progress and general ineptitude. Baranova complained that little was being done to train women within the factories. Women who had worked for years in unskilled positions were passed over for promotion in favor of new, younger workers or the wives of workers. Managers had not opened up the factory training schools to women, and older women workers in particular felt bitter about their prospects. The discussion about training quickly broadened to include a familiar array of problems, including lack of planning, managerial intransigence, and the failure to hire women into jobs that had been redesignated as "female." Samoilov, a representative from VTsSPS, stated, "We must note the extraordinarily slow tempo of involving women in industry." He criticized NKT not only for dragging its feet in developing a plan but also for its inability to implement it locally.

---

[13] Ibid.   [14] Ibid., 51.

"The plan is poorly fulfilled," he declared. "The responsible organizations must immediately begin to fill the existing lists of jobs with women by substituting female for male labor." Samoilov and other representatives noted that women were not being brought into jobs listed as "female" but instead were being deployed in the most unskilled sectors of the labor force. The brigades had offered specific recommendations the previous fall, but factory managers had failed to comply with them. Sergeeva, a local KUTB representative from the Proletarskii *raion* in Moscow, testified that when a brigade had returned in the spring to the largest factories in her district, AMO, Dinamo, and Serp i Molot, it had discovered that not one factory had put its suggestions into practice. The introduction of mechanization at AMO made it possible to involve women in every single shop, yet the factory had no plan for doing so. Management had no control over the labor force: workers transferred rapidly from one factory to another, and women were hired *samotek* by managers desperate for workers.[15] Baranova contended that the main problem was the lack of coordination between NKT and VSNKh (the Supreme Council of the National Economy) – in other words, between the organizations responsible for labor and economic development. The planning organizations had no idea what was happening in the factories, and the factories themselves were operating without plans. "They don't know how many women should be or will be hired," said Baranova. The planners could neither assess the demand for labor nor control its deployment. "A half a year has already passed," Baranova exploded. "When will women be brought in? Everything is murky." Moirova, an ex-Zhenotdel member now in KUTB, complained that there were no social services for women, and not a single organization had developed a plan to establish any. Baranova angrily summed up KUTB's dissatisfaction: "On April 27, we heard a plan for provisioning the labor force with women. As the presenter himself remarked, no plan has been adopted up to now in the localities. Today we heard another report. Although we bandy about loud phrases about the training and involvement of women, we never accomplish these things."[16] Women were in fact entering the labor force in record numbers, but Baranova, aware only of the chaos at the local level, had little sense of those numbers or of how the new women workers were being deployed.

Once again, KUTB passed a series of censorious resolutions. Branding NKT's and VSNKh's efforts to train women "unsatisfactory," the agency noted that VSNKh had made no attempt to apply NKT's plan for female labor to the economic organizations or the factories. The plan had thus come to a halt at the national level. Moreover, the absence of *byt*

---

[15]   GARF, f. 6983, o. 1, d. 165, "Zasedaniia Komiteta po Uluchsheniiu Truda i Byta Rabotnits i Krest'ianok pri Prezidiuma VTsIK," 48 ob–49.
[16]   Ibid., 49.

institutions and women in training programs "threatened" the state's decision to draw 1.6 million women into the workforce. KUTB set a new deadline for NKT and VSNKh, giving them until June 10 to develop a plan to train and hire women. The new plan, based on the national control figures affirmed by SNK on April 30, would provide projections for women's participation in each industrial branch within every region and district. KUTB further ordered NKT and VSNKh to work out a plan for *byt* institutions to serve the needs of the women who were projected to enter the labor force. Given VSNKh's notable failure to implement previous plans in the workplace, KUTB suggested that NKT also develop enterprise-level plans by June 10. It instructed VSNKh, VTsSPS, and NKT to ensure that all training courses met the quotas set earlier for women's participation. NKT was to mobilize workers in the factories to make certain that the plans for women were carried out. KUTB also urged the press more broadly to publicize the issue of women's labor-force participation. Finally, in light of the "weak work" of local Party organizations, KUTB vowed to provide them with clear instructions about mobilizing women to enter the workforce.[17] Throughout 1931, KUTB, the last organizational stronghold of women's interests, lashed a reluctant NKT into action. Well aware that national plans were meaningless if they were not implemented locally, KUTB repeatedly set deadlines for NKT in an attempt to meet national targets, develop training programs, and create *byt* institutions. NKT, as ever, responded slowly. Romanov appeared well disposed, but he had little control over his own labor departments, which were widely perceived as hostile and disorganized by women's advocates, and no control at all over managers and union officials. Lenau, the head of VTsSPS's Department for Mass Campaigns, summed up the state's achievements in the early summer of 1931: NKT and VSNKh had no idea how many women had entered or would enter production by region or by industry that year. NKT's directives had been "unsatisfactorily" fulfilled. The unions had done nothing to combat managers' prejudices against female labor. The enterprises had not created local plans. "There is no operative plan," Lenau explained. "*Samotek* rules this work."[18]

Central Directives, Local Inertia

KUTB's irritation and impatience with NKT were replicated at the local level by NKT's own frustration with various local authorities. NKT fired off endless directives and instructions, only to have them be completely

[17] Ibid., 49 ob–52.
[18] "Na Prezidiume VTsSPS. Il'ichevtsy Dobilis' Vovlecheniia v Proizvodsto 3,000 Zhen Rabochikh," *Trud*, July 7, 1931, p. 1; "Za 1,600,000 Rabotnits," 2.

disregarded by managers and local officials. A closer look at the relationship between central and regional authorities reveals the obstacles that NKT faced. The inertia and ineptitude that prevailed in the town of Nizhnii Novgorod (which would be renamed Gorky in 1932) and its surrounding district (*krai*) were typical of many localities. Located east of Moscow on the Volga River, the Nizhegorod district was then an important center for industrial development, encompassing a huge new auto plant, locomotive, railroad-car, and shipbuilding industries, a large chemical factory, a glass factory, metallurgical shops, machine-tool plants, and several light industries. The majority of its industrial workers, both men and women, were employed in metallurgy. As a center of both new and older industries, the Nizhegorod district was chronically short of labor and thus offered numerous opportunities for women seeking work. The local authorities, however, seemed incapable of organizing a plan for either recruitment or deployment.

In early February 1931, the Nizhegorod KUTB met to hear local officials from the labor department and VSNKh present the district's plan for women for that year. At first glance, the plan, which provided current statistics on women's participation by industrial branch, along with projections for 1932, appeared to show an increase in the number and share of women in almost every industry. But in reality, it omitted figures for the total number of workers and thus masked the fact that several industries were shrinking rather than expanding. It gave the false impression that women claimed a growing share of industry, when the truth was that in chemical, paper, textiles, clothing, and toiletries, women's share had increased only because these branches were contracting and losing workers overall. The increase in women's share was directly attributable to the fact that men were fleeing these industries in droves, presumably to take jobs in better-paying sectors of the economy. Upon close examination, the plan revealed that women were coming to dominate the more neglected, lower-paying industries. Thus the plan, rather than reflecting organizational efforts to pull women into the labor force, in fact demonstrated the apathy that left women stranded in contracting industries. The statistical projections seemed to have been quickly cobbled together in an effort to satisfy the demands of NKT, rather than in a genuine attempt to involve women in newly expanding heavy industry.[19]

Not surprisingly, members of the Nizhegorod KUTB were not happy with the plan. Although no one pointed out that the statistics gave a misleading impression of women's gains, the KUTB officials did remark that "there was an extraordinary slowness in meeting the control figures"

---

[19] GARF, f. 6983, o. 1, d. 165, "Postanovlenie," 65.

and noted "insufficiencies in the work of the planning organizations and managers." Women continued to constitute "an extremely insufficient share of skilled workers" because managers refused to move them into skilled work. The Nizhegorod KUTB ordered the local labor department to set target figures for women in every factory, establish a quota of no less than 50 percent female enrollment in the factory schools, and develop a plan for *byt* institutions, all by March 8. It stressed that all workplaces must pay close attention to NKT's list of jobs reserved for women.[20]

The Nizhegorod labor officials, like those in other areas of the country, did not heed the March 8 deadline. Little was done to recruit women into production, develop *byt* institutions, or meet the quotas for women's participation in the factory schools. The district labor department issued control figures for women but made scant effort to meet them. In April, the Nizhegorod district Party committee and soviet executive committee pledged to involve fifteen thousand women in industry and to increase women's share from 24 to 30 percent of the workforce. Women were also to comprise 40 percent of the trainees in the factory schools. Yet none of these targets was translated into concrete efforts. The enterprises received explicit instructions, but they ignored them.[21]

On May 4, representatives from Nizhegorod district unions met with planners and local labor department officials to discuss the deployment of women workers. The meeting quickly slid into the familiar routine of mutual recrimination. The representatives agreed, however, on one point: the unions, the labor department, VSNKh, and managers had all done a poor job. The economic and union organizations had ignored the instructions of the district labor department, the district planning organization had no plan, and no one had done anything to involve women in production. Throughout the spring, local officials had engaged in their own version of that old children's game "pass the hot potato." After the Nizhegorod KUTB ordered the labor department to develop more specific factory-based statistics on women by March 8, the labor department extended the deadline to April 1 and passed the assignment on to the factory managers. But as of May, no one had done anything. Lacking other ideas, the representatives to the meeting decided to repeat the process all over again with a *new* deadline. They instructed the labor department to compel the managers to develop plans for women no later than May 12. This time, anyone who did not comply would be subject to criminal penalties. The representatives planned a large conference of managers and union

20   Ibid., 65–65 ob.
21   GARF, f. 6983, o. 1, d. 165, "Materialy o Vnedrenii Zhenskogo Truda v Promyshlennost'," 1.

officials for mid-May and pledged to check up on the progress of the plan in the factories.[22]

By late fall, a report to the Russian Central Executive Committee from the Nizhegorod district noted that women were still "a largely untapped resource," though they were coming into the labor force in significant numbers. Scattered data from approximately one quarter of the district's enterprises indicated that between January and August 1931, women increased their share of the workforce in the electrical, lumber, metallurgical, chemical, leather and fur, and printing industries. According to the control figures, women were to constitute 30 percent of industrial workers by December, and preliminary data suggested that their share had already reached 26 percent in August. The report made it clear, however, that local authorities had played a negligible role in these advances. In not a single local organization had managers discussed the practical implementation of the control figures developed by the labor department. Women were still concentrated in unskilled and semiskilled jobs, with their share of the former having increased from 34 to 44 percent. The Nizhegorod labor department still did not have a coherent plan, and industrial managers ignored the instructions they received. "As a result," the report concluded, "lack of planning, spontaneity, and irresponsibility characterize this entire issue."[23] In other words, women had indeed moved into the labor force in the Nizhegorod district, but not as a consequence of official efforts. Rather, they took jobs because they needed the wages. Managers, operating without any plans for training, regendering jobs for, or promoting women, hired them as unskilled labor. By August 1931, they comprised about one quarter of all industrial workers, and almost half of the unskilled labor force.[24]

Reports from Moscow's factories showed a similar pattern: managers and factory committees simply disregarded plans or directives from the center. In April 1932, a volunteer worker from VTsSPS researched the status of women at Dinamo and found that the mighty machine-building and electrical factory still had no plan in place for hiring or deploying women. The number of women employed had jumped from 338 to 827 by 1931, but the new women workers had entered *samotek*. The factory committee kept no records of the number of female employees and had never discussed the issue of women's labor. Its social sector, organized to improve daily life for workers, "knew nothing about any plans to involve female labor in 1932." The factory newspaper had never printed a

[22] GARF, f. 5451, o. 15, d. 362, "Protokol. Zasedanie KSPS," and "Protokol, Soveshchanie Sektora Kadrov KSPS," 143.
[23] GARF, f. 6983, o. 1, d. 165, "Doklad o Vnedreniiu Zhenskogo Truda v Promyshlennost' v Nizhegorodskii Krai," 1–3.
[24] Ibid., 1.

single article on women. The cadre (personnel) department had no data on women's skill levels, training, or productivity, and no plans for their promotion to skilled positions. The 16 percent of the factory's workforce that was female emerged briefly from the shadows once a year on International Women's Day, only to disappear again when the holiday was over.[25]

In an attempt to force local authorities to create plans for the recruitment and promotion of women, the press began exposing the apathy of individual managers. One journal sent a group of worker correspondents (*rabkory*) into the Kalinin iron foundry and machine-building factory to report on conditions there. Until 1927, when six females had entered the foundry, Kalinin had never employed any women at all. By 1930, the original six had grown to thirty. By 1931, the foundry had become all-female, and women began to enter the mechanical shop as well. In 1931, the women from the mechanical shop cooperated with the press to plead for greater female employment in the factory, more attention to female labor, and an end to work "in general." In a widely publicized letter, the women demanded that every factory and enterprise develop and implement a concrete plan to involve women in production within a specific time frame. The women, hoping to set an example for other factories, pledged to take responsibility for supervising both the factory committee and management. Ten women from the mechanical shop and foundry signed the petition, promising "to involve 1,600,000 women in this third decisive year of the five-year plan."[26] Yet the appeals from below did not presage the usual campaign from above. The women of Kalinin, organized from above to place pressure on local authorities, did not spark campaigns in other places. Neither NKT nor the unions attempted to replicate the Kalinin campaign as a means to change the behavior of managers, labor officials, or factory committees. Quickly ignited, the tiny movement soon flickered and faded.

Reports from farther-flung areas showed a similar pattern of growing women's employment coupled with official indifference. A conference of women shock workers in Baku announced that "neither the local department of labor nor the unions have created a single initiative to involve women in production. All goes *samotek;* plans are absent." A brigade formed by VTsSPS in Siberia discovered that not one district had a plan for the recruitment or deployment of women.[27] The unions simply ignored the steady stream of decrees and instructions from above.

25 GARF, f. 5451, o. 16, d. 557, "Akt," 65–68.
26 "My, Rabotnitsy Liteinogo Tsekha i 1-go Mekhanicheskogo Otdela Zavoda im. Kalinina," *NTF,* 1931, no. 18: 7. For information on the Kalinin plant, see "Zhenshchina na Zavode im. Kalinina," *NTF,* 1931, no. 28: 9.
27 Ritov, 4.

In April 1931, VTsSPS called a meeting of union representatives to discuss the campaign to involve women. Almost all reported that the local and district (*raion, oblast*) union councils had done nothing. One representative noted that her district council had issued only two directives on women since it was first established, and one of the two was recycled yearly on International Women's Day. Summing up the attitude of the unions, she explained, "In general, the issue of female labor receives no attention, and there are no consequences for the fact that no one takes an interest."[28] The decrees from above were ignored; no one ever checked to see if they had been fulfilled. When the Leningrad district union council was asked to gather information on the skill level of women in the area, it disregarded the request. Eventually it did provide a few skimpy figures, but the report omitted a comparison with the previous year, and the council never developed a plan for further training. In part, the district union council was at the mercy of the factory training schools (FZUs), which had ignored the council's requests. Without figures from the schools, the council was unable to assemble a report on current conditions or plan for the future.[29] A representative from Zlatoust explained that the local unions were ignorant of the most basic statistics on women in production; they did not even know how many were employed in the factories.[30] Work in Magnitogorsk was especially disorganized. The local (*raion*) bureau of the Party developed a plan for female labor and sent it to local organizations with clear instructions that it be implemented by March. Yet when Party representatives visited Magnitogorsk, they discovered that though the plan had been published in the newspapers, the representatives of the unions and the local soviet had not bothered to read it. The Party representative declared in exasperation, "This is typical of how they regard this work."[31] Reports from the Middle Volga noted that the majority of enterprises had no plans at all for involving women. Many factories had failed to meet the target goals set for women's employment, and jobs that could have been filled by women were still held by men. Some factory managers worked with local labor departments to develop plans that were then never implemented. When representatives from the local labor department went into the largest factories to check on implementation, they found "a very poor picture." Most managers lacked data on their women workers, made no effort to improve women's skills, "arbitrarily deviated" from the regendering decrees in making job assignments, and failed to remove men from jobs listed as being reserved "exclusively" for women. Suggestions on recruiting women issued by the labor department "languished in a file."

[28] GARF, f. 5451, o. 15, d. 361, "Soveshchanie o Podgotovke," 23, 31.
[29] Ibid., 32.   [30] Ibid., 28.   [31] Ibid., 19 ob.

And the labor department itself did little to ensure that managers implemented the plans.[32]

New Patterns or Old? Regendering
at the Local Level

The lack of central control over the localities was apparent not only in
planning and recruiting but in the deployment of the workforce as well.
The central authorities and KUTB struggled with managers throughout
1931, trying to force them to implement the lists of jobs for women and
the recommendations of the brigades. Progress was slow. KUTB feared
that women were being used almost exclusively as unskilled labor and
that they would remain at the bottom of the factory hierarchy unless an
aggressive campaign was undertaken to regender skilled and semiskilled
positions. The Fifth Plenum of VTsSPS, in February 1931, specifically
stressed that all plans for involving women were to follow the regendering
strategy: "Brigades should be set up to replace men with women wherever
possible."[33] Women were to replace men in areas where "male labor is
inefficient due to the easiness of the work," and groups of men were to
be transferred from lighter to heavier labor.[34]

The government continued to send brigades into the factories in 1931 to
determine which jobs might be reclassified as "female." Numerous studies
conducted in factories, including Krasnyi Putilovets, Southern Shipyards,
a Moscow electrical plant, the Podol'skii machine factory, and the Rostov
agricultural machine plant, suggested that the "mechanization of entire
shops and sectors" would permit 40 to 80 percent of positions to be
filled by women with only one to three months of training.[35] Lengthy
investigations were also carried out in the chemical factories Krasnyi
Bogatyr, Promtekhnika, Shinnyi, and Regeneratnyi to ascertain in which
areas women could replace men. By summer, the researchers had targeted
thirty-six jobs for the exclusive employment of women, including weigher,
greaser, milling machine operator, planer, turner, light mechanic, motorist,
soaker, weaver, rubber roller, and rubber press operator.[36] Managers

---

[32] B. Ban'kovskii, "Plan Vnedreniia Zhenskogo Truda po Srednei Volge Ne Vypolnen. Ne
Est' Li Eto Rezultat Slaboi Raboty Organov Truda?," *NTF*, 1932, no. 5: 16; S. Zh.
"Est' Plany Direktivy po Net Zhenshchin na Proizvodstve," *NTF*, 1932, no. 4: 18.
[33] GARF, f. 5451, o. 15, d. 363, "Material k n. 5 Zasedanie Prezidiuma," 67.
[34] GARF, f. 5451, o. 15, d. 362, "O Vnedrenii Zhenskogo Truda v Narodnoe Khoziaistvo
v 1931," 159.
[35] GARF, f. 5451, o. 15, d. 362, "Proizvoditel'nost' Rabotnits i Deistvitel'nost' Zhenskogo
Truda," 32.
[36] GARF, f. 5451, o. 15, d. 362, "Material o Vnedrenii Zhenskogo Truda v Proizvodstvo,"
70.

facing shortages of labor were encouraged to replace men with women by means of a *funktsional'naia sistema* ("functional system"), or *funktsional'ka*. The *funktsional'ka* was used to transform entire lists of jobs from "male" to "female." Implemented successfully in the textile and construction industries, it was also applied throughout 1931 in machine building and metal.[37] In a Moscow electrical factory, for example, managers solved their labor shortage by filling up to 90 percent of the positions in certain shops with women. In the new Ukrainian machine tractor factory, Bolshevik, only 700 out of 5,500 workers were women, but the bolt shop and auxiliary turners were exclusively female.[38] At Magnitogorsk, workers, foremen, and managers agreed that only women would fill the positions of groom and coachman.[39] In some factories, special brigades of women replaced men en masse as the men were transferred to heavier work.[40] By the summer of 1931, the mobilization of women into production had become almost synonymous with the regendering of the labor force. When a union representative from Magnitogorsk complained that nothing was being done to involve women, she put it in the following terms: "No one is occupied with replacing male with female labor."[41]

Yet the regendering process moved slowly. NKT sent an angry letter to its local labor departments in March, accusing them of "either completely ignoring or giving very little attention to the introduction of female labor into industry and to the creation of a skilled cadre of women workers in production." The letter was accompanied by instructions addressed to local labor departments, stating that men were not to be assigned to any position deemed "primarily" for women unless *women were unavailable*. This interpretation of the law effectively erased the line between jobs designated "exclusively" and "primarily" for women, and thus closed an entire category of jobs that had once been open to men: women would now fill both categories. NKT's letter further instructed its local labor departments to ensure that *managers replaced men with women in all jobs not forbidden to them by law*. In other words, every job that did not specifically prohibit female labor was to be filled by a woman. Men were to be transferred "to more difficult or more highly skilled work." Finally,

37   "Za 1,600,000 Rabotnits Otvechaiut Prezhde Vsego Soiuzy," *Trud*, July 10, 1931, p. 2.
38   GARF, f. 5451, o. 15, d. 362, "VTsK, VKP (b) O Massovoi Rabote Sredi Zhenshchin Sviazan s Vnedreniem Novogo Sloia Zhenshchin v Promyshlennost'," 86; "Za 1,600,000 Rabotnits Otvechaiut Prezhde Vsego Soiuzy," *Trud*, July 10, 1931, p. 2.
39   GARF, f. 5451, o. 15, d. 361, "Soveshchanie o Podgotovke Materialov Vnedreniiu Zhenskogo Truda v Proizvodstvo," 15–15 ob.
40   GARF, f. 5451, o. 15, d. 362, "VTsK, VKP (b) O Massovoi Rabote Sredi Zhenshchin Sviazan s Vnedreniem Novogo Sloia Zhenshchin v Promyshlennost'," 85.
41   GARF, f. 5451, o. 15, d. 361, "Soveshchanie o Podgotovke Materialov Vnedreniiu Zhenskogo Truda v Proizvodstvo," 15.

NKT considerably expanded the list of women's jobs that it had issued in December 1930. If managers and local labor departments followed these instructions, they would be forced to reclassify almost every job, hire women into lower- and middle-echelon jobs currently filled by men, and transfer men into heavier, hazardous, or more highly skilled work. The letter ordered local organs to support these instructions by ensuring that as many women as possible were trained for "female" jobs. If managers were resistant to employing women, the labor departments were "to hold them responsible." This vaguest of threats was intended to encourage the labor departments to place managers under closer supervision.[42]

The letter, despite its threatening tone, appeared to have little effect. Problems and complaints continued to mount throughout the spring. Despite a national list and sweeping recommendations by local regendering brigades, managers often failed to convert jobs from "male" to "female," and the unions and local labor departments did not enforce the law. Managers still adhered to older patterns in hiring and deploying women: brigades found that women continued to be placed in the least skilled jobs. In Leningrad, the district union council resolved to establish a committee to help every workplace develop a plan for training women and for regendering its workforce. The committee, however, never met.[43] A report to the Leningrad soviet noted that managers and labor officials paid no special attention to recruiting women or raising their skills. A survey of twenty Leningrad enterprises showed that while women had substantially increased their share of the workforce in the first six months of 1931, there had not been a corresponding increase in their skills. The percent of men holding skilled jobs had increased from 33 to 39 percent, but the percent of women had risen only from 28 to 30 percent.[44] Another study of eighteen Leningrad enterprises in the summer of 1931 revealed that 94 percent of newly hired men but only 19 percent of newly hired women were transferred to skilled work. Reports from other Leningrad factories pointed to similar lags. At Elektrosila, an electrical factory that hired large numbers of women, not one woman was employed in a highly skilled job. Moreover, the number of women in middling skilled jobs actually dropped in the first seven months of 1931, from twenty to fourteen, or from 1.3 percent of women workers to a mere .9 percent, and women's share of semiskilled jobs barely increased, from 31.5 to 32 percent. Northern Shipyards, a notorious bastion of antifemale prejudice, did not employ a single highly skilled woman, and the overall number of skilled women

---

[42] GARF, f. 6983, o. 1, d. 165, "Tsirkuliarnoe Pis'mo Vsem Oblastnym i Kraevym Otdelam Truda i NKT Avtonomnykh Respublik," 78.

[43] GARF, f. 5451, o. 15, d. 361, "Soveshchanie o Podgotovke Materialov Vnedreniiu Zhenskogo Truda v Proizvodstvo," 31.

[44] GARF, f. 6983, o. 1, d. 165, "V Prezidium VTsIK," 6.

had fallen by almost half. The number of semiskilled women employees, however, had increased, as had the number of unskilled. Moreover, there was little change in the shipyards between January and July of 1931: women continued to constitute almost half of all unskilled workers. By October 1932, 14.2 percent of the shipyard's workers were female, but managers still had no plan for recruiting, training, or promoting women. In Krasnyi Putilovets, the situation was somewhat better. Managers were slow to regender jobs, but they did gradually promote women out of the ranks of the unskilled. By July 1931, the number of women working at the fourth grade had almost tripled. Summarizing the efforts of Leningrad's managers and labor officials overall, the report noted that "efforts are unsatisfactory." Women working in highly skilled positions in Leningrad's plants and factories could be "counted in the single digits."[45] Flouting the state's decrees and instructions, managers hired women to sweep, clean, load, haul, and repair, and continued to place women in unskilled positions outside of production.

In May, worker-journalists (*rabkory*) once again dragged the Kalinin factory into the news. The chairman of the factory committee admitted in an interview that he had done nothing to recruit or promote women: all 260 women employees at Kalinin had arrived *samotek*. When one worker-journalist asked him whether women's issues were discussed at production meetings, he snapped, "Perhaps you can remember everything! Look at the minutes of the meetings. I never remember." Checking the minutes, the workers found that the factory committee had never once discussed the issue of female labor. According to Bukhanov, the head of the cadre (personnel) department, most women workers in the factory were not in production jobs. When the worker-journalists asked him, "Which jobs, Comrade Bukanov, do you consider the most suitable for women?" he answered, "We have women working as turners, clerks, charwomen, and corers in the foundry." And when they politely followed up, "And how do you see the further involvement of women?" he answered brusquely, "With the transition to three shifts, we will hire ten more women." The workers concluded, "It is possible to say in advance and with surety that given the views advanced, the ten new women will be used to clean the factory!" Kalinin's union, factory committee, and management failed to set target figures for women's employment or draw up a list of jobs in which women were to replace men. The decrees and plans from the center had never found their way to the factory. A woman organizer in the factory summed up the situation with a long sigh: "It is difficult to struggle with the apathy and conservatism of our administrators," she said. "They neglect women's labor, and they do not believe in the capability of

[45] GARF, f. 6983, o. 1, d. 165, "V Prezidium VTsIK," 6 ob, 7 ob; GARF, f. 5515, o. 17, d. 189, "Vnedrenie Zhenskogo Truda v Tsenzovaia Promyshlennost' g. Leningrad," 78.

women workers. Every woman who comes to the factory they consider a burden."[46]

Observers of different industries remarked on the slow pace at which women were promoted – "an indisputable index," in the words of one reporter, "of the negligent attitude of the economic organs and the unions toward training a skilled female labor force."[47] As of the fall of 1931, most factories still lacked plans for the deployment, training, or promotion of women. At Elektroapparat, a few women would be promoted to low-paid jobs in a production shop every March 8 in celebration of International Women's Day. When women protested, the administration countered by invoking the principle of *edinonachalie,* or one-man rule. "Don't forget, comrades, about *edinonachalie!*" the manager would counsel. "If a master or a brigadier does not want to hire women, no one has the right to force him to do otherwise." And many shop bosses refused to accept women. One reporter noted, "For a woman to be promoted to [factory] brigade leader is an unrealizable dream."[48] Managers in the Rabochii factory disregarded the central lists of jobs in which women might have replaced men, instead hiring and deploying women spontaneously, or *samotek.* In Baku, factories received instructions "from above," but nothing was done to implement them locally. Neither the factory committees nor the Party collectives "had a single conversation about the role of women in production." In some plants, such as Russian Diesel, managers deliberately sabotaged the promotion of women by assigning them to work on machines that even some of the stronger men could barely handle.[49] At Magnitogorsk, even skilled women were routinely used in unskilled jobs requiring heavy lifting. Female stonemasons, carpenters, and plasterers were placed in jobs that required the lifting and hauling of stones and timbers weighing more than eighty pounds. Few women were placed in the more mechanized sectors of production, which did not require great strength. In general, managers in construction gave little thought to how best to deploy women.[50] In the Moscow and Leningrad regions in 1932, about 70 percent of women workers held unskilled jobs, and in the Ural machine-building factories, the figure was 100 percent.[51] In the

---

[46] Brigad Rabkorov (Kuznetsova, Askinazi, Adrianov), "Medlennym Shagom, Robkim Zigzagom," *NTF,* 1931, no. 18: 6.

[47] N. Aristov and Tolchiev, "Dorogu Zhenshchine na Proizvodstvo na Kvalifitsirovannuiu Rabotu," *NTF,* 1932, nos. 26–27: 22.

[48] K. Silin, "Samodury Meshaiut Vnedreniiu Zhenskogo Truda," *NFI,* 1931, nos. 17–18: 48–50.

[49] "Zabyli o Glavnom," *NTF,* 1931, no. 28: 8; "Metallicheskii Trud na Proizvodstve," *NFI,* 1931, nos. 17–18: 47–48.

[50] V. Brumshtein, "Zhenskii Trud na Magnitostroi," *Okhrana truda,* 1931, nos. 23–24: 17–22.

[51] GARF, f. 3316, o. 51, d. 7, "Ocherednye Zadachi Organizatsii Zhenskogo Truda i Bytogo Obsluzhivaniia," 43.

Konstantinovskii chemical factory, women worked as charwomen and in other unskilled jobs outside of production: the head of the materials department had never considered hiring them in any other capacity. More than nine hundred women worked in the Gorlovskii mine, but primarily as unskilled labor; there were no plans to train them. Although the mines had received specific instructions about replacing men with women, nothing was done toward this end.[52] A national survey prepared by VTsSPS for the Central Committee concluded, "The increase in women's skills has been completely unsatisfactory." Among male workers, 11 percent were highly skilled, and 21 percent had midlevel skills. Among women workers, however, less than 2 percent possessed high-level skills, and only 8 percent midlevel skills. The report blamed managers and labor officials for these stark differentials: women lagged behind men because of "cultural prejudices against female labor in heavy industry and particularly in skilled work."[53] One reporter noted, "Neither the managers nor the unions have done any systematic planned work."[54]

Managers generally took action only when challenged by women workers. At Elektrosila, a new factory, women workers organized themselves into groups of five (*piaterki*) and went from shop to shop identifying those jobs in which women could work. They brought their suggestions to production meetings and tried to gain wider support among the workers at large. When management offered to hire and promote a certain percentage of women, they advanced a counterproposal. The workers rejected management's plan in favor of the women's. Like the brigades formed earlier in the fall, the *piaterki* took direct action within the factory by developing a "counterplan" for women's labor.[55] Yet the *piaterki* never became a mass phenomenon. In most workplaces, women did not collectively challenge long-standing discriminatory practices, and managers continued to deploy women according to older patterns.

On May 31, NKT USSR published a new list of positions to be filled exclusively or primarily by women, regendering 340 additional jobs. Newspaper headlines broadly advertised the new opportunities, calling "wives and daughters of workers to the bench." G. Ritov, a journalist for the labor press, insisted that the Party could meet its goal of 1.6 million women in the labor force only if women replaced men "in a series of jobs." Yet he pointed out that recent research by brigades revealed that

52 Pukhova, "Bol'she Initsiativy v Udarnom Vnedrenii Zhenskogo Truda," *NTF*, 1931, no. 20: 17.
53 GARF, f. 5451, o. 15, d. 362, "O Massovoi Rabote," 82–83.
54 Pokhebaev, "Plokhoe Kachestvo Verbovki – Vot Glavnaia Prichina Tekuchesti, "*NTF*, 1932, nos. 8–9: 19.
55 Trubnik, "1,600,000 Zhenshchin v Proizvodstvo k Kontsu 1931 g.," *NTF*, 1931, no. 28: 8.

women were being used primarily as unskilled labor. Women were supposed to comprise 50 percent of the trainees in factory schools, but this
quota was rarely met. Managers simply ignored the lists of designated jobs
for women. The economic trusts followed the "path of least resistance,"
hiring women in unskilled jobs to fill labor shortages as needed. The
real obstacle to employing women, in Ritov's opinion, was the attitude
of men. "In many enterprises," he wrote, "women are greeted at times
with bayonets, not only by management but by backward male workers."
The "women's question" was relegated to overburdened *zhenrabotniki*
(women's activists), while the union organizations, the Party collectives,
and the organs of labor remained "indifferent." In Ritov's view, the "solution to the problem of women's labor in production still lies in agitation-
propaganda work among ... men."[56] Although Ritov did not mention
the Zhenotdel directly, he repeated arguments that its members had once
cited in its defense.

G. Serebrennikov, a prominent labor economist, later summed up the
transformation in the workforce in 1930 and 1931. The quotas set for
women in almost every branch of industry were exceeded, he wrote. Yet
"despite the successful figures, sufficient practical work was not devoted
to fulfilling the plan. In reality, the plan never reached the enterprises."
Even plans generated by managers for their own factories "never attained
operational significance and did not become the basis for the planned
composition of the female workforce." According to Serebrennikov, this
lack of planning had "unpleasant consequences." Managers used women
primarily as unskilled labor. He concluded, "The mass streams of women
[entering] production in 1931 entered, as a rule, independent of the concrete planned actions of the leading managers and union organizations,
often under conditions of prejudice against women's labor – i.e., they
entered *samotek*."[57] Prejudice, not plan, ruled the factories.

Throughout 1931, women's activists pushed hard to implement the
lists of jobs for women and the recommendations of the brigades. Yet
they did not fully foresee the consequences of the regendering strategy.
As managers slowly reclassified jobs as "female," they opened up "male"
positions to women but also regendered whole shops. New patterns of
sex segregation emerged, effectively resegregating rather than integrating
factories and enterprises. In Krasnyi Putilovets, 1,300 women were hired
into the tractor department, a new part of the factory.[58] The shovel shop
in the Stalin factory, the box shop in the Rykov factory, and the winding

---

[56] Ritov, 3–5.
[57] G. Serebrennikov, "Zhenskii Trud v Sotsialisticheskom Stroitel'stve," *Udarnik*, 1932,
      no. 10: 24–27.
[58] "6 Mesiatsev Proshlo, a Rezultaty?" and "Strana Dolzhna Znat' Svoikh Geroev," *NTF*,
      1931, no. 18: 8, 10.

shop at Elektrosila rapidly became exclusively female.[59] Once women were hired into the Kalinin foundry, it, too, quickly became all female. Milling-machine operator, lathe operator, and plater were identified as women's jobs in many factories.[60] In macaroni production, a traditionally male sector of the food industry, very few women held skilled jobs. Women in the OGPU macaroni factory in Moscow were carefully steered into jobs as folders and cutters, which soon became known as *bab'ii*, or women's work.[61] When women first entered Serp i Molot, a huge steel and machine-building plant in Moscow that employed 5,780 workers in 1930, their numbers expanded from 370 to 1,564 (6.4 to 17 percent of the workforce) in less than two years. The cable and press shops were soon identified as "female." More than four hundred women were steered into the steel-wire shop and segregated by job, working as turners, electricians, crane operators, haulers, and bolters. The vast majority were concentrated in the two lowest grades. A report from Serp i Molot in 1931 noted that shop foremen consistently "undervalued women in both a political and an economic sense."[62] The regendering strategy, effective though it was in moving large numbers of women into the factories, carried a cost. The appearance of women in jobs and shops designated for both sexes created a "contamination" effect whereby certain areas rapidly became inappropriate for men.

In July 1931, NKT once again tried to establish plans for every enterprise. This time, however, it shifted responsibility from its local labor departments, which had been unsuccessful in enforcing the mandate, to the economic organs. The latter were instructed to develop plans for women at the factory and shop levels, based on the lists of jobs in which men were to be replaced by women.[63] But the economic organs fared no better in this task than the local labor departments. By late fall, few workplaces had come up with a strategy for regendering. In some cases, labor shortages interfered with any attempt to divide jobs by gender: restrictions on sending men to work in "primarily" female jobs made it impossible to fill those jobs at all. The regendering lists demanded that unskilled women replace skilled men, who would then be sent to unfamiliar unskilled positions. In an economy short of skilled labor, managers had few incentives to make such changes. The situation proved especially problematic in the Caucasus, where the Supreme Court was forced to decide whether it was fair to establish jobs for women only. The procurator of the Supreme

[59]   GARF, f. 6983, o. 1, d. 165, "V Prezidium VTsIK," 7.
[60]   Iasvin, "Golos Zhenorganizatsii Dolzhen Byt' Usl'yshan!," *NTF*, 1931, nos. 8–9: 16.
[61]   Beregovoi, "Opyt Vnedreniia Zhenskogo Truda v Proizvodstvo," *NTF*, 1931, no. 7: 15.
[62]   GARF, f. 5451, o. 15, d. 362, "Zavod Serp i Molot," 1; S. Gudkov, "Zhenshchina Stala Aktivnym Boitsom za Piatletki v Chetyre Goda," *NTF*, 1931, no. 7: 15.
[63]   "Vnedrenie Zhenskogo Truda," *NTF*, 1931, no. 20: 18.

Court rendered the opinion that the practice would be "very harmful to industry."[64] In the fall, NKT USSR retreated from the regendering strategy in a memo it sent to SNK Russia, explaining that legislation that created jobs "exclusively" for women was "incorrect at the present moment of sharp shortages in skilled cadres" because it resulted in the dismissal of skilled men. NKT asked SNK to rescind its decree of December 8, 1930, mandating "the exclusive use" of women in certain jobs.[65] The regendering decree had been "premature," according to NKT's memo, which further noted that women's labor would still be broadly or "primarily" applied to certain jobs and categories. NKT suggested that the Uzbek and Caucasus republics should likewise countermand the decree.[66] Despite NKT's objections to "exclusivity," however, the state continued to rely on the strategy of regendering through the end of the first five-year plan. A decree from SNK Russia in August 1932 once again ordered managers to work out plans to replace men with women.[67]

On October 20, 1931, one year to the day after the Party declared the elimination of unemployment, the state made yet another attempt to force managers and local officials to obey its directives. The Russian Central Executive Committee (CEC) issued a new decree establishing an elaborate system of review and control at every level. Because the local labor departments and the economic organs had failed to compel workplaces to develop plans for women, the CEC now turned to the soviets. Local soviet officials were to survey the workplaces in their districts, identify those jobs in which women could replace men, count the unemployed women, and mobilize them for work through housing cooperatives. The republic, regional, and local soviet executive committees were to ensure that local authorities met their goals for female labor, *byt* institutions, and training for women. The local soviets were to verify that every labor contract between a factory and a collective farm contained a set quota for women. Managers would be held *personally* responsible for the fulfillment of the 1931 control figures. SNK Russia was instructed to increase the targets for 1932 over the 1931 figures for women in every branch of industry. Gosplan, NKT, and the economic commissariats were to ensure greater female participation in 1932 in machine construction, food, railroads, and local and water transportation; develop plans for *byt* institutions; and account for female labor at the local level. Representatives of the economic commissariats were to make certain that the control figures were met. NKT and the Commissariat of Health

---

64 GARF, f. 5515, o. 13, d. 18, pp. 1–12. This material covers an exchange between NKT USSR and the Procurator of the Supreme Court and NKT of the Caucasus.
65 GARF, f. 5515, o. 13, d. 18, "Ot: NKT SSSR, V: SNK RSFSR," 17.
66 GARF, f. 5515, o. 13, d. 18, "Proekt Postanovlenii Kollegii NKT SSSR," 17.
67 GARF, f. 5451, o. 16, d. 557, "Postanovlenie SNK RSFSR," 1–1 ob, 3.

(NKZdrav) were to expand the list of jobs in which women would replace men. The CEC stressed that women constituted a valuable "local labor resource," a means to reduce labor turnover and "to free industry and local budgets from the superfluous expenses of supporting an imported labor force." The state's record in bringing women into industry was "not sufficient." As a result of "poor work," the control figures for women had not been met in several branches. The government and the economic organs had failed to produce an accurate accounting of the reserves of female labor, failed to train sufficient numbers of women and promote them to skilled work, and failed to develop social-*byt* institutions. In sum, they had been unable to surmount "the sluggish opposition to involving women and the prevailing view of female labor as inefficient."[68] The CEC's new decree, aimed at establishing responsibility in the chain of command between central and local authorities, tried to position the local soviets as watchdogs over the workplaces. Yet its very remedies suggested that little had changed in either the attitudes or the behavior of local officials.

Assessing the Plans

At the end of the period covered by the first five-year plan, the central planners claimed that many of the plan's goals had been realized. Although their figures were not entirely consistent, officials from key government agencies agreed with NKT that the campaign to bring 1.6 million women into the workforce had been a success.[69] VTsSPS asserted that the number of women in the waged labor force had risen from 3.7 million in September 1930 to 5.7 million by September 1931 – an increase of 2 million, including 1.4 million in the nonagricultural sector.[70] The CEC, for its part, announced that while 1.3 million women had initially been targeted for the nonagricultural sector, 1.5 million had actually taken jobs, well exceeding the target. According to the CEC's statistics, 93 percent of the target for industry had been met, as had 78 percent of the target for construction, and 75 percent for transport. In retail trade and socialized dining, over four times as many women as initially projected had found jobs.[71] Fuller, more reliable statistical data later confirmed that the goals of the campaign had been met: more than 1.8 million women had entered

---

[68] GARF, f. 6983, o. 1, d. 165, "Postanovlenie Prezidiuma Vserossiiskogo Tsentral'nogo Ispolnitel'nogo Komiteta," 29–31 ob.
[69] RTsKhIDNI, f. 17, o. 10, d. 496, "Predvaritel'nye Dannye NKTruda," 19.
[70] Serebrennikov, 24–25.
[71] GARF, f. 6983, o. 25, d. 968, "Itogi Vnedreniia Zhenskogo Truda v 1931–1932g. Planovye Nametki v Etoi Oblasti na 1932g.," 262.

the economy in 1931, with almost one third taking jobs in industry.[72] Yet such numbers alone begged the question of whether the government's campaign was truly responsible for women's growing participation in the workforce. As late as 1934, one planner could remark that the majority of industrial managers still hired *samotek*. A system of "hiring from the gate" thus stood in for organized recruitment. In other words, in the peculiar climate of planning and anarchy that prevailed, the state's numerical targets were themselves achieved *samotek*!

For women, every step in the planning process had been a struggle: NKT had failed to set accurate regional control figures, the regions themselves had been unable to meet them, and local managers, union representatives, and labor-department officials had balked at hiring and promoting women. Although KUTB blamed NKT for its ineptitude, NKT was in fact paralyzed by a lack of data from the localities, a factor beyond its control. A meeting called by NKT in March 1931 revealed that neither the unions nor VSNKh nor the local labor departments had ever bothered to gather data on women workers. As late as the summer of 1931, one writer noted that the data NKT received were "extraordinarily sparing and distinguished by their thinness and lack of clarity." A significant number of local labor departments were not involved with female labor at all. Even the Moscow labor department, situated at the epicenter of state power, did nothing in this regard. The writer concluded harshly, "All of it reveals a wretched picture, stressing that up to now there has been no turning point in involving women in production."[73] In the fall, a report from VSNKh on the localities reiterated the same problems. Organizational work with women was proceeding at "an insufficient tempo." Not enough women were enrolled in the factory training schools, and *byt* institutions, especially day-care centers, were so "extraordinarily weak" as to constitute "the main obstacle to involving women in industry." There were too few dining halls and laundries, and many barracks and dormitories lacked kitchens, electricity, and running water. Local organs were not taking the directives about women "seriously enough."[74] Even the CEC conceded that the achievement of its target figures could not be attributed to planning, given that "throughout 1931, no one in the localities was actually occupied with the practical fulfillment of these plans."[75] And numerical success, in any case, made no claims for deployment. In the summer of 1932, NKT reported that local officials showed little interest in moving

[72] "Chislennost' Zhenshchin po Otrasliam Narodnogo Khoziaistva v 1929–1935 gg.," in *Trud v SSSR. Statisticheskii spravochnik* (Moscow: TsUNKhU Gosplana, 1937), 25.
[73] "6 Mesiatsev Proshlo, a Rezul'taty?," *NTF,* 1931, no. 18: 8.
[74] GARF, f. 6983, o. 1, d. 165, "V Prezidium VTsIK," 13.
[75] GARF, f. 3316, o. 51, d. 7, "Ocherednye Zadachi Organizatsii Zhenskogo Truda i Bytogo Obsluzhivaniia," 54.

women out of the unskilled jobs they had initially been hired into. The officials still had no system to track female labor: they did not know how many women worked in their districts or by which enterprises they were employed.[76]

Drawing on NKT's report, SNK issued a decree that aimed to break the older patterns of hiring and deployment. Once again urging managers to substitute female for male labor and to promote women out of unskilled jobs, it set astounding new quotas requiring that 60 to 80 percent of all promotions be reserved for women. By 1933, enrollment in the factory schools was to be 50 percent female. Gosplan and the economic organs were to include a category for gender in all their national and regional projections for industry in 1932 and 1933, and NKT was to develop monthly plans for involving women in the labor force.[77] The decree, a familiar variation on the numerous directives and orders fired off from the center over the past two years, showed that the central authorities continued to rely on planning – in the form of monthly plans, target figures, and quotas – to counter local inertia. If local authorities had failed to comply with earlier plans, SNK would simply generate new versions. In place of national plans, it ordered plans for every workplace, and in place of annual plans, it demanded monthly ones. The local authorities would be forced to comply if the target goals could be broken down to microlevels that could not be ignored. According to SNK, higher quotas and targets coupled with stricter methods of surveillance would eventually force the local authorities to obey central directives.

The record of the previous two years, however, suggested that more specific planning did not necessarily generate higher levels of compliance. Women had entered new branches of the economy in great numbers. Their share of heavy industry had increased impressively. Yet by all accounts, they had entered the workforce independent of the efforts of local labor-department officials and managers. In fact, the local authorities had proved to be a stumbling block in the implementation of central plans. They had failed to gather the statistical information required for meaningful planning, and blithely disregarded instructions, orders, and even threats from above. Overwhelmed by high production targets and a multitude of new workers, they lacked the statistical skills to calculate or project the demand for labor. The local labor departments were unable to recruit workers or dispatch them to regions or industries that needed them. Ultimately, NKT was forced to relegate the task of managing the labor force to managers themselves. But managers did not, as a rule,

[76]   GARF, f. 5451, o. 16, d. 557, "Postanovlenie SNK RSFSR," 1–3 ob; "Informsvodka," 28–31.
[77]   Ibid.

view the state's unending directives regarding women as a priority. Despite plans, lists, and counterplans, the regendering of the labor force in industry occurred slowly, and prejudice ensured that a large percentage of women remained in unskilled jobs. Although KUTB won a place for women in the national plans, the plans themselves proved difficult to implement. KUTB did not exist as a mass organization in the factories. The Central Executive Committee specifically noted that "the elimination of the Zhenotdel and KUTB" shifted responsibility for women's issues to a variety of organizations "in general," meaning to none in particular. The main problem with deploying female labor during the first five-year plan, in the CEC's own estimation, was that "no one has any particular responsibility or feels the need to realize the directives of the Party or the government."[78]

[78] GARF, f. 3316, o. 51, d. 7, "Ocherednye Zadachi Organizatsii Zhenskogo Truda i Bytogo Obsluzhivaniia," 54.

Tromova, a woman worker in the transformer shop of Elektrozavod, a large electrical plant in Moscow. A brigade of women's activists struggled to open this shop to women. 1931.

7

Gender Relations in Industry:
Voices from the Point of Production

> With *babas*, there is a lot of trouble. It is not worth it to put them to work at the bench.
>> Master of the mechanical shop in Lavshchutskii factory[1]

> When we raise the question of hiring women in transport, the union officials and managers refuse with every bone in their bodies and say, "We do not want women," even though they have the same skills as men and are able to work. This shows that the old life still lives among us, that the exploitation of women by men still has not disappeared.
>> Vinogradova, female switchman on the Northern railroad line, working since age sixteen[2]

Women workers and activists were well aware of the failure of local authorities to implement the plans generated in Moscow, but they did not attribute the failure to disorganization or inadequate statistics. To them, the single most important factor influencing women's opportunities in the workplace was male prejudice. The number of women hired, the jobs they received, their access to skilled work, and their treatment on the shop floor were all affected by male attitudes toward female labor. Women were fiercely critical of planners, union and labor-department officials, managers, local Party leaders, foremen, shop heads, brigade leaders, and even their male coworkers. In their view, these men shared powerful prejudices that shaped, and limited, the world of female labor.

Prejudice against female labor was not unique to Russia. In the late nineteenth and early twentieth centuries, capitalist employers in Europe,

---

[1] GARF, f. 5451, o. 15, d. 362, "Orgbiuro Ts.K. VKP (b)," 84.
[2] GARF, f. 5474, o. 10, d. 337, "Ts.K. Soiuz Zheleznodorozhnikov. Stenograficheskii Otchet Vsesoiuznogo Soveshchaniia po Rabote Sredi Zhenshchin na Transporte," 51. Hereafter cited as "Soiuz Zheleznodorozhnikov."

America, and China frequently used women to lower wages, deskill and replace men, and break strikes. In an effort to protect men's jobs and wages, unions launched campaigns against female labor and sought to expel women from the workplace. Everywhere, workers' movements were fraught with gender conflict created and exacerbated by employers seeking to reduce labor costs. In 1869, Susan B. Anthony, a leader of the woman suffrage movement, urged women to break a printers' strike in New York in order to gain access to skilled jobs that the union denied them. In 1925, a bitter strike was sparked in a Shanghai cotton mill when fifty male workers were fired and replaced with cheaper female trainees. And after 1890, employers in Russia increasingly used women to replace men, driving down wages for all workers.[3] Nor did the revolution in 1917 eliminate these conflicts among Soviet workers. In the 1920s, unions sought to shield their largely male membership from female competition. Women's activists received some protection from the Party, but union officials proclaimed their Party-sanctioned efforts a blow against union democracy.[4] During the first five-year plan, women entered the labor market on a large scale at a time of rapidly expanding employment, but prejudice persisted nonetheless. As women took jobs traditionally reserved for men on construction sites and in mines, shipyards, metal and machine factories, and timber camps, men were forced to adjust quickly to radical changes in the gender composition of the workforce. Male peasant migrants brought patriarchal and conservative views of women into the workplace. They were not alone in their hostility: men at every level of industry reacted strongly to the regendering policy. And Soviet women fought back.

Historians of many countries have found the voices of women workers notoriously elusive. What did women workers think about male prejudice? How did they view the demand for a male "family wage," or union campaigns to bar them from the workplace? Even studies devoted to women workers have concluded that these are difficult questions to

---

[3] Mary Blewett, *Men, Women and Work: Class, Gender and Protest in the New England Shoe Industry, 1780–1910* (Urbana, Ill.: University of Illinois Press, 1990), 172–73; Christina Gilmartin, *Engendering the Chinese Revolution.: Radical Women, Mass Movements and Communist Politics in the 1920s* (Berkeley, Calif.: University of California Press, 1993), 131; Rose Glickman, *Russian Factory Women: Workplace and Society, 1880–1914* (Berkeley, Calif.: University of California Press, 1984), 84–104.

[4] Elizabeth Wood, "Class and Gender at Loggerheads in the Early Soviet State: Who Should Organize the Female Proletariat and How?," in Laura Frader and Sonya Rose, eds., *Gender and Class in Modern Europe* (Ithaca, N.Y.: Cornell University Press, 1996), 294–310. On the attitudes of male workers toward women in the 1920s, see Diane Koenker, "Men against Women on the Shop Floor in Early Soviet Russia: Gender and Class in the Socialist Workplace," *The American Historical Review* 100, no. 5 (December 1995): 1438–1464.

answer.[5] The evidence is skimpy; the records are few. Women, occupied as they often were with child rearing, were less likely to be organized, to attend meetings, to write, or to participate in activities that left written records. Industrial workers under both capitalism and socialism were involved in gender conflicts, but unique to Soviet workers is the ample documentation that exists of women's experiences and opinions. This chapter draws extensively on the actual words and speeches of women workers and activists. The voices here are strong and clear, the sources rich. The records show that women workers had a distinct perspective, but the records themselves owe their existence to an unusual confluence of interests: women wanted to be heard, but the Party also had its motives for encouraging women to speak and then publicizing their testimonies.

Women had complained frequently throughout the 1920s about discrimination within the factories, labor exchanges, and unions, but their grievances had received little attention. The Party's decision in November 1930 to mobilize 1.6 million women to fill the labor shortage, however, cast a harsh new light on the behavior of local officials. The mobilization campaign abruptly elevated women, a group long scorned for its "backwardness," to a crucial position in the industrialization drive. If large numbers of women were to enter the labor force, the Party would need to dispel the prejudices against female labor. With this aim, the Party gave women workers and activists strong public support, encouraging them to air their views in large official meetings and widely reprinting their comments, speeches, and ideas. It sought to use women workers, first, to combat male managers' reluctance to employ female labor; second, to shake up local officials; and third, to create a fairer climate in the workplace. Women, for their part, seized the moment to speak frankly and furiously about gender relations, boldly denouncing factory managers, union and Party officials, and male workers.

The All-Union Meeting for Work among Women

VTsSPS (the All Union Central Council of Trade Unions) had complacently presided over two years of "liquidationist" activity, doing little to prevent local union officials from systematically dismantling women's

---

[5] Different interpretations of the "family wage" demand include Heidi Hartmann, "Capitalism, Patriarchy, and Job Segregation by Sex," in Zillah Eisenstein, ed., *Capitalist Patriarchy and the Case for Socialist Feminism* (New York: Monthly Review Press, 1979), 206–47; Jane Humphries, "Class Struggle and the Persistence of the Working-Class Family," *Cambridge Journal of Economics* 1 (1977): 241–58; and Colin Creighton, "The Rise of the Male Breadwinner Family: A Reappraisal," *Comparative Studies in Society and History* 38, no. 2 (1996): 310–37.

organizations. M. Lenau, the head of the Sector for Mass Campaigns in VTsSPS, noted that the unions had understood the elimination of the Zhenotdel as a "signal to liquidate all work with women."[6] The Party's call to bring 1.6 million women into the workforce compelled the national union leadership to reassess its position. In the absence of the Zhenotdel, women's union organizers, and delegate meetings, VTsSPS had lost its organizational links with women. In an attempt to respond to the Party's call, VTsSPS leaders began, late in 1930, to plan a large meeting with representatives from the unions. Officially, the meeting had several aims: to focus attention on the new importance of women; to develop a plan for mass recruitment; and to revive the organizational links that local unionists had destroyed.[7] VTsSPS recognized that unless local union officials changed their attitudes, they would be worse than useless in the upcoming campaign. The meeting was intended to send a clear message that male prejudice, discrimination, and apathy would no longer be tolerated. In the words of the labor newspaper *Trud*, VTsSPS wished "to strike a powerful blow against the conservative elements that undermine the role of female labor for industrialization and defense."[8]

Two years of union-sanctioned liquidationism, however, had left their mark. Union leaders had no interest in attending the meeting. VTsSPS had initially hoped to convene the delegates in January, but it was forced to postpone the date several times because the unions were so slow to gather material on women.[9] These difficulties hinted at the situation on the local level. A VTsSPS report to the Central Committee after the meeting noted that despite the repeated postponements, the union leaders had still been unprepared: "The meeting showed the complete lack of preparation of the economic, union, and Party organizations." In conducting its own research prior to the meeting, VTsSPS had uncovered "conservatism toward female labor not only among managers, union officials, and backward workers, but among many leading Party workers" as well.[10]

The All-Union Meeting for Work among Women was finally convened on February 1, 1931, bringing together about one hundred union representatives for five days of speeches and testimony. Among the delegates were many former Zhenotdel organizers and women shock workers, the remnants of the *zhenskii aktiv* that had organized women in the

---

6   "Promyshlennost' Trebuetsia 1,600,000 Novykh Rabotnits," *Trud*, February 3, 1931, p. 1.
7   "Soveshchanie Profsoiuzov po Rabote Sredi Zhenshchin," *Trud*, December 11, 1930, p. 4.
8   "Promyshlennost' Trebuetsia 1,600,000 Novykh Rabotnits."
9   GARF, f. 5451, o. 15, d. 363, "Vsekh TsK Profsoiuzov i Sovapparatov," 166.
10   GARF, f. 5451, o. 15, d. 362, "Orgbiuro TsK VKP (b)," 80.

factories throughout the 1920s. Andrei Zhdanov, the young leader of the Nizhegorod district Party committee, who had helped purge Tomsky from VTsSPS in 1929, spoke bluntly and forcefully about the Party's decision to mobilize 1.6 million women. He stressed that the basic task that lay before the unions now was to recruit women. In a stunning parallel to the popular political call for the "liquidation of the *kulaks* as a class," he announced that it was time to "liquidate women as housewives" or to eliminate housewives from the working class. The task demanded, in his view, "a total change in the consciousness of male unionists." If women were to enter production and contribute to industrialization, the apathy, discrimination, and hostility that characterized union attitudes toward women would have to be eradicated. Just as Stalin and his supporters had attacked Tomsky for trying to maintain the independence of the unions, Zhdanov now fiercely attacked the old union leaders for women's problems, charging that "the question of women's mobilization into the industrial proletariat had almost no place in the work of the old leadership." Yet Zhdanov admitted that the purge had changed little with regard to women: the entire union apparatus was still guilty of indifference. Refusing to attend the meeting, they had sent the ex-Zhenotdel organizers in their stead. "We come to this meeting with shameful results," Zhdanov thundered. "The role of the unions is not to chatter about the backwardness of women" or moan about "objective reasons" for their failure to work among women. The time had come for local organizations, the economic organs, and the commissariats to pay attention to the issue of female labor. "The task of every woman worker," Zhdanov boomed, "of every more or less comprehending unionist, is to change the consciousness of unionists on the issue of work among women."[11]

Given such powerful license from above, the meeting quickly turned into an explosive and angry exposé of the abuse, discrimination, and indifference that women suffered from men at every level. Local Party leaders, managers, and officials in NKT (the Commissariat of Labor), the labor exchanges, the economic organs, and VTsSPS were all the subject of the delegates' scathing criticisms. For a brief moment, the aims of Party leaders coincided with those of women at the local level, resulting in an explosion of frustration and bitterness. In permitting women to speak fully and freely, VTsSPS skillfully sought to use their anger to unsettle local officials. The unions, having delegated the old *zhenotdelki* to attend what they clearly viewed as an insignificant "women's meeting," were unexpectedly subjected to fierce public denunciations by their own representatives. As women rose, one after another, to describe the angry

[11] GARF, f. 5451, o. 15, d. 358, "Stenogramma Vsesoiuznogo Soveshchaniia po Rabote Sredi Zhenshchin" (hereafter cited as "Stenogramma"), vol. 2, p. 15.

and troubled gender relations within the factories and at new industrial sites, the meeting provided a rare glimpse into their consciousness and experiences.

Stuck at the Bottom: The Obstacles to Becoming a Skilled Worker

On the second day of the meeting, E. S. Serina, NKT's chief inspector for women's labor and a strong advocate of women's interests, gave a lengthy speech on skill that provoked much subsequent discussion. She noted that mass participation of women in the labor force would not in itself end their segregation into low-skilled jobs. The crucial objective, in her view, was to raise women's level of skill. Serina, like Zhdanov, employed the language of the purge, blaming "the old, opportunistic leadership of NKT" for women's current difficulties, though she conceded that the training of women had also been "overlooked" by leaders in the economic organs and the commissariats. "Everyone talks," she declared, "but no one does anything." The commissariats agreed in principle to train women, but they often resisted raising the quotas for female enrollment in the factory training schools (FZUs). The Central Committee had decreed that women were to compose 30 to 40 percent of incoming classes, but "due to insufficient effort," NKT had failed to meet that target, and the Supreme Council of the National Economy (VSNKh) had actively opposed NKT's plan to recruit two hundred thousand girls for training.

Serina advanced a radical proposition: women's share of promotions in every branch of industry should equal their general share of the labor force. Thus, if women constituted one third of the workers in the chemicals industry, then fully one third of promotions for trainees in chemicals should be reserved for women. According to this scheme, women would rapidly move out of the lowest (unskilled) sector of the workforce as their distribution across the skill hierarchy came to resemble their representation in the industry as a whole. This aggressive "affirmative action" plan distributed the opportunity for higher positions on the basis not of seniority but of gender. By establishing quotas for promotion in proportion to representation by sex, it would rapidly eliminate sex segregation by skill. Yet current practice was far removed from this proposal. According to Serina, the industrial unions, Narpit (the Union of Public Dining and Dormitory Workers), and the economic organs were all "sluggish" in promoting women. NKT had tried repeatedly to discuss the recruitment of women, but the union leaders always refused. "No matter how many times you call a meeting on female labor," Serina noted with exasperation, "the central committees of the unions do not show up."[12]

The old leaders of NKT and the unions, who had recently been purged for "Right opportunism," provided several of the main speakers with a convenient target for blame. Lenau, the head of VTsSPS's Sector for Mass Campaigns, claimed that the purges had eliminated the sources of discrimination. Scapegoating the "old, opportunistic leadership" and "rightists" such as Tomsky, the former head of VTsSPS, he implied that new leaders would chart a new direction. Yet the women representatives from the factories expressed a different view. The problem, as they saw it, was not politics at the highest level but rather the discriminatory practices engaged in by men from top to bottom.[13] Berdakina, a representative from the Crimea, openly challenged the idea that the problem rested with the old leadership. "I would say that we do not see any new leadership," she remarked tartly. In her estimation, the new leaders had not taken a fresh approach to women's issues; leadership on the local level "absolutely has not changed its attitudes." Women, for example, could not enter the FZUs without learning to read, but no attention was given by the new leaders to literacy training. Women were still being placed in the lowest-skilled, most physically arduous jobs. Ordered to hire women, managers complied by sending them to work as stevedores. When Berdakina questioned this practice, union officials contemptuously brushed her off: "You asked about female labor," they said. "Well, now it is being used." She concluded, "There is a definite unwillingness to understand and fulfill the directives correctly."[14]

Women described an industrial world rigidly stratified by skill. Workers in skilled positions commanded higher wages, greater respect, more autonomy, and more control over the work process. Women, however, were rarely admitted into the apprenticeships that opened up access to more skilled positions. They worked in "support" or janitorial services – cleaning, mopping, loading, and hauling – rather than in production. They did heavy physical labor, unskilled and poorly paid work, but they seldom worked "at the bench." They held the lowliest positions even in those industries, such as textiles, where they constituted the majority of workers. Soviet labor analysts in the 1920s and 1930s explained women's concentration at the bottom of the industrial hierarchy as a consequence of their family responsibilities, poor education, and physical weakness.

---

12 GARF, f. 5451, o. 15, d. 357, "Stenogramma," vol. 1, pp. 7–13, 23–24.
13 Women never used the contemporary term "male chauvinism," though it describes the attitudes of unions officials, male workers, foremen, bosses, and local Party leaders perfectly.
14 GARF, f. 5451, o. 15, d. 357, "Stenogramma," vol. 1, pp. 49–52.

0

14   *Women at the Gates*

They were aware of discrimination against women, but few troubled to
explore men's role in maintaining the gender hierarchy within the factories. Favoring "objective" structural over "subjective" cultural explanations, they assumed that training for women would quickly eliminate
inequality. Women workers themselves, though, insisted that plans, quotas, and targets were implemented, in the final analysis, by men, who were
bound by their own cultural prejudices.

Plant managers commonly held that women *belonged* in janitorial or
"support" work rather than in production, simply because they were men-
tally and physically incapable of skilled work. Women would eventually
leave the factory to marry or have babies, so training them was a waste of
valuable resources. Such prejudices were so strong that even when NKT
trained women outside the factory, many managers refused to place the
graduates in skilled positions. Spivak, a delegate from East Siberia, noted
that most of the women in the factories in his region did janitorial work.
"We have met with extraordinarily conservative attitudes," he reported.
The director of one porcelain factory believed that in hiring them as janitors, he had fulfilled the directives of the Party to involve women. This
director declared, "Enough with [this talk of] the involvement of women;
there is no place else to put them." Spivak explained, "They think that if
they involve women in janitorial work in the enterprises, this means they
have involved women in production." Fully 30 percent of the workers in
the porcelain factory were women, but there were no female turners or
molders, both skilled positions. Spivak said that the leaders of the economic organs were also opposed to women's entering skilled jobs. The
Committee to Improve the Labor and Life of Women (KUTB) in his region had tried to force VTsSPS and the local labor department to survey
the status of women in the factories, but neither had complied. Spivak
also cited "the sluggishness" of the unions and cooperatives. Expressing
his own view of local conditions, he noted, "If this question took the
economic organs in the center by surprise, what do you expect in East
Siberia?"[15]

Delegates to the meeting enumerated the many tactics used to discour-
age women from taking skilled jobs. Managers placed women on old,
faulty equipment, which lowered their output and their earnings. They
pointedly ignored women and refused to place them in appropriate positions. Lisenkova, a delegate from Krasnyi Sormovo, reported that "no
work at all" was done with the chemical plant's thirty-three hundred
women. Even after women returned from three-month training courses,
managers claimed that they had no machines available and sent them back
to unskilled jobs. "This is how we approach female labor," Lisenkova

[15] Ibid., 38–42.

exclaimed angrily. "Women study a certain skill, and they put them back to work with a broom. ... What did they study for?"[16] And even when managers did permit women to enter skilled positions, they often made it impossible for them to work effectively. Nazarova, a delegate from the Donbas, told the story of four women who were finally promoted to turners. "They very much wanted to be turners," Nazarova recalled, "but the proper conditions were not created for them." Placed at the faultiest machines, they were ultimately forced to quit after six months. The union then cited this incident as evidence that "women cannot be turners."[17]

Managers and union officials were not alone in their opposition to training women. Delegates spoke repeatedly about foremen and male workers who denied women apprenticeships and abused them on the job. Acting together, men created an insurmountable barrier to women's advancement through the factory hierarchy. Gudrova, a woman metalworker in the Mekhanicheskii State Factory, noted that not a single woman had been promoted to a leadership position in her factory since the revolution. The only two production workshops (*mastera*) composed of women had been eliminated. Although there were many suitable jobs, no women worked in the production sector. When several women were finally promoted to the machine shop (*avtomat*), the men harassed them interminably. "*Nu,*" they said, "here come the hairy machinists [*avtomatchiki*]." Gudrova explained the result: "The women had to listen to endless such remarks, and at the end of the year, they left."[18] Kravchenko, a delegate from Dneprostroi, a huge dam and hydroelectric station under construction on the Dnieper River, noted that many skilled male workers shared management's view that the promotion of women represented a waste of resources. One central mechanical master, a member of the workers' committee, had told him, "You know, it is better not to raise this issue. That trick won't work here. There is a good reason that I won't permit more than two women at the bench: you skill them, and then they get married, and the work is ruined. What does the government want to spend money on this for?"[19] Lenau supported the arguments made by the women delegates. Men, he argued, were promoted much more rapidly than women because of prejudice against female labor. "A woman can sit in a trivial job for more than a year," he said, "while a man stays no more than two to three weeks before they promote him."[20]

Newspaper reports corroborated the testimony of the delegates to the All-Union Meeting for Work among Women. Prejudice against the promotion of women was widespread in every industry, including textiles, which employed a majority of women. From plant director to skilled worker, men believed that women should not do skilled work. One woman,

[16] Ibid., 52–53. [17] Ibid., 99. [18] Ibid., 26. [19] Ibid., 35. [20] Ibid., 285.

reporting on work conditions in Stalinskii *okrug,* termed the attitudes of men toward women workers "uncomradely." Women were subjected to "hooligan attacks and abuse [*khuliganskie vynady i rugan'*]." In the rolling-rail shop of the Stalingrad plant, after several women were promoted to the position of crane machinist, male workers, Party members included, had denounced the promotions as a "pointless waste of resources." The head of the coke shop had told the shop bureau that he would not take any responsibility for the work of women promoted to soakers (*namotchitsy*) in his shop. In his view, unskilled wages were sufficient for women, and "a higher salary would spoil them." Many male workers agreed with the notion that a woman should not earn more than a man. There was similar resentment in other factories and workplaces. Skilled male workers did not want to train women. In one mining school, the instructor explained, "Girls do not need to study to be masters. They should study only stockings and lace."[21]

The widespread bias against skilling women and placing them in production jobs was not motivated by a protective desire to shelter them from heavy or hazardous work. Their placement in jobs requiring heavy unskilled labor outside the shops belied claims that they could not cope with the physical requirements of skilled work in production. In the chemicals industry, for example, large numbers of newly hired women began to work as weighers, turners, light mechanics, rubber press workers, greasers, milling-machine operators, planers, weavers, and winders, mainly semiskilled nonproduction or "support" jobs that had been identified as "suitable" for women.[22] Yet their lowly place in the chemical plants was not determined by safety considerations. Out of 1,713 women in the Chernorechenskii chemical complex, only 181 performed skilled work in production. The remainder held "support" jobs such as janitor and washerwoman, or worked as haulers of pyrites and anthracite waste, heavy and hazardous work. Women worked with unsealed containers of poisonous chemicals in unmechanized jobs under unsanitary conditions. The manager had a plan to promote 633 women, but only fifty of these were targeted for skilled support positions such as mechanic and electrician. He planned to "promote" the others to the positions of yard worker, cleaner, janitor, and watchman.[23]

Women workers on the railroads also complained bitterly about their inability to move into better jobs. Throughout the 1920s, railroad work had been primarily "male" (only 7 percent of the labor force in 1928 was female). Most women worked in white-collar or service jobs, as

---

21   Cherevadskaia, "Trud i Byt Rabotnits," *Kommunistka,* 1928, no. 6: 60–63.

22   GARF, f. 5451, o. 15, d. 362, "Material o Vnedreniiu Zhenskogo Truda v Proizvodstvo Vmesto Muzhchin," 70.

23   N. Aristov and Tolchiev, "Dorogu Zhenshchine na Proizvodstvo na Kvalifitsirovannuiu Rabotu," *Na trudovom fronte,* 1932, nos. 26–27: 22–23.

washerwomen, loaders, guards, telephonists, or clerks. The railroad work-shops were almost entirely male, and there were virtually no women in skilled positions. The railroads were one of the few sectors in which the central planners had hesitated to challenge men's hegemony. Women charged that they were never encouraged or given the opportunity for promotion. Vinogradova, a worker on the Northern line, explained, "I have worked since I was sixteen years old as a switchman, and for ten years I heard, 'What use are you, and what are you doing there?' Yet I never received a single reprimand, as did the men who often came to work drunk." One worker half jokingly suggested that great strides could be made simply by replacing all the men who violated labor discipline with women. Many women noted that they could easily fill the job of conduc-tor, but managers considered the work too difficult. One woman on the Moscow–Baltic line said with a laugh, "What do conductors do? They sit at the end of train and gossip. The work is not very hard. Women can do this." Another woman suggested that only men were employed as conductors because women were expected to spend their "whole lifetimes with a floor rag." Women questioned why they were used to replace men who left temporarily on vacation, but were never given the opportunity to win permanent positions. Why were unskilled men hired directly from the labor exchanges into apprenticeships that were closed to women who were already working on the railroads?[24]

Women also mentioned the problems created by their lack of education. Women generally had higher rates of illiteracy than men. Artiukhina, the former head of the Zhenotdel, called illiteracy "our sore and our shame." After the revolution, the Party had launched mass campaigns to eradi-cate illiteracy, setting up short courses in factories and villages. By 1931, the overwhelming majority of new union members claimed some degree of literacy. Soviet schools were highly effective in teaching basic skills to working-class and peasant adults and children: literacy rates among women union members had risen from 44 percent in 1918 to 94 percent by 1931. Yet new women workers in industry and construction in the Moscow region still lagged behind men: women were twice as likely as men to be illiterate. Illiteracy was most prevalent among both sexes in construction, a seasonal sector that employed many peasant migrants.[25] Moreover, the ability to sign one's name or read a simple newspaper article did not necessarily equip a worker to comprehend instructions, minutes from a meeting, or blueprints. Zenikova, a worker on the Southeastern railway line, explained how crippling and shameful illiteracy could be. Elected to the presidium of the railway committee, a rare honor for a

24 "Soiuz Zheleznodorozhnikov," 51, 73, 61, 101, 84.
25 Ibid., 128; RTsKhIDNI, f. 17, o. 10, d. 496, "Sostav Chlenov Profsoiuzov," 28; "Sostav Uchashchikhsia," 30; Goltsman, "Sostav Novykh Rabochikh," *Udarnik,* 1932, nos. 3–4: 69.

woman, she had attended her first meeting and three days later had received the protocols of that meeting, which she in turn was to explain to her fellow workers. "I went home, I saw the protocols, and I cried," she remembered, "because, truly, I had no idea what they said, and I knew they would expel me." A man noted that many of the women who were sent to his shop to enter apprenticeships were illiterate and could not be trained. Although training normally took four months, the administration would often send over women just three days before the exam was given. Clearly they were bound to fail. Women complained that in place of help, they got only "sneers and mockery" from men. And it was hard to study, to work, and to cope with the demands of a family. As one railroad worker remarked, "Naturally, after work a woman is very tired. And yet she has to go and stand in line to get bread, and if she has a large family, she has to cook and do laundry."[26]

Many women testified that women's promotions were reserved for March 8, International Women's Day. On this day, a few women would invariably be singled out, only to be swiftly forgotten again. One woman railroad worker noted, "On March 8, the bosses give women some kind of promotion, but it is taken away after March 8." Many of the promotions were awarded for the sake of appearance only; the promoted women often were not prepared to do their new jobs. One worker described what happened in such cases: "On March 8, we promote a woman to this or that job, and within six months, the woman runs back with tears in her eyes and says that they fired her." She explained, "We call for forward movement [*prodvizhenie*] and upward movement [*vydvizhenie*], but what we have is backward movement [*zadvizhenie*]." She added, "Our achievements are very miserly. We take steps like a turtle." Zacharova, a woman worker on the Baikal line, angrily concurred: "Our promotions are timed to March 8. But what kind of promotion is this? Last March 8, a woman from a group of janitors was promoted to be the brigade leader of the janitors. In other words, she went from one bucket of slop to the same exact bucket of slop."[27] Not only did women not feel honored by the March 8 celebration, but they saw it as a pretense and a sham, a cover for the absence of real change on every other day of the year.

Women reported that it was much harder for a woman to qualify for a promotion than a man. According to Ivanova, a worker on the Southern line, "When they promote a man, they weigh his negatives and positives. Maybe he is barely literate and cannot cope with the job immediately, but all the same, they declare that he can cope and will work. When the same issue comes up with a woman, though, they say she should receive the job only if she does not have a single negative quality." Savanenko, a worker

[26]   "Soiuz Zheleznodorozhnikov," 82, 70, 92–93, 101.
[27]   Ibid., 50, 65, 67–68, 147.

on the October line, suggested that it was almost impossible for women to qualify for promotion. When a woman on the railway was put up for a promotion, the administrator said, "'How can we promote her? She is too short,'" Savanenko recalled. "But when you look at the administrator, he is even shorter. He is simply insulting. Once, I could not help it, I said to him, 'Look at yourself, comrade, you are even shorter. If you can become the boss of a section, why can't you allow a woman to work?'" Even after women received training, managers often refused to assign them to skilled jobs. A woman worker said, "The girls come to us in tears. They [the bosses] tell them that they don't have to listen to the government."[28]

Artiukhina noted that when women were selected for promotion [*vydvizhenie*], they were more timid, less sure, and less comfortable than men were in their new positions, even if they were equally qualified. In part this was because women felt more personal insecurity about their talents and their abilities, but it was also because they faced greater hostility. Zueva, a worker on the Riazan–Urals line, explained, "Men see the woman worker as an enemy, a wrecker of production, not a comrade. In our section there is a woman driller. Next to her stands a man who laughs and jeers at her, who does not understand that she has a right to master production just as he does." Not only did men not help, but they made the women's jobs harder. Zueva continued, "You all know that the eleventh spring coil weighs about one hundred ninety-six pounds. You go toward the coil, and the men go also. You approach it. The man begins to roll a cigarette, and of course you are not going to wait for him, so you lift the coil onto your shoulders and you leave. The man laughs at you and says, 'It's nothing, she has the strength of a horse. Let her strain a little.'" Women frequently lifted loads that exceeded the legal weight limits. In the boiler shop on the Southeastern line, for example, they moved rings weighing more than 270 pounds. When they complained, their boss would ask, "Why did you come to work?"[29] Men offered a wide variety of reasons not to hire, train, or promote women. Yet regardless of their reasons, men at every level actively maintained a hierarchy of skill and gender, in the factories, on worksites, and in plants and mines, that kept women at the bottom.

Unions, Factory Committees, Labor Exchanges

The hostility that women faced on the shop floor was exacerbated, after the elimination of the Zhenotdel, by the absence of any organization willing to counter discrimination or promote women's interests. Unions,

---

[28] Ibid., 56, 75–76, 72.   [29] Ibid., 120, 71, 72, 81.

factory committees, local labor departments, and even Party committees not only failed to challenge male attitudes and actions but tacitly accepted, overlooked, or even supported gender inequality. Delegates to the All-Union Meeting for Work among Women repeatedly testified that the unions refused to recognize women as a constituency. "Our union organizations treat women coldly," declared one delegate. "They say our women cannot cope with work, but I would say that our unions do not know how to lead our women."[30] Artiukhina, accusing the unions of "colossal sluggishness," noted that it was almost impossible to get a woman promoted to a position of regional leadership in the printing, chemicals, or metal unions.[31] Even though millions of female workers had entered the labor force and joined the unions, women were still poorly represented among the leadership. As late as 1935, women constituted only 6 to 10 percent of representatives to factory and shop committees in machine building, the industrial branch that absorbed the single greatest number of new women workers. In sewing and cotton, two branches that employed an almost exclusively female labor force, only about half the local shop-floor leaders were women.[32] One report on the railroad workers' union pointed to significant differences between male and female workers: "Women work as scrubwomen, they can barely read, and they do not understand most of what goes on at union meetings."[33] Staffed by men, the unions reflected men's concerns. The relationship between women and their unions was characterized by mutual apathy.

Several delegates linked the decision of the Eighth Trade Union Congress to abolish separate women's organizers in the factories with the subsequent collapse of union work among women. One delegate from the Ukraine observed, "In the past several years, a great coldness toward work among women has been felt."[34] The liquidation of the Zhenotdel in 1930 had reflected and intensified this mood. The unions, receiving no guidance and no leadership from above, had promptly jettisoned *byt* issues such as child care, education, promotion, training, and gender relations in the factories. When the delegate assemblies tried to take on the extra work, the unions ignored them.[35] Nazarova, a delegate from the Donbas, angrily commented that the chairman of her own factory committee had refused to help with the reelection campaign for the delegate assembly. When she asked him to participate, he told her, "You go to your meetings. We have our own work." She bitterly concluded, "This shows that

---

30 GARF, f. 5451, o. 15, d. 357, "Stenogramma," vol. 1, p. 31.
31 "Soiuz Zheleznodorozhnikov," 117.
32 *Zhenshchina v SSSR. Statisticheskii sbornik* (Moscow: TsUNKhU, 1937), 158–59.
33 "Soiuz Zheleznodorozhnikov," 34.
34 GARF, f. 5451, o. 15, d. 357, "Stenogramma," vol. 1, p. 63.   35 Ibid., 80.

the union organizations do not consider women's work their business."[36]
Railway union leaders were irritated by women's constant complaints and
demands for special attention. Union officials on the Baku line noted with
impatience, "[We] do not feel the need to consider such separate issues
as who sits at our meetings, who speaks, and whether men or women
are participating."[37] When women challenged union officials about their
refusal to do work among women, they responded with the same line the
Party had used to liquidate the Zhenotdel: "We do not carry on separate
work among women. We carry on work *in general.*" Pimenova, a metalworker, announced, "I think it is time to put an end to this 'in general.'"
She demanded that unions and factory committees take responsibility for
work among women.[38] The mine workers' union was hostile to the new
women workers and refused to process their applications for union membership. Union leaders in the OGPU mine proclaimed, "*babas* are in the
mine only temporarily, to fill gaps in the labor force"; accordingly, their
applications were left to "marinate" for a while.[39] Many women repeated
the view that "the unions do poor work among women."[40]

On the rare occasions when the unions did deal with "women's issues," they invariably assigned the work to women. After eliminating the
Zhenotdel, the Party had stressed that all organizations were to become
broadly responsible for women's issues. Yet the unions interpreted the decision differently. Kochkina, a worker on the Perm railway line, strongly
criticized her union's leaders: "I came to Moscow this summer, sacri-
ficed my holiday, in order to discuss questions relating to women's work
[*zhenrabota*]. It turned out that nobody on the union's central committee,
with the exception of comrade Murav'eva [the sole female representa-
tive], knew anything. In the central committee, they declared, 'Murav'eva
leads work among women. Talk to her.' So stands this business: they promote one woman, and she is responsible for this." Murav'eva confirmed
Kochkina's account, saying, "Yes, every piece of paper that has the word
woman on it, they dump into my lap. The higher organs say, 'You are
supposedly a woman, so you should do it.'"[41]

In organizing the All-Union Meeting for Work among Women, VTsSPS
had encouraged women to vent their anger toward and frustration over
men in the Party, the government, and the unions. If the problems that
the delegates outlined were clear, however, the solutions were less so.
The overwhelming sense of the meeting was that male prejudice against

36 Ibid., 99.   37 "Soiuz Zheleznodorozhnikov," 32 ob.
38 GARF, f. 5451, o. 15, d. 357, "Stenogramma," vol. 1, pp. 103–4. On this issue, see also
    Lenau's speech, ibid., 230.
39 "Dovol'no Passuzhdenii," *Na trudovom fronte*, 1931, nos. 23–24: 12.
40 GARF, f. 5451, o. 15, d. 357, "Stenogramma," vol. 1, p. 36.
41 "Soiuz Zheleznodorozhnikov," 49, 98.

women helped maintain a hierarchy of skill within the factories that systematically deprived women of the opportunity to advance. Prejudice was firmly entrenched at every level of the factory and could be countered only by organizing women separately from men. But the delegates were not invited to develop a plan for "reconstructing the consciousness of the male unionists," as Zhdanov had suggested. Although the delegates had vividly detailed the problems they encountered, the official list of resolutions, duly approved at the end of the meeting, offered few cures.

Within a week, the resolutions were adopted by the presidium of VTsSPS to serve as directives for the unions. The resolutions addressed the unions' general apathy toward women, making it clear that the decision to eliminate women's organizers in the factories had had disastrous results: "*Zhenrabota* [women's work] has not found a place within the central committees of the unions, VTsSPS, union councils, or factory committees." Yet VTsSPS did not reinstate the system of women's organizers. Following the Party's approach to the Zhenotdel, VTsSPS permitted separate women's organizers to operate only in the national republics of Central Asia, Kazakhstan, and Karelia, not in the industrialized regions. Instead, it designated one organizer on every town and district union council to oversee work among women. It suggested that the unions call separate women's meetings, particularly for wives of workers, peasant women, and the unskilled. The unions were ordered to revive the delegate assemblies, which they had unofficially eliminated in many localities, but these assemblies were to mobilize women to "face toward production"; they were not to address women's issues. Finally, VTsSPS recommended that the unions follow the example set by the women's brigades earlier in the fall, and go into the factories to determine in which jobs women might replace men.[42]

The resolutions offered few organizational remedies for the unions' traditional hostility toward women. With the exception of designating one member of each union council to oversee women's work, VTsSPS made no substantive organizational changes. It sought to preserve the delegate assemblies, but only in order to reorient them to mobilizing support among women for Party policies. The unions were encouraged to "reconstruct their work," but few concrete guidelines were provided. The resolutions ultimately did not address the myriad organizational deficiencies that the delegates had described. The problem, as one woman put it, was that "everyone recognizes that women need to be a part of socialist construction, but no one is doing much about it."[43] It was doubtful that the consciousness, attitudes, or practices of men could be altered in the absence of strong new organizational forms and programs focusing on women. The

---

[42]   GARF, f. 5451, o. 15, d. 359, "Postanovlenie k n. Zasedaniia Prezidiuma VTsSPS," 54; "Massovoe Vnedrenie Zhenskogo Truda i Ocherednye Zadachi Profsoiuzov v Rabote Sredi Zhenshchin," 55–63.
[43]   GARF, f. 5451, o. 15, d. 357, "Stenogramma," vol. 1, p. 28.

resolutions, curiously disconnected from the actual conditions detailed by the delegates, did little to restructure a system of long-standing inequality buttressed on every level by deeply held male prejudices.

Reports from the Factories: "We Need Workers, Not Women"

In March, VTsSPS and KUTB launched a major campaign organized around the twin slogans "1.5 Million Women in the Economy!" and "Live to Serve the Five-Year Plan!"[44] The labor newspaper *Trud* popularized the campaign by urging unions to train women and replace male with female labor. B. Marsheva, a prominent expert on female labor, wrote that the broad use of women's labor depended on a reconfiguration of gender segregation in the workforce: "We must transfer all workers in order to free up positions for women, and use men for those jobs in which female labor is impossible or less efficient." The pace of involving women in production, she exhorted, "must literally increase tenfold."[45] For all this publicity, however, the campaign seemed to have little effect on managers' attitudes toward women. Throughout 1931, published and unpublished reports from the factories indicated that women were still experiencing discrimination. Many managers were unwilling to accept women, skilled or unskilled, in *any* position. The administrator of the Podol'skii machine factory, for example, flatly declared, "We don't need *babas*." Another proclaimed, "*Babas*? I don't train them, and I don't want to train them."[46] A manager in the mines announced, "A *baba* can do nothing in mining." And one director of a glass factory said that he considered "the arrival of women in a factory the highest measure of punishment."[47]

Managers and male workers were even more resistant to the idea of skilling women. Despite the high quotas imposed by VTsSPS, men simply refused to allow women into skilled positions. Women *rabkory* (worker-journalists) sent troubling stories of discrimination to the labor press. In the instrument shop of Krasnyi Putilovets, a woman worker named Grivneva spent the better part of a year "sharpening pencils." When she requested a transfer to more complex work, the master yelled, "You women can never be good turners!" When another woman asked to be placed in more skilled work after eight months of removing drill cones, the master told her, "Nothing can be done here by *babas*, work is a

44 GARF, f. 5451, o. 15, d. 362, "Orgbiuro TsK VKP (b)," 80.
45 B. Marsheva, "Poltora Milliona Zhenshchin Vovlechet v Stroitel'stvo Sotsializma," *Trud*, March 3, 1931, p. 4.
46 Ibid.
47 "Na Prezidiume VTsSPS. Il'ichevtsy Dobilis' Vovlecheniia v Proizvodstvo 3,000 Zhen Rabochikh," *Trud*, July 7, 1931, p. 1.

serious business." Even girls trained outside the factories by the Central Institute of Labor were assigned to unskilled positions. They demanded to be tested and promoted, but the foreman (*nachal'nik*) acceded only after considerable pressure was exerted by the institute. After testing them at poorly functioning machines, he refused to promote them, claiming, "Girls are completely worthless!"[48]

In April, a small group of representatives who had just returned from a tour of factories in the North Caucasus and Leningrad, several mines, and Magnitogorsk, the giant iron and steel complex, gathered to discuss the campaign for female labor. The mood of the meeting was pessimistic. Simonova, delivering the report on Magnitogorsk, spoke with disgust about the treatment of women on the site. "At Magnitogorsk," she asserted angrily, "attitudes toward women workers are absolutely revolting." Women were placed in the worst-paid and most physically difficult jobs. "The least of it is that they don't promote women," she said. "When a woman comes to work, they treat her horribly. They give her a thirty-six-pound stone to lift. This is what they call involving female labor." The head of the cadre department, responsible for personnel throughout Magnitogorsk, had publicly announced, "We are not interested in women; we do not need them, and we do not take them into account." Although fully half of the unskilled workers at Magnitogorsk were women, nothing was being done to train them. There were no women at all among the metal craftsmen (*slesari*), and only a tiny percentage among the construction engineers (*armaturshchiki*). The unions were doing nothing about any of it. Simonova concluded bitterly, "They have the opinion that 'we need workers, not women.'"[49]

Shcherbatiuka described better conditions in an older mechanical factory in Zlatoust. Almost one third of its workers were women, most of them new to the factory. Initially the shop foremen and masters had threatened to leave if women entered the shops, but the director had taken a hard line, telling one master, "Either the woman goes to the bench, or you will not be permitted in the shop." The woman in question proved to be an excellent worker. In this case, a strong director had forced the masters and foremen to accept skilled women.[50] The situation in Zlatoust, however, appeared to be the exception rather than the rule. At Northern Shipyards, most women worked as janitors or in backbreaking, unskilled jobs that regularly required them to lift 145-pound loads. Work on machines, more highly skilled and less physically taxing, was done by men.

[48] "Razognat' Brigady Rabotnits," *Trud*, March 24, 1931, p. 3.
[49] GARF, f. 5451, o. 15, d. 361, "Soveshchanie o Podgotovke Materialov Vnedreniiu Zhenskogo Truda v Proizvodstvo," 21, 22.
[50] Ibid., 25–25 ob.

One master sent five women who had already completed their apprenticeships back to the apprentice level, even as he placed several men at the
bench as drillers. In another shop, one brigade leader declared, "What
use can come from a *baba*? She should be home cooking cabbage soup,
not working in a factory." He pointedly ignored the one woman in his
brigade for three months, refusing to let her see drafts and isolating her
from his men. When women in the shipyard began to train as heaters
(*nagreval'shchitsy*) and dress in pants, they were subjected to widespread
derision from male workers. The master, recently informed that the job of
heater was to be reserved for women, refused to train them, arguing that
the younger ones would marry and the older were incapable of learning.[51]

Unpublished reports sent by the factories to VTsSPS noted similar patterns of resistance. A report from Serp i Molot, the metallurgical plant
in Moscow, complained that women were not trained to enter skilled
positions and that skilled women were not appropriately placed. After Andreeva, an unskilled woman worker, was trained as a cable machinist (*kanatchitsa*), the head of the shop informed her, "I don't need
kanatchitsy. Why did you study this? Who asked you?" The report added
that this was hardly an isolated incident: "Such examples of repulsive
behavior toward women we can enumerate endlessly."[52] Many managers
openly disavowed the campaign to involve women in production and
simply refused to hire them. The director of a ship-remodeling factory in
Arkhangelsk insisted, "We don't need women. I will countermand these
absurd directives. Women cannot prove themselves here, and they do not
work as well as men." The head of the bottling shop in the Konstantinovskii glass factory announced that he considered himself "above all
measures of punishment." And the manager of the Berezniakovskii chemical complex curtly swore, "There will be no fussing with women here."
Often the factory committees supported their directors. In a striking display of male solidarity's cutting across hierarchical lines, workers in the
Lavshchutskii factory in Belorussia, proclaimed, with the full support of
their director, that "the only work for women here is to wash windows
and clean out the wagons."[53]

Gender Resegregation and Conflict

Male hostility toward the skilling and promotion of women had long
been embedded in the male work culture, but it had been exacerbated
by recent Soviet policies. The strategy of replacing men with women had

[51] Ibid., 34–35.   [52] GARF, f. 5451, o. 15, d. 362, "Zavod Serp i Molot'," 3–6.
[53] GARF, f. 5451, o. 15, d. 362, "Orgbiuro TsK VKP(b)," 84–85.

created competition, animosity, and conflict among workers, especially when women took men's jobs and men were sent to heavier work. When women went into the mines in the Shakhtinskii district, for example, men were forced to vacate a range of jobs to take on the backbreaking work of extracting coal at the mine face. In the understated words of Tserlina, an ex-*zhenotdelka* who visited the mines, "Men do not greet this move with benevolence." She noted that neither the union nor the Party had bothered to explain to the workers why women were going underground. "I am not afraid to say it loudly," Tserlina commented with regret: "I think it's very bad that we no longer have the Zhenotdel."[54] The railroad workers' union in the Moscow region decided to replace 90 percent of its (male) conductors with women. In Leningrad, the union went even further, reserving the jobs of conductor and streetcar driver exclusively for women. The plans provoked a great deal of anger among male workers, who seized upon the differences between the two cities to protest the decisions. A *Trud* editorial queried, "Who is wrong here, who is right? Who is responsible? Who is in charge?"[55] In the Ukraine, male drivers and conductors were removed from the tram cars, replaced with women, and relegated to unskilled jobs that paid them considerably less. The male workers were furious about it and openly protested "these unceremonious transfers."[56] Job allocation, closely but not exclusively tied to the matter of skill, became a fiercely contentious issue between men and women workers.

The issue of heavy physical labor also provoked constant squabbles between men and women. Members of both sexes believed that they performed the dirtiest, heaviest, most unpleasant work and that management unfairly favored the other sex. The strategy of regendering the labor force exacerbated this perception on both sides. Because labor legislation set weight limits on what women could lift or haul, the state redesignated jobs that did not require heavy lifting as "female." Men naturally resented being moved to heavier work to make way for women. Women, for their part, surveyed the sharply gendered hierarchy of skill that existed in every workplace and concluded that men held the greater share of more skilled, lighter jobs, leaving them with the heaviest, dirtiest, and least desirable work. In Magnitogorsk, for example, twenty housewives were mobilized for unskilled work and sent to the electrical station, where they hauled bricks, boards, and long, heavy crossties. One woman, staggering beneath a cumbersome load of crossties, fell and split her head open. Her workmates were outraged; after accusing management of providing men

[54] GARF, f. 5451, o. 15, d. 361, "Soveshchanie o Podgotovke," 1.
[55] "Za 1,600,000 Rabotnits Otvechaiut Prezhde Vsego Soiuzy," *Trud*, July 10, 1931, p. 2.
[56] "Programma Vnedreniia Zhenskogo Truda Sorvana," *Na trudovom fronte*, 1931, nos. 23–24: 13.

with lighter, easier work, they walked off the job.[57] Almost a year into the campaign to involve women in production, VTsSPS concluded, "Bad relations between men and women arose when women replaced men, and men were given heavier work."[58]

Not all conflicts between men and women, however, had such clear explanations. Often men simply did not want to work with women. After a man and a woman were allegedly caught having sex in a tunnel in a Shakhtinskii mine, the workforce buzzed with ugly rumors for weeks.[59] If nothing else, the rumors were evidence of men's extreme discomfort at working closely with women underground. Men in many jobs had difficulty conceiving of women as workmates rather than sexual partners, and the atmosphere at work was often tense. Men frequently regarded women's presence not only as an infringement of their privileges as male workers but also as a sexual transgression, and their resentment in turn took on a sexualized form. They subjected women to sexual advances and obscenities expressly intended to force them off the job. In Magnitogorsk, a woman was placed on the night shift among five hundred men, all of them hauling bricks from one spot to another. A report noted, "First one, then others, began to pester her." She responded with growing anger, the conflict quickly escalated, and finally she spat in their faces. The men wanted "to beat her to death." One worker said that the woman herself was responsible for the situation. She managed to get through the shift, but in the morning she told the foreman, "Transfer me to day work, I cannot work nights." "You do not *want* to work," he retorted, and fired her.[60]

Although women workers did not use the modern term "sexual harassment," they described situations of "abuse" (*rugan'*) that carried the same meaning. When a brigade of Komsomol girls arrived to work at Magnitogorsk, the male attendant in the baths refused to leave while they undressed; he made obscene comments and reduced them to tears.[61] In Krasnyi Putilovets, a mechanic (also a Party member) and his friend, an instrument calibrator, physically molested every woman who entered their shop and subjected her to a stream of obscenities. When one woman protested this treatment, the instrument calibrator hooted sarcastically, "A baroness has shown up in the factory! There is no place for her here." Women workers retaliated by writing up the incident in the factory-wall newspaper, prompting the male workers in turn to attack them as "intriguers and scandalmongers tied to the *rabkory* [worker-journalists]."

---

[57]   GARF, f. 5451, o. 15, d. 361, "Soveshchanie o Podgotovke," 15 ob.
[58]   GARF, f. 5451, o. 15, d. 363, "Itogi Vnedrenie Zhenskogo Truda v Promyshlennost' za 1-oe Polugodie 1931," 12.
[59]   GARF, f. 5451, o. 15, d. 361, "Soveshchanie o Podgotovke," 9.   [60]   Ibid., 15 ob.
[61]   Ibid., 21.

The men yelled, "We will drive you out of the factory!"[62] Foremen often met women's requests with obscene propositions and insinuations; when the women complained, they were accused of provoking the offensive behavior. One member of the Workers' Control Commission, which was responsible for investigating such incidents, coolly observed, "They themselves are guilty. Where there are women, this always happens." Invoking the unassailable logic that where there were no women, there was no sexual harassment, he concluded, "Look, when they were not in the workshop, we never had these squabbles." If women's presence provoked men to behave uncouthly, women were naturally at fault. Not surprisingly, the commission refused to act on the complaints.[63]

Forces for and against Change

Male resentment toward women had multiple causes – legal, political, structural, and cultural. Managers were loath to hire and train women because they feared the loss of their investment if they left the factory to marry or have children. Generous Soviet maternity benefits proved to be a strong economic disincentive. The regendering strategy of employing blocs of women through the creation of exclusively or primarily "female" lines was guaranteed to create animosity between men and women. Male workers resented the women who displaced them, especially if they themselves were moved to heavier work. The redefinition of certain jobs as "female" did little to address male prejudice, which itself was rooted in a system of gender segregation. Throughout the 1920s, women's organizers had received scant support from men within the factories. Male union officials, directors, and workers shared the view that the Party was forcing them to hire, train, and promote women. Yet male hostility toward women was not solely the result of policies promulgated from above. Male prejudice ran deep, predating the Soviet regime and its policies. Men regarded the workshop as essentially "male," and the introduction of women therein as a violation of a "natural" order. Because they benefited directly from the gender hierarchy within the factories, men were anxious to preserve and maintain their exclusive right to skilled work. Male workers understood skill as a "male" attribute; they objected to women's being trained and actively tried to push them out of skilled positions. Women were subjected to sexual innuendo, obscene comments, derision, and physical molestation, behaviors consciously designed to maintain the gender hierarchy in the factory, to prevent women from advancing, and to bar them from skilled work. Long-standing cultural traditions mingled with

---

[62] "Razognat' Brigadu Rabotnits," *Trud*, March 24, 1931, p. 3.   [63] Ibid.

politics. Stalinist leaders did not hesitate to excoriate union officials for their apathy toward women workers in their purge of "rightists," and union officials were not ashamed to defend their "apathy" as democracy.

Male prejudice was difficult to eradicate because it was embedded in every level of the factory hierarchy. Directors, shop bosses, foremen, masters, and skilled male workers all held similar views of women. Directors therefore did not rebuke foremen who refused to accept women in their shops; foremen did not force masters to train them; and masters did not compel skilled workers to cooperate with them. Everyone turned a blind eye to harassment and discrimination. If women could not cope with the ugly treatment meted out by men, then "women themselves were guilty." Even after the Party changed its approach to women workers, local officials remained sympathetic to the views of skilled male workers, their main constituency in the 1920s, and fought hard to protect their interests. Although Party leaders encouraged women to speak out, they refused to revive the system of separate women's organizers that they had earlier eliminated.

In the context of a widely popularized state ideology stressing class, women workers demonstrated a strong and independent consciousness of gender. If the Party urged them to think of themselves only as "workers," men did not allow them this luxury. Every obscene proposition, every slight, every inequality reminded them that they were women as well. Unlike men, they never accepted the gender hierarchy of the factory as "natural." They were fiercely critical of their male fellow workers; they felt the men's lack of respect, they were keenly aware of discrimination, and they were angry about how they were treated. Although they lacked a specific language to critique male privilege and prerogatives (they did not speak of "male chauvinism," "sexual harassment," or "gender politics"), women workers had no trouble expressing their anger at abuse (*rugan'*) and inequality. Even when women, for lack of a better word, termed men's sexual advances "wooing" (*ukhazhivan'ia*), it was clear that they took such propositions as insults, not as marriage proposals.[64] Women's fury at their treatment was unmistakable. They spoke out strongly against men at all levels, holding their fellow workers no less accountable than local officials and managers. Critical of the unions, NKT, and local labor departments, they declared themselves disgusted by the general apathy toward women. They repeatedly directed their anger at the Party for liquidating the Zhenotdel and thus eliminating the one organization that would have been capable of addressing their concerns and advancing their interests. Outspoken in their complaints and dissatisfaction, they

---

[64] For women's use of this word, see, for example, "Razognat' Brigadu Rabotnits," *Trud*, March 24, 1931, p. 3.

used wall newspapers, meetings, *rabkory* in the factories, and visiting officials to make their grievances known. Many former Zhenotdel activists had entered KUTB and the unions, becoming an important conduit of information between individual workplaces and the central authorities. Any investigator who was sent to collect material on local conditions would be quickly apprised of the behavior of foremen, managers, and officials, thus ensuring that discrimination and abuse in local areas would be heard about in Moscow.

Throughout the early 1930s, newspapers, journals, and reports from the factories were filled with examples of discrimination against women workers. Clearly, the introduction of women into industry was painful, and the skilling process was even more so, challenging as it did deeply entrenched ideas about the very nature of "male" and "female" work and the place of women. Women were eager and determined to enter skilled positions, to move up in the factories, to make more money, and to improve their collective and individual positions. Yet they frequently acceded to harassment by just giving up. There were numerous stories of women who asked to be transferred back to their old jobs, to be put back on the day shift, to be removed from the hostile atmosphere of a particular shop, even at great cost to themselves and their future. Advancement was not worth the misery and isolation imposed by male workers. These stories received much critical attention in 1931 because the cost to the Party, the state, the enterprise, and the overall industrialization effort was also considerable. Female labor was an essential means of meeting the labor shortage. Each woman who was prevented by male prejudice from using her training represented a financial loss to the state. By 1931, Party leaders had realized that it was in the interest of the industrialization drive to deploy and train women. Yet these leaders never quite grasped one simple truth understood by every former Zhenotdel activist and woman worker: prejudice was deeply ingrained in the culture of male workers. The state could not legislate equality merely by regendering a list of professions, setting high quotas for women's participation in training programs, or filling more positions with female workers. Prejudice, abuse, and discrimination had to be confronted directly. Given the previous record of the unions, labor departments, and factory committees, it was unlikely that these organizations would be successful in this task without a strong organization of women.

The large-scale introduction of female labor in the Soviet Union, even in the context of the rapid expansion of the labor force, was accompanied by many of the same transformations that marked the deployment of women workers under capitalism: falling wages, deskilling, attacks on the unions, the loss of collective bargaining power. Even the policies promulgated from above bore an uncanny resemblance to those promoted by capitalist drives for accumulation. The state's strategy of employing blocs of women through the creation of exclusively or primarily "female" jobs echoed the replacement of men by women in whole sectors of capitalist industry; the transition provoked animosity under capitalism and socialism alike.[65] In the Soviet case, Party leaders targeted women as a key reserve of labor and made a strong initial attempt to break the barriers erected by local officials, managers, and workers. At the end of 1931, however, the Party proclaimed the drive to recruit 1.6 million women a success. Its initial interest in eradicating prejudice and discrimination faded. Fearing that separate women's organizations would distract women from production, it refused to permit the development of any organizational forms capable of addressing women's special interests and concerns. By the end of the first five-year plan, public discussion of sex segregation, gender relations, and structural inequalities in the workplace was no longer heard.

[65] On gender and capitalist industrialization, see, for example, Kathleen Canning, *Languages of Labor and Gender: Female Factory Work in Germany, 1850–1914* (Ithaca, N.Y.: Cornell University Press, 1996); Mary Blewett, *Men, Women, and Work: Class, Gender, and Protest in the New England Shoe Industry, 1780–1910* (Urbana, Ill.: University of Illinois Press, 1990); Ava Baron, ed., *Work Engendered: Toward a New History of American Labor* (Ithaca, N.Y.: Cornell University Press, 1991); and Laura Frader and Sonya Rose, eds., *Gender and Class in Modern Europe* (Ithaca, N.Y.: Cornell University Press, 1996).

A woman worker hauls stones at Ural'mashstroi, a construction site for the Urals machine-building factory in Sverdlovsk. This work was typical of the unskilled labor performed by women on construction sites. 1931.

A brigade of workers that initiated a movement to raise production targets in the Karl Marx machine-building factory in Leningrad. Seven of the ten brigade members were women. 1931.

8

Rebuilding the Gates to the Working Class

The creation of a new communist state demands from all participants in socialist construction a firm, genuinely proletarian labor discipline, the fullest use of every working day, every working hour, and the decisive elimination of all types of disorganized production, in particular absenteeism. *Trud*, labor newspaper, 1932[1]

Why do we need a second five-year plan when we have not gotten anything from the first one?
Worker in a mechanical factory in Briansk, 1932[2]

Purge the Towns of Social [i.e., Human] Garbage!
Headline in *Trud*, 1932[3]

By the end of the term of the first five-year plan, 10.7 million new workers had entered the labor force. The cities and construction sites were teeming with people, but housing, running water, electricity, sewage disposal, and food distribution were all still woefully inadequate for the needs of the new population. People lived amid horrific conditions: crowded into single rooms and corners in subdivided apartments, in hastily erected, rickety barracks, in primitive tent and cave dwellings, even in the factories and shops themselves. Thousands of new, badly needed workers arrived each day at the country's sprawling construction sites, only to leave again for lack of housing. Turnover rates soared as workers sought better living situations in other places. Everywhere labor was on the move, trudging from building site to city, thronging the railroad stations, packing the trains. The plants and sites were extremely disorganized. Dining halls and kitchens built to serve several hundred workers now turned out meals for thousands. Record keeping was chaotic.

[1] "V Nastuplenie na Proguly," *Trud*, November 17, 1932, p. 1.
[2] GARF, f. 5451, o. 43, d. 12, "Ob Otritsatel'nykh Nastroenniiakh Vyiavleniiakh v Kampanii po Zaimu," 112.
[3] "Ochistit' Goroda ot Sotsial'nogo Musora," *Trud*, December 29, 1932, p. 2.

The second five-year plan (1933–1937) was distinguished by its slower rates of growth, mass layoffs of workers, intensification of capital accumulation, and replacement of men with women workers. Female labor was critical to the new drive for higher productivity and stability. At the beginning of 1932, managers negotiated collective contracts with the unions according to a prototype distributed by VSNKh (the Supreme Council of the National Economy) and VTsSPS (the All-Union Central Council of Trade Unions). The contracts stressed the importance of female labor: each contained a prominent section on women in production, specifying the number of women to be hired, trained, and promoted to skilled work.[4] State and Party leaders identified male workers' wives and family members as the solution to labor turnover, housing shortages, and the lack of municipal and social services. Urban women, they argued, were vastly preferable to migrant peasants, since they did not require housing and were already accustomed to factory discipline and urban life. Women offered a flexible reserve of labor, already lodged in the cities, that could be used to curb peasant migration.

At the beginning of the second five-year plan, the state enacted draconian laws aimed at eliminating worker mobility, slowing migration from the countryside, intensifying labor discipline, and creating strict systems of record keeping and control. It purged the factories, promulgated punitive laws regarding absenteeism, set higher production norms, curtailed the wage fund, and established a compulsory internal-passport system. Wages, rations, and even *byt* institutions were used as new instruments of labor discipline to increase productivity. Workers in "leading professions" and sectors, as well as shock workers with high productivity, were rewarded with greater access to day care, dining halls, vacations, education, and other services, now collectively termed the "social wage." New gates to the working class were built on these administrative orders, tying labor to the factory and erecting barriers between countryside and town. As the state began to rebuild the gates to the cities and waged work, women became the single most important source of new labor in the second five-year plan.

Labor Turnover and Living Conditions

For managers and Party leaders, one of the greatest obstacles to production and social stability was the high rate of labor turnover that persisted throughout the first five-year plan. The great building projects and

---

[4] A. P., "Shest' Uslovii Tov. Stalina – v Osnovu Koldogovora," *Na trudovom fronte*, 1932, no. 3: 10–11. Hereafter cited as *NTF*.

seasonal industries experienced a particularly large influx and outflow
of people. In the fall of 1931, Magnitostroi, the rising iron and steel
giant, lost 129 percent of its new arrivals, while Cheliabtraktorstroi, a
huge new tractor plant, lost 123 percent, and Uralmashstroi, a machine-
building plant, 142 percent.[5] The lack of housing, food, and services led
to disruptions everywhere. Timber, a seasonal industry that was essential to construction, had the highest levels of turnover. In the first half of
1932 alone, 962,200 workers entered the industry, and 1,395,200 left.
In the heavily forested region around Leningrad, timber workers had no
housing and went a month without meat, fish, or sugar. The funds allocated for housing were never spent because *there was no available lumber.*
Like the coal miners with "no coal to heat the shack" in the American
folksong "The Banks Are Made of Marble," Soviet timber workers had
no lumber with which to build themselves shelter. In the Urals, meanwhile, the wagon drivers who hauled the timber received no fodder for
their horses;[6] hungry workers had to share their meager rations with their
half-starved animals. In the summer of 1932, thousands of workers in the
Moscow region fled the textile factories to work on collective farms because there was no food in the towns. Many of them were older *kadrovye*
workers who had been working in the mills for years. Large numbers
of textile workers lived in wooden huts heated by wood-burning stoves;
because the steel industry was not producing ax heads for consumer use,
and there were thus no axes available to chop wood, workers froze. The
factory barracks, too, were dark and cold, and "thievery, drunkenness,
and hooliganism flourished."[7] In large factories critical to the industrialization drive, including the Stalin factory, the Rostov agricultural machine
plant (Rostovsel'mash), and the Andre Marti factory, over 50 percent of
newly hired workers left for other jobs within a year. Studies conducted
in 1930 at twelve large factories showed that labor turnover was so high
that even older factories with established procedures, such as Krasnyi
Putilovets in Leningrad, were unable to maintain accurate attendance
records.[8] In many factories, up to one third of the workers never returned
from vacation.

The living conditions produced by rapid industrialization and the influx
of millions of people into towns and cities contrasted sharply with the revolutionary vision of the *novyi byt,* or "new life," promised by socialism.
In a visit to Magnitogorsk in 1933, Grigorii Ordzhonikidze, a Politburo
member and the people's commissar of heavy industry, refused to call the

---

[5] Z. Mordukhovich, "Uzlovye Voprosy Privlecheniia Rabochei Sily v 1932g.," *NTF*, 1931,
no. 34: 5.

[6] Aristov, "Likvidirovat' Tekuchest' na Lesozagotovkakh," *NTF*, 1932, nos. 31–32: 8.

[7] A. Anserov, "Bol'she Vnimaniia Bytovym 'Melocham'!," *NTF*, 1932, no. 33: 10–11.

[8] GARF, f. 6983, o. 1, d. 165, "Zhenskii Trud v Promyshlennosti," 141–142.

new town a socialist city, fuming, "You have named some manure a socialist city. A 'socialist city,' and it's impossible to live in it."[9] There were severe shortages of housing, running water, baths, kitchens (both private and communal), dining halls, laundries, sewage facilities, and municipal services. Even in older cities such as Moscow and Leningrad, the flood of new workers quickly swamped existing infrastructures. Moscow and Leningrad both had fewer than half the number of public baths they had before World War I, despite massive increases in population. In 1930, there were only fifty-one public baths in Leningrad, and only forty-four in Moscow. There were no laundries for the general population. One report to the Central Committee noted, "The business with baths and laundries is catastrophic." Reports from many industries indicated that the high turnover in the workforce was directly linked to poor living conditions.[10]

In Moscow's Krasnyi Bogatyr factory, for example, where women constituted about 80 percent of the 11,840 workers, more than 2,000 workers lacked any living quarters at all. Factory administrators planned to build more housing, but they were desperately short of lumber and building supplies. They built three barracks in 1931 and 1932 to house 300 workers, but living conditions in them were horrendous. The barracks themselves were filthy, the windows were broken, and the stoves did not work. More than 800 workers' children were packed into crowded day-care centers, and the demand for places was five times greater than the number enrolled. Administrators were working on a new plan to create space for 1,000 more children. In the entire factory settlement, the only laundry was located in an orphanage. Women workers washed their families' clothing and linens in streams, rivers, or the few communal sinks in the barracks that supplied running water. The dining room, equipped to serve 3,500 meals a day, now served 18,000; workers used it because food was so difficult for them to buy and prepare. Although the dining hall was heavily subsidized by the state, workers could still barely afford its meals. Older women workers with seniority reaching back to the tsarist period were paid between 120 and 138 rubles per month; they could only just survive on what they termed their "unsatisfactory" wages. All of these problems led to high turnover. During a two-week period in August 1932, 459 workers left the factory, and 318 others arrived. Projected over a year, this amounted to a loss of 11,016 workers, a turnover rate of almost 100 percent.[11] At Serp i Molot, a large Moscow metallurgical plant, many

---

9   For vivid descriptions of building and life at Magnitogorsk in the 1930s, see Stephen Kotkin, *Magnetic Mountain: Stalinism as a Civilization* (Berkeley, Calif.: University of California Press, 1995). Quote from p. 120.
10 GARF, f. 5451, o. 15, d. 362, "Orgbiuro TsK VKP (b)", 90.
11 GARF, f. 5451, o. 16, d. 557, "Zav. Sektor po Rabote Sredi Zhenshchin pri VTsSPS," 71–71 ob.

workers had no place at all to sleep. Some women workers lived in over-crowded barracks, while others slept in the public baths, on the streets, in "red corners" of dormitories and public buildings, and even on the plant floor.[12] A report from a representative of the Union of Agricultural Machine Production Workers noted that 85 percent of the demand for child-care services in the plant could not be met. More than 5,000 places were needed for infant care, and more than 17,000 for day care.[13]

The situation was no better in Leningrad. Krasnyi Putilovets, one of the city's oldest metal and machine plants, was overwhelmed by incoming workers and a demanding production schedule. Services on the factory grounds were rudimentary: there were no baths or laundries, and 4,500 workers were in need of housing. More than 14,000 workers lived some distance from the plant and had to walk miles to work. Three hundred workers lived in the factory itself, sleeping among the machines. The shops were filthy, cold, drafty, and littered with broken glass; the windows were broken and blackened with grime. The toilets in the "hot" shops were "disgusting." Krasnyi Putilovets had one dining hall and forty-two smaller buffets, but the quality of the food was poor. The dining hall was crowded and dirty, and there were no knives or forks. Gastrointestinal illnesses periodically swept through the workforce as a result of unsanitary conditions in the kitchen. Yet the situation slowly improved. The number of workers without housing dropped by 2,000 between 1930 and 1931. The factory built barracks for 240 workers and planned shelter for 800 more, though construction was temporarily stalled for lack of building materials.[14]

Conditions in smaller towns were equally bad. In the Nizhegorod district, 60,000 workers entered industry in 1930–1931. The district boasted one laundry, a few child-care centers, and a chronic shortage of building materials.[15] In the Petrovsky metallurgical factory in Zaporozh'e, some workers were beginning to bloat from malnutrition. In a factory settlement that was home to 30,000 families, dinner was usually three to six hours late because the dining halls, designed to serve 150 people, now fed 4,000. Up to 400 people stood on line at any one time. Workers often had to leave the line without eating in order to get back to work. There was no

12 GARF, f. 5451, o. 15, d. 362, "Zavod Serp i Molot," 9–10.
13 GARF, f. 5451, o. 15, d. 362, "Soiuz Rabochikh S.Kh. Mashin Prod.," 19.
14 GARF, f. 6983, o. 1, d. 165, "Dokladnaia Zapiska – o Sostoianii Sots.-Bytov. Obsluzhivaniia Rabotaiushchikh i Rabochego Snabzheniia na Zavode 'Kr. Putilovets' po Materialiam Provedennogo Obsledovaniia ot 7–9 Oktiabria 1931 g.," 33–34, 37–38; "Zhenskii Trud v Promyshlennost'," 143. Workers were in general poorly skilled. The shortage of specialists and technical personnel, especially on the night shift, resulted in a high accident rate. In the first half of 1931, there were 7,137 industrial accidents and three deaths in Krasnyi Putilovets.
15 GARF, f. 6983, o. 1, d. 165, "Materialy o Vnedrenii Zhenskogo Truda v Promy-shlennost'," 3.

silverware; people ate straight from their plates, using their dirty hands. In one dining hall that offered spoons, workers had to hand over their hats, mess kits, and union and even Party cards as collateral. In March, there was no water in the dormitories, so workers melted snow for drinking and washing. They relieved themselves around the broken outdoor toilets, next to the dormitories, and in the courtyards. The chairman of the factory committee jokingly dubbed the growing piles of waste "the Egyptian pyramids." A. Abolin, an important Party official sent to investigate conditions in Zaporozh'e, was appalled: "We must ask, how can people live such lives? Where are the union and Party organizations?" he demanded.[16] Workers in a small oil manufactory wrote a desperate letter to a labor journal, explaining that the walls of their barracks were collapsing. The barracks were so crowded that workers had to sleep in heaps on the floor because there was no room to squeeze in even one more cot. There was no hot water because the boilers were broken.[17]

The worst living conditions and the harshest shortages, however, were on the huge new construction sites. At Magnitostroi, the barracks erected to house workers during the freezing winter months were nothing but flimsy wooden skeletons. Crawling with vermin, they were impossible to disinfect because of the large gaps between the unseasoned boards. The health department finally ordered that the gaps be closed, and some plaster was slapped on the structures. Inside, no one cleaned the floors, shook out the mattresses, or washed the sheets for months at a time. The dining halls were falling apart, but because they served workers around the clock, it was impossible to undertake any repairs. The workers considered the food a public health hazard. As in other places, there was a chronic shortage of silverware in the dining halls. When the dining hall received 2,000 knives, the workers, acting on an ingrained "shortage mentality," quickly pocketed them for personal use and resale; within two weeks, there was not a single knife left. The state's emphasis on heavy industry at the expense of producing consumer goods had its costs in terms of labor productivity. Workers at Magnitostroi, could be found in the mechanical shop at all hours of the day and night, crafting personal utensils out of scrap metal. Ten baths served 100,000 people.[18] For workers arriving at the Kuzbas mines, meanwhile, there was no housing at all: new arrivals were placed in overcrowded barracks built hurriedly from unseasoned logs and branches. The wood warped as it dried, creating huge cracks.

[16] GARF, f. 5451, o. 43, d. 30, "VTsSPS N. M. Shverniku. Pis'mo No. 2," 118–14 (pages numbered backward).

[17] "Khodyzhenskie Nefte-Promysla Apsheronskogo Raiona," *Okhrana truda*, 1930, nos. 8–9: 16.

[18] N. Ulasevich, "Nuzhno Sozdat' v Magnitogorske Khoroshe Bytovye Usloviia Dlia Rabochikh," *NTF*, 1931, no. 34: 14.

The barracks lacked windows, heat, toilets, and running water and were virtually uninhabitable in the winter. The workers soon fled to other mines in the region.[19]

The state faced great difficulties in feeding the new labor force. The systems that governed the distribution, sale, and mass preparation of food were beset by constant breakdowns and shortages. Public dining halls were serving workers millions of meals by the beginning of the second five-year plan. Reports repeatedly noted that the dining halls themselves were dirty, the food and tables crawling with flies, and the meals unappetizing and monotonous. Cabbage soup was the mainstay of every menu. There were persistent shortages of dishware, silverware, food, cooking utensils, teapots, tables, chairs, coal, and firewood. Dining halls initially established to serve several hundred people routinely served more than a thousand. Food service was so chaotic that it frequently interfered with production in the factories. Workers stood on lines that snaked out into the streets, missing work in the attempt to get fed. On the railroads, conductors and railway workers, finding no food available at the stations along the lines, would often stop their trains and walk for miles to the nearest village in search of something to eat.[20] Industrial cargo, agricultural goods, and passengers sat for hours while the railroad workers scoured the countryside for bread.

The state required the industrial enterprises to meet high goals. Unlike capitalist factories, which were never expected to provide food or social services, Soviet factories assumed broad responsibilities. Moreover, in the early years of industrialization, jurisdictions were often confused. The Commissariat of Enlightenment, the Commissariat of Health, the municipal soviets, and individual factories were all involved in child care, for example. Krasnyi Putilovets funded and ran a small day-care center, but of the sixty children it served, only twenty belonged to women who worked in the factory. In April 1931, the Council of People's Commissars (SNK) decreed that every newly built residence must allocate space for a child-care center. Building plans for social services were drawn up without any coordination among planning organizations, industry, the economic organs, and other agencies. Rykov, a member of the Central Committee, urged that social services receive their own allotments within the larger industrial plan.[21] Factory directors, overtaxed by high production targets and new machinery, frequently ranked *byt* as the lowest of their priorities. In the Podol'skii machine factory, for example, managers squabbled

[19]   GARF, f. 5515, o. 17, d. 649, "Obespechenie Zhilishcham Rabochikh Kuzbassa," 36.
[20]   Val'ter, "Obshchestvennoe Pitanie – Vazhneishee Zveno v Bor'be za Promfinplan," *Voprosy truda*, 1931, nos. 11–12: 85–87. Hereafter cited as *VT*.
[21]   GARF, f. 6983, o. 1, d. 165, "O Meropriiatiiakh Bytovogo Obsluzhivaniia, Obespechivaiushchikh Vovlechenie Zhenshchin Proizvodstvo v K. Ts. na 1932 g.," 39–40.

constantly with the factory committee over the unwanted responsibility for social services. Podol'skii, which had a workforce of 10,000, provided only fifteen places for child care. Although the factory's director saw women as the key to filling his labor shortage, he had no idea how many of the factory's 3,300 women workers needed child care. With the elimination of women's organizers from the factories, the factory committees were generally hostile to "women's issues." One report exhorted the unions to take control of social services, a move that would free up managers to concentrate more narrowly on production. Most managers had no plans to create laundries, dining halls, day care, housing, or public baths. The report confided, "There is complete confusion about this issue."[22]

The lack of building materials was a serious obstacle to the development of any project in the early 1930s, including *byt* institutions. The state allocated money for social services, but it made little difference: lumber, nails, bricks, mortar, and glass simply could not be obtained at any price. In the region surrounding Moscow, for instance, thirty new buildings were funded in 1930, but two years later, construction had begun on only nineteen of them. In Moscow itself, not one of the twenty-seven buildings funded was yet under way. In Kuznetsstroi, the great mining and steel site in West Siberia, the plant administration had no building materials to devote to child-care centers.[23] At the national level, only 70 percent of the housing plan for 1931 was fulfilled, despite the allocation of funds, and only 14 percent of the 1932 plan for baths and laundries was realized.[24] Directors of construction sites and factories commonly diverted funds for social services to production and housed homeless workers in buildings set aside for child care. One report to the Central Executive Committee (CEC) described the status of *byt* institutions as "catastrophic."[25]

Part of the problem was that the plans created for the factories were often unrealistically ambitious. The Stalin metal plant in Leningrad, for example, was expected to feed all its workers *and their families* in the communal dining hall. The dining hall served more than 6,500 people daily, but its kitchen was too small, fuel was short, and the lack of plates and silverware resulted in long lines. Elektrosila, an electrical plant in Leningrad, likewise struggled to provide services. More than 2,000 of the plant's 11,000 workers were women, but the plant offered only a

[22] GARF, f. 6983, o. 1, d. 165, "Zhenskii Trud v Promyshlennosti," 145–146 ob, 148 ob.
[23] GARF, f. 6983, o. 1, d. 165, "Material Dlia Doklada VTsIKa po Vovlecheniiu Zhenshchin v Promyshlennost'," 12–13.
[24] "Shest' Uslovii Tov. Stalina – Osnova Bol'shevistskikh Pobed," *NTF*, 1932, no. 6: 9; N. Solov'ev, "Usylim Vovlechenie Zhenshchin v Proizvodstvo," *NTF*, 1932, no. 33: 13.
[25] GARF, f. 3316, o. 51, d. 7, "Ocherednye Zadachi Organizatsii Zhenskogo Truda i Bytovogo Obsluzheniia," 50; f. 3316, o. 25, d. 986, "V Orgkomissiiu TsIK SSSR," 32.

small number of places in a local day-care center run by the education department. Four dining halls served 5,600 meals a day, and the lack of utensils led to long lines. Three shops had showers, which were used by workers from the entire plant. Although factory directors were reluctant to make social services a priority, the absence of such services was closely linked to labor turnover. The lack of housing, in particular, resulted in the hemorrhage of tens of thousands of newly hired workers every year. Elektrozavod, an electrical plant in Moscow, could not house the new workers it hired. An estimated 6,000 additional workers were needed to fill production targets for 1931, but the plant had no place to put them; the few barracks that it maintained for unmarried men were already full. New workers quit immediately after learning that there was nowhere for them to live. Elektrozavod planned to build an entire town, designed to house 8,000 new workers, close to Moscow. (The plant already served 12,000 meals per day and had its own shoe shop.) In the meantime, however, family members of workers were targeted as the best possible source of new labor.[26] Huge numbers of workers continued to arrive at factories and construction sites, only to leave again because they could not find a place to lay their heads.

Stalin's Six Conditions: Blueprint for Class Discipline

Party leaders, highly sensitive to the impact that labor turnover had on production, sought to stabilize the labor force by using every material incentive at their disposal, including wages, rations, and the "social wage." Stalin provided the "blueprint" for stabilization in a speech he gave on June 23, 1931, before an economic conference of industrial managers. Focusing on the transition from the first to the second five-year plan, he called for a shift from construction to production, from introduction to mastery of new machinery, and from unskilled to skilled labor. He urged the replacement of prevailing wage scales with sharp new pay differentials between unskilled and skilled and easy and difficult jobs. He blamed the incessant movement of workers on "the leftist leveling of wages, or *uravnilovka*," a holdover from the revolutionary program of 1917. In Stalin's view, the lack of wage differentials between skilled and unskilled work gave workers no incentive to stay in one factory, master skills, or increase production. "We cannot tolerate that a rolling-mill worker in ferrous metallurgy should get the same wages as a sweeper," Stalin declared. Increasing wages for skilled work would provide an incentive for

[26]   GARF, f. 6983, o. 1, d. 165, "Zhenskii Trud v Promyshlennosti," 143–49.

skilled workers to stay in the plant, and for unskilled workers to become more skilled. Acknowledging that labor turnover was not just the result of "wage leveling," Stalin also noted that better housing and social services were necessary. He enumerated six conditions that he said were critical to reducing turnover and increasing productivity: organized recruitment of labor and mechanization of the labor process; reorganization of the wage system; personal accountability for tools, machines, and quality of work; development of a new *Soviet* engineering and technical intelligentsia; respect for the old technical intelligentsia; and an increase in capital accumulation through strict methods of cost accounting.[27] The speech, which quickly became known by the shorthand phrase "Six Conditions," was officially disseminated as the new labor policy for the second five-year plan.

Although Stalin did not specifically mention women in his speech, Party and state leaders realized that women, too, could play an important role in stabilizing the labor force. Individual studies by brigades showed that women had lower overall turnover rates than men. In Krasnyi Putilovets, for example, out of the 18,339 workers hired in 1930, about half left within the year. But of the 1,613 women hired, only 7 percent left. In the large plants and factories, turnover rates among newly hired women were about 25 percent. Moreover, studies showed that not only were women more likely to stay on the job, but their productivity was equal to or greater than men's. One study suggested, "Women stabilize the workforce and stabilize male labor. Their productivity in mass work is not lower than men's." In fact, when men and women were placed in the same job on the same shift, women's productivity was higher. These short-term experiments did not, however, take into account time lost to childbirth and children's illnesses (both major complaints among managers about female labor).[28] KUTB (the Committee to Improve the Labor and Life of Women), always eager to promote women's labor, tailored its arguments to the new concerns over turnover, deeming women "a managerial necessity."[29] If labor turnover for both sexes was figured into productivity, KUTB maintained, "the advantage gained by employing women covers all losses tied to their deployment in production."[30] In other words, women's productivity and stability on the job outweighed the costs associated with childbirth and child rearing. Anxious to reduce turnover and to foster greater stability within the workforce, NKT (the Commissariat of Labor) urged all plants to hire the family members of their workers first. Labor officials assumed that if a plant employed several workers from the same

---

[27] Joseph V. Stalin, *The New Russian Policy* (New York: Stratford Press, 1931).
[28] GARF, f. 6983, o. 1, d. 165, "Zhenskii Trud v Promyshlennosti," 141–42.
[29] GARF, f. 6983, o. 1, d. 165, "O Planovom Vovlechenii Zhenskogo Truda v Promyshlennost'," 166.
[30] Ibid., 170.

family, they would be less likely to leave their jobs.[31] The Central Committee instructed KUTB to prepare guidelines for the construction of social services within the factories and on construction sites. The purpose was "to free women, primarily the wives of workers, to enter the labor force and to eliminate turnover."[32]

Party and state officials also turned to urban women to relieve the pressure placed on housing and services by new migrants. By the fall of 1931, officials were anxious to stop the flood of peasant migrants to the cities. The Central Executive Committee decreed in October that urban women were critical to "reducing the turnover of the labor force and freeing industrial and local budgets from the extra expense of providing housing and social and cultural services for an imported labor force."[33] Cost accounting showed that it was cheaper to provide social services to enable the wives of workers to enter the labor force than to construct additional housing and services for new migrants and their families. In the words of two economists, "It is true that the use of women always involves more expenditure on day care, etc., but these expenses are significantly offset by economizing on housing. The use of women creates the conditions for a permanent workforce in the factories."[34]

Wages

After Stalin's "Six Conditions" speech, economists began to consider how to refashion wages to extract maximum productivity from workers. The speech quickly became the basis for a powerful attack on "wage leveling," a new term for the old socialist idea that significant wage differentials among workers were antithetical to class solidarity. Stalin urged a new policy whereby skilled, difficult jobs in heavy industry would be sharply differentiated from easier, unskilled work in light industry by means of higher wages and better benefits. Stalin's suggestion was promptly elaborated by labor economists to include new and complicated plans for progressive, productivity-based wage increases, piecework, the elimination

[31] GARF, f. 6983, o. 1, d. 165, "Tsirkuliarnoe Pis'mo Vsem Oblastnym i Kraevym Otdelam Truda i NKT Avtonomnykh Respublik," 78.

[32] GARF, f. 6983, o. 1, d. 165, "Osnovnye Vyvody iz Soveshchaniia po Voprosu o Prakticheskikh Meropriiatiiakh, Neobkhodimykh dlia Vypolneniia Reshenii TsK o Vypolnenii v Planovom Poriadke Zhenskoi Rabochei Sily v Promyshlennosti i o Bor'be s Tekuchest'iu," 218–19 ob.

[33] GARF, f. 6983, o. 1, d. 165, "Postanovlenie Prezidiuma Vserossiiskogo Tsentral'nogo Ispolnitel'nogo Komiteta," 31.

[34] L. Sabsovich, "Rost Gorodskogo Naseleniia i Sotsialisticheskaia Rekonstruktsiia Byta," *NTF*, 1930, no. 5: 29; N. Aristov and Tolchiev, "Dorogu Zhenshchine na Proizvodstvo na Kvalifitsirovannuiu Rabotu," *NTF*, 1932, nos. 26–27: 22.

of paid overtime, and other methods for achieving a less egalitarian distribution of the wage fund. The new wage policy encompassed several of Stalin's six conditions. It used wages as a spur to labor productivity. It attempted to attract workers into heavy or leading sectors of industry and skilled jobs. It sought to decrease turnover. And less obviously, it promoted an increased level of capital accumulation. By funneling benefits and higher wages to a smaller number of workers at the upper end of the wage scale, it aimed to conserve the wage fund overall.

The new wage policy marked a divergence from earlier Bolshevik conceptions. The Labor Code of 1918 initially relegated the determination of wages to unions and managers through joint contracts; NKT merely approved the contracts on behalf of the state and set wages in state institutions. But in 1920, in the midst of civil war and industrial disintegration, NKT usurped the roles of both unions and managers and assumed responsibility for setting wages in industry as well. As the money economy collapsed, workers were increasingly paid in rations or in kind, and differentials between skilled and unskilled workers became inconsequential. Then, with the end of the Civil War, the rebuilding of the economy, and the reintroduction of a stable currency, wage differentials reappeared. They grew between 1920 and 1926, though the gap between highest and lowest never became as great as it had been before the revolution. A new Labor Code, promulgated in 1922, reinstated the wage contract between unions and managers, but then a series of subsequent decrees increased the role of the state in setting upper limits on the wage. In 1926, the unions and the state began actively seeking to reduce differentials. Wages varied considerably from one industry to another, and even within a single factory, where two turners working at similar jobs in different shops might receive different wages. Tomsky branded wage norms, especially in state institutions, "a scandalous mess." The state's role in promoting standardization and wage leveling was aided by new technologies of mass production, which eliminated the need for very skilled workers.[35] The state aimed to level differences between industrial branches, eliminate variation among plants, narrow the wage gap between skilled and unskilled workers, and promote *uravnitel'nost'*, or wage equality. As a result of new national wage standards, the percentage of workers at both the lowest and the highest ends of the wage spectrum shrank, yielding ground to a growing middle by 1928. Wage equality, both as a socialist principle and as a practical goal, was firmly supported by many groups, including Communist managers, union leaders and activists, labor officials, economists, Party

[35] I. Troitskii, "Gosudarstvennoe Normirovanie Zarabotnoi Platy," *VT*, 1929, no. 6: 20–31; E. El'iashevich, "K Voprosu o Sootnosheniakh Mezhdu Zarplatoi Kvalifitsirovannikh i Nekvalifitsirovannikh Rabochikh," *VT*, 1930, no. 6: 42–48.

leaders, and workers. Throughout the 1920s, union leaders strongly promoted the idea of *uravnilovka,* or "the elimination of excessive differences between top and bottom wage rates."[36] They did not advocate paying all workers the same wages immediately, but they viewed wage leveling as a laudable and achievable goal.[37]

After Stalin's speech, a number of prominent labor economists launched a sharp attack on *uravnilovka,* deriding the idea and its proponents as "petty bourgeois" and "opportunist." Wages were to be defined by the productivity of labor as expressed through piecework, meaning that workers would "be paid according to their work." Stalinist economists made every effort to discredit the socialist belief in *uravnilovka;* one even suggested that it "opportunistically perverts the line of the Party, which is to pay labor by results." Many Soviet labor economists still considered the adoption of piecework "a surrender of the central principles of socialism." Stalin retorted in kind, characterizing the opponents of piecework as anti-Party and anti-Lenin: "Marx and Lenin said that differences between skilled and unskilled labor would exist even under socialism. Only under communism will these differences disappear. In view of this, wages should be paid according to work, not need. But our *uravnilovtsi* among the unions and the managers do not agree. Who is right? Marx and Lenin or the *uravnilovtsi?* Clearly, Marx and Lenin." Opponents of steep wage differentials and piecework were seen not only as opponents of Marx and Lenin but even as "traitors."[38] Throughout the fall of 1931, the attacks on *uravnilovka* became more and more vituperative. In addition to revising the wage grids, economists conceived numerous schemes to create ever sharper differentials between workers. They proposed, for instance, that all workers be transferred to piecework, a system they called "payment for results." They paired piecework itself with inventive new methods of compensation, including "progressive piecework," which paid more for each item produced, and "progressive premium piecework," which paid increasing sums for each item or batch of items produced over the norm (20 kopecks for the first five above the norm, 25 kopecks for the second five, etc.). The feverish enthusiasm for piecework extended even

---

[36] A. Runov, "Trud Ne Dolzhen Byt' Obezlichen," *NTF*, 1931, no. 15: 3.

[37] See, for example, Iu. Kalistratov, *Za Udarnyi Proizvodstvennyi Kollektiv* (1931); A. Pavlov, *Za Sotsialisticheskuiu Organizatsiiu Trudy* (Moscow: VTsSPS, 1931); I. Burdianskii, *Osnovy Ratsionalizatsii Proizvodstva* (Moscow: Gosudarstvennoe Sotsial'no-Ekonomicheskoe Izdatel'stvo, 1931); A. Mokson, "Ot Sdel'noi k Povremmenoi Oplate Truda," *VT*, 1931, no. 2.

[38] For the attack against *uravnilovka,* see, for example, Runov, "Trud Ne Dolzhen Byt' Obezlichen"; V. Razyminskii, "Oplata Truda po Rezultatam," *VT*, 1932, no. 1: 22–28; Z. Sokolov, "Protiv Melkoburzhuaznoi Uravnilov'nosti," *VT*, 1931, no. 6: 10–11; Z.A., "K Voprosam Perestroiki Zarplaty v SSSR," *VT*, 1931, nos. 11–12: 20–26; M. Iampolskii, "Voprosy Zarabotnoi Platy na Sovremennom Etape," *Problemy ekonomiki*, 1931, no. 6: 3–31.

to the assembly line, in the form of a peculiar scheme dubbed "collective piecework"![39]

Stalinist economists argued that "payment by results" would not only increase productivity but also "educate workers by means of the ruble." Increasing wages at the higher end of the scale would encourage workers to better their skills. Moreover, the system could be manipulated both to encourage training and to move workers from one branch of industry to another. The first five-year plan had targeted key branches of industry for wage increases. In 1928, for example, the printing, leather, metallurgy, and food sectors had paid the highest wages, in that order, while textiles, women's traditional domain, paid the lowest. The first five-year plan had rearranged this ranking, raising wages in metal above those in printing, leather, and food and moving mining from eighth to fifth place. Textiles remained last.[40] After Stalin's speech, the priority industries were rearranged once again, to favor, in order, machine building, ferrous metallurgy, coal mining, oil, blooming mills, chemicals, and ore extraction.[41] Neither the printing nor the food industry was designated a "leading branch." Workers in "leading professions" within "leading branches" were to receive even greater privileges. Advocates of the new system explained that the Soviet Union could not be accused of fostering a labor aristocracy because it offered its workers enormous opportunities for upward mobility. The creation of favored professions within privileged sectors would simply encourage workers to take advantage of new opportunities. Stalinist economists thus substituted the promise of mobility for equality. Improvement now lay within the grasp of the individual, not the class. In fact, advocates of the new policy actively sought to break up the collectivity of workers, attacking the older system of "brigades," in which workers organized themselves into teams and pooled their wages, as well as other forms of voluntary collectivism, including production communes. The brigades were "liquidated" and the production communes shifted onto an individual rather than a collective system of output.[42]

Economists even urged that the "social wage" – access to child care, health resorts, vacations, housing, food, and work clothes – be used as a lever to boost productivity. The social wage, like the money wage, should be distributed to workers not according to need, they argued, but according to skill, sector, and productivity.[43] A single mother with several dependents who worked in an unskilled job in light industry was less

[39] Runov, 3.   [40] N.V., "K Voprosy Planirovanii Zarplaty," *VT*, 1929, nos. 3–4: 45.
[41] "Shest' Uslovii Tov. Stalina – Osnova Bolshevistskikh Pobed," *NTF*, 1932, no. 6: 7.
[42] Iampolskii, 3–31; "Pervye Rezultaty Perestroiki Sistemy Zarabotnoi Platy," *NTF*, 1931, no. 34: 17; "Dobit' Uravnilovku," *NTF*, 1931, nos. 32–33: 18.
[43] Z.A., "K Voprosam Perestroiki Zarplaty v SSSR," *VT*, 1931, nos. 11–12: 20–26; A. Aluf, "Protiv Izvrashchenii v Regulirovanii Zarabotnoi Platy," *VT*, 1932, no. 2: 22–26.

deserving of the "social wage" than a single, highly skilled man in heavy industry. The new system was clearly disadvantageous to women, who were disproportionately concentrated in less skilled jobs in light industry and bore a greater burden of care for children and elderly parents. Whereas the Zhenotdel and the *bytoviki* had once hoped that new institutions of *byt* would become the basis of women's emancipation, the very phrase "social wage" now reduced this earlier vision of state support for the most vulnerable – women, children, the elderly – to a reward for the most productive workers.

Advocates of the new wage policy called for the reorganization of the current wage grid, or salary scale, which set a maximum differential of 1:3 between the lowest and highest wages. "The grid itself," noted one critic, "does not encourage workers to increase production or their skills." Moreover, the grid did not provide a progressive increase in wages. A metalworker who moved from the first to the second level, for example, received a 20 percent increase in wages, but a promotion from the seventh to the eighth level yielded only a 12 percent increase. The greater increases were concentrated at the lower end of the grid, which accounted for the majority of workers, rather than the upper end, with its highly skilled minority. The grid also worked to the advantage of women, who were disproportionately represented at the lower end. A new variant of the grid proposed that wage increases rise at each subsequent level: there would be a 16 percent increase between levels 1 and 2, for example, and a 25 percent increase between levels 7 and 8.[44] The new weighted wage increases clearly favored the small minority at the top of the wage scale. By targeting a smaller number of workers for larger wage increases, the new system reduced the overall wage bill, one of its unpublicized advantages. It thus permitted the state to spend less on wages and to invest more in industrial development. It was an excellent strategy for increasing capital accumulation, the one among Stalin's six conditions that was least favored by a hungry working class.

Economists directly endorsed capital accumulation as a rationale for the new policy, explaining that labor productivity alone could not determine wages. The material standard of living of the working class would rise only with "the maximum tempo of socialist accumulation" – that is, only industrial development could guarantee an improvement in living standards. Wage policy, in other words, would have to be subordinated to greater investment and development. If workers would defer consumption in favor of continuing investment in the new industrial system, living standards would eventually rise.[45] The economists strongly advised that

[44]   Runov, 3–5; B. Tsekhanovich, "Otchenit' Uravnilovku i Razbit' Staruiu Tarifnuiu Sistemu," *NTF*, 1931, no. 21: 4.
[45]   Iampolskii, 6–15.

every job be reevaluated to increase production norms and rates. Norming should no longer be done by "eyeballing" the job (*na glazok*); instead, a "scientific process was needed."[46] The sixth Plenum of VTsSPS (the All-Union Central Council of Trade Unions) actually criticized the printing, paper, leather, sewing, and food unions for not "counteracting the rise of wages in their own industries" – possibly the first time that a national labor organization ever chastised its member unions for allowing wages to rise![47]

The new policy – imposing the mass application of piecework, higher production norms, and overall wage conservation through less egalitarian distribution – yielded higher productivity of labor in the mining, machine-building, and chemical sectors, but it also produced widespread disgruntlement and protest. By the fall of 1931, 20 to 30 percent of all workers were on some form of progressive piecework, and in December, piecework was widely introduced into the textile industry. Workers and central authorities were locked into a major conflict of interest. The workers were literally hungry for higher wages and consumption, while the central authorities craved capital investment. Workers were not opposed to higher tempos if wages kept pace with output, but they protested strongly when the implementation of the new *progressivka* resulted in lower wages. In one state sewing factory, workers resisted the new system so strongly that it was scrapped. The metalworkers' union, too, proved to be a particularly stubborn opponent of all forms of piecework.

The struggle over capital continued under socialism with new and unexpected alliances.[48] Plant directors, foremen, local labor officials, and even norm setters often joined workers in opposing central Party authorities. Managers, anxious to retain workers and avoid stoppages, wildcat strikes, and protests, continued to overspend their wage funds – a form of self-protection that became a "mass phenomenon," according to one critic. In Leningrad's Promtekhnika factory and in Kharkov's electromechanical factory, managers and foremen reclassified the overwhelming majority of jobs as "leading professions," thus placing them in higher wage categories. In some factories, managers even designated unskilled jobs as "leading professions." Norming, in theory

---

[46] Runov, 4.   [47] Aluf, 23.

[48] Some historians argue that workers were allowed openly to discuss topics of interest to them and even to criticize their bosses. See, for example, Robert Thurston, *Life and Terror in Stalin's Russia* (New Haven, Conn.: Yale University Press, 1996), 192. In the Soviet Union, however, the primary conflict over the accumulation and allocation of capital was not between bosses and workers but between the highest levels of the Party, popularly termed "Moscow," and the workers. Stalin and the Politburo were the firmest adherents of high capital investment in heavy industry. Directors, caught between Moscow and their workers, were fair targets for criticism, but criticism of Stalin and the Politburo had severe consequences.

an unassailably "scientific" assessment, in practice produced fierce arguments, prompting Kaganovich to remark, "In practice, we do not have norming as such, we have conflict."[49] And local labor officials, responsible for implementing the reforms, blunted Moscow's sharp intentions with their customary disorganization. In Leningrad, for example, "social inspectors" were charged with reorganizing wages in the factories. Yet not a single person in Leningrad's labor department knew where these "social inspectors" were, or even if they existed.[50] Finally, "progressive piecework," based on an increasing rate of payment for each successive item produced over the norm, was designed to stimulate workers to greater productivity through monetary incentives. The system was premised, however, on workers' ability to calculate the relationship between their wages and their output. It required that workers be informed of their daily output and earnings, which in turn demanded a clear accounting system for individual production. But many foremen and shop bosses simply could not master the accounting necessary to calculate output for each worker. In some cases, they retained the old brigades and production communes under a cover of "fictive piecework." Foremen, managers, and even norm setters, anxious to keep workers on the job, made every effort to maintain wage levels, paying full wages and premiums even when workers did not meet production norms. Often, the *progressivka* was actually used to raise wages without a corresponding increase in output by decreasing norms. The *progressivka* was thereby transformed from a spur to productivity into a means for overspending the wage fund.[51] The Party's move to use the wage "as a lever of production" was thus countered, contested, and twisted at every level of production through outright protest, reclassification of jobs, and quiet fiddling with norms.

A special commission discovered that the wage fund for 1932 had been overspent by over 1.2 million rubles. Much of this overspending was the direct result of various "fictive" efforts at many levels of the factory to maintain the wage. In December 1932, NKT sent SNK and the Central Committee a secret letter containing several suggestions for controlling spending. The letter proposed that plant directors be placed under stricter supervision by being forced to set and adhere to clear wage limits in every

---

[49] A. M. Tsikhon, "Pravil'naia Sistema Zarabotnoi Platy," "Shest' Uslovii Tov. Stalina –
     Osnova Bol'shevistskikh Pobed," *NTF*, 1932, no. 6: 3–8; "Srevkhurochnye, Brak,
     Prostoi, Izlishki Rabochei Sily Priveli k Pereraskhodu Fondov Zarplaty," *NTF*, 1932,
     nos. 8–9: 18.

[50] N.M., "Borot'sia za Realizatsiiu Ukazanii t. Stalina," *NTF*, 1931, no. 25: 4.

[51] E. Levi, and E. Lysenko, "Zarabotnaia Zarplata v Tekstil'noi Promyshlennosti," *VT*,
     1932, no. 3: 57; "Pervye Rezultaty Perestroiki Sistemy Zarabotnoi Platy," *NTF*, 1931,
     no. 34: 17; V. Gornostaev, "Protiv Iskazhenii 'Progressivka'," *NTF*, 1931, nos. 23–24:
     9; idem, "K Voprosy o Perestroike Regulirovaniia Zarplaty," *NTF*, 1931, no. 25: 6;
     A. M. Tsikhon, "Pravil'naia Sistema Zarabotnoi Platy," *NTF*, 1932, no. 6: 3–4.

shop and department. The main thrust of NKT's memo, however, was a scheme to shift costs currently borne by the state to the workers. If factories failed to meet their production targets due to a lack of raw materials, fuel, or electricity (three resources that commonly ran short), wages were still to be pegged to productivity. Workers would not receive wages in the absence of production, *no matter what the cause*. If workers were temporarily idled due to shortages or bottlenecks in production, directors were to lay them off. Directors were instructed to reduce overtime by 75 percent and to compel workers to pay for the defective items they turned out. Given the high level of waste (*brak*) produced by inexperienced workers on new, unfamiliar machinery, these costs constituted a considerable burden that workers could ill afford to shoulder.[52] By 1934, Party leaders were also disenchanted with progressive piecework, which led directly to overspending and gave too much discretionary power to the managers. It was largely eliminated in all sectors with the exception of mining, and directors were instructed not to introduce any progressive bonuses without raising norms.[53]

Rations and Labor Discipline: "Those Who Don't Work Don't Eat!"

Piecework, progressive bonuses, and steeper wage differentials were each intended to reduce turnover and increase productivity, but their strategic efficacy was limited by the fact that the money wage accounted for only part of workers' subsistence in the early 1930s. The incentive of wage increases for leading workers was undercut by food shortages, as workers who sought to spend their new raises in state stores found little to buy. In an economy beset by severe shortages, rations rather than wages secured the staples of working-class consumption. On the continuum of state support, the ration fell somewhere between the wage and social welfare. Although rations, like wages, were remuneration for production, they also covered the reproduction of the working class by providing separate allotments for the dependents of workers, invalids, and other members of the nonlaboring population. The Party had instituted rationing in 1929 to ensure its control over food distribution during times of severe shortage. Rations entitled workers to basic foodstuffs, including bread, sugar, fats, and meat, while wages purchased additional foods and goods in

---

[52] GARF, f. 5515, o. 33, d. 50, "Postanovlenie Ekspertnoi Komissii po Voprosu o Pereraskhode Fondov Zarplaty v 1932 g.," 2; "Postanovlenie TsKa VKP (b) o Planirovanii Fondov Zarabotnoi Platy," 209–14.

[53] GARF, f. 5451, o. 43, d. 31, "Material dlia TsK Partii. Materialy k Dokladu 'Zarabotnaia Plata za 3 goda, 1930–1933'," 28–30.

state stores and the higher-priced peasant markets. Workers survived on a combination of ration cards and wages, but the ration ensured the basic measure of survival. Like wages, rations, too, were subject to a hierarchy of distribution.[54] After the introduction of rationing, Party leaders tried to use the ration system as well as the wage to tie workers to the factories and guarantee greater productivity.

Absentee rates, like turnover, soared during the first five-year plan. The Party claimed that it was peasant migrants, with their "petty-bourgeois psychology and self-seeking tendencies," who were largely responsible for the trend. Yet absenteeism had many causes. Chaotic, interrupted distribution of food, clothing, and basic services such as baths often forced workers to stand in line for hours and miss work. The lack of simple but necessary consumer items such as tools, silverware, shoes, mugs, and thread sent workers scrounging through factory grounds and urban markets on plant time. The hunt for housing invariably consumed days. The factories themselves were disorganized, and foremen had no fixed system for recording attendance. The enormous influx and outflow of new labor rendered almost any system of accounting useless. The discipline of the clock, the bell, and the time card had yet to rule the masses of new workers, and conditions of daily life regularly undercut what little work discipline existed.

In most towns and cities, workers received their ration cards from a *snabotdel,* or provisioning department, after showing a *spravka* or certificate attesting to their residence or workplace. The ration card was good for three months. Many workers, in moving from place to place, would collect and use several cards at the same time. The opportunity to amass cards by changing jobs not only "squandered the larger rationing fund" but encouraged turnover. Ration cards, aimed at eliminating exorbitant prices amid shortage, fueled their own lively private trade as workers began to use them as a new currency. Two enterprising stonemasons, for example, reported for work in one factory just long enough to receive ration cards. Soon after, they disappeared from the factory and sold the cards on the private market, getting an outrageous price from desperate buyers. Living on the proceeds, they moved on to the next "job." Workers also did a brisk trade in "shock worker" awards and banners, trading them for extra ration cards procured through various scams and swindles. People who had never once set a production record waved "their" new shock-worker banners and boldly exercised their right to move to the head of every line. Some factories distributed coupons (*zabornye knizhki*), tokens, or monthly passes for meals in the factory dining halls. Only workers were

[54] For an excellent treatment of the rationing system, see E. A. Osokina, *Ierarkhiia potrebleniia. O zhizni liudei v usloviiakh stalinskogo snabzheniia,* 1928–1935 (Moscow: Izdatel'stvo MGOU, 1993).

supposed to use them, but all sorts of people showed up to eat: a surprise visit to one state farm found 160 people working and 280 people eating dinner. Workers also sold their meal passes outside the factory, creating an active market in "coupon currency." Relatives and friends concocted elaborate cons using falsified certificates of residence, and phony kinship and residence claims got large numbers of people undeserved rations. The cities were teeming with thousands of hungry, sharp-eyed migrants living one short step ahead of the law. Short rations and hunger spawned an infinite variety of inventive, ingenious schemes designed to defraud the state.

In the summer of 1932, the administration of a large Kharkov factory undertook an experiment aimed at reducing turnover by directly tying ration cards to good attendance. Timekeepers in the shops were given responsibility for the distribution of bread cards. In order to receive a bread card, a worker had to hand over his or her personal documents to the timekeeper as collateral. Workers who quit could not get their documents back until they returned their bread cards. Moreover, the timekeepers had to validate the bread cards every five days. Thus, even if a worker absconded with a card, it soon expired. The timekeepers were given the considerable power to reduce workers' rations for violations of labor discipline or unexplained absences. The goal of the program was to reduce absenteeism and eliminate the various scams that had developed around "bread-card currency." By transferring the distribution of cards to the workshops, management weeded out from the ration lists thousands of "dead souls" who collected rations without working, as bread cards were strictly limited to those actually working in the factory and their families. After the timekeepers assumed responsibility for the bread cards, they discovered that six thousand fraudulent cards were in circulation, belonging either to "double dippers" or to people who were no longer employed at the factory. A "*troika*" of workers was set up to ensure honesty in the shops. The Party presented both the *troika* and the new system as examples of "workers' control" over the distribution of food. From the state's perspective, the experiment was a success, "leading to a significant increase in labor discipline."[55]

In November, workers in Moscow, Leningrad, and the machine-building industry voted to adopt the new system. Individual factories began experimenting with even harsher forms of labor discipline in the same spirit of control. In Moscow's Malenkov factory, for instance, workers voted to endorse strict new controls over bread cards and the coupons that entitled them to enter the factory dining halls each day. The coupons were to be distributed by the timekeepers in the shops on a daily, rather than a monthly, basis. Any worker who was fifteen or more minutes late to

[55] "V Nastuplenie na Proguly," *Trud*, November 17, 1932, p. 1.

work would not receive a coupon: barred from the dining hall for the day, late workers would go hungry.[56] Following this well-publicized display of "support" from below, the state transformed the ration card into a new national weapon for labor discipline.

On November 15, 1932, the Central Executive Committee moved to punish absenteeism with a harsh new law. Any worker who missed even a single day of work without "an important reason" was subject to dismissal and the loss of all privileges associated with his or her job, including housing, ration card, and other social services.[57] In 1933, even stiffer penalties for absence were imposed on workers in defense, chemicals, military transport, electrical, and water supply. Workers could be demoted, fired, and even arrested for being late, refusing to work, leaving work early, drinking on the job, being careless with tools or machinery, participating in a work stoppage, creating too much waste in production, or being absent without sufficient reason.[58] The labor press strained to convince workers of the importance of good attendance: "Absenteeism is a sore on the body of socialist industry, gnawing away a huge part of the production necessary to the country every year," the papers luridly proclaimed. "Hundreds of thousands of tons of lost coal, metal, and machines, millions of meters of lost cloth – these are the results of absenteeism for frivolous reasons."[59] The Party was straightforward and unapologetic about the connection between capital accumulation and labor discipline: "If the plan for labor productivity is not met and there are excess expenditures of the wage fund, prices will rise, and this will lead to a decrease in internal industrial socialist accumulation."[60] Yet ideological appeals had their limits when workers did not expect to benefit in the foreseeable future. Capital investment, according to plan, was directed toward production of heavy industry, not consumer goods.

In December 1932, the Central Executive Committee and SNK passed a decree that elevated the Kharkov experiment to the law of the land and transformed the entire food-distribution system into a lever for exacting productivity and enforcing labor discipline. It transferred all the stores, inventories, monies, goods, gardens, rabbit hutches, piggeries, milk and poultry farms, and fisheries under the control of the closed workers'

[56] "V Stolovuiu Zavodu im. Malenkova Vkhod Dlia Progulshchikov Zakryt," *Trud*, December 5, 1932, p. 3.

[57] "Ob Uvol'nenii za Progul bez Uvazhitel'nykh Prichin," *Sobranie zakonov i rasporiazhenii* (Moscow: Gosudarstvennoe Izdatel'stvo, 1934), 765–66. The new law replaced another which stipulated that workers could be dismissed for three days' unexplained absence in a single month. This law had been widely flouted by workers and managers.

[58] GARF, f. 5515, o. 33, d. 54, "Postanovlenie TsK SSSR ob Instruktsii NKT SSSR," "V SNK SSSR," and "Instruktsiia NKT SSSR," 15, 17, 18–22.

[59] "V Nastuplenie na Proguly," *Trud*, November 17, 1932, p. 1.

[60] "Protiv Izvrashchenii Politiki Zarplaty," *Trud*, December 4, 1932, p. 2.

cooperatives (ZRKy) to newly created departments of workers' rationing *within* the factories. ZRK was to be eliminated. Timekeepers in the shops took over control of the coupons that permitted workers to enter the factory dining halls. Any worker fired from a factory was deprived of the right to use its facilities, including housing, dining halls, ration cards, or day-care centers; workers found using ration cards after their dismissal were subject to criminal prosecution. A new system designed to tighten control over the printing and distribution of cards was instituted. Workers who changed jobs could not receive new ration cards until they obtained certificates proving they had returned their old ones. Every worker was to be attached to a particular store and would be given a ration card for that store only.[61] The newspapers proclaimed, "Workers of Moscow and Leningrad Warmly Greet the Decree."[62]

Implementation of the new system did not go as smoothly as its "warm" reception might have implied. Foremen, timekeepers, and factory administrators, forced to regularize attendance records, quickly discovered that they did not know *who* was working in their shops. Factories hastily began counting workers, trying to create order out of the prevailing chaos.[63] Managers on construction sites faced a particularly difficult task because of their massive rates of turnover.[64] The law set December 28, 1932, as the last day for distribution of the new ration cards, but few of the large factories met the deadline. Many housing authorities were slow to issue workers' residence certificates, which plant managers had to have before they could distribute the new cards. Timekeepers in the shops were unsure just *how* to draw up a basic attendance roster. Moscow's huge machine factory Serp i Molot suffered from all these problems and more. New cards were printed and ready for distribution, but no rationing department had been created to dole them out. The administration did not know which workers were supposed to receive cards. Certificates from the housing authorities, attesting to the size of every worker's family, were late, and no one in the factory knew how many rations to provide. Hundreds of hungry, angry workers crowded the corridors outside the offices of the factory committee and the director, desperate to get their ration cards; no

61 "O Rasshirenii Prav Zavodupravlenii v Dele Snabzheniia Rabochikh i Uluchshenii Kartochnoi Sistemy," *Trud*, December 5, 1932, p. 1; "O Prakticheskikh Meropriiatiiakh po Provedeniiu v Zhizn' Postanovleniia SNK Soiuza SSR i TsK VKP (b) ot 4 Dekabria o Rasshirenii Prav Zavodupravlenii v Dele Snabzheniia Rabochikh i Uluchshenii Kartochnoi Sistemy," in *Sobranie zakonov i rasporiazhenii* (Moscow: Gosudarstvennoe Izdatel'stvo, 1934), 802–4.
62 "Za Luchshuiu Postanovku Rabochego Snabzheniia na Predpriiatiiakh," *Trud*, December 6, 1932, p. 1.
63 "Razvernem Besposhchadnuiu Bor'bu s Tekuchest'iu i Progulami," *Trud*, November 18, 1932, p. 1.
64 "Bor'ba s Progulami Otlozhena ... do Zasedaniia," *Trud*, November 27, 1932, p. 2.

one seemed to know who was responsible for distributing them. In other places, chaos ensued when officials prepared to transfer the property of the workers' cooperatives (ZRKy) to plant managers. The space between the hands of one official and the next turned into a "Bermuda Triangle" into which much of the inventory simply vanished. In many areas, officials swiftly eliminated the workers' cooperatives but did not set up rationing departments to take their place. In the transition from the old system to the new, many workers were left without any food at all. In one factory in East Siberia where workers were provided with flour in lieu of bread, the transfer of property from ZRK to the factory administration was accompanied by a new order that workers would no longer receive flour in advance, but only after ten days of work. As a result, workers got no flour at all for almost two weeks, and they and their families went hungry. The mechanical shop and the foundry stopped work for two hours, and the remaining workers went out on strike in protest. There were riots, wildcat strikes, and work stoppages in many places. And before the new system was even in place, fresh scams for trading and stealing ration cards and coupons were being hatched. Timekeepers, the new enforcers of labor discipline and rationing, had already been caught stealing coupons.[65]

In 1933, Tsikhon, the commissar of labor, wrote a long letter to Stalin, Molotov, and Kaganovich in which he summarized the effects of the new law. Beginning with its "successes," he noted that absenteeism had dropped significantly in many factories, and that managers were developing new systems of accounting and control. Yet Tsikhon argued that the intent of the law was being sabotaged at many levels. Plant managers were afraid to punish workers too harshly; anxious above all to retain their labor force, they preferred to overlook absences, especially of highly skilled workers.[66] Workers themselves gaily summed up this collusion in a popular ditty, or *chastushka*:

I work when I like	*Khochu – rabotaiu*
I stroll when I like	*Khochu – guliaiu*
It's all the same	*Vse ravno*
They won't fire me!	*Menia ne uvoliat!*[67]

[65] "Otvetstvennost' Profsoiuzov za Snabzhenie," *Trud*, December 16, 1932, p. 1; "Profsoiuzy Obiazany Vziat' Vydachu Prodkartochek Pod Samyi Zhestkii Kontrol'," *Trud*, December 14, 1932, p. 1; GARF, f. 5515, o. 33, d. 50, "Sektor Informatsii Otdela Orgraboty i Proverku Ispol'neniia VTsSPS. Svodka No. 4," 116.
[66] "Razvernem Besposhchadnuiu Bor'bu s Tekuchest'iu i Progulami," *Trud*, November 18, 1932, p. 1; "Progulshchiki Pod Zashchitoi Nach. Tsekha," *Trud*, November 27, 1932, p. 2; "V Stolovuiu Zavodu im. Malenkova Vkhod Dlia Progulshchikov Zakryt," *Trud*, December 5, 1932, p. 3.
[67] *Chastushka* in headline, *Trud*, December 18, 1932, p. 3.

Shop heads were unsure how to interpret and apply the new law, in particular the phrase "absent without sufficient reason." One woman, with her boss's approval, took twelve days off to search for living quarters. Managers understood that workers could not keep working without housing, which was notoriously difficult to find. Was this an "insufficient" reason? Interpretations of the decree varied widely. In Krasnyi Proletarii, the director understood the decree as giving him "the right but not the obligation to fire workers." His deputy added, "Punishment is not a good means of struggling with absence." Other managers, not wanting to "spoil their relations with the workers," transferred those who were frequently absent to the factory's "comrade courts" for a lesser punishment rather than firing them. Many factory directors considered dismissal "inefficient." In a period of high labor turnover, intense pressure for productivity, and terrible living conditions, managers realized that wide and brutal use of the stick would only encourage more workers to flee the factory. Tsikhon claimed that the directors' hesitancy to fire workers infected the shop heads, masters, cadre-department officials, and timekeepers as well. At all levels, he said, there was "direct resistance to applying the law."

In many places, managers colluded with workers in an attempt to cover up absences. In the Dinamo factory, for instance, the master of the foundry refused a direct command from the Party organization to fire a woman worker. Shop masters connived to transfer workers who got fired from one shop to another. Union officials, factory-committee representatives, comrade-court members, labor inspectors, and state-court judges all resisted the new law by overturning decisions to dismiss workers. Widespread disobedience of the law was coupled with a lack of supervision to ensure compliance. No one, Tsikhon noted indignantly, checked to make certain that absentee workers were thrown out of workers' housing or deprived of their ration cards. Many workers considered the new law a joke. When one worker was fired for absenteeism from the Paris Commune factory, he playfully organized his own "*artel* of absentees" and placed a sign on his dormitory door: "I am now enrolling a labor force." Tsikhon, lacking in humor, considered this an example of anti-Soviet activity.[68] The Party made a concerted effort to encourage workers to police one another; comrade courts within the factories, in which workers judged their mates for infractions, were one initiative in this line. Yet the comrade courts, too, were reluctant to dismiss fellow workers,

---

[68] GARF, f. 5515, o. 33, d. 50, "V TsK VKP (b) – Tov. Slainu i Tov. Kaganovichu. SNK SSSR – Tov. Molotovu," 57–64; "V TsK VKP (b). Dopolnitel'nye Punkty Predlozhenii NKT SSSR o Bor'be s Progulami," 70; "Profsoiuzy v Bor'be za Trudovuiu Distsiplinu," *Trud*, January 8, 1933, p. 1; "Na Shelkovskikh Zavodakh Proguly ne Snizhaiutsia," *Trud*, January 5, 1933, p. 1.

preferring to issue reprimands or even impose fines. Shirin, the head of the Moscow labor department, explained to Tsikhon, "This is a mass phenomenon." And workers in general were dubious about the value and the purpose of the new law. In shop meetings throughout the Moscow region, workers "made unhealthy declarations" against it. One worker in the Kalinin railroad-car construction factory exclaimed, "Why are they throwing workers out of their homes the way they do in America? To hell with this decree. What the workers need is decent food and clothing." Workers, forced to endorse the new law in shop meetings, were afraid to vote against it, so many refrained from voting at all. In the words of one mechanic, "Why would I vote against it when, if I did, they would immediately arrest me?" Another, referring to the need to scrounge for food, declared, "What forces us to be absent is the prices in the market." Shirin reported all these comments directly to Tsikhon, along with the name, shop, and factory of every worker who spoke out.[69] Even Party members opposed the new law. One railroad worker and Party member ventured, "The decree on absence is wrong. The whole thing should be shot down." Another sharply noted, "In the USSR we have compulsory labor, otherwise they will seize your ration card." Many thought the penalty was too harsh. A worker in a beer factory in Ivanovo, after being censured for absenteeism, angrily retorted, "The decree of the government is very cruel in regard to taking away your home and also dismissing you from work. No one will hire you [after that]; you must become a thief. If they try to throw my things out of my room and put my children in the street, I will first cut them with an ax." When a woman was fired for absence, the rest of her brigade of eight went out on a sympathy strike. Even the head of the Party committee sided with the brigade. The whole brigade was fired, and the members of the Party committee were expelled. Workers understood that the new law was more than merely a weapon against individual absence; it could also easily be used to punish workers who protested wages, rations, or conditions through work stoppages or strikes. As one machinist saw it, "This noose around our necks gives the administration the chance to chase out whomever they want."[70]

In Tsikhon's opinion, the weakest link in the new law was not unwillingness to enforce it, but inability. Directors could account for their workers only on a monthly basis; they had no idea how many were working from day to day. "Statistical work in the factories is a chaotic mess," Tsikhon

[69] GARF f. 5515, o. 33, d. 50, "Tov. Kaganovichu, Ryndinu, Kaminskomu, Tsikhonu," 83–87.

[70] GARF, f. 5515, o. 13, d. 50, "Sektor Informatsii Otdela Orgraboty i Proverki Ispolneniia VTsSPS. Svodka No. 5," 114–114 ob; "Sektor Informatsii Otdela Orgraboty i Proverki Ispolneniia VTsSPS. Svodka No. 4," 117 ob.

wrote. The timekeepers were barely literate, and the time sheets were filled with "dead souls." People who did not work in the shops were regularly marked present; attendance was often recorded in advance. Tsikhon suggested that the Central Committee order the Central Statistical Branch to develop new procedures for taking daily attendance. "The factory should know how many people are working or absent every day," he explained. "The factory director should closely monitor his timekeepers, using Party members to oversee their work."[71] Shirin, the head of the Moscow labor department, and Tsikhon both recognized that without a standardized system of attendance taking within the factories, the new law could not be applied. Accordingly, NKT moved quickly to petition the Central Committee for stronger, clearer procedures.

In January 1933, the Central Committee compiled a set of suggestions aimed at improving record keeping. Timekeepers were required to be literate and competent, and their wages were upgraded. The provisions on absence, moreover, were henceforth to extend to lateness as well: any worker who was more than fifteen minutes late more than once a month or late by less than fifteen minutes more than twice a month without having "sufficient reasons" could be fired. Only the shop heads could deem an absence "important" enough to excuse. New accounting systems for attendance were established. Control booths were set up at the gates to the factory to stamp workers' time cards upon their entering and leaving. Timekeepers within each shop were to check attendance daily and keep accurate records of absences. The timekeepers were responsible for correlating their records with those of the gatekeepers. Thus two parallel systems of control – one within the larger factory and within individual shops – were established. Each worker was logged in a total of four times every day, on entering and leaving both the factory and the shop.[72] In effect, the regularization of standards for attendance originated in a punitive campaign for labor discipline. The entire system of timekeeping, clocking, and record keeping was inextricably linked to the need to control the movement of workers in order to increase capital accumulation.

Although the Party was candid in its emphasis on labor discipline, it was less scrupulous in mobilizing support. Pitting one group of workers against another, the press explained that food was scarce because

---

[71]   GARF, f. 5515, o. 33, d. 50, "V TsK VKP (b) – Tov. Slainu i Tov. Kaganovichu. SNK SSSR – Tov. Molotovu," 57–64; "V TsK VKP (b). Dopolnitel'nye Punkty Predlozhenii NKT SSSR o Bor'be s Progulami," 70.
[72]   GARF, f. 5515, o. 33, d. 50, "Postanovlenie Tsentral'nogo Komiteta VKP (b) ob Organizatsii Ucheti Iavki na Rabotu i Meropriiatiiakh po Real'nomu Ukrepleniiu Trudovoi Distsiplinii," 133–35; "Instruktsiia NKTa SSSR ob Uchete Iavki Rabochikh i Sluzhashchikh na Rabotu," 136–37.

"absentees, idlers, rolling stones, aliens, pseudo-workers, and loafers" ate at the expense of those who worked. Shortages were blamed on all the people who were undeservedly dipping into the ration fund; the elimination of double dippers, swindlers, and other schemers would, so the argument went, make more food available to "honest" workers. The decree on rations was thus presented to workers as a means for increasing the food supply. While cheating was in fact partially responsible for food shortages, it was shortage itself that spurred hungry, chronically undernourished workers, migrants, and their families to cheat. Literally thousands of workers were involved in cheating schemes. In Leningrad, after the new distribution system for ration cards went into effect, fifty thousand fewer cards were given out in the large factories. In Rostov, another fifty thousand fraudulent cards were withdrawn; in Baku, twenty thousand; and in Moscow's Paris Commune factory alone, five thousand.[73] The numbers suggested that abuse of the ration system was ubiquitous, providing a critical (if unfairly distributed) supplement to thousands of workers and their families.

The rhetoric surrounding the new rationing system echoed the unions' denunciations of peasant migrants in the 1920s, invoking once again a two-tiered system of settled "protected" workers versus mobile and disruptive migrants. The Party encouraged workers to write in support of the new laws and to denounce "idlers" for stealing food from the "hardworking." One editorial starkly counterposed "yesterday's peasants," "undigested by the proletarian cauldron," against "the heroic strength of *kadrovye* workers." The article demonized the new migrants for their purported view of the factory "as a temporary stage, merely an occasionally 'profitable place' in which they can snatch a little more from the state." These "professional deserters and rolling stones, constantly absent from the factories, wander from one factory to another, earning money everywhere but actually working nowhere."[74] In tarring migrants as chronic cheats and "rolling stones," the rhetoric refused to acknowledge the deeper social reasons for labor turnover: lack of housing, poor living conditions, and short rations. By 1932, the consequences of collectivization were everywhere: chronic food shortages, dispossessed *kulaks*, migrants fleeing the countryside. In its virulent condemnations of labor mobility and its increasingly frantic efforts to stamp out the petty private trading schemes and swindles of a hungry population, the state subordinated the ration to production and rebuilt the gates to the factory. Ration card and worker were both tied to the clock.

[73] "Pravo na Prodkartochku Tol'ko Rabotaiushchim," *Trud*, January 6, 1933, p. 2.
[74] "Vkliuchit' Tsekhi Pitaniia v Bor'bu za Vysokuiu Trudovuiu Distsiplinu," *Trud*, January 6, 1933, p. 3; "Za Ukreplenie Edinonachaliia," *Trud*, November 20, 1932, p. 1.

Passportization and the Gates to the Cities

The new decrees on lateness and absenteeism were quickly followed by even broader measures to control labor mobility. On December 27, 1932, the state issued a decree reviving the internal personal passport, a system of control used in both Europe and tsarist Russia and despised by revolutionaries everywhere. The purpose of the decree was to purge the towns and construction sites of people "not involved in productive work or socially useful labor." Aimed at dispossessed *kulaks,* private traders, former NEPmen, people deprived of voting rights, criminals, and thieves, the internal passport offered the state a means for tracking and controlling the population. It replicated the new attendance procedures in the factories on a larger, national level. The decree introduced a compulsory passport for every citizen sixteen years or older who was living permanently in a town, on a new construction site, or in a workers' settlement, or was employed in transport or on a state farm. Everyone who was either engaged in waged labor or dependent on the state also had to register for a passport, which henceforth would be the only valid proof of identity. Children would be listed on the passports of their parents, orphans with their institution, and soldiers with the military. Peasants did not need to register for passports unless they intended to move to an urban area. The internal passport listed the citizen's full name, date and place of birth, nationality, social position, permanent residence, dates of compulsory military service, and dependents, and identified the original documents on which it was based. Citizens were required to have their passports with them at all times. Anyone found without a passport was subject to a large fine or criminal prosecution. In order to take a job, get urban housing, or move from one area to another, a citizen had to register with the militia and present his or her passport. A peasant wishing to leave the countryside had to request a passport from the rural militia. The passport system was instituted gradually throughout 1933. It was first applied to residents of Moscow, Leningrad, Kharkov, Kiev, Odessa, Minsk, Rostov na Donu, and Vladivostok; within two months, the populations of Kuznetsk, Stalingrad, Baku, Gorky-Sormovo, and Magnitogorsk were added. Large areas around Moscow and Leningrad, and all population centers within one hundred kilometers of the Western border, were also incorporated, as were additional towns, regions, workers' settlements, and construction sites.[75]

The passport system affected both urban dwellers and peasants, but in different ways. Officials initially used the decree as a weapon against

[75] "Ob Ustanovlenii Edinoi Pasportnoi Sistemy po Soiuzu SSR i Obiazatel'noi Propiski Pasportov," in *Sobranie zakonov i rasporiazhenii* (Moscow: Gosudarstvennoe Izdatel'stvo, 1934), 821–23.

people who were living in the towns but not working for wages. It aimed to flush out the "social garbage," the "thieves, swindlers, speculators, and lovers of easy profit" who "hid in the labyrinths of the towns." It sought to purge the towns of *byvshie liudi,* or members of the former upper classes; dispossessed *kulaks*; *lishentsy,* or those deprived of voting rights; former NEPmen; and private traders. These people, who were frequently denied jobs because of their social backgrounds, joined with the freewheeling swindlers, thieves, criminals, and homeless street children to support a shadowy private market that traded in shortage at the expense of the state. The decree spotlighted those who found themselves, either by choice or by necessity, trading, stealing, and siphoning goods at the margins of the state economy. The passport system strove to separate the "honest" waged worker from the private trader by fixing the former in place and driving out the latter. As one editorial noted, "Passports will reveal the underlying social face of their owners."[76]

The decree was also used to purge the factories of workers who came from "suspect" backgrounds. In February 1933, NKT informed the unions, labor departments, and local soviets that all workers without passports were to be fired within ten days. Moreover, the reason for their dismissal was to be noted in their official documents. Factory directors were encouraged to comb their personnel records to ensure that former *kulaks,* traders, small-business owners, and others deprived of voting rights (*lishentsy*) were not masquerading as workers. One director reported that a search in his factory uncovered two hundred "foreign elements" who had not received passports. He queried NKT about how he was to fire them, pointing out that unless a clear notation about the reason for their dismissal was made in their documents, they would "work in other places." Local organizations, including the labor department, had counseled the director not to write the "real reason" in the documents, suggesting that many officials considered the purge too harsh. Defying the directive from the center, they tried to leave other employment options open to those who were fired. But in a secret memo, the deputy commissar of labor dispelled any ambiguity about the decree: those without passports were to have their papers marked so that future employment would be impossible.[77] In Moscow, the union soviet explained that it was actively purging the factories of the traders and *kulaks* who had "crawled into them." All purged workers received a certificate stating the reason for their dismissal, such as "concealing social origins as a dekulakized person." Throughout the spring, many factories were purged. About 500

[76] "Ochistit' Goroda Ot Sotsial'nogo Musora," *Trud,* December 29, 1932, p. 2.
[77] GARF, f. 5515, o. 33, d. 54, "Direktoru Zavoda No. 37," "NKT SSSR," "Tsirkuliar NKT SSSR ob Uvol'nenii Lits, ne Poluchivshikh Pasportov," 3–10.

people were expelled from Izhorsk, a defense factory employing more than 11,000 workers, and 350 from Elektrosila, an electrical plant of similar size. Workers were fired without warning and without pay. Any worker who participated in a work stoppage or protest automatically ran the risk of a background check.[78]

Passportization also affected peasants who wanted to leave the countryside. The state told local militias to advise people that they would not be able to get housing in towns without a valid passport or a document from their local militia. The militia launched a broad informational campaign, but peasant migrants continued to arrive without passports. The instructions given to town militias were firm: "These citizens must be removed." Yet the militia was not pleased at the prospect of having to round up thousands of peasants and ship them back to their villages. It urged the local rural soviets to educate peasants about the consequences of arriving in town without a passport. In 1934, Usov, the deputy director of the militia, wrote to the Central Executive Committee, noting, "There are still mass arrivals of citizens without passports from the agricultural areas to the towns. People are also arriving at worksites *samotek.*" Undeterred by the new law, peasants persisted in migrating without documents or with invalid certificates from their rural soviets. Seeking "to avoid the pointless detention and removal of citizens," Usov once again called on the local soviets to stop giving out worthless papers and instead to direct peasants to their rural militias. Correspondence between Usov and the soviets indicated that passportization did little to dam the stream of migrants.[79] Throughout 1934 and 1935, the state attempted to tighten the restrictions on migration from the countryside through the passport system and organized labor recruiting. Collective-farm workers who had not been officially recruited to work for wages under a collective-labor contract were not permitted to leave without permission from their farm manager and a valid certificate of residence from their local militia. Peasants with proper documents would receive temporary passports, which would have to be renewed by their factory every three months. Any peasant who left a collective farm without permission from the farm manager would be deprived of the right to live in his or her chosen locality.[80]

---

[78]   GARF, f. 5515, o. 33, d. 55, "V VTsSPS Tov. Shverniku i NKT SSSR Tov. Tsikhon," 78; "Narkomtrudam Soiuznykh Respublikov: o Poriadok Uvolneniia Klassovo-Chuzhdykh Elementov," 219–20; "Sektor Informatsii – Otdel Orgraboty i Proverki Ispolneniia VTsSPS," 128, 125.

[79]   GARF, f. 3316, o. 25, d. 193, "Postanovlenie SNKa SSSR," 27; "Protokoly SNK SSSR," 29; "Protokol Zasedaniia Sekretariata TsIKa SSSR," 61; "Spravka," 63–64; "V Sekretariat Prezidiuma TsIKa SSSR," 65; "V Prezidium TsIK SSSR," 73; "Sekretariat Prezidiuma TsIK Soiuza SSR," 77; "Tsirkuliarno TsIK SSSR," 79.

[80]   GARF, f. 5446, o. 1, d. 91, "O Propiske Pasportov Kolkhoznikov-Otkhodnikov, Postupaiushchikh na Rabotu v Gorod na Predpriiatiia bez Dogovorov s Khozorganami," 149.

Statistics suggest that passportization did enjoy a very brief success in controlling peasant migration to the towns. In 1932, 10,505,000 people arrived in the towns; of these, 7,886,000 left again, and 2,719,000 settled. In 1933, however, the numbers were substantially reduced: 7,416,000 arrived, 6,644,000 left, and only 772,000 settled. But then, in 1934 and 1935, the numbers began to climb again. In 1935, 14,374,100 people arrived, 11,909,700 left, and 2,464,400 settled. Thus, by 1935, the number of people settling in the towns was once more approaching the 1932 (pre-passport) level. This implies that though passportization considerably reduced settlement in the towns in 1933, it failed to stop or even slow the high mobility of the population for very long. Passportization had no apparent effect on the gender composition of the peasant migrations: women comprised about 40 percent of all those who arrived in the towns, and this percentage remained roughly constant from 1932 to 1935. The percentage of women among those who stayed (about 50 percent), though, was consistently greater than the percentage of women among those who arrived or left, indicating that women settled down more quickly and were somewhat less mobile than men.[81] Although 100 percent of the workers entering waged labor in 1932 and 1933 were women, there was no increase in the percentage of women among migrants to the towns in those years. In other words, the exclusively female composition of the newly hired labor force cannot be attributed to a sizable increase in the share of migrants who were women. This suggests either that women migrants found it easier to get jobs than men did, or that women who were already based in the towns – that is, wives and daughters of workers – represented an increasingly important source of labor in these years.

Over time, the new passport system also served to turn the peasantry into second-class citizens forbidden to leave the countryside. The second five-year plan, unlike the first, was based not on the extensive construction of new plants but rather on the mastery of new techniques, the acquisition of skills, and an increase in labor productivity. Planners expected the rate of growth to decrease: the labor force would expand more slowly, they predicted, and workers would produce goods of better quality. According to the second five-year plan, only 390,000 new jobs would be created in 1933, of which 127,000 would be in industry, 100,000 in transport, 100,000 in trade, and 63,0000 in communications, socialized dining, and municipal services. Some sectors would actually contract: 400,000 waged workers in agriculture and 700,000 construction workers were projected to lose their jobs. Thus, according to the plan, 390,000

[81] "Zhenshchiny Sredi Pribyvshikh v Goroda i Vybyvshikh iz Gorodov SSSR," in *Zhenshchina v SSSR. Statisticheskii sbornik* (Moscow: Soiuzorguchet, 1937), 69.

jobs would be added and 1,100,000 eliminated, leaving 710,000 waged workers unemployed.[82] If the second five-year plan was implemented successfully, the labor shortage could be expected to turn into a labor glut. The plan in fact understated the magnitude of the contraction in 1933: in reality, only 77,000 new jobs were created in the national economy. No new jobs were added in industry; on the contrary, 10,000 were lost. Only in construction did the plan overestimate the contraction: just 303,000 jobs were eliminated, instead of the anticipated 700,000 (see Tables 8.1, 8.3 and 8.4). Passportization was a logical adjunct to an economic plan that aimed to slow the rate of growth. Because new migrants would only increase competition for a reduced number of jobs, it was in the state's interest to stop the flood from the countryside and allow urban working-class wives and daughters to fill whatever gaps might remain in the labor force.

Passportization was a complex system of internal monitoring that affected many sectors of the population. While historians have focused primarily on its effect on rural peasants, its initial target was actually the urban population. The system sought to purge the cities of traders, *kulaks*, criminals, and others involved in criminal and recently criminalized activities based in trade. The state's struggle to control the food supply and deploy it as a tool of labor discipline fueled the campaign to eliminate the unwaged from the cities. The system was also used to purge the factories of members of these same groups who had taken "honest" employment as workers. Hounded from the cities and the factories, they became a "hunted" people, driven from place to place, unable to settle or to find work without concealing their pasts. The constant threat of investigation also helped keep workers in the factories in line. Fear of exposure, or "unmasking," helped mute labor protest. Finally, passportization was also intended to stop the constant movement of workers from one city to another. By introducing a system of checks and registration, the state aimed to put an end not only to the continuing migration of peasants but to the geographical mobility of workers as well.

The Second Five-Year Plan: Almost Women Only

The purges of the cities and the factories, like the new gates between town and country, were consonant with the slower rate of growth set by the second five-year plan. Yet a new and flexible source of labor was still needed to fill gaps created by growth and to replace the workers purged from the factories. The Party quickly found its solution in urban

---

[82] "O Narodnom-Khoziaistvennom Plane SSSR na 1933 – Pervyi God Vtoroi Piatiletki," in *Sobranie zakonov i rasporiazhenii*, 50–58.

Table 8.1. *Workers and* sluzhashchie *(white-collar workers) in the national economy 1932–1936 (January 1)*

Year	Total number	Number of men	Number of women	Percentage women
1932	21,923,000	15,916,000	6,007,000	27.4
1933	22,649,000	15,741,000	6,908,000	30.5
1934	22,726,000	15,522,000	7,204,000	31.7
1935	23,844,000	15,880,000	7,964,000	33.4
1936	24,976,000	16,484,000	8,492,000	34.0

Source: Excerpted from "Chislennost' Zhenshchin – Rabotnits i Sluzhashchikh – po Otrasliam Truda," in *Zhenshchina v SSSR. Statisticheskii sbornik* (Moscow: Soiuzorguchet, 1937), 51.

Table 8.2. *Workers and* sluzhashchie *entering the national economy, 1932–1935*

Year	Total number	Number of men	Number of women	Percentage women
1932	726,000	−175,000	901,000	100
1933	77,000	−219,000	296,000	100
1934	1,118,000	358,000	760,000	68
1935	1,132,000	604,000	528,000	47

Source: Excerpted from Table 8.1.

women. Women played an unprecedented role in the economy during the second five-year plan. In 1932 and 1933, *their number provided the sole source of incoming workers: 100 percent of the new workers were female.* Moreover, not only did they provide the sole source of incoming workers, they also actively began to replace men. The substitution of female for male labor began in 1932, even before the tempo of growth slowed or passportization took effect. For men, 1932 was a year of layoffs, despite the overall expansion of jobs: 175,000 men left waged labor, and 901,000 women entered. In 1933, the trend of male layoffs coupled with female hiring continued as the rapid tempo of growth slowed. Only 77,000 new jobs were created in 1933, versus 726,000 the previous year. An even larger number of men lost their jobs in 1933 (219,000), while women kept being hired, albeit in smaller numbers (296,000). Hiring improved in 1934 and 1935 for both men and women, but women retained their predominance: in these two years, 1,288,000 women were hired, and 962,000 men. In 1934, 68 percent of new workers were women (see Tables 8.1 and 8.2).

Table 8.3. *Workers and* sluzhashchie *entering large-scale industry, 1932–1935*

Year	Total number	Number of men	Number of women	Percentage women
1932	52,000	−112,000	164,000	100
1933	−10,000	−77,000	67,000	100
1934	464,000	114,000	350,000	75
1935	644,000	360,000	284,000	44

Source: Excerpted from "Chislennost' Zhenshchin – Rabotnits i Sluzhashchikh – po Otrasliam Truda."

The trends that emerged in these years in the national economy – the slowdown in growth, the large layoffs of men, the unprecedented use of women – were even more apparent in industry. Between 1932 and 1936, the total number of women working in industry increased by 865,000, while the number of men rose by only 285,000. At 75 percent, women constituted the overwhelming majority of the 1,150,000 workers who entered industrial jobs in this period, and they comprised fully 100 percent of new workers in 1932 and 1933. In these two years, 189,000 men lost their jobs, and 231,000 women were hired (see Table 8.3). In 1933, even the influx of women could not make up for the large layoffs of men: industry lost a total of 10,000 workers. This contraction of the male labor force was partly a result of passportization, which purged the factories of "undesirables," tightened controls on movement into the cities, and shifted the focus of labor recruiting from the populations of the villages to the wives and daughters of urban workers.

The second five-year plan reflected Stalin's call, in his "Six Conditions" speech, for a shift from construction to production. The contraction of the labor force was most deeply felt in the construction industry, which shrank steadily between 1932 and 1936 as 864,000 workers lost their jobs. But the overall loss concealed the fact that while the number of men working in construction sharply plummeted, the number of women actually increased. Men bore the brunt of the layoffs, with 886,000 of them being thrown out of work. The combination of male layoffs and female hiring, however, marked only the beginning of the second five-year plan; by 1934 and 1935, women, too, were leaving construction (see Table 8.4).

Workers were keenly attuned to the slowdown in the economy, the mass layoffs, the substitution of female for male labor, and the state's attempts to raise production norms and curtail the wage fund. In defiance of the state, they constructed their own understandings of policy. At a meeting

Table 8.4. *Workers and* sluzhashchie *entering
construction, 1932–1935*

Year	Total number	Number of men	Number of women	Percentage women
1932	−238,000	−295,000	57,000	100
1933	−303,000	−320,000	17,000	100
1934	−144,000	−140,000	− 4,000	—
1935	−179,000	−131,000	−48,000	—

Source: Excerpted from "Chislennost' Zhenshchin – Rabotnits i
Sluzhashchikh – po Otrasliam Truda."

in a mechanical factory in Moscow, for example, one worker intimated
that what the state really wanted was to drive workers out of the factory:
"There is no money; wages are held down. Truly, they want some of the
workers to leave the factory without their having to lay them off." Another added, "They have begun to chase the workers out of production.
It was the workers who built the five-year plan, but now they no longer
need them. Again we will have unemployment. They chase the workers
out because they have nothing to feed them." Workers attributed the new
draconian legislation covering ration cards, absenteeism, and lateness to
the end of the labor shortage. Another worker noted, "At the beginning,
they said they would fire only absentees, but now they are letting good
workers go. The decree of the government [on absenteeism] comes out
of the fact that they no longer need a workforce."[83] Workers intuitively
understood that the state's need for labor during the first five-year plan
had protected them from harsher forms of labor discipline. And now the
state had chosen to enact new laws at precisely the moment when workers
were no longer required. Labor discipline and layoffs were inextricably
linked.

Ironically, the mass layoffs of male workers, the contraction of economic growth, the attempt to control rural migrant labor, and the increase
in labor discipline during the second five-year plan were also accompanied
by a continuing expansion of opportunities for women in every branch
of the economy (Table 8.5). The only category of waged work that almost disappeared was domestic service/day labor. In 1929, 16 percent of
waged women had worked in this lowly sector; by 1936, the figure was
down to only 2 percent. Industry, always the largest employer of women,

[83]   GARF, f. 5515, o. 33, d. 50, "Sektor Informatsii Otdela Orgraboty i Proverki Ispolneniia
VTsSPS. Svodka No. 5," 114.

Table 8.5. *Women in the main branches of the national economy, 1929–1935*

Sector/year	1929	1930	1931	1932	1933	1934	1935
Industry	939,000	1,236,000	1,440,000	2,043,000	2,207,000	2,274,000	2,627,000
Construction	64,000	156,000	189,000	380,000	437,000	454,000	450,000
Agriculture	441,000	425,000	221,000	394,000	508,000	605,000	685,000
Transport	104,000	146,000	173,000	243,000	322,000	358,000	384,000
Trade	97,000	179,000	233,000	374,000	432,000	408,000	473,000
Socialized dining	37,000	100,000	172,000	301,000	354,000	358,000	349,000
Enlightenment	439,000	482,000	514,000	692,000	790,000	859,000	919,000
Health	283,000	320,000	358,000	426,000	466,000	506,000	537,000
State administration	239,000	332,000	373,000	475,000	510,000	499,000	522,000
Domestic service/day labor	527,000	312,000	283,000	279,000	241,000	200,000	192,000
Total	3,304,000	3,877,000	4,197,000	6,007,000	6,908,000	7,204,000	7,881,000

Source: "Chislennost' Zhenshchin po Otrasliam Narodnogo Khoziaistva v 1929–1935 gg," in *Trud v SSSR. Statisticheskii spravochnik* (Moscow: TsUNKhU Gosplana, 1936), 25.[84]

[84] Data from 1929 and 1930 are given as the annual average; data from the years 1931–1935 are figures as of January 1. The figures given for women in *Trud v SSSR* (p. 25) are identical to those shown in table 8.1, with the exception of 1935. *Zhenshchina v SSSR* may be more accurate for 1935 because it was published a year later.

expanded its employment of female waged workers from 28 percent in 1929 to 34 percent in 1936.[85]

Between 1932 and 1936, women also increased their share of jobs within large-scale industry from 33 to 40 percent. Indeed, their share of *every* branch grew. Textiles and sewing, branches that had always contained large percentages of women, now became even more predominantly female. In 1928, 61 percent of textile and sewing workers were female; in 1936, 72 percent were. And by 1936, women workers would also be the majority in printing, a traditionally "male" branch, and in animal-product processing. Thus, even as long-established "female" branches became even more intensely feminized, historically "male" industries crossed the gender line as well. Lumber, metal and machine production, mining, and mineral extraction, industries that had employed negligible percentages of women in 1928, would all expand their female workforces to 25 percent or more of their workers by 1936.[86]

The distribution of women throughout industry also shifted considerably. In 1913, the largest group of women workers (63 percent) was employed in textiles; only a tiny minority worked in metal and machine production (2 percent) or mining (4 percent). By 1936, this pattern had changed: just 30 percent of women workers remained in textiles, while 20 percent were now located in metal and machine production, and 12 percent in mining. Women were more evenly distributed over many branches of industry, including those previously dominated by men.[87] These parallel trends – the increased feminization of traditionally "female" industries, alongside female expansion into traditionally "male" ones – began during the first five-year plan and extended into the second. These two trends marked the female experience in Soviet industrialization. Together they produced a paradox: wider opportunities for women workers overall, combined with more intense sex segregation of traditionally "female" industries. For the workers (mostly women) "left behind" in undercapitalized light industries, these parallel phenomena also brought a worsening of conditions and living standards.[88]

[85] "Raspredelenie Zhenshchin – Rabotnits i Sluzhashchikh – po Otrasliam Truda," *Zhenshchina v SSSR*, 52. The vast majority of women employed by large-scale industry in 1936 (82 percent) were workers. The remainder were service personnel or MOP (5 percent), white-collar employees (7 percent), engineers and technicians (3 percent), and apprentices (3 percent). See "Chislennost' i Sostav Zhenshchin v Krupnoi Promyshlennosti po Kategoriiam Personala," 56.
[86] "V Protsentakh k Chislu Rabochikh i Uchenikov Oboego Pola Kazhdoi Otrasli," in *Zhenshchina v SSSR*, 58.
[87] "Raspredelenie Zhenshchin-Rabotnits Krupnoi Promyshlennosti po Otrasliam," in *Zhenshchina v SSSR*, 59.
[88] See, for example, Jeffrey Rossman, "Worker Resistance under Stalin: Class and Gender in the Textile Mills of the Ivanovo Industrial Region, 1928–1932" (Ph.D. Diss., University of California, Berkeley, fall 1997).

As women entered new industries such as machine building and electrical, and older "male" ones such as metallurgy and printing, they continued to be overrepresented in the ranks of the unskilled, underrepresented among the skilled, and clustered within certain jobs. Yet they made rapid and significant advances in the ranks of skilled workers. In machine construction, for example – an important new branch that took in more women than any other – 28 percent of the workers were women in 1934, in contrast to a mere 4 percent in 1927. Women still constituted 56 percent of the unskilled workforce, but they also held a fair share of the skilled positions. They became blacksmiths, stampers, press operators, welders, fitters and assemblers, turners, painters, and greasers, all positions in which they had figured as less than 1 percent of the workforce before the first five-year plan. They comprised a significant majority in certain jobs, including mechanical operator, pourer, driller, and stamp presser, and they were represented in every skill, with the sole exception of revolvers. In the electrical industry, another new and rapidly expanding branch, women made up 39 percent of the workers in 1934, compared to 18 percent in 1927. Here again, though still overrepresented among the unskilled (at 42 percent), they also entered many skilled jobs. The positions of lamp maker, lamp pumper, and wire cable worker were filled almost exclusively by women, and most revolvers, drillers, stamp pressers, coil winders and insulators, spool winders, assemblers, and machinists were female as well. In ferrous metallurgy, a traditionally "male" industry, women constituted only 22 percent of the workforce in 1934, but they were represented in every shop: blast furnace, open-hearth steel furnace, Bessemer and Thomas shops, rolling mill, transport, and skilled support. Here, too, they were disproportionately concentrated in unskilled work, but they also could be found in well-paid skilled positions in even the hottest, heaviest, and most dangerous shops.[89]

It is difficult fully to assess Soviet women's advances in industry. Statistical breakdowns of industry in the 1930s show women's shares of many skills but do not disclose how many people were employed in each. As a result, it is often unclear precisely how important any job or skill was to a particular industry. In printing, for example – a "male" industry that became heavily feminized – women made up 58 percent of the workers by 1934 and held many skilled jobs. The only skilled job that retained its male character (with only 9 percent women) was "printer." If "printer" encompassed the vast majority of skilled workers in this industry, and women remained excluded from its ranks, then their share of other skilled jobs may not have meant very much. A full accounting

[89] "Zhenskii Trud v Otdel'nykh Professiiakh Mashinostroeniia," "Elektrotekhnicheskaia Promyshlennost'," and "Zhenskii Trud v Otdel'nykh Professiiakh Chernoi Metallurgii," in *Zhenshchina v SSSR*, 83, 84, 87.

of female advancement must await more extensive statistical data from every branch of industry. From the published statistical accounts that are available, however, it appears that women made impressive gains in both "male" and "female" industries, moving into skilled positions that had once been closed to all but the tiniest minority. The Party made strenuous efforts to enroll women in its many technical schools, training programs, and courses, including institutes of higher education (Vyshie Uchebnye Zavedenii, or VUZy), technicums, and *rabfaks* (workers' faculties). By 1936, women constituted 40 percent of the students in the VUZy, 43 percent in the technicums, and 35 percent in the *rabfaks*. Their growing share of skilled jobs attested to the Party's success in promoting their strong participation in worker training and education.[90]

The Levers of Production

The idea that people would create a *novyi byt* ("new life") under socialism enjoyed widespread popularity in the 1920s and 1930s. The term "*novyi byt*" encompassed many ideals, including the liberation of women from dependence and housework; the creation of new forms of culture for and by workers; the transformation of daily life and personal relationships; and the provision of free access to leisure, education, and culture for all citizens. At the heart of these plans was the socialization of *byt*, or daily life. The labor that women traditionally performed in the home without monetary compensation – cooking, cleaning, washing, caring for children, the sick, and the elderly – would be transferred to the public sphere, where it would be undertaken by waged workers. People would eat food prepared by waged workers in public dining halls. The meals themselves would be subsidized, appetizing, and nutritious; children would be fed them at day care or school, and adults at work. Large industrial laundries would wash linens and clothing. Women, relieved of the weight of household chores, would be free to enter the waged labor force and public life. One writer explained, "Housing will be transformed from a place of work (food preparation, washing linens, etc.) exclusively into a place for

---

[90] "Zhenskii Trud v Otdel'nykh Professiiakh Poligraficheskoi Promyshlennosti," in *Zhenshchina v SSSR*, 91. This statistical collection shows women's share of skilled positions in many industries (pp. 83–100) but does not specify the number of workers in each position. On worker training, see "Chislennost' Zhenshchin – Uchashchikhsia VUZov, Teknikumov i Rabfakov," 121, and "Zhenshchiny Sredi Uchashchikhsia VUZov v SSSR i v Kapitalisticheskikh Stranakh," 127. Soviet women had better access to higher education than European women and constituted 38 percent of university students in 1935, in comparison to 14 percent in Germany, 26 percent in England, and 14 percent in Italy. In technical fields, women in these European countries constituted less than 3 percent of students, compared with almost 25 percent in the Soviet Union.

daily rest." Clubs, rest-and-recreation resorts, and public dining facilities would transfigure public spaces, offering amenities never before available to workers. Architects, designers, educators, planners, and women's activists elaborated this vision in futuristic designs for "green towns," collective living spaces, clothing, furniture, resorts, and palaces of culture that aimed to liberate both men and women from their traditional roles and burdens.[91] The socialization of *byt* promised men and women a new freedom. For women workers in particular, it offered the possibility of a life without endless toil. *Novyi byt* excited practical schemes and utopian fantasies, stimulating the visionary side of the socialist imagination.

Many writers expanded on these notions during the 1920s, but little was done to realize their visions. The meager resources of the state were instead devoted to rebuilding the industrial base that had been shattered during the war years. With the first five-year plan, the socialization of *byt* found a sharp new impetus. Artiukhina, the former head of the Zhenotdel, stressed its importance in the context of rapid industrialization. Addressing a meeting of the Moscow Party committee, she dismissed suggestions that industry should begin producing new labor-saving devices for individual consumption. "Our task," she reminded everyone, "is not only to improve individual life, but to build a communal life. Why should we imitate the bourgeoisie who are still oppressing women workers with saucepans and consigning them to their own individual kitchens?" Artiukhina urged the Party to make the production of washing machines for communal laundries its number-one industrial priority.[92] In stark contrast to the 1920s, a period of high unemployment, the early 1930s were a time of labor shortages, when the state's ideological commitment to socializing *byt* was revived by pressure to bring women into the workforce. Socialized dining halls were an imperative when hundreds of thousands of new workers were housed in temporary tents, barracks, and dormitories without kitchens; apartments with separate kitchens and baths were expensive to build. During the rapid industrialization drive, the demand for cheap, basic communal services thus reinforced earlier commitments to the socialization of *byt*. The massive increase in the labor force, coinciding as it did with the production demands of the state, turned many early visions of women's liberation into necessities. Working-class women put the problem to the state directly. When managers tried to hire housewives in the barracks in Magnitogorsk, the women replied, "We will agree to work if you build child-care centers, organize dining halls with decent food and no lines, set up laundries, and eliminate the lines in the stores."[93]

[91] I. Gorskii, "Sotsialisticheskii Gorod i Rekonstruktsiia Byta," *VT*, 1930, no. 2: 13–21.
[92] A. Artiukhina, "Za Sotsialisticheskuiu Peredelku Byta," *Rabotnitsa*, 1930, no. 4: 3.
[93] B. Brumshtein, "Zhenskii Trud v Magnitostroe," *Okhrana truda*, 1931, no. 23–24: 20.

The plans for socializing women's domestic work were initially highly ambitious. An early version of the five-year plan for women proposed that Narpit (the Union of Public Dining and Dormitory Workers) serve 50 percent of all meals eaten by the urban population in communal dining halls. Its plans for workers were even more ambitious: socialized dining was targeted to cover 90 percent of workers in the industrial districts and over half of their families. Workers would eat not only their midday meal in a dining hall, but their breakfast and dinner as well. Every child, urban and rural, would be fed a hot breakfast at school. And Narpit was not the only organization responsible for the socialization of *byt*: the Commissariat of Enlightenment intended to provide preschool places for all workers' children by 1931.[94] The Central Committee called for a complete transition from individual cooking and food preparation to socialized dining by the end of the first five-year plan. In 1932, the number of dining halls in Leningrad alone was to increase from 1,355 to 19,555![95] The second five-year plan aimed higher still, projecting that "100 percent of all the basic aspects of daily life in the towns will be communalized."[96]

Construction was slow, but by the end of the first five-year plan, the state had made considerable progress toward providing millions of people with social services. By 1932, almost 9 million people in the towns ate some or all of their meals in communal dining halls. Three million children were served a hot breakfast in school every morning.[97] Between 1928 and 1933, the number of dining halls expanded by a factor of 64, to 387,000 facilities serving more than 25.5 million people. The number of children in child-care centers meanwhile increased tenfold, from 104,386 in 1928 to 1,048,309 in 1936.[98] Between 1930 and 1931, the percentage of workers' children enrolled in child-care centers in the Leningrad region more than tripled, rising from 17 to 52 percent. There were similar increases in the regions of Moscow, Nizhegorod, Ivanovo, and the Urals.[99]

The establishment of such services represented the first step toward creating a material base for *novyi byt*. Yet by 1934, dreams of a new life were no longer encouraged or discussed. The old *bytoviki*, the women who had emerged triumphant from the factories in the heady days of revolution, were stripped of the opportunity to organize and make their

---

[94] GARF, f. 6983, o. 1, d. 159, "Perspektivy Zhenskogo Truda," 327–28, "Itogi Vnedreniia Zhenskogo Truda v Promyshlennost' za 1-oe Polugodie 1931," 23.

[95] V. Val'ter, 85, 88.

[96] G. Serebrennikov, "Zhenskii Trud v SSSR za 15 et," *VT*, 1932, nos. 11–12: 67.

[97] V. Val'ter, 85.

[98] M. Goltsman, "Uchastie Zhenshchin v Sotsialisticheskom Stroitel'stve," *Voprosy prof-dvizheniia*, 1934, no. 3: 88; "Set' Detskikh Sadov i Chislo Detei v Nikh," in *Zhenshchina v SSSR*, 138–39.

[99] GARF, f. 6983, o. 1, d. 165, "Itogi Vnedreniia Zhenskogo Truda v Promyshlennost'," 22–23, 28.

voices heard. The Central Committee liquidated the Zhenotdel in 1930. The last elections to the delegate assemblies were held in 1931, and after 1933, the delegates stopped meeting entirely.[100] KUTB was eliminated by the end of the first five-year plan. After 1934, it became difficult to hear even the faintest echo of these vibrant, working-class voices, drowned out as they now were by the ever-louder drumbeat for production. After Stalin's "Six Conditions" speech, the voices of economists replaced those of working-class women. These men spoke not of the "socialization of *byt*" but rather of the "social wage." Subsidized meals, dining halls, day-care centers, medical and maternity care, and other social services were now calculated as part of a "wage" and routinely enumerated as part of a larger argument that workers' wages were rising.

Just as wages and rations were used to tie workers to the factory and to spur productivity, the social wage, too, became a reward. The state made a concerted effort to concentrate the distribution of food and social services under the control of factory administrations. The shift of resources to the factory administration was a direct result of the campaign to increase labor discipline and limit workers' mobility. No longer a program to liberate women, the socialization of *byt* had become an instrument for exercising labor discipline over the working class as a whole. As the factory began providing meals, housing, and child care, usurping the unpaid domestic labor of women, it also gained an important new weapon: managers were now able to tie the provision of these essential services to attendance, timeliness, productivity, and good behavior. Workers who were absent too often, who engaged in work stoppages or strikes, or who did not "work well" might find themselves evicted from factory housing, their children expelled from factory day care, and their families barred from factory dining halls. The socialization of *byt,* initially intended as a means to individual liberation, was reinvented as a new form of labor discipline, transformed from a revolutionary principle into a privilege for productive workers.

By the time the second five-year plan was implemented, a new ideological definition of the worker had emerged to replace the older political emphasis on "male, hereditary, *kadrovye*" workers. Women, peasants, and young people had entered the working class in unprecedented numbers, irretrievably altering its composition. The new definition had to be broadened to include previously excluded categories. Yet fears of the peasantry – itinerant, hostile, dispossessed – persisted. As the gates to the working class were rebuilt during the second five-year plan, urban women replaced peasants as a new labor reserve. The large-scale use of urban female labor allowed the state to establish a passport system that

[100] *Sovetskie zhenshchiny i profsoiuzy* (Moscow: Profizdat, 1984), 96.

sought to stop new migration from the countryside and to slow workers' movement from town to town. Women not only filled gaps in industry but also replaced men who were already working. In 1932 and 1933, almost 400,000 men lost their jobs, and nearly 1.2 million women were hired. In industry, 189,000 men were laid off, and 231,000 women were hired. The trends that had marked the first five-year plan – increased feminization of traditionally "female" industries, alongside a growing female presence in every branch – intensified during the second five-year plan. Women moved into new skilled positions, shouldering the responsibilities of both waged and household labor. Their wages helped maintain the standard of living for the working-class family. Providing the state with two workers for the cost of one, they contributed a new source of capital accumulation and investment.

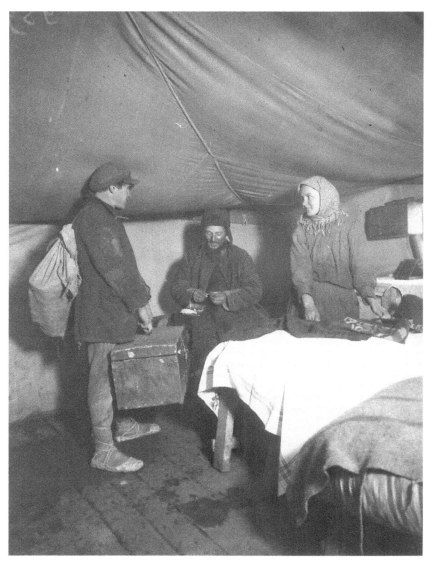

A woman dormitory worker makes a bed in a crowded tent for a
peasant new arrival at Magnitogorsk. 1931.

Conclusion

This story begins and ends at the gates to the working class. These "gates" have served as a metaphor for policy, or, more specifically, for the state's attempts to define and control the size, composition, and behavior of the working class. By dividing those who were permitted to enter from those who would remain outside, the state used the gates to construct the working class from above. The gates were not, however, maintained by the state alone. Put up in the 1920s to exclude women and peasants, the gates also privileged and revived an older "*kadrovye*" working class that had all but disappeared during the civil war. The gates were staunchly defended by the unions and contested by the Zhenotdel. In 1930, they were toppled by a vast and mobile crowd of peasants, women, and other unemployed people in search of work. As job opportunities opened up and managers everywhere faced severe labor shortages, new workers streamed into jobs and onto construction sites, forming a new working class that now encompassed formerly excluded elements. The Party struggled to keep pace with a labor-market expansion that its own industrial policies had created. Veterans of the Zhenotdel, organizers from KUTB, and female members of the planning brigades cheered as the gates fell and women edged forward toward the best of the once-protected working-class positions: production jobs in heavy industry. The unions, labor exchanges, and local labor organizations all lost their place as gatekeepers. Yet the gates did not remain open for very long. Within a few short years, the Party erected new entrance barriers to the cities and to the working class. The state rebuilt the gates to slow the growth of the working class, to create obstacles to labor mobility, to control workers in the factories, and to prevent the creation of vast urban slums. It also established a passport system, bound workers to the factories through the use of ration cards, and introduced the "social wage" as a lever of production, barring many from the cities and from the working class. As growth slowed, the state drew on urban women as an additional and highly flexible new source of labor. Labor newspapers and journals helped prop up the gates by convincing workers that the expulsion of "class aliens" and

278

"double dippers" would ensure greater prosperity for those who were now "inside."

At each of these junctures, gender was critical to the way the gates helped structure the working class. The working class was not a loose aggregation of autonomous individuals but rather a network of people embedded in families. The family served as a unit to support the unwaged at the expense of the waged – to raise children and care for the sick, the disabled, and the elderly. In the 1930s, the Soviet worker's family was a key source of waged labor by virtue of its making a reserve of women available to the state. This in turn had serious implications for state expenditure, capital accumulation, gender roles, and the composition of the working class. Viewing the family as a source of labor, on a par with the peasantry or the urban working class, affords us new theoretical insights into the relationship between gender and class formation. In the 1920s, the working class was defined through a process of exclusion, keeping out those who had never worked for wages (such as unemployed women) or who lacked skill or long *stazh* in the factories. During the first five-year plan, women were critical to the unprecedented growth and recomposition of the working class. Their wages offset the sharp cuts in family consumption caused by the dramatic decline of real wages. Women's waged labor not only allowed the working-class family to survive, but also proved to be a critical and unacknowledged resource for capital accumulation by the state. And during the second five-year plan, the state could not have enacted its harsher laws governing labor mobility, absenteeism, and turnover without having women as a key reserve of labor within the urban working class. Quite simply, the construction of the Soviet working class cannot be understood apart from the deployment and contributions of women.

As the Party constructed the working class in the 1920s and 1930s, it remained haunted by fears about the reliability of its putative social base. Despite the enormous expansion and recomposition of the working class, Party leaders still feared those social groups that threatened, in its view, to dilute the "purity" of the proletariat. These fears took two forms. The first and perhaps the bigger specter was the peasant. Official presentations of the passportization program in the early 1930s replayed the same anxieties expressed by labor officials in the 1920s. Well into the second five-year plan, in newspapers, journals, and speeches, the peasant in search of work continued to be demonized as a conniving, thieving "rolling stone" and "opportunist in search of the long ruble." The second specter was female, the "backward woman" invariably depicted as unskilled, illiterate, and unable to understand politics or to imagine a socialist future beyond the empty larder. The Party worried that "class enemies" could easily manipulate her to "help the anti-Soviet element." Such warnings played well among male workers, foremen, labor-exchange officials, and local union activists, who sought to protect a range of employment and skill privileges against the claims of women. True, women's bread riots had brought down the autocracy in February 1917, but how long would women's commitment to Soviet power last under trying conditions of food shortage, short rations, and endless lines?[1]

The Party's concern over its main social and political base was not simply a figment of its political imagination, but was grounded in real changes in the composition of the working class. During the civil war, a new, more feminized proletariat, composed of urban traders, small shop-keepers, women, youths, and peasants, had taken the place of the heredi-tary *kadrovye* workers of the revolution. In 1921, the Party and the labor unions had struggled to revive the surviving older, cadres. Women had been fired en masse and replaced with Red Army veterans. Throughout the 1920s, the unions had fought hard to guard the privileges of their members against new workers who were "sneaking and oozing" into the working class. The Party's fears both reflected reality and helped to shape it. The protection of the union worker was transmuted into the demoniza-tion of the job seeker. Between 1929 and 1930, the Party was paralyzed by its own anxiety. The economy was expanding, and managers were hungry for labor, but labor and union officials continued to enforce the old policy, seeing themselves as "gatekeepers" to the working class. Managers, in-tensely responsive to the new demands of production, began bypassing the labor exchanges and hiring peasants and working-class women directly from the factory gates. Amid severe labor shortages, Party and union offi-cials still grumbled about the need to close off Narpit, and the construction and sugar industries as "conduits" into the working class. Not until the late fall of 1930 did the Party finally alter its labor policy to reflect the new realities of the economy and the labor market, with its declaration of the end of unemployment and its announcement of the campaign to bring 1.6 million women into the workforce. By this time, the working class was well on its way to being remade from below, as hundreds of thousands of male and female peasants, and urban women entered the workforce "*samotek*," or independent of state planning. Labor policy thus struggled to catch up with changes that were already taking place.

But if labor policy was not initially responsible for remaking the work-ing class, how can its growth and gender recomposition be explained? The answer to this question lies in a tangled knot of state policy and social

---

[1]   Elizabeth Wood, in *The Baba and the Comrade: Gender and Politics in Revolutionary Russia* (Bloomington, Ind.: Indiana University Press, 1997), notes that Party leaders, ex-plicitly conscious of women's backlash against the French Revolution, asked this same question during the civil war (p. 44). On women's reactions against the French Revolu-tion, see Olwen Hufton, *Women and the Limits of Citizenship in the French Revolution* (Toronto: University of Toronto Press, 1992).

consequence that linked peasants, women, and workers in new, dynamic, and complex relationships. The Party's ongoing struggles with the peasantry over entry into the unions, the price and extraction of grain, trade and the elimination of the private market, collectivization, and passportization were central to the creation and recomposition of the working class. Similarly, the behavior of workers and women (both working-class and peasant) figured prominently in the great contest for control over agriculture. Throughout NEP, the interests of urban workers and peasants had often been sharply opposed. On the one hand, workers wanted to keep unemployed peasants out of urban labor markets. On the other, high prices for grain and other produce and the inability of the state to dictate retail or wholesale pricing hurt urban workers but benefited peasants. Riots and protests in the late 1920s among workers over high prices and shortages exerted strong pressure on the Party to solve the food problem. In eliminating the private market and collectivizing the peasantry, the Party acted to protect the urban working class, its main base of political support, at the peasants' expense.

Collectivization and the elimination of private trade in turn affected women by pushing them into the labor force. The disappointing harvest of 1928, the decision to extract grain forcibly, the peasants' sharp reaction in reducing production, and the precipitous decision to launch mass collectivization all led, step by lurching step, to a massive food crisis that lasted into the second five-year plan. Millions of peasants fled the countryside, and urban working-class and newly arrived peasant women alike quickly discovered that a man could not feed a family on his wages alone. As prices for food rose, real wages fell, and women were compelled to enter waged labor in order to maintain their families' overall income. The ratio of dependents to earners dropped steadily in tandem with food shortage and rising prices. The fall in real wages was the result of an unplanned inflation, which itself resulted from a severe disruption of the rural-urban exchange nexus. The most successful recruiter of women into production, at least at the outset, was hunger.

State policies regarding urban women and peasants were inextricably linked. The campaign to involve women reflected a choice about which labor reserves the Party could tap most profitably and reliably: women within working-class families or rural peasants. The Party opted for urban women over peasants at two critical points: in the fall of 1930, when it launched the campaign to recruit 1.6 million new women workers, and after passportization in 1932, when it needed a flexible labor reserve already based in the cities. In both instances, the Party openly admitted that urban women were preferable to peasants because they required no additional outlay for housing, water, sewage, electricity, social services, schools, or other urban infrastructures. Urban women represented an ideal reserve of labor during the slower growth of the second five-year plan. They allowed the state to halt movement into and between cities and to begin to stabilize the workforce. Passportization extended the struggle over the relative privileges of urban life, including access to better housing, schools, medical care, and food distribution within urban areas. The peasantry could never have become the second-class citizens of the passport system if the state had not been able to count on the labor reserves provided by women already settled in the cities.

The Party's campaign to involve women in waged labor also endeavored, with much élan and some success, to transform a labor imperative into an initiative for women's emancipation. It appealed to women to get out of the kitchen, widen their horizons, obtain education and training, and build a new society. It elevated to new, national importance the long-standing efforts of women's activists to open up skilled jobs to women. KUTB's relentless insistence on increased labor-force participation by women in every locality, the work of the female planning brigades in reassigning previously "male" jobs to women, and the open discussion of discrimination, harassment, and the male monopoly of skill were all made possible by the economy's need for women workers. The decision from above to mobilize 1.6 million women briefly reinvigorated a genuinely feminist, populist activism that had been in danger of disappearing with the elimination of the Zhenotdel. Women's activists seized the moment. Maintaining considerable faith in waged labor as a basis for women's independence and emancipation, they fought hard to open up skilled, highly paid jobs in many factories and professions to women. If women initially entered the waged labor force because of the fall in real wages, they nonetheless found expanded opportunity because of the efforts of women's activists. For a brief period, the Party's campaign to involve women, the growing need for skilled labor, and the feminism of the women's activists came together to create new and vast opportunities for hundreds of thousands of women workers. The woman worker smiled confidently from posters, postage stamps, and the front pages of newspapers. An object of scorn, pity, and condescending philanthropic zeal under capitalism, she was praised, respected, and extolled for her contributions in the Soviet Union.

The moment of confluence between feminist plans and the Party's need for labor was fleeting, however. By the end of the first five-year plan, it was over. As large numbers of women entered new jobs and new skills, the intense need for labor lessened. KUTB was eliminated, and the local planning brigades left off their regendering work in the factories. By 1933, few organizational bases for women's activism remained. Without bases to sustain activism, women's issues quickly faded from view. And without the Zhenotdel and KUTB, the problems of discrimination, harassment, skill, promotion, and deployment were left to the unions, the economic organs, local Party and factory committees, managers, and foremen, whose interest in these questions was demonstrably weak. The question of female labor ceased to be urgent to anyone but women workers themselves, and they no longer had organizations that would voice their perspectives, needs, or grievances. The powerful combination of feminism and socialism, which had emerged for the first time among revolutionary women textile workers and laundresses in 1917, found its last expression in the planning brigades and KUTB during the first five-year plan. Thereafter, the vitality of the feminist perspective was slowly extinguished. After the elimination of the Zhenotdel, KUTB members offered only a weak critique of state planners' proposals to gender as "female" entire poorly paid sectors of the economy. The femininization of light industry and service jobs (MOP) in the industrialized Soviet economy bore a striking resemblance to the sex segregation that marked its Western capitalist counterparts.

Yet in the Soviet Union, unlike the West, the concentration of women in low-paying service jobs and light industry was planned from above, by the state. Beginning with the blueprints for regendering the economy in 1930, we have traced the entire planning process from conception to implementation. The blueprints, more than just a faded artifact of the planners' shining surety and reach, raise critical questions about the efficacy of the planning process. Did the plans shape the labor force? Was the state able to force a vast and messy reality to conform to its tidy target figures? What was the relationship between plan and reality, between planners in Moscow and local officials? Steady complaints from labor, union, KUTB, and Party officials suggested that the plans were not readily or easily implemented. Yet as the tremendous turmoil and chaos of the first-five-year-plan period receded, the national and local variants of the "Five-Year Plan for Female Labor" had some influence on women's labor-force participation. The carefully elaborated target figures for localities were seldom met exactly, but the plans did regender the economy and open up new industries and professions to women. The quotas set for training schools and jobs in heavy industry helped to integrate previously "male" sectors, while the sectors regendered as "female" became largely the preserve of women. The statistics show that women's participation in the Soviet labor force was defined by parallel trends: traditionally "female" industries such as textiles and sewing became almost entirely female, even as women also moved into traditionally "male" industries such as metal, mining, and machine building. The shape of the labor force blurred and bled beyond the precise lines of the plans, but it resembled the original template in its general configuration. In no area was reality grossly different from the general outline offered by the plan.

And herein lies one of the many paradoxes of Soviet planning. Historical documents reveal a messy process characterized by poor communication between Moscow and the localities. The central planners could not plan without data from below, and local officials were so overwhelmed by the rapid pace of industrial transformation that they could not collect meaningful data. Planners at every level, from Moscow to the factory shops, generated statistics that had little relation to one another. And yet somehow, from these endless ink-stained columns of figures drawn up by planners large and small, a bottom line emerged to prove the Party's success in creating a plan that shaped a new reality. It pulled millions of men and women into a new working class that made bricks out of sand and clay in the wastelands, built cities on the steppes and the tundra, dug coal pits in the Kuznets basin, harnessed the power of the Dnieper River, and forged steel from iron ore in Magnitogorsk. And by 1935, almost 40 percent of these workers were women.[2]

In the struggle to create a new reality, planners offered a vision of a world transformed. A simple primer for children on the first five-year plan explained, "We change Nature, but as yet we have not changed our own selves. And this is the most essential thing. Why have we begun all this tremendous work? Why do we mine millions of tons of coal and ore? Why do we build millions of machines? Do we do these things merely to change Nature? No, we change Nature in order that people may live better."[3] The industrialization of the 1930s presented a model of development that continues to fascinate working people, students, union activists, peasant organizers, and feminists around the world. It laid the groundwork for enormous achievements, including a modern, globally competitive Soviet state; the victory over a powerful, highly mechanized Fascist army; higher living standards; urbanization; and democratic access to health care, literacy, and education. Yet in the struggle to transform the world, to produce, to meet the target figures, the women's activists who had once dreamed of a *novyi byt* – the old *bytoviki,* as they were called – were forced to redirect their energies, too, toward production. After the elimination of the Zhenotdel, Party leaders repeatedly made it clear that women were no longer to concern themselves with issues of *byt.* By the end of the first five-year plan, the dreams of *novyi byt* had been transformed into a "social wage," a set of rewards and privileges for high productivity, another lever of production.

If one of the old *bytoviki* could step out of the factory in which she worked from childhood, and stand before us in her flowered kerchief

[2] *Trud v SSSR. Statisticheskii spravochnik* (Moscow: TsUNKhU Gosplana, 1936), 95.
[3] M. Ilin, *The Story of the Five-Year Plan: Russia's Primer* (Cambridges, Mass.: Houghton Mifflin, 1931), 148.

and her dark-blue coverall, what would she say to us across these many years? How would she sum up a lifetime shaped by work, by revolutionary dreams, by the drive to industrialize and to build socialism? Perhaps she would have first learned to read in one of the thousands of courses and schools the Party established to liquidate illiteracy. Perhaps she would have found an old pamphlet in one of the many workers' libraries established by the Party in dormitories, factories, and clubs. And perhaps she would paraphrase for us the words of William Morris, a nineteenth-century English radical:

> ... I pondered all these things, and how people fight and lose the battle, and the thing that they fought for comes about in spite of their defeat, and when it comes turns out not to be what they meant, and other people have to fight for what they meant under another name ... [4]

[4] William Morris, *A Dream of John Ball* (London, 1888).

Postage stamp of a woman worker with the factories' smoking chimneys behind her. Issued from 1929 to 1931.

Index

wage fund, 245, 248–9, 254, 267
wage policy, 245–51
wage scale, 246–8
wages, 3, 6, 7, 22, 60, 68, 87, 88, 96,
    103–15, 107, 237, 242–52, 275, 281
  differentials in, 16, 145, 156, 242,
    245–6, 248
  equality of (*uravnilovka*), 156, 242–3,
    244–51
  fall of, 74, 76–82, 138, 279
  planning for, 77–82
women
  in Central Asian republics, 55, 60
  in Communist Party, 47
  employment opportunities for, 92,
    94, 96, 97, 103, 154, 156, 166,
    175–6, 183, 188, 212, 222, 268, 270,
    282
  in industry, 9–15, 22–4, 88–102, 135,
    150, 154, 157–60, 161–3, 166, 169,
    174–6, 182–6, 188–94, 204, 217,
    268–70
  in labor force, 88–92, 265–70
  as labor reserve, 126–39, 265–72
  mass mobilization of, 129–40, 163
women's activists, 8, 14, 21, 33, 40, 41, 42,
    43, 44, 45, 47, 48, 49, 50, 52, 56, 57,
    58, 59, 60, 61, 64, 68, 93, 144–5, 147,
    148, 159, 175, 199, 207, 210, 273,
    282, 284
Women's Congress, 38–9, 40
Women's Department of the Central
    Committee, *see* Zhenotdel
women's emancipation, 15, 17, 34, 35, 36,
    40, 64, 149, 153, 155–6, 248, 272–5,
    282
women's factory organizers, 43, 45, 46, 48,
    65, 68, 175, 210, 220, 241
women's movement, 33
women's separatism, 37, 39, 40, 41, 42,
    46, 230
wool industry, 15, 96, 97, 98

workers (*see also* women, in industry)
  identity, 2, 10
  kadrovye, 2, 7, 8, 11, 30, 236, 260, 275,
    278, 280
  non-industrial, 11
Workers' and Peasants' Inspectorate
    (Rabkrin), 5, 8, 27, 62
Workers' Control Commission, 228
working class
  consumption, 78–81, 83–5, 248–9, 251,
    273, 279
  definition of, 6–7, 10, 24–5, 32, 125,
    139–40, 152–3, 275, 278–80
  formation of, 3, 71, 72, 140, 278–85
  historiography of, 2, 208–9
  in industry, 88–98
  protests, 76, 80, 81, 84, 208, 249–50,
    254–8, 263, 265, 267–8, 275, 282
  size of, 1, 7–8, 9, 88–98, 103
  social composition, 1, 6, 7–8, 11, 31, 70,
    72, 88–102, 104–5, 110, 143, 199,
    208, 279–81
  standard of living, 81–3, 88, 103–5, 248
World War I, 9, 31, 34

Zhdanov, A., 211, 212, 222
Zhenotdel, 8, 22, 23–4, 31, 33, 34, 46, 50,
    52, 54, 65, 68, 150, 170, 175, 186,
    199, 205, 210, 211, 217, 219, 220–1,
    226, 229–30, 248, 278, 284
  activities, 39–42
  delegate assemblies, 39, 47, 48, 49, 51,
    56, 60, 61–3, 210, 220–1, 222, 275
  elimination of, 47, 48, 49, 51–68,
    220–1, 275
  history of, 35–9
  social composition, 36–7
  women's commissions, 39, 45, 48
Zhukrov, 123, 124
Zimichev, 119
Zlatoust, 192, 224
Zvonkov factory, 46